PERFECTION

PERFECTION
Coming to Terms with Being Human

Michael J. Hyde

BAYLOR UNIVERSITY PRESS

Cover Design by Nicole Weaver, Zeal Design Studio
Cover image © Fotosearch
Book Design by Diane Smith

The Last Supper, 1495–1497 (fresco) (post restoration) by Leonardo da
Vinci (1452–1519)
Santa Maria della Grazie, Milan, Italy / The Bridgeman Art Library

Mona Lisa, c.1503–6 (oil on panel) by Leonardo da Vinci (1452–1519)
Louvre, Paris, France/Giraudon / The Bridgeman Art Library

The Proportions of the human figure (after Vitruvius), c.1492 (pen & ink
on paper) by Leonardo da Vinci (1452–1519)
Galleria dell' Accademia, Venice, Italy / The Bridgeman Art Library

Library of Congress Cataloging-in-Publication Data

Hyde, Michael J., 1950-
Perfection : coming to terms with being human / Michael J. Hyde.
p. cm.
Includes index.
ISBN 978-1-60258-244-6 (cloth : alk. paper)
1. Perfection. I. Title.

BD233.H93 2009
179'.9--dc22
2009029959

Printed in the United States of America on acid-free paper with a
minimum of 30% recycled content.

For my wife, Bobette,
and my students at Wake Forest University

"This union may never be perfect, but generation after generation has shown that it can always be perfected."

PRESIDENT BARACK OBAMA
A More Perfect Union
"The Race Speech"
Philadelphia, PA
March 18, 2008

"That is our calling. That is our character."

PRESIDENT BARACK OBAMA
Health Care Speech to Congress
September 9, 2009

CONTENTS

ACKNOWLEDGMENTS

I am indebted to the faculty, staff, and students of the Department of Communication and the Program for Bioethics, Health, and Society, School of Medicine, Wake Forest University, for providing me with communities that make teaching and research an immense joy. For their wisdom, inspiration, caring guidance, and psychological support, special thanks are due to Pat Arneson, Ron Arnett, Art Bochner, John Bost, Melissa Cook, Annette Holba, Beth Hutchens, Lisa Keranen, Joe Fennell-Lowe, Nancy King, Seth Maheu, Ananda Mitra, Peter Rosenquist, Calvin Schrag, Joe Verga, and Eric Watts. I also thank those groups who heard earlier versions of some of my chapters at the University of South Florida and the University of South Carolina, as well as at Duquesne, Villanova, Wake Forest, and Yale universities. I am grateful to Wake Forest University for awarding me an Ethics, Leadership, and Social Responsibility grant that enabled me to complete the writing of certain sections of this book. And for their expertise and kindness, I wish to thank Carey Newman, Director, Baylor University Press, and those from whom I have received outstanding assistance in working with the Press: Abby Collier, Jenny Hunt, Karen Helgeson, and Diane Smith.

Chapters 3, 4, 6, 8, and 9 contain portions of previously published material: "Searching for Perfection: Martin Heidegger (With Some Help from Kenneth Burke) on Language, Truth, and the Practice of Rhetoric," in *Perspectives on Philosophy of Communication*, edited by Pat Arneson (West Lafayette, Ind.: Purdue University Press, 2007), 23–36; "Coming to Terms with Perfection: The Case of Terri Schiavo" (with Sarah McSpiritt), *Quarterly Journal of Speech* 93 (2007): 150–79; "Ethos and Rhetoric," in *The International Encyclopedia of Communication*, edited by Wolfgang Donsbach, vol. 4 (New York: Wiley-Blackwell, 2008), 1604–6; and *Perfection, Postmodern Culture, and the Biotechnology Debate* (The Carroll C. Arnold Distinguished Lecture, 2007) (New York: Pearson/Allyn & Bacon, 2009). Grateful acknowledgment is made to the editors and publishers of this material for their permission to use it here. The present adaptation represents various degrees of revision and expansion of those first versions.

PREFACE

This book evolved from two earlier works (*The Call of Conscience* and *The Life-Giving Gift of Acknowledgment*) that, as they were researched and written, headed me in the direction of having to struggle with the issue of perfection.[1] The first book explored how human existence discloses a moral directive, a "call of conscience," and how this call is further facilitated by humankind's communicative and rhetorical abilities. The ongoing debate in the United States over the justifiability and social acceptability of euthanasia and physician-assisted suicide served as the major case study there. Whether one is on the side of the "right to die" or the "right to life," this debate, among other things, forces one to come face-to-face with the question, what would life be like if no one *acknowledged* your existence? The second work addressed this specific question. Various case studies drawn from religion, science (cosmology), literary and film criticism, research on computer-mediated communication, and the politics of public address were offered to illustrate how acknowledgment is a "life-giving gift" and how it, too, is facilitated by the communicative and rhetorical abilities of human beings. With each of these case studies, I kept confronting the issue of how, as beings in need of acknowledgment, we embody a metaphysical desire for perfection, *achieving a state of completeness in our lives whereby, at least for the moment, we feel secure, comfortable, and at home with ourselves, others, and our immediate surroundings.* This issue warranted more careful consideration than I had so far given it.

As indicated by dictionary definitions of the phenomenon, the "completeness" of perfection can be associated, for example, with the "integrity," "soundness," and "flawlessness" of a given object. Thus, a triangle (with its three sides that connect to form three angles totaling 180 degrees) is, by definition, perfect. When, however, this geometric form is employed aesthetically in a work of art, such as a painting, only an equilateral or right-angled triangle may be the appropriate (perfect) choice. The completeness of perfection can also be associated with the "contentment" and "satisfaction" that people experience when, for example, attending a social gathering, such as an art exhibit, at which the atmosphere is exciting and friendly, and the featured artist's use of triangles in her paintings is perceived to be both fitting and fascinating.

Like both conscience and acknowledgment, the phenomenon of perfection functions to bridge objective and subjective levels of experience. Moreover, like both conscience and acknowledgment, perfection admits a certain ontological significance: perfection is essential to our well-being. Life would be hell if it was never informed by moral consciousness (conscience); if no one cared enough to give us the time of day (acknowledgment); and if we lacked any desire to improve the human condition, to perfect whatever goodness (perfection) it is capable of producing. A metaphysical desire for perfection is at work not only when artists answer their calling, but also when religious souls pray to God, scientists formulate mathematical equations in an attempt to identify the ultimate laws of nature, and philosophers address the question of what it means to be a human being. Indeed, the workings of perfection are present in our everyday lives—in our thoughts and actions—as we attempt to sustain and advance whatever progress we have achieved in the struggle to survive, understand the world, be better persons, and live the good life. We metaphysical creatures have a desire, a longing, for the completeness that living such a life is supposed to produce. This desire, in fact, informs the definition of health offered by the World Health Organization: "a state of *complete* physical, mental and social well-being and not merely the absence of disease or infirmity."[2]

There is something "heavenly" about this definition of health. For where but in heaven (at least as this place is commonly understood in Western religious traditions) does such a state forever exist? The story I have to tell about perfection encourages readers to ponder this question and a host of related ones, although not primarily for religious reasons. Rather, my story is about how we have been instructed throughout history to come to terms with perfection. This activity involves us in the educational and rhetorical process of learning how to formulate and express in the most effective (perfect) way possible our understanding of the phenomenon's presence and significance in our everyday lives. The history and rhetoric I examine provide strong evidence for the ontological significance of perfection—how it is essential to our well-being. The uniqueness of my story lies in its specific integration of history, rhetoric, and ontology. I write in the belief that the relationship between perfection and human existence is too important to be taken for granted, overlooked, or forgotten.[3]

Many fine minds from both the humanities and the sciences have significant roles to play in my narrative. I have tried to integrate and expand on their insights and arguments in such a way that readers, academics and nonacademics alike, might find the story "entertaining" in both senses of the term simultaneously: amusing and thought provoking. Given what it means and does to us, perfection is not simply a matter for credentialed scholars.

I owe much to the renowned social critic Kenneth Burke for bringing this last point home to me, both in his writings and in one particular interaction that I had with him in 1988, a few years before he died in 1993. I was invited to conduct a public interview with Burke at Purdue University. The interview centered on Burke's reaction to the first book-length study comparing his research program to the philosophical investigations of Martin Heidegger.[4] At times during the interview, Burke's age overtook his narrative coherency, and a noticeable number of audience members displayed looks of confusion and a lack of patience. The scene did not escape Burke's attention. When the interview and subsequent kindly applause ended, I escorted the professor off the stage of the lecture hall and into the lobby. As we walked, he looked up at me, a wily smile on his face, and asked, "Well, how do you think we did?" My response was immediate: "It was an honor to share the stage with you, Professor Burke. You were great." To which he replied, "Young man, you are more optimistic than I am."

It was a funny, sad, and educational moment. The wit was still there, but so was the realization of imperfection—which, for Burke, was not necessarily a bad thing to experience. The realization of imperfection is a necessary step for improvement. Burke would have us remedy our imperfections, but not to the point of contracting the disease of becoming "rotten with perfection." For Burke, succeeding in this task is a true sign of "progress," of perfecting our goodness without letting it turn evil. Burke consistently maintained that if the endeavor "could be perfected by many kinds of critics and educators and self-admonishers in general, things might be a little less ominous than otherwise."[5] I agree, hence my effort to tell a story about the historical and rhetorical process of coming to terms with perfection.

When all is said and done, my story, of course, will not be perfect. Just how far away it is from this praiseworthy goal will depend, at least, on how much readers agree and disagree with what I have to say about perfection, how well I say it, what they think about the quality of scholarship that supports my positions, and the practical relevance of my illustrations. Faced with the topic of perfection staring me in the face day and night, it has been impossible not to have moments of despair about the (in)completeness and (un)worthiness of my expressive endeavors. Still, I believe the endeavor is worth the effort. Coming to terms with the nature of perfection defines a requirement for maintaining the health of our personal and public existence. Human survival and dignity call for some degree of perfection operating in our lives, although how we define and express—*come to terms with and understand*—whatever this perfection is can be quite problematic. Indeed, the rhetorical nature of perfection is a complex phenomenon that necessarily involves us in a paradoxical task. Specifically, there is something fundamentally antirhetorical (or at least unrhetorical) about the notion of perfection: it presents itself as beyond debate, which of course is what makes debate that relies on it so difficult, intractable, but all the more necessary.

In chapter 1, I expand on the introductory comments offered so far in order to define more specifically the nature of my project. The story I have to tell about perfection includes an account of how our understanding of the phenomenon has developed with the help of Western religion, philosophy, science, and art and how this development entails an appreciation of rhetorical theory. This account, which unfolds throughout all of the chapters of this book, is intended to be more provocative than strictly chronological and comprehensive, although I do spend some considerable time in chapters 2 and 3 dealing with the supposed source of perfection: God. More often than not, this most holy of subjects and its corresponding rhetoric are somewhere on or behind the scenes when the issue of perfection is at hand. "God" *is* the most famous *term* that readily comes to mind when people think about the nature of what the dictionary defines as "freedom from fault or defect: flawlessness," "the quality or state of being saintly," "an exemplification of supreme excellence."

Perfection calls attention to itself in moments of awe and wonder, moments that are beneficial, burdensome, cosmic, mystical, holy, and quite concrete and secular. Whether we realize it or not, the presence and absence of perfection is an everyday occurrence, a phenomenological happening that is contextualized by all the otherness (people, places, and things) that comes with the experiences of day-to-day existence. In chapter 2, I speak of this fact of life as it is expressed primarily in religious rhetoric, with its emphasis on the "otherness" of God. Chapters 3 and 4 are concerned with how we hear and interpret the call of otherness, be it God's or that of other things and other people. In chapter 4, I also specify in more phenomenological detail how perfection is rooted empirically in the ontological workings of our everyday temporal, spatial, and purposive existence. Perfection first comes to us in what is described as an original disclosing or "saying" (*logos*) of human being: an evocation that brings us face-to-face with our freedom and that functions eloquently, beautifully, sublimely as a call of conscience in need of acknowledgment. Perfection, in other words, shows itself first and foremost as a primordial communicative and rhetorical event that expresses a fundamental truth and admits a moral quality. The event, however, is itself not a human creation (which is not to say that God necessarily deserves the credit), although human beings are needed in order for the event to transpire in a meaningful and reasonable way.

In chapter 5, I focus on the relationship between reason and perfection. Here my discussion is informed primarily by philosophers, scientists, theologians, rhetorical theorists, and artists whose works help to define and advance the progressive inclinations of the Age of Enlightenment. Mary Shelley's classic work of science fiction, *Frankenstein: Or, The Modern Prometheus*, is used to illustrate how rhetorical competence can and must facilitate the relationship between reason and perfection. Aided by such competence, the workings of this relationship function to open people to the truth.

In chapter 6, I discuss how this entire process is rightly seen as an event of beauty. Beauty and perfection have long been recognized by philosophers, scientists, theologians, rhetorical theorists, and artists as complementary phenomena. Beauty is oftentimes understood to be a sign of perfection (especially when it is more than simply skin-deep). This point is clarified as I turn to a discussion of Leonardo da Vinci's interest in the "lived body" and how his scientific and aesthetic theory of painting informs this interest and its resulting artistic productions.

Chapter 7 extends Leonardo's concern with the lived body by identifying the ontological structures of existence that inform this body's struggle with the chaos and order of everyday existence. My discussion of this matter expands on specific phenomenological concerns that will have already been introduced and developed to a certain extent and that constitute what I term "a rhetoric of perfection." The major terms of this rhetoric include the spatial and temporal structure of human existence, freedom, otherness, conscience, emotion, truth, acknowledgment, interpretation, salvation, heroism, beauty, reason, and justice.

With this discussion of the lived body at hand, it should be clear how our impulse for perfection lies at the empirical heart of our existence. This placement and witnessing of perfection defines a necessary condition for all other conceptualizations of the phenomenon that one finds in the rhetoric of Western religion, philosophy, science, and art. These conceptualizations are the result of our coming to terms with perfection—*our making use of our rhetorical ability to find the right and fitting words and other symbolic devices for communicating to others in the most enlightening and effective ways possible whatever it is that we understand and hold to be worthy of reverence and respect.* Chapter 8 presents a real-life case study of this rhetorical operation. The focus here is the recent landmark legal case of Ms. Terri Schiavo, a young woman who lived in a persistent vegetative state for fifteen years before she was allowed to die the "dignified" death that she supposedly wanted all along. The Schiavo case offers a vivid illustration of the rhetoric of perfection at work.

The life and death of Terri Schiavo fueled an ongoing debate in this country that is exceptionally relevant for a project like mine: how far we should go in developing and using biotechnology to sustain and perfect our lives. In this debate, the stakes are quite high regarding the "fate" of human being; expressing perfection as perfectly as possible is a major moral obligation for those who wish to enter the debate and influence its outcome. Chapter 9 examines how this debate informs and is informed by today's "postmodern" culture, in which the rhetoric of "our posthuman future" is being worked out and questioned by scientists and a vast assortment of proponents and critics of biotechnological advances. Here arguments abound over the benefits and burdens that accompany the perfection-driven impulse of medical science and technology.

Chapter 10 concludes my story about perfection by giving further consideration to an observation about human beings that takes form throughout this book and that I initially associate with the eighteenth-century philosopher David Hume: in the great scheme of things, we are fated to live a life of significant insignificance, being no more important to the cosmos "than the life of an oyster." Unlike Hume, however, I find such an oxymoronic existence to admit a greater worth than that. Human being is perfectly structured as an imperfection that constantly speaks to us of our crucial role in the rhetorical process of keeping ourselves and others open to the truth of all that stands before us. As far as we know, oysters neither hear nor respond to the evocative and provocative "saying" going on here. Human beings, on the other hand, are fated to meet this moral challenge head-on in their everyday lives.

CHAPTER ONE

COMING TO TERMS
WITH PERFECTION

Have you ever perceived perfection in yourself, in others, in human inventions and artistic creations, in the workings of nature? At the moment of discovery, some change in consciousness, in perception and thought, likely occurred that moved your attention away from its habitual and routine involvements in the everyday world and toward something else at work in this world that was particularly captivating and special. The experience could be as simple as walking outside your home at dusk to do some chore (e.g., sweeping the patio), glancing up at the sky for a moment, and responding silently: "Good God, look at that sunset. Beautiful." God, nature, beauty, and silence are known to work together to stimulate experiences of at least some degree of perfection. The experience feels good. The feeling helps to cultivate a passion for perfection. This passion plays a fundamental role in our social and political lives as we attempt to sustain and advance the progress we have achieved in the struggle to survive, understand the world, be better persons, and live the good life. Our passion for perfection is admirable; it defines who we are as metaphysical animals, creatures who have a longing, a nostalgia, for security, comfort, and completeness in our lives.

This same passion is humbling, too. The eighteenth-century philosopher David Hume put it this way: a human being "can form an idea of perfections much beyond what he has experience of in himself; and is not limited in his conception of wisdom and virtue. He can easily exalt his notions and conceive a degree of knowledge, which, when compared with his own, will make the latter appear very contemptible." Our passion for perfection not only speaks of potentially great things to come but also puts us in our place. "Man falls much more short of perfect wisdom, and even of his own ideas of perfect wisdom, than animals do of man; yet the latter difference is so considerable, that nothing but a comparison with the former can make it appear of little moment."[1]

Hume speaks of a truth of human being that is quite telling in what it discloses about our species. No matter how great and important we think ourselves to be, we are still animals, fallible creatures fated to fall short of ever having it "all together." Perhaps such human imperfection was on Hume's mind when, while considering the debate over the morality of suicide and how "God-fearing" souls used their ultimate understanding of perfection to decry the sinfulness of this final act, he claimed that "the life of man is of no greater importance to the universe than that of an oyster."[2]

Still, the passion for perfection persists. Its impulse permeates the very fabric of language that allows us to think and talk about whatever this passion (or anything else) may truly be. As the social and literary critic Kenneth Burke notes, "The mere desire to name something by its 'proper' name, or to speak a language in its distinctive ways, is intrinsically 'perfectionist.' What is more 'perfectionist' in essence than the impulse, when one is in dire need of something, to so state this need that one in effect 'defines' the situation?"[3]

Like any author who has a truth to tell to an audience and who wants this truth to be thought provoking, influential, and memorable, Hume had to be concerned with finding the most appropriate, convincing, and effective way of expressing himself about the matter at hand. This rhetorical task calls for an appreciation of "eloquence," a phenomenon that Hume praised as being essential for the well-being of any civil society that values freedom and that is bent on achieving genuine social, political, and moral progress. For Hume, eloquence is "the rapid harmony [of discourse], exactly adjusted to the sense: It is vehement reasoning, without any appearance of art: It is disdain, anger, boldness, freedom, involved in a continued stream of argument. . . . The principles of every passion, and of every sentiment, is in every man; and when touched properly [by eloquence], they rise to life, and warm the heart, and convey that satisfaction, by which a work of genius is distinguished from the adulterate beauties of a capricious wit and fancy."[4] Eloquence is rhetoric functioning wisely, as perfectly as possible, in helping people to understand what something is and what, if anything, we are obliged to do in light of this knowledge. Hume is being eloquent as he conveys with "rapid harmony" and "vehement reasoning" how something that makes our species significant—the conceiving of perfection—is also something that signals our insignificance in the great scheme of things.

Granted, what Hume has to say is not likely to "warm the heart[s]" of readers who do not share his skepticism about human perfectibility and his rhetorical taste for oysters. Still, Hume was on to something as he used his rhetorical competence to help readers come to terms with the beneficial and burdensome character of perfection. Hume was critical of institutions like the church that added to this burden by using their own esteemed notions of perfection in a fanatical way to manipulate and persecute the masses. Burke uses the oxymoron "rotten with perfection" to describe such an unethical event.[5] Hume's reaction to the event echoes the general assessment of Enlightenment philosophers who, like him, saw the church as a threat to freedom and the reasonable thought that was needed to guide this fundamental source of liberty in a rational and progressive way. Here, for example, is Hume putting it mildly:

> There is no method of reasoning more common, and yet none more blameable, than in philosophical debates to endeavor to refute any hypothesis by a pretext of its dangerous consequences to religion and morality. When any opinion leads us into absurdities, 'tis certainly false; but 'tis not certain an opinion is false, because 'tis of dangerous consequence. Such topics, therefore, ought entirely to be foreborn, as serving nothing to the discovery of truth, but only to make the person of an antagonist odious.[6]

What I have been emphasizing about Hume points to the central and related concerns of this book. I intend to tell a story about how we have been instructed throughout history to come to terms with perfection: a state of being that is both a benefit and a burden, life fulfilling and life threatening, and that can be conceptualized and called into question by rhetorical means. I thus hope to stimulate an awareness of a process that is too easily taken for granted, ignored, or forgotten by people who are satisfied with their particular take on what they understand perfection to be and who therefore are too easily blind to the negative (rotten) consequences that may follow from their respective and rhetorically constructed worldviews. I submit that it is important to keep these specific matters in mind, especially in an age like ours when, for example, science and technology are being employed more than ever before to create what has been termed our ever-growing "instant-makeover," "self-improvement" culture in which "anything less than perfection is pathology." The disease of being rotten with perfection seems to be spreading fast.[7]

As my story about perfection unfolds, I emphasize a point that too often escapes the attention of those who offer remedies for the disease and, as will be detailed in chapter 9, motivates biotechnological progress: although too much perfection can lead to disaster, not having enough of this specific *pharmakon* can also be dangerous to our health. Along with the ailment of being rotten with perfection, we must also take seriously the disease of what I term being "rotten with imperfection." This fact of life is given a humorous twist in an episode of the television comedy *Seinfeld* as the funny but irritating character George reflects on his "pathetic" existence:

> Why did it all turn out like this for me? I had so much promise. I was personable, I was bright . . . oh, not academically speaking, but I was perceptive. I always know when someone's uncomfortable at a party. It all became very clear as I was sitting [alone] out there [on the pier] today. . . . Every decision I've ever made in my entire life has been wrong. My life is the complete opposite of everything I want it to be. Every instinct I have in every aspect of life, be it something to wear, something to eat . . . it's all been wrong. Every one. . . . I'm disturbed! I'm depressed! I'm inadequate! I got it all! And, yeah, I'm a great quitter. It's one of the few things I do well. I come from a long line of quitters. My father was a quitter, my grandfather was a quitter. . . . I was raised to give up.[8]

George is rotten with imperfection. His outlook toward the future is cynical and hopeless, uninformed by careful reasoning and lacking in moral responsibility. His character is not enriched by such attributes as faith, intellect, or ethics. That George is still able to feel bad about his situation is, however, an indication that a desire for perfection still flickers in his soul. Being rotten with imperfection is not a particularly praiseworthy way to be; in fact, it goes against human nature. I will have occasion to expand on this last point throughout the book.

A Benefit and a Burden

Achieving some degree of perfection in our everyday existence is known to be a satisfying and pleasant experience—so much so, in fact, that people will fight for its presence in their own lives as well as in the lives of others. As a graduate student, I read Saul Alinsky's *Rules for Radicals* and came across a saying that has remained unforgettable, especially as it applies to this fighting spirit: "Better to die on your feet than to live on your knees." Adopted from the Spanish civil war, the saying was used by Alinsky as a credo for his activities as a social reformer dedicated to helping people on the margins of society "realize the democratic dream of equality, justice, peace, cooperation, equal and full opportunities for education, full and useful employment, health, and the creation of those circumstances in which man can have the chance to live by values that give meaning to life."[9] The specific goal here, of course, heads one in the direction of "a better world." Social reformers have some degree of faith in the goodness and perfectibility of human beings. People like Alinsky put themselves through ordeals that offer no guarantee of success because they believe the struggle is worth the potential and real psychological and physical suffering. No pain, no gain, it is said. The dedicated athlete, artist, businessperson, construction worker, teacher, student, or any other "hard worker" knows how true this saying is. It is not necessarily a bad thing to have what less-devoted souls might simply dismiss as "masochistic" tendencies. Achieving some degree of perfection in life can at least help people feel a bit better about themselves and the world, unless the perfection has something to do with finding ways to make oneself more miserable than he or she already is. Here the burden of perfection becomes especially alarming.

People suffering from obsessive-compulsive disorder (OCD) are a case in point; they have become rotten with perfection. Making sure *over and over again*, for example, that one's hands are *truly* washed clean, or that the front door of the house is *actually* locked before one can go to work are behaviors that can drive one (as well as others) crazy. Although such craziness serves a purpose for the sufferer of OCD—it grants the person a way to cope with some past social and psychological trauma that has yet to be properly and perfectly understood by the person—it nevertheless also serves as a stimulus to be uncomfortable with and oftentimes depressed about who he or she *really* is. In the case of OCD, a person's masochistic and perfectionist tendencies expose him or her to the danger of becoming his or her own worst enemy. That others may also suffer because of the habits at work here makes the perfectionism of the person all the more imperfect and burdensome. If these others feel like they are being made to live on their knees because of this perfectionism, if they take exception to this state of subservience and "sadomasochism," and if they, goaded by their own impulse for perfection and a sense of dignity, decide to react, no matter the consequences, by rising to their feet, then the situation at hand might become rather unpleasant.

Indeed, perfection can turn tragic, ironic, and rotten. In the United States and other affluent quarters of the world today, people (especially women) who need not go hungry will literally starve themselves to ill health and even death in order to achieve with "perfect control" the "perfect look."[10] On September 11, 2001, the world (and especially the United States) was given a lesson in how high the costs and how tragic the irony can be. Terrorists, people rotten with perfection, killed thousands of others who, at least for the terrorists, were the true carriers of the disease. The backers of these terrorists argued that the presence and influence of the United States in the Islamic cultures of the Middle East was sacrilegious and destructive. Things must change. Better to die on your feet than live on your knees. Shortly after the World Trade Center twin towers collapsed, the United States took the same position and acted accordingly. Listening to both sides tell their version of the story, the lesson is clear: terrorism and counterterrorism will continue for as long as it takes until one of the warring parties achieves its goals. Then things presumably will be perfect, complete, finally "right with God." Both sides claim that "God is great" and that "God is on *their* side." What a potentially perfect situation for things to remain rotten.

How well do we understand the workings of perfection? How do we know perfection when we perceive it? How good are we at expressing the meaning and significance of the awesome matter at hand? Do we have an obligation to make things as perfect as possible for ourselves and others? These are some of the questions that readers are asked to consider as they work their way through this book. The questions are intended to encourage critical reflection on a state of being that has much to do with all that is good and bad about human existence and that thereby warrants our careful and undying attention.

A God Term

Perfection is a "god term," an ultimate standard meant to define states of completeness that can be used to direct us toward the good, the just, and the true. We thus tend to think of the completeness of perfection in terms of virtue. But as noted above, perfection can also drive us crazy and lead to troublesome (if not disastrous) consequences in our lives. We live in a world in which the "perfect day" might be ruined by the "perfect storm" or some "perfect villain." Perfection can be both a benefit and a burden. We even find this contradictory nature of perfection displayed in God's "true" character, at least as this character is presented and developed in the narrative of the Old Testament: God's perfect unity includes such imperfect traits as jealousy, indecision, and vengefulness. Still, we are given reassurance. In Psalms 19:7-11, for example, we are told that "The law of the Lord is perfect, converting the soul: the testimony of the Lord is sure, making wise the simple. The statutes of the Lord are right, rejoicing the heart: the commandment of the Lord is pure, enlightening the eyes. The fear of the Lord is clean, enduring for ever: the judgments of the Lord are true and righteous altogether. . . . Moreover by them is thy servant warned: and in keeping of them there is great reward."[11] God, it seems, has a perfectly good reason for exhibiting imperfect traits: they incite the fear that is needed to ensure that we walk the straight path toward the truth.

Coming to a complete understanding of perfection is no easy matter. Still, as will be discussed throughout this book, it lies in our nature to keep on trying to achieve this goal and thus to be able to say with some degree of confidence, for example, that, yes, that person over there is a "perfect lady" or a "perfect gentleman," or that we hold in our hands the "perfect picture" of someone or something. A baseball fan knows at least a form of perfection when he or she sees it, for, as indicated in the dictionary, there is such a thing as a "perfect game": one in which a pitcher allows no hits, no runs, and no opposing batter to reach first base. Pitching a perfect game is a remarkable accomplishment: the stuff of baseball heroes whose athletic achievements are "unbelievable" as soon as they actually happen.

Along with the examples of the perfect lady and gentleman, this last example of perfection demonstrates a crucial fact about the matter: the achievement of certain forms of perfection presupposes predetermined and agreed upon rules and standards of excellence concerning human activities that enable us to gauge when a given endeavor is complete, without fault or defect, thoroughly made, and thus lacking no essential detail. Perfection is something that human beings define and attempt to perform. In establishing the rules and standards of excellence that are needed here, we show ourselves to be metaphysical creatures: longing for stability, security, and completeness.

PERCEIVING PERFECTION

The example of holding the "perfect picture" of someone or something, however, requires that we refine a bit what has just been said about perfection and human beings.

Perfection is not simply a condition made possible by rules and standards of excellence. For, as any decent photographer will tell you, one's state of mind and the ways in which such a state can either open one up or close one off to the world will have much to do with one's ability to perceive something of the truth of any given subject matter. Being in a "bad mood," for example, is not generally conducive to the openness that is required to experience the "perfect" day and to capture something of its grandeur on film, on a canvas, or in words.[12] But perfection may also incite disgust and hatred, as when it shows itself ironically in the character of someone like Hitler. In either case, however, the experience of perfection works to encourage our stepping back from the preoccupations of our everyday routines and habits in order to catch at least a glimpse of some matter's essential character, what truly makes it what it is. The artist has an "eye" and a "feel" for catching this glimpse and a "talent" for being at the right place at the right time when it might present itself. Sometimes the experience requires more than a bit of luck; other times one has a brief second or longer to better position himself or herself before the subject matter such that the best angle and lighting can be secured for disclosing the subject matter's own disclosure, its being and truth. Perfection, in short, is inextricably tied to the workings of subjectivity. And, this being so, another refinement regarding the relationship between perfection and human beings is in order.

The "best" picture of a person, for example—"best" in the sense that it truly (perfectly) captures what is considered to be the person's genuine character—need not be one of a face showing a loving smile and a body dressed in gorgeous attire. The truth, as they say, is not always pretty; hence, the same can be said of the perfect picture of this truth. Which pictures of 9/11 and its aftermath (e.g., the United States' invasion of and "victory" over Iraq) are most effective in disclosing the truth of the situation? Or, to use a related example, who showed more respect for the truth—the well-positioned photographer who snapped the picture of the ruthless and smiling dictator, Saddam Hussein, coiffed and dressed in military apparel, waving a sword, firing a gun, and being admired by all, or the photographer who clicked the shutter once this dictator, having emerged from his hiding place in a hole in the ground, was captured and showed himself to be a rather miserable-looking and disgusting creature? Which of the two, in the best sense of the term, was a more perfect picture of the "real" Saddam?

Perfection is not something that can be talked about in a meaningful and realistic way without taking into consideration all that its witnesses bring to the scene: the lived experiences of everyday existence; the habits, attitudes, beliefs, and prejudices that inform and are informed by these experiences; and a sense of history that necessarily has its own peculiar ways of interpreting and judging the "good" and the "bad" of things. I say "necessarily" with the teachings of Kenneth Burke once again in mind. Any given history presupposes the appropriation of a language and its sundry definitions. Although these definitions constitute vocabularies intended to be "reflections" of reality, they also are "selections" of reality. And any selection of reality must function as a "deflection" of reality.[13] Hence, for example, exists the reality of racist language that first and foremost classifies people not as human beings but rather as something "lower" and "dirtier." Racism deflects humanity away from those who, by definition of the racist thought and language at work, "deserve" to be, at the very least, marginalized for the "good" of society.

This is not to say, however, that perfection, tied as it is to human subjectivity, is an issue that simply dead-ends in a realm of relativism in which people are left to claim anything they want about truth or error without any attempt to arrive at a mutual agreement on whatever problematic circumstances are at hand. The chaos that is cultivated by such a state of affairs is conducive neither to who we are as metaphysical creatures nor to our need for orderly environments. Relativism aside, more-realistic threats to perfection are posed by the reified social and political relations that such environments can foster and whose "Big Brother" authorities (e.g., Hitler, Saddam) gladly define the terms that regulate human community.

COMING TO TERMS WITH PERFECTION

I agree with the philosopher John Rawls, who notes, "One difficulty with perfectionism is that while it seems quite evident that there is an intuitive idea of perfection, it is hard to make it sufficiently clear."[14] What I have to say about the topic necessarily involves me in this task. I hope to clarify how perfection is at work in our lives whether we realize it or not, whether we are purposively struggling to improve ourselves in certain situations or just trying to make it through the day with as little effort as possible. Being perfectly lazy on occasion, and feeling good about it, can be a well-deserved reward for even the most conscientious, hard-working, and obsessive souls. Being perfectly lazy throughout one's life, on the other hand, will warrant objections from anyone who believes that dedication to a respectable work ethic is truly the way to perfect one's moral character. Perfection has its rules, and they operate on a sliding scale. Sometimes our actions are complete failures; sometimes they are stunning successes—so stunning, in fact, that others who *really* know us might describe them as "being too good to be true." At other times, the way we behave is meant only to be "good enough" to pass whatever test is at hand. This specific measurement comes into play when, for example, feeling a bit under the weather, we still get dressed up for a night on the town and are satisfied with our looks, although we could have done a much better job choosing the appropriate attire if we had felt better. "This tie doesn't really go with my shirt and coat. Oh well, it's good enough for tonight."

In concluding his book *The Perfectibility of Man*, the philosopher John Passmore notes that writing a book, whether about perfection or any other topic, "can be a 'vital joy,' but a joy which is inevitably united with the thorns of anxious care. It is not a contribution to perfection, as perfection is classically understood. To write anything worth writing is to arouse opposition, controversy—writing does not promote the classical perfectibilist ideals of unity and harmony or contentment; it is to abandon all hope of self-sufficiency, to make oneself dependent on a multitude of other human beings, to surrender one's peace of mind, to stir up one's passions, to struggle with time."[15] I find these words reassuring. Passmore's work provides the most extensive intellectual history of perfection found in the literature. His narrative served as an invaluable reality check for gauging my awareness, understanding, and ignorance of matters that warrant consideration in the study of perfection. My story about the topic, however, differs from his in that it emphasizes an existential and phenomenological perspective that allows for a robust and empirically oriented appreciation of the ontological nature of perfection and its presence in everyday life. Moreover, my story makes much of a matter that I take to be essential in the history of perfection and that escapes Passmore's attention: the theory and practice of the orator's art, rhetoric. The human capacity for rhetorical competency enables us to *come to terms* with the nature of perfection.

Coming to terms with perfection defines a rhetorical process that calls on our ability to find the right and fitting words and other symbolic devices for communicating to others in the most enlightening, truthful, and effective ways possible whatever it is that we understand and hold to be "right," "good," and "true": something that is especially worthy of consideration and respect and inspires us to better our lives and the lives of others, to achieve our full potential. Directed by what the book of Genesis reports—"The Lord appeared to Abram and said unto him, I *am* the Almighty God; walk before me, and be thou perfect" (Gen 17:1-2)—the discourse and teachings of Western theology are well known for trying to express as perfectly as possible a conception of perfection that supposedly is the source of all things perfect. From this source shines "the perfection of beauty" (Ps 50:2) that is seen throughout the *cosmos* (the Greek term for "world" that means "fitting order" or "beautiful arrangement"). Science seeks to display this beauty in its mathematical equations of the laws of nature—be these laws divinely inspired or not.

RHETORICAL ELOQUENCE

Both theology and science have a role to play in my story about perfection, as do philosophy, psychology, art history, literary and film studies, and rhetorical theory and criticism. The eighteenth-century philosopher John Locke dismissed rhetoric as a "perfect cheat" when it comes to understanding and expressing as perfectly as possible "ideas" that are "clear and distinct."[16] Locke employs his rhetorical competence (i.e., the use of an oxymoron) to condemn certain uses of this competence. This condemnation, contributing as it does to the age-old conflict between philosophy and rhetoric, was and is unfortunate.

More than any other tradition in the arts and sciences, the rhetorical tradition pays homage to our ability to deal symbolically with particular matters that we recognize as pressing and that require careful deliberation and judgment, but whose meaning and significance are presently ambiguous, uncertain, and contestable. Because of the contingency of human existence, we inhabit a world in which the practice of rhetoric is genuinely necessary. This point has been made by many theorists, among them the philosopher Hans Blumenberg: "Lacking definitive evidence and being compelled to act are the prerequisites of the rhetorical situation."[17] The orator's art defines a realm of existential "know-how" that enables us to find the most appropriate ways to use and arrange symbols in order to inform others about and move them toward what is held to be the "correctness," the "truth," of some matter of importance. The ancient Greek philosopher (fifth century B.C.E.) and teacher of rhetoric Isocrates refers to the entire process when he writes,

> Because there has been implanted in us the power to persuade each other and to make clear to each other what we desire, not only have we escaped the life of wild beasts, but we have come together and founded cities and made laws and invented arts; and, generally speaking, there is no institution devised by man which the power of speech has not helped us to establish. For this [power] has laid down laws concerning things just and unjust, and things honorable and base, and if it were not for these ordinances we should not be able to live with one another.[18]

Rhetoric finds application throughout the arts and sciences. As Professor of English and Comparative Literature George Steiner notes, "There is a part of rhetoric in every communicative act and visitation. Rhetoric is the craft of charging with significant effect the lexical and grammatical units of utterance. A statue, a building, have their rhetoric of self-presentment. So does the sound-structure and projection in a piece of music. The actual proceedings of persuasion are built of the relevant grammar."[19]

Such proceedings can, of course, be used to manipulate and deceive others, hence rhetoric's long-standing reputation as being the "harlot" of the arts. But rhetoric at its best, striving for perfection, also shows itself to be a source of eloquence and the instructive beauty that comes with it. As students of the orator's art have long understood, rhetorical eloquence "is made up of the methods which reflection and experience have evolved to make a discourse such as to establish the truth and to arouse a love for it in the hearts of [human beings]. Things which strike and arouse the heart . . . eloquence is just that."[20] Whether one likes it or not, the study of perfection, especially the expression of perfection, requires an appreciation of eloquence and the competence, the know-how, that makes it possible.

The employment of this competence is supposed to show itself—for the best of social, political, and moral reasons—in the public discourse of a democratic nation's leaders as they inform, persuade, and guide their fellow citizens along proclaimed paths of righteousness. Rhetorical competence, however, is also seen in the humdrum of our everyday existence, although much of the time its happening is hidden in the simplicity and familiarity of those ways of being that we have become good at performing and that we thus tend to take for granted in order to make it through the day as efficiently and successfully (perfectly) as possible. Knowing how to display the right smile, taste in apparel, and logical and emotional ways of being with others whenever the situation calls for such "appropriate" behavior are cases in point. So, too, is knowing how to end a conversation without insulting the person who is "boring you to death" with his stories. The "decorum" that promotes the social practices of civil society presupposes rhetorical talents.

Being skilled in the employment of such know-how can help prevent an otherwise perfect day from going wrong. An inner-city gang member, for example, might not survive the day if he or she does not perfect a certain way of being with others, of giving the right "signs," wearing the "true colors," and speaking the proper "slang." Religious souls, who take exception to associating perfection in any way with such a "pagan" lot, might not hear and answer correctly God's call to do the good if they have not perfected their "spirit" enough in the right way. The civilizing effect of "normal," "proper," and "righteous" behavior cannot establish itself in any domain of culture until members, employing a certain ability of know-how, communicate in a rhetorically effective way and agree about what is bad, good, better, perhaps best, if not perfect, about their everyday existence and all they hold to be just, true, and worth living and dying for. Sending a condolence card to a friend or acquaintance is a "nice" thing to do. Are the words on the card genuine, fitting, truthful—reflecting the authentic sincerity of your heartfelt compassion? The card seems perfect. Are you?

When considering how human beings actually come to terms with perfection, the issue of rhetorical competence is necessarily before us. Ever since the ancient Greeks "officially" began creating the Western rhetorical tradition, the bottom line of the rhetorician's calling has been to analyze and clarify humankind's symbolic endeavors in order to further an appreciation of how these endeavors succeed and fail in advancing our social, political, and moral well-being. Rhetorical critics attend to the body politic as physicians attend to the pathophysiology of a patient's disease: with the goal of improved health in mind. Rhetoric, without a sense of perfection to guide it, can be a dangerous thing. With this point in mind, the rhetorical theorist Lloyd Bitzer emphasizes that rhetorical discourse is called into being by some "exigence": "an *imperfection* marked by urgency." An exigence is "a defect, an obstacle, something waiting to be done, a thing which is other than it should be." An exigence is rhetorical when it "invites the assistance of discourse" as a way of finding and implementing change that can result in some "positive modification" of the imperfection at hand.[21]

A Phenomenological Approach

I am interested in the origins, practices, and ethics of such perfection-oriented know-how. Western religion is well known for equating the origins of perfection with God. Directed by the Darwinian theory of evolution, Western science, on the other hand, feels compelled to associate perfection more simply and soundly with our species' biological and evolutionary drive for survival. Cognitive scientists, in fact, have identified structures in the human brain that can account for our metaphysical tendency to associate this drive with "God's call." This is not necessarily to say that God exists, but only that the evolved "wiring" of our brains allows us to invent and use this linguistic construction and, then, feel comfortable and secure with its mysterious referent and supposedly ultimate form of perfection. Language, claims the cognitive scientist Steven Pinker, is first and foremost "the product of a well-engineered biological instinct," an "evolutionary adaptation" that consists of "a form of mental software" (grammar) made possible by specific genetic structures in the brain.[22]

Perfection, of course, can and does extend beyond the empirical boundaries of science to the realm of metaphysics where, with the help of religious ideology, it retains its most humbling influence while gaining the attribute of "loving-kindness." Sure, we are "nothing"—a significant insignificance—when compared to the Creator of the universe: God. But this ultimate source of perfection, who can strike us down without any notice and for no understandable reason, is known (by definition!) to "have a heart" for creatures like us. In God's presence, there is fear and trembling as well as a sense of hope and redemption. We need only respond to God's call ("Where art thou?") and follow God's way ("Here I am!").

Western religion teaches that the significance of human being lies in our unique ability to perform this task, no matter how insignificant it appears to be in the ever-expanding vastness of the cosmos that began with a big bang approximately 15 billion years ago. Indeed, coming to terms with God's truth takes place on a small planet in a galaxy that shares space and time with approximately 10^{11} other galaxies in the observable universe. Each galaxy contains about as many stars, and each is typically one hundred thousand light-years across. Still, the Old and New Testaments tell stories about how our evolving power of consciousness has an essential role to play in God's plan for the universe to become aware of itself, better itself, and, in so doing, achieve as much perfection as possible as we make our way from our home on earth to our home in an even better world to come.

As my story unfolds, I will have more to say about this interplay between religion and science as it regards perfection. My specific interest in the origins of perfection, however, favors a phenomenological and ontological appreciation of the matter: one that necessarily encourages us to be as open-minded as possible to both metaphysical and empirical explanations of the true source of perfection. Phenomenology is a way of thinking devoted to interpreting, analyzing, and describing how the immediate content of experience actually presents itself to human consciousness. It seeks to disclose with "demonstrative precision" the appearing or "presencing" of some phenomenon: "to let that which shows itself . . . be seen from itself in the very way in which it shows itself from itself."[23] Phenomenology, in other words, attempts to generate a discourse that is especially attuned to the way in which some phenomenon happens, to how it reveals or manifests itself within the temporal and spatial horizon of human understanding. The discourse of phenomenology assumes the task of disclosing a phenomenon's own disclosure, *its* being and truth. Phenomenology thus offers itself as a truth-telling activity, for the happening of any truth takes place first and foremost as a disclosing of the world, a revealing or uncovering of the "givenness" of something that is perceived *to be*.[24]

I thus intend to develop an understanding of perfection that is informed by the ontological workings of everyday human existence. Here, at this most fundamental level of our being, is where the actual practice and ethics of perfection take form. Thus here, too, is where religion, science, and the other intellectual domains of expertise that inform my story must stand as they express their respective understandings of perfection—the very thing that is supposed to be driving their teaching and research. Striving for perfection is a fundamental moral obligation of the academy—one that demands, as Immanuel Kant is famous for emphasizing, "scholastic precision . . . even if such precision is denounced as meticulosity. Only in this way can precipitate reason be brought to understand itself before making its dogmatic assertions."[25] One must not forget, however, that scholastic precision is only one way of being rhetorically competent. Authors of "do-it-yourself" and "self-help" books also display such competence as they write in everyday "commonsense terms" instructions for helping others to perfect their physical, mental, social, and spiritual abilities.

Indeed, rhetoric needs to have a sense of perfection about it in order to do good. But fulfilling this need can itself become a problem when rhetoric becomes too enthralled with its own sense of perfection. In such a situation, rhetoric may serve to condition its possessors to marginalize what is other than itself and to see this otherness and its difference as being threatening, perhaps requiring extermination, whether this is truly the case or not. The process is most obviously at work whenever genocide is advocated and practiced by the ideological and perhaps religious zealots of some political regime. In this way, rhetoric contributes to perfection's role as both a benefit and a (potentially horrendous) burden.

CHAPTER TWO

GOD ON A GOOD DAY

During the early stages of researching and writing this book, I had an experience that spoke directly to my interests. I was sitting in an auditorium listening to the chairman of the board of trustees of my university explain to students and faculty how the search was going for hiring a new university president. After detailing all of the professional accomplishments that this person had to have achieved and the personal qualities that he or she had to possess, the chairman summarized his description by noting, with a smile on his face: "What we seem to be looking for is 'God on a good day.'" The chairman admitted that the task at hand—finding the "perfect" person for the job—was daunting. Indeed, no matter how close we are to the Almighty's presence, God is other than a human being, something that is always more than what we can completely comprehend. God's otherness transcends our earthly existence.

"God on a good day"—or, as one of my graduate students once put it, "God on Prozac." The teachings of Western religion are not known for advocating this distinction between God and goodness (let alone God being on drugs). Nay, God *is* goodness in its most complete—perfect (from the Latin *perficere*: *facere*,

"to make"; *per*, "thoroughly")—form. God is the *highest* reference point for coming to terms with perfection. Something that
is perfect, by definition, cannot get better than it already is. The
Oxford English Dictionary thus instructs us that describing
something as "most perfect" is redundant, not "proper" English,
not a "perfect" way of expressing "perfection." The human tendency to *emphasize* and, beyond that, to exaggerate and become
hyperbolic, is certainly related to who we are as metaphysical
beings bound for perfection and the progress it affords. "If the
idea of progress" ever dies in the West, writes historian Robert
Nisbet, "so will a great deal else that we have long cherished
in this civilization."[1] The same can be said about what progress
presupposes. A sense of perfection, as it is sometimes phrased,
is "absolutely essential" to the well-being of humankind. Our
mindless acceptance of the unneeded adjective found in this common expression is evidence of how perfect we want perfection to
be (at least sometimes). What is the difference between something
that *is* essential to some being's existence and something that is
absolutely essential to this existence? God on a good day?

I find this last expression to be one of the better (if not "most
perfect") ones for encouraging people to begin thinking about a
state of being that is both a benefit and a burden to human existence and that presupposes how human beings are, among other
things, purposive and metaphysical creatures. "Blessed" with
these ontological characteristics, we are fated to struggle with the
ever-present challenge of "getting things right," "making things
better," "improving" ourselves, and being as "complete" as we
can be as we grow, mature, and become wise with experience.
We are beings who must continually engage in the process of acting and planning, planning and acting, in order to sustain the
best of times and to overcome the worst of times. A person who
admits that he or she has no purpose in life is likely to be considered irresponsible, if not worthless. Even a person who, owing
to some accident, is in a persistent vegetative state but who is
still being kept alive artificially by the technologies of medical
science is recognized by right-to-life advocates as serving a crucial purpose: encouraging a heartfelt respect for God's gift of life
and the struggle that is needed to put this gift to its proper and
perfect use. The benefit we receive from God can amount to an

abject burden as we faithfully adhere to God's laws for achieving perfection, no matter the costs.[2]

A well-known saying of progress is associated with this struggle: "Practice makes perfect." Athletic coaches and trainers are fond of correcting this saying: " 'Practice makes perfect?' No way! *Perfect* practice makes perfect!" Indeed, we are capable of performing activities that, although at times quite demanding, are nevertheless satisfying because they are perceived as advancing our "goodness" and thereby testify to our hope that humankind's potential for perfectibility can continue to be actualized. Especially when coupled with past successes, the metaphysical strength of this hope registers itself as a longing or nostalgia to feel secure and at home with ourselves and others—in short, to have it, as they say, "all together." A state of perfection is a state of completeness.

METAPHYSICS AND GOD'S OTHERNESS

As a formal philosophical doctrine, such "all togetherness" is what metaphysics is all about: it seeks a unifying perspective of the totality of what is—the Being of existence. Human beings are born philosophers, whether or not they are ever awarded advanced degrees in the discipline. Everyday existence calls us to this vocation, especially when things go wrong. The philosopher Karl Jaspers emphasizes this point when he notes that the "philosophical life springs from the darkness in which the individual finds himself, from his sense of forlornness when he stares without love into the void, from his self-forgetfulness when he feels that he is being consumed by the busy-ness of the world, when he suddenly wakes up in terror and asks himself: What am I, what am I failing to do, what should I do?"[3]

If only for a moment, we are likely to lose our bearings in life when, for whatever reason, we find ourselves in situations that disrupt our current "comfort zones" such that we must address these questions "for our own goodness," as well as for the goodness of others. The disruption exposes a lack in our being and thus triggers a metaphysical impulse. We are creatures whose nostalgia (from the Greek *nostos*, "to return home") for security and completeness makes us susceptible to the ailment of becoming homesick for familiar and welcoming surroundings, for places in which compassion, civility, and justice help to ensure our well-being. The philosopher and theologian Charles Hartshorne makes the point this way: "In the absence of metaphysics . . . [humans] are likely to feel confused as to their basic aims and aspirations. They do not know how to combine the sense of the importance of their actions with the essential facts of life, such as the inevitability of death, the conflicts of aims among men, and the partial or complete failure of many of these aims, if not perhaps all of them, when looked at from the widest perspective in space-time. Accordingly, there is a tendency toward dull despair or cynical indifference."[4] The Enlightenment philosopher, social critic, and Deist Francois-Marie Arouet, better known as Voltaire, certainly was thinking along these lines when he proclaimed, "If God did not exist, it would be necessary to invent him."[5] God's holy otherness—the benefits it offers and the burdens it poses—allows for the hope of better things to come.

The question is whether God is the "first cause" of our metaphysical tendencies or some ultimate effect of these tendencies, informed as they are by the warp and woof of human evolution. This question sets the sides of the long-standing debate between religion and science over the "true" origins and workings of the cosmos. In the end, both sides might be correct. The late sixth-century (B.C.E.) philosopher Xenophanes is credited with offering the first statement in Western history of the idea of progress: "Truly the gods have not revealed to mortals all things from the beginning, but mortals by long seeking discover what is better."[6] By discovering "what is better," might we be fulfilling God's (or the gods') evolutionary plan for perfection, which, although perfect in theory, remains incomplete on a practical level until we learn to live our lives in accordance with this plan? Might our actions be a necessary ingredient for God becoming what God (according to God's ultimate plan) is supposed to be? What makes God perfect? Is it God alone? Do we set the terms? Are all parties needed? Xenophanes had an answer: "There is one god, among gods and men the greatest, not at all like mortals in body or in mind. He sees as a whole, thinks as a whole, and hears as a whole. But without toil he sets everything in motion, by the thought of his mind. And he always remains in the same place, not moving at all, nor is it fitting for him to change his position at different times."[7]

Xenophanes admits that this understanding of God's perfection is "conjectural only," for when it comes to understanding God's "certain truth, no man has seen it, nor will there ever be a man who knows" everything there is to know about the matter.[8] God's otherness transcends human comprehension. The struggle to connect with this otherness, however, is worth the effort. Progress is at hand! Indeed, as the classics scholar Charles Kahn points out, what we encounter with Xenophanes "for the first time in surviving literature, is a total rejection of the basis upon which . . . traditional [Greek] theology rests."[9] This popular tradition was the culture of Homer, the poets, and the early sages, who all promoted an anthropomorphic understanding of "the gods": deities were said to have human form and emotional characters. Influenced by the natural philosophers (the Milesian scientists or *physikoi*) of his day, Xenophanes rejected this view. His "one god" is itself the ruling principle of a rational and orderly cosmos, the divine intelligence that orchestrates the harmony of everything that exists. God's intelligence is always otherwise than even the highest cognitive capacity of human being. Xenophanes does not see this intelligence as did the biblical Daniel, whose description has influenced numerous illustrators of the Christian "God the Father": "I beheld till the thrones were cast down, and the Ancient of days did sit, whose garment was white as snow, and the hair of his head like pure wool: his throne was like the fiery flame, and his wheels as burning fire" (Dan 7:9).

One of Xenophanes' contemporaries, the philosopher Heraclitus, associated this intelligence with "wisdom": "the plan" that "steers all things through all things." Moreover, in his critique of traditional theology, Heraclitus emphasizes that "the wise is one alone, unwilling and willing to be spoken of by the name Zeus (*Zenos onoma* 'the name of life')."[10] The point here is that the "wise one" allows Itself to be *named*, but Its true and perfect nature forever escapes the limitations of human discourse. Further progress regarding the matter is made by another contemporary philosopher, Pythagoras, whose teachings emphasize that the orderliness of nature is best understood and expressed in terms of numbers. The true beauty of the cosmos is thus comprehended most completely by way of mathematics. God, literally, is "the One," perfection "pure and simple." With those like

Xenophanes, Heraclitus, and Pythagoras, there is never talk of "God on a good day."

To know God as perfectly as possible and to do the Almighty's work certainly defines what religious souls consider to be humankind's most esteemed moral accomplishment. Considering the difficulty of this task and the time it might take to achieve it, the nineteenth-century philosopher Frederick W. J. Schelling wondered, "Has creation a final purpose at all, and if so why is it not attained immediately, why does perfection not exist from the very beginning?"[11] The question may incite frustration, if not anger, on the reader's part. As one of my students once remarked, "Really, all this struggle, all the pain and suffering in the world. It seems like God is playing an 'amazing game' with us for 'His' amusement. That's sadistic! I'm certainly not amused." Another student responded, "Neither was Job, but it all worked out in the end, right? Perfection takes time!" Schelling agrees: "God is a *life*, not a mere being. All life has a destiny and is subject to suffering and development. God freely submitted himself to this too, in the very beginning. . . . All history remains incomprehensible without the concept of a humanly suffering God. Scripture, too, . . . puts that time into a distant future when God will be all in all, that is, when He will be completely realized. For this is the final purpose of creation, that which could not be in itself, shall be in itself."[12]

Schelling holds to an evolutionary metaphysics: the notion of an evolving God who has it all together but still needs the thinking and acting of human creatures in order to complete, *completely*, the task of *all being One with the cosmos*. Owing to our cognitive abilities, we are the creaturely means whereby the cosmos becomes aware of itself. Such self-awareness is needed in order to determine the progress of our moral status. There is no telling for sure how and when this task will be completely accomplished. But we must never give up the struggle to endure its suffering moments. We are here on earth to answer God's call: "Where art thou?" Not answering this call risks the wrath of the Lord. As made clear in the story of Adam and Eve, a "Here I am!" is definitely expected whenever the call is sounded. God demands acknowledgment. Consequences *will* follow. They need not be pretty. Remember what happened to the murderer Cain:

"And the Lord said unto Cain, Where is Abel thy brother? . . . What hast though done? The voice of thy brother's blood crieth unto me from the ground." And God "cursed [Cain] from the earth": "When thou tillest the ground, it shall not henceforth yield unto thee her strength; a fugitive and vagabond shalt thou be in the earth." Cain's punishment is the denial of receiving the life-giving gift of acknowledgment from others. God, too, would no longer be a source of this gift and the hope that comes with it. "And Cain said unto the Lord, my punishment *is* greater than I can bear" (Gen 4:10-13). But improvement is possible. In *Paradise Lost*, for example, John Milton has Adam speak these words after the fall:

> O goodness infinite, goodness immense!
> That all this good of evil shall produce,
> And evil turn to good; more wonderful
> Than that which by creation first brought forth
> Light out of darkness! Full of doubt I stand,
> Whether I should repent me now of sin
> By me done and occasioned, or rejoice
> Much more, that much more good thereof shall spring,
> To God more glory, more good will to men
> From God, and over wrath, grace shall abound.[13]

We pray, "God help us!" The prayer also works as a question: "Where art thou?" We wait for a reply. We have hope and faith, but still we worry: God forbid that God should *decide not* to answer our desperate call here and now. If, however, this holy option ends up happening, and if we still feel the strength of the Lord's "loving-kindness" in our souls, then we might admit that, despite the heartbreak of the moment, it all happened for the best, for the good. Life will eventually get better. Indeed, when suffering strikes and our metaphysical impulse to feel at home in the world goes full throttle and upward—toward God, our Maker, the One who holds a place for us in the "most perfect" home of all (Heaven)—we really want to hear God say "Here I am!" (if only to reassure us that our loss was not in vain). Contributing substantially to the power of religion is the institutionalized belief that when no one else is willing to heed our call for help, we can turn to God for the life-giving gift of acknowledgment. What would life be like if *no one* took the time to acknowledge your existence? The concept of "god" without the life-giving gift of acknowledgment is rather vacuous.

THE HEART OF CONSCIENCE

God acknowledges. God declares, "Let there be . . . !" The cosmos came into being with the uttering of the Word. God's plan is in the works. We actualize the potential of the plan and its narrative and moral integrity by "having a heart" and acting accordingly. The Old Testament speaks of conscience in terms of the "heart": "I will give them a heart to know Me, that I am the Lord" (Jer 24:7). God orders Abraham to "walk before me, and be thou perfect [Hebrew, *tamin* or 'wholehearted']" (Gen 17:1-2). Gifted with a heart (conscience), we are made capable of being open to, concerned with, and awed by the happenings and mysteries of life. According to Rabbi Abraham Joshua Heschel, awe "is the cardinal attitude of the religious Jew." The emotional experience of awe draws one near to that experience's inspiring object; it is "evoked not in moments of calculation but in moments of being in rapport" with what is being witnessed.[14] In a moment of awe, one's orientation toward the world assumes a way of being whose watchword is this: let there be! The moment is "holy," for now the manner in which one experiences the presence of things is most like the "saying" that first called life into being: "And God said, Let there be light" (Gen 1:3).

In moments of awe, things "speak" in mysterious ways. The experience is humbling. It is a time of wonder. What does this mystery mean? What should one do? For the religious Jew, wonder "is the state of our being asked," the state in which one is addressed and acknowledged—"Where art thou?" (Gen 22:1)— and in which one's capacity for moral feeling is called forth and directed: "And now . . . what doth the Lord thy God require of thee, but to fear the Lord thy God, to walk in all his ways, and to love Him, and to serve the Lord thy God with all thy heart" (Deut 10:12). Wholeheartedness is the way toward perfection— at least in theory.

The Old Testament teaches us how a person's conscience may call with the wisdom it has acquired over the years, but the voice of God calls from beyond the heartfelt and interpretive workings of one's moral sense: "His is the call, ours the paraphrase."[15]

Whatever God's otherness *is*, is beyond words. Moreover, the Old Testament teaches that our moral sense is not infallible; its paraphrase may be utterly mistaken ("The heart is deceitful above all things, and desperately wicked: who can know it?" [Jer 17:9]).

In the New Testament, this fact of life is acknowledged by the Apostle Paul in 1 Corinthians 8 and 10 when he discusses how the socially conditioned "conscience" of certain Christian converts forbade them to eat meat that had been offered in sacrifice to idols. Paul considers this conscience to be misguided and therefore "weak," for "we know that an idol is nothing in the world, and that there is none other God but one" (1 Cor 8:4). It is significant, however, that Paul advises against the use of force to enlighten those of a "weak conscience" because this could lead to their destruction (1 Cor 8:11). For Paul, conscience (Greek, *suneidesis*) is a person's knowledge ("consciousness") of his or her own conduct, especially as this conduct is consistent with whatever moral standard the person has appropriated. Conscience thereby functions to inform and defend one's psychic health, self-respect, and personal integrity.[16] Requiring the "weak" to disobey their conscience is thus tantamount to inflicting a potentially fatal wound on their well-being. Paul regards such an act as sinful (1 Cor 8:12) and encourages the weak, whenever they learn that the meat before them is sacrificial, to behave according to their own standards so as to avoid the pangs of conscience (1 Cor 10:28-29). An individual's conscience is not something to be taken lightly. As Thomas Aquinas, a true believer in God's perfection, would later put it, "Every conscience, whether it is right or wrong, whether it concerns things evil in themselves or things morally indifferent, obliges us to act in such a way that he who acts against his conscience sins."[17] When the paraphrase of the call of conscience is in error, Paul recommends a showing of respect for the circumstances at hand and preaches tolerance and patience as ways to reform. For him, conscience calls for such virtues.[18]

The heart, conscience, and perfection go hand in hand. So say the Scriptures. But the relationship is not without its problems. Situated as it is in the contingency of experiential reality, hearing the call of conscience may end up effecting errors in judgment. Conscience, therefore, must be cultivated and instructed. As in

the case of Paul and the Corinthians, this approach of directing conscience favors collaborative deliberation that takes into
account the attending circumstances of those who seek to be in
good conscience. We have an obligation to remain open to others and respect their existence. Tolerance and patience are ways
of being in the world that serve this obligation. Perfection calls
for open-mindedness (tolerance) and a willingness to remain in
this state for however long it takes (patience) for all concerned to
reach a satisfactory conclusion. Collaborative deliberation helps
to keep the process going, thereby providing some safeguard
against the disease of becoming rotten with perfection.

THE POWER OF THE WORD

The lesson is made clear long before Paul speaks of Christ. It was
previously demonstrated when God ordered Moses (around 1400
B.C.E.) to confront Pharaoh, gave the Jewish leader "the words"
(devarim) to speak to the Egyptian ruler, and then, in a moment
of Almighty manipulation, "harden[ed] Pharaoh's heart" (conscience) so that he would not "listen" to what Moses had to say
(Exod 7:3-4, 13). Bad things can happen to people when they
refuse to engage in collaborative deliberation, especially when
the order comes from One who, although supposedly perfect (all-
good, all-compassionate), is known to be jealous and vengeful.
In the Old Testament, God (Yahweh) has good and bad days—
mood swings that are not fully worked out until the narrators of
God's story begin writing the narrative of the New Testament.[19]
Throughout the Scriptures, however, punishment is due to those
who are not open to God's teachings and who thus might treat
others as the Jewish people were treated in Egypt: "Thou shalt
neither vex a stranger, nor oppress him: for ye were strangers
in the land of Egypt. Ye shall not afflict any widow, or fatherless child. If thou afflict them in any wise, and they cry at all
unto me, I will surely hear their cry; And my wrath shall wax
hot, and I will kill you with the sword; and your wives shall be
widows, and your children fatherless" (Exod 22:21-24). A most
fitting (perfect) punishment, to be sure: don't do to others what
you would not have others do to you. God values otherness.

Moses knew himself to be "slow of speech" and "slow of
tongue"; he was not "eloquent" enough to preach and prophesy

to Israel and her enemies (Exod 4:11). Moses, in short, lacked the requisite rhetorical competence to spread the word of God in a moving and truthful way. Remedying this problem with God's help was part of Moses' heroic struggle. Rabbi David Wolpe makes much of this point in his telling of the story of Moses: "Rather than the gentle comfort of rolling phrases and smooth oratory, God's leader has to prove by his inner struggle that he shares the people's plight. The leader must also have a catch in his throat, not spread ready rhetoric like a salve over all wounds. Moses cannot lead by means of the easy fluency of the demagogue. His is a hard-earned eloquence. His is less the mastery of the word than the heroism of the word."[20] Hard-earned eloquence: I understand this to mean a form of rhetorical competence that one acquires not simply by knowing and talking theory, but instead by being open and devoted to God's call and the effort that it takes to spread the Word in a convincing and honest way. Moses is set on a path where coming to terms with perfection must take place in the muck and mire of everyday existence. Here, in this world of ever-changing circumstances and innumerable contingencies, all of God's messengers must find ways of employing words to help people understand and move toward the truth. To speak for God truthfully and effectively, one must be open not only to God's otherness but also to the immediate concerns of one's audience, for attending to these concerns is how speakers gain and maintain the attention of their listeners, thereby heightening the chance of moving them toward the truth, for their *own* good. Hard-earned eloquence helps to bring God's otherness to others. The skill was also employed by Moses in persuading God not to annihilate the Jewish people when they broke the law and worshipped an idol (the golden calf) at the base of Mount Sinai. In this case, we learn of the importance of keeping God open to the otherness of others. A closed-minded God allows for the possibility of being rotten with perfection, a condition that begins to materialize whenever God's creatures think that they know it all.

Within Christian tradition, the parables of Christ offer "perfect" illustrations of this entire rhetorical process. And let us not forget that the first parable (the Sower and the Seed, Matt 13:1-23) is about spreading the Word as one would spread the seed. The activities require that we consider and attend to the nature of the "soil" (the "heart" of an audience) wherein we intend to have our seeds (ideas) grow and flourish. This heart may be "hard," "shallow," "strangled" by the "thorns" and "weeds" of everyday life, or, in the best case, "open." The open heart is most receptive to and welcomed by God: it receives the gospel like good soil receives seed. Soil, especially when it is hard, shallow, and strangled by other matters, is always in need of cultivation. We are here on earth to carry on the work of "the divine Gardener."[21] The Bible is a "self-help" ("how-to") book with a heavy dose of metaphysics.

The notion of the "heart" present in the parable of the Sower and the Seed reflects a fundamental teaching of Christ's Jewish heritage. Recall that this notion is related to "conscience"—that gift from God that enables us to hear and heed God's call. In Judaism, being open-hearted to the call of conscience is essential if we expect to reach and feel at home in the "promised land." Moses and his people wandered in the desert for forty years, but not without the hope of achieving this goal. Wanderlust can certainly have its rewards, but having what in Judaism is called a "dwelling place" (*makom*) where some reprieve is offered from the grind of everyday life and that we can call home defines a deeply felt need of human being.

The Hebraic term *makom* is also a word that refers to God's presence here on earth—a presence that is spoken of in the Hebraic notion of the *shechinah*, which literally translates as "the dwelling place of God." Such a dwelling place is most commonly associated with the tabernacle (*mishkan*) or portable synagogue that God told Moses and his people to build and to carry with them in their nomadic wanderings as a reminder of God's presence in the world. The *shechinah* also is understood to be situated in the human heart and makes itself known with the wondrous happenings of life that present themselves to us and inspire moral consciousness. Our open-heartedness and God's presence go hand in hand. "*God [is] in search of man*," writes Heschel.[22] Even God needs a place (e.g., the planet Earth) to be heard and responded to ("Where art thou?" "Here I am!"), a home away from home—heaven—if you will, hence the gift of the heart, of conscience, and its capacity to be open to what is other than itself. The art and practice of rhetoric serve this end.

THE RELIGIOUS ORATOR

One of the most famous and influential religious defenses of this art is developed in Augustine's *On Christian Doctrine*:

> For since by means of the art of rhetoric both truth and falsehood are urged, who would dare to say that truth should stand in the person of its defenders unarmed against lying, so that they who wish to urge falsehoods may know how to make their listeners benevolent, or attentive, or docile in the presentation, while the defenders of truth are ignorant of that art? Should they speak briefly, clearly, and plausibly while the defenders of truth speak so that they tire their listeners, make themselves difficult to understand and what they have to say? Should they oppose the truth with fallacious arguments and assert falsehoods, while the defenders of truth have no ability either to defend the truth or to oppose the false? Should they, urging the minds of their listeners into error, ardently exhort them, moving them by speech so that they terrify, sadden, and exhilarate them, while the defenders of truth are sluggish, cold, and somnolent? Who is so foolish as to think this to be wisdom?[23]

Augustine, of course, is being rhetorical with the instructive questions that he asks. Christianity needs the art of rhetoric to sustain and spread the Word, especially as this homiletic endeavor must take place before so many others whose discourse, although eloquent and entertaining, promotes misunderstandings and falsehoods about the true meaning of the Word. Augustine calls for hard-earned eloquence to counter this ever-present danger and, in the process, to contribute to an "ecclesiastical literature" that can instruct readers about God's truth and the ways it is best said and practiced. God's word lives with the help of words expressed by "teachers" who remain open both to its truth and to those who have yet to understand and appreciate this truth. Clarity of expression, which he understands to lie at the heart of teaching, is especially important for Augustine. He councils, anyone "who teaches should thus avoid all words which do not teach." So, for example, "good teachers have, or should have such a desire to teach that if a word in good Latin is necessarily ambiguous or obscure, the vulgar manner of speech is used so that ambiguity or obscurity may be avoided and the expression is not that of the learned but of the unlearned. . . . What profits correctness in a speech which is not followed by the listeners when . . . what is said is not understood by those on whose account we speak?"[24]

It is important to note here that Augustine is not counseling teachers to give priority to style over correctness. Finding a fitting (eloquent) way of presenting God's word to audiences characterized by various competing interests and cognitive abilities is a valuable means to a much greater end: God's truth. Augustine writes, "This eloquence is that to be used in teaching, not that the listener may be pleased by what has horrified him, not that he may do what he has hesitated to do, but that he may be aware of that [truth] which lay hidden." The teacher's style must always be inclined to serve the greater good of helping people to "feast delightedly on this truth, for it is a mark of good and distinguished minds to love the truth within words and not the words."[25] The authenticity of eloquence lies in its capacity to move people beyond its perfect presentation of words toward that which is perfect in the highest sense. Indeed, Augustine teaches that it is a mistake to ever insist that we have reached perfection in our everyday lives, for the true function of perfection is to make us acknowledge our imperfection. We have here a prescription for treating the disease of being rotten with perfection. Coming to terms with the perfection of God's truth is a lifelong endeavor—one that is facilitated by teachers who know how to spread the Word effectively to others. Augustine further emphasizes the point: "Of what use is a gold key if it will not open what we wish? Or what objection is there to a wooden one which will, when we seek nothing except to open what is closed? But since there is some comparison between eating and learning, it may be noted that on account of the fastidiousness of many even that food without which life is impossible must be seasoned."[26]

Augustine's use of metaphors, analogies, and wit here owe much to his understanding and appreciation of the extant rhetorical tradition, especially as this tradition was developed in the writings of Cicero. Like the philosophers Socrates, Plato, and Aristotle before him, Cicero held firmly to the belief that "if we bestow fluency of speech on persons devoid of . . . [the] virtues [of integrity and supreme wisdom], we shall not have made orators of them but shall have put weapons into the hands of madmen."[27] Hence, Cicero insisted that "philosophy is essential to a full, copious and impressive discussion and exposition of the subjects which so often come up in speeches and are usually treated meagerly, whether they concern religion, death, piety, patriotism, good and evil, virtues and vices, duty, pain, pleasure, or mental disturbances and errors."[28] Augustine admits that Cicero's "exhortation to study philosophy" helped to change his life: "It gave me different values and priorities. Suddenly every vain hope became empty to me, and I longed for the immortality of wisdom with an incredible ardour in my heart."[29] Cicero's praise of philosophy directed Augustine toward its most metaphysical limits: God.

But Cicero also insisted that "we are not born for ourselves alone," that "our country claims a share of our being," and that if we intend "to contribute to the general good," we must not disparage and retreat from the politics of public life but instead use "our skill, our industry, and our talents to cement human society more closely together, man to man."[30] The obligation stated here speaks to the importance of rhetoric. Philosophy is essential for the education of the orator, but it is the "art of eloquence" (*oratio*) practiced by this advocate of the *vita activa* that instructs one on how to equip (*ornare*) knowledge of a subject in such a way that it can assume a publicly accessible form and function effectively in the social and political arena. For the good of the community, philosophy and rhetoric must work together. Cicero—who admitted "that whatever ability I possess as an orator comes, not from the workshops of the rhetoricians, but from the spacious grounds of the Academy"[31]—would have it no other way. "To be drawn by study away from active life is contrary to moral duty."[32] No wonder Cicero felt obliged to offer counsel in the ways of rhetoric. For "what function is so kingly, so worthy of the free, so generous, as to bring help to the suppliant, to raise up those who are cast down, to bestow security, to see free from peril, to maintain men in their civil rights? . . . The wise control of the complete orator is that which chiefly upholds not only his own dignity, but the safety of countless individuals and of the entire State."[33]

Being much less concerned with the social and political workings of the state than with the heavenly kingdom of God, Augustine stressed that he did not read Cicero "for a sharpening of [his] style . . . and literary expression." Rather, he "was impressed" by the author's "content": Cicero's instructions for getting at the truth of things as much as possible. Rhetoric at its best serves the truth, which for Augustine ultimately requires that we "leave earthly things and fly back to [God]."[34] Eloquence, however, is not to be forsaken, for it serves a valuable purpose in helping to establish a way for others to come to terms with the Almighty. Augustine put it this way:

> [S]ince infants are not taught to speak except by learning the expressions of speakers, why can men not be made eloquent, not by teaching them the rules of eloquence, but by having them read and hear the expressions of the eloquent and imitate them in so far as they are able to follow them? Have we not seen examples of this being done? For we know many men ignorant of the rules of eloquence who are more eloquent than many who have learned them; but we know of no one who is eloquent without having read or heard the disputations and sayings of the eloquent.[35]

Rhetoric helps to construct and cultivate on earth a dwelling place for God's truth. The twentieth-century theologian Dietrich Bonhoeffer, who was executed by the Nazis for his resistance to Hitler, spoke of this dwelling place as "the goal of all Christian community":

> God has put this Word into the mouth of men in order that it may be communicated to other men. When one person is struck by the Word, he speaks it to others. God has willed that we should seek and find His living word in the witness of a brother, in the mouth of man. Therefore, the Christian needs another Christian who speaks God's Word to him. He needs him again and again when he becomes uncertain and discouraged, for by himself he cannot help himself without belying the truth. He needs his brother man as a hearer and proclaimer of the divine word of salvation.[36]

HOLY SPARKS AND THE PHYSICIAN

The goal of Christian community is inextricably tied to the spreading of the Word and to the advance of understanding and personal reassurance made possible by this rhetorical activity. Rhetoric may thus be credited as an art form that is capable of what in the Judaic tradition of Kabbalah (the mystical core of Judaism, and ultimately of Christianity and Islam) is described as raising "holy sparks." As Rabbi David Cooper notes, the theory of holy sparks emphasizes that "every particle in our physical universe, every structure and every being, is a shell that contains sparks of holiness"—that is, "the light of divine consciousness" that is needed to experience the disclosing of the truth of anything that exists. The holy task of humankind "is to release each spark from the shell and raise it up, ultimately to return it to its original state. The way these sparks are raised is through acts of loving-kindness, of being in harmony with the universe, and through higher awareness." Clarifying the nature of these acts, Cooper stresses that "in each moment of existence we have the potential to raise holy sparks. . . . The choices we make for our activities, the interactions we have with our family, friends, neighbors, business associates, and even strangers, the way we spend our leisure time, the books we read, the television we watch, the way we relate to food, everything in daily life presents sparks locked in husks awaiting release."[37]

Raising holy sparks is the fundamental activity that cultivates and heightens religious awareness and messianic consciousness of the Word and its teachings in the dwelling place (*makom*) of one's community. Talmudic sages (interpreters of the Torah, the five books of Moses) point to this vocation as being essential to our ability to make a place in our hearts for the reception of God's truth. This embodied dwelling place for God, where the pangs of conscience are felt at a moment's notice, is the matter at hand when the Holy One, with memorable metaphorical and rhetorical competence, says, "My children, give me an opening of repentance no bigger than the eye of a needle, and I will widen it into an opening through which wagons and carriages will pass."[38] The practice of rhetoric lends itself to the raising of holy sparks, the fostering of wholeheartedness, the creation and maintenance of community, and thus to the perfection of humankind.

The struggle for perfection is a common theme in both the Old and New Testaments; it defines a fundamental aspect of God's design. Augustine puts it this way: "You stir man to take pleasure in praising you, because you have made us for yourself, and our heart is restless until it rests in you."[39] Blessed with a heart and the cognitive ability to understand and express our feelings, we are fated to struggle to know and enact God's ways of being good, just, and true. Augustine is completely committed to this struggle, hence his "confessions" to God: "You are being in a supreme degree and are immutable. In you the present day has no ending." Our ever-passing years are "your Today," a constant presence that grants "the measure and condition" of human existence. "If anyone finds your simultaneity beyond his understanding, it is not for me to explain it. Let him be content to say 'What is this?' (Exod 16:15). So too let him rejoice and delight in finding you who are beyond discovery rather than fail to find you by supposing you to be discoverable."[40] "Faith," of course, is essential in dealing with this paradox of finding One who is "beyond discovery." Augustine describes this One as "the Physician whose help has kept him from falling sick, or at least enabled him to be less gravely ill." God has "prepared the medicines of faith [found in the Bible] . . . applied them to the sicknesses of the world, and . . . given them such power."[41] God says as much in the Old Testament: "I am the Lord that healeth thee" (Exod 15:26).

In his *Confessions*, Augustine is coming to terms with God, "the Physician," who has always been and who will always be here "Today" but who is "beyond discovery." Indeed, God was here before "here" had a name. God's truth transcends the symbolic representations that struggle to give meaning to this truth. God's truth is always otherwise than whatever can be said about it. Although Augustine admits that "it is not for [him] to explain [this truth]," he nevertheless is hopeful that his ways of representing the matter will encourage others to hear and respond to its call of conscience. He prays to God: "[M]ake it clear to me, physician of my most intimate self, that good results from my present undertaking. Stir up the heart when people read and hear the confessions of my past wickedness, which you have forgiven and covered up to grant me happiness in yourself, transforming my soul by faith and your sacrament." Augustine desperately wants his confessional rhetoric to have effect, and he believes that God's gift of goodness will aid him in achieving this goal: "Good people are delighted to hear about the past sins of those who have now shed them. The pleasure is not in the evils as such, but that though they were so once, they are not like that now."[42] God, the Physician, brought us into being and is always on call to attend to and remedy our ills. Augustine assumes the responsibility of helping to dispense the medicaments at hand. Having a way with words—rhetorical competence—has a significant role to play in this holy task of coming to terms with perfection.

How best to spread the Word, to make it memorable so that it will live on in our hearts and minds and show forth in our behavior? As noted above, Augustine would have us think of God in terms of medicine and its practitioners. The physician's healing powers offer the best approximation of God's gift of life. Without these powers, "physicians [are] of no value" (Job 13:4). Such was the case, for example, with those physicians who could not cure "a certain woman, which had an issue of blood twelve years. And had suffered many things of many physicians, and had spent all that she had, and was nothing bettered, but rather grew worse" (Mark 5:25-26). When, however, this woman of faith was able to touch Jesus' garment as he stood before a crowd of people, she became "whole." And Jesus said, "Daughter, thy faith hath made thee whole; go in peace, and be whole of thy plague" (Mark 5:28, 34).

This life-saving act of grace takes place as Jesus is on his way to help the dying daughter of Jairus, one of the rulers of the synagogue: "My little daughter lieth at the point of death: I pray thee, come and lay thy hands on her, that she may be healed; and she shall live" (Mark 5:23). Jairus' wife and friends believed that the child was already dead; they scorned Jesus, who entered her house and maintained that she was only asleep. But then "he took the damsel by the hand, and said unto her . . . arise" (Mark 5:41). And as the miracle unfolded, a lesson was once again demonstrated: there are physicians, and there is "the Physician," the One whose healing powers treat the *whole* person, both body and soul. The perfectibility of humankind requires that we become "wholehearted" by opening ourselves to God's call and its gift of salvation.

Augustine confesses to God and to all who would read his words, "Many and great are those diseases, many and great indeed. But your [God's] medicine is still more potent. We might have thought your Word was far removed from being united to mankind and have despaired of our lot unless he had become flesh and dwelt among us."[43] In coming to terms with God, Augustine's rhetoric makes use of a powerful analogy—one that *really makes a difference* as it provides a sense of humankind's "godlike" (although still painfully deficient) capacity to "heal thyself." The analogy is rooted in the Scriptures, especially in the New Testament (Luke 4:23). But the history of the analogy is older than these holy writings; it goes back at least to the beginnings of Western philosophy. Five hundred years before the birth of Christ, Socrates spoke of God, medicine, and rhetoric when instructing his students on how they should attempt to speak the truth as perfectly as possible. For Socrates, it all begins with a certain interpretation of the call of conscience that comes from One who is beyond having good and bad days and whose presence brings benefits and burdens.

CHAPTER THREE

INTERPRETING THE CALL

Socrates describes the call as a "prophetic voice" that first came to him in early childhood and remained his "constant companion."[1] The voice commanded his "service to God (23b), which he took to mean that his life's calling must be that of "leading the philosophical life" (28e), of "elucidating the truth" for others (29d) and encouraging them "not to think more of practical advantages than of . . . [their] mental and moral well-being" (36c). To those who accused him of corrupting the minds of the youth, Socrates said, "I am . . . a gift from God" (31a). He could not say this if he did not believe it to be true, he said, for the voice, his daemon, always spoke up and prevented him from committing any wrongdoing (40a–b). When the call came, lying was out of the question, as was any involvement in the politics of public life, "corrupted" as they were by the teachings of those (the sophists) who were eloquent but unwise, who were skilled in the oratorical practice of making "the weaker argument defeat the stronger by employing flowery language . . . decked out with fine words and phrases" (17b–18b).

Although he accepted being called an "orator" as long as that was defined to mean "one who speaks the truth" (17b), Socrates "would much rather die" as the result of his philosophical ways and commitments than engage himself in the unethical maneuvers of sophistry (38d–e). His daemon never balked at this decision, nor did the companion balk when Socrates turned to the teachings of Hippocrates (the father of scientific medicine) as a remedy for curing rhetoric's ills. Socrates' diagnosis and prescription are clear: in performing its principal function of influencing men's souls, rhetoric is suffering from the malady of sophistry, of granting priority to opinion, appearance, and probability over science, knowledge, and truth. As science is currently developing a rational understanding of the body and its diseases, so must rhetoric develop a rational understanding of the soul and of any topic that is discussed to influence it. If rhetoric is to be cured of its ill-mannered behavior such that it will no longer insult the intelligence of those who "know the truth about things" or further infect those who do not, it must acquire the healthy status of a *techne*. It must become scientific in scope and function; it must know itself to be a true medicament of the soul.[2]

Hippocratic physicians made use of the orator's art. Whether in spoken or written form, rhetoric enabled these first men of scientific medicine to define and defend their *techne* during public debates and while treating patients in their homes or in the physicians' workshops. It thus served the important purpose of calling into being a "medical public" that, owing to its new scientific education, could stand with the Hippocratic physicians in their initial fight against traveling sophistic lecturers and those quack doctors whose practice still admitted the use of magical charms.[3]

Plato commended this rhetoric of science in his *Laws*.[4] Hippocratic physicians employed it, however, so as to be done with it. The author of the Hippocratic and *rhetorical* treatise *The Art* gives testimony to this fact when, in concluding his defense of scientific medicine, he willingly discredits what he has been engaged in by noting with approval that "the multitude find it more natural to believe what they have seen than what they have heard."[5] Once a physician's medical skills are demonstrated not in words but in action, rhetoric becomes superfluous for the Hippocratics, or at best something that must be uttered to patients whose opinions and fears reflect their ignorance about the truth of medicine and about the trust they should have in their healers' diagnostic and prognostic abilities.[6] As the author of the Hippocratic text *Decorum* notes, the wisdom that these healers possess and that they must constantly seek as their first priority makes them "the equal of a god. Between wisdom and medicine there is no gulf fixed."[7]

Under Hippocratic doctrine, rhetoric is destined to lose its status as medical science flourishes. Indeed, according to the author of the Hippocratic *Law*, "There are in fact two things, science and opinion; the former begets knowledge, the latter ignorance."[8] Medicine is a science and must remain a science by continuing to give witness and proven remedy to the body. For the good of the patient, life must be protected and prolonged, and in the process no harm should be committed against the one who is seeking health. This injunction, found in the Hippocratic *oath*—"Do no harm!"—is not an invention of science. Rather, it is rooted in Pythagorean religious beliefs that some argue are themselves influenced by the more ancient Hebraic law of Moses and that emphasize, among other things, how physician-assisted suicide, as well as an unrestricted zeal to keep people alive even when their plight is hopeless, is sacrilegious and thus an immoral act. Hippocratic physicians had their own way of answering the call of conscience.[9]

Plato's *Dialogues* detail Socrates' commitment to the Hippocratic distinction between science and opinion. The science and healing powers of physicians are called for by God. The physician is a model for the orator who seeks to perfect his skill when coming to terms with the truth of the matters at hand. The truth, for the physician, is identified with the body and its diseases. Treating the soul is left to those who are willing to struggle with the ways of rhetoric. Socrates and Plato made use of the art in their pursuit of philosophical truth, be this truth that of God or the transcendental "forms" that define the essence of other lesser matters. Augustine confined his attention to God. All three taught that the paths toward the truth should become ever more barren of rhetoric as the ultimate goal is approached. The prophetic voice of God's call of conscience demands as much. Still, the practice of rhetoric warrants recognition as an art that can serve the truth. Socrates' personification of this art gets to the point: "I never insist on ignorance of the truth on the part of one who would learn to speak; on the contrary, if my advice goes for anything, it is that he should only resort to me after he has come into possession of truth; what I do however pride myself on is that without my aid knowledge of what is true will get a man no nearer to mastering the art of persuasion."[10] With this art, we are given a way of opening people to the truth, of having them hear the call and respond in a proper manner.

Creating Openness

Creating openness is the key. Such openness is at work when Augustine speaks to God about this specific matter, especially as it applies to understanding how Moses "perfectly perceived and had in mind all the truth we have been able to find in [the Bible], and all the truth that could be found in it which we have not been able, or have not as yet been able, to discover."[11] One particular (albeit lengthy) passage is worth quoting:

> May I hear and understand how in the beginning you make heaven and earth (Gen. I, I). Moses wrote this. . . . He is not now before me, but if he were, I would clasp him and ask him and through you beg him to explain to me the creation. I would concentrate [keep open] my bodily ears to hear the sounds breaking forth from his mouth. If he spoke Hebrew, he would in vain make an impact on my sense of hearing, for the sounds would not touch my mind at all. If he spoke Latin, I would know what he meant. Yet how would I know whether or not he was telling me the truth? If I did know this, I could not be sure of it from him. Within me, within the lodging of my thinking, there would speak a truth which is neither Hebrew nor Greek nor Latin nor any barbarian tongue and which uses neither mouth nor tongue as instruments and utters no audible syllables [much like the prophetic voice that directed Socrates]. I would say: "What he is saying is true." And I being forthwith assured would say with confidence to the man possessed by you: "What you say is true." But since I cannot question him, I ask you who filled him when he declared what is true; you my God I ask. "Spare my sins" (Job 14: 16). You have granted to your servant to utter these things; grant also to me the power to understand them.[12]

For his own sake as well as that of others, Augustine struggles to come to terms with God, to understand the One who is the whole truth: perfection. Augustine admits that "the language" of God that inspires the Scriptures is "rich in meaning," allowing for a "diversity of true views." He also confesses, "I would not be using the language of my confessions if I fail to confess to you that I do not know" which of these views correspond "supremely" (perfectly) "both to the light of truth and to the reader's spiritual profit."[13] The word "confess" is from the Latin *confiteri*, meaning "to acknowledge." A genuine act of acknowledgment functions to open us to the otherness of people, places, and things so that we can "admit" (Middle English, *acknow*) its wonders into our minds and hearts and then "admit" (Middle English, *knowlechen*) to others the understanding we have gained and that we believe is worth sharing. Put another way, the act of acknowledging is a way of attuning consciousness toward others in order to make room for them in our lives. With this added living space comes the opportunity for a new beginning, a second chance, whereby we might improve our lot in life and feel more at home with others. There is hope to be found with this transformation of space and time as people opt to go out of their way to make us feel wanted and needed, to praise our presence and actions, and thus to acknowledge the worthiness of our existence. Such consideration and respect heightens the chance that in the company of others a "knowing together" (*con-scientia*) of the truth of some matter of importance will take place.[14]

Augustine acknowledges God. He is dedicated to remaining open to the Word. He seeks wholeheartedness and wants to teach the truth of that call of conscience that was first disclosed to Moses in a burning bush. Truth, be it holy or not, happens first and foremost as an act of disclosure, a "showing-forth" (*epi-deixis*) or epideictic display of something that discloses itself to us and that, in turn, can be disclosed by us to others in some symbolic manner. The assertion and validity of *any* "truth claim" presupposes the occurrence of such an act and thus the acknowledgments that initiated and continue to sustain its status. "Knowledge," insists the philosopher Ludwig Wittgenstein, "is in the end based on acknowledgments."[15] The philosopher Stanley Cavell stresses the moral implications of this central claim of "ordinary language" philosophy in arguing that acknowledgment is "something owed another simply as a human being, the failure of which reveals the failure of one's own humanity." Indeed, for Cavell, the "crucified human body is our best picture of the acknowledged human soul."[16] With the narratives of the Old Testament in mind, the

Talmudic scholar and philosopher Emmanuel Levinas would have us think about acknowledgment as what is going on when we are abruptly awakened to the presence of "otherness" in our lives, especially when this presence is in need of a caring response. "Where art thou?" "Here I am!" Acknowledgment of otherness is a moral act that "accomplishes human society" as it promotes "the miracle of moving out of oneself," of egoism becoming altruism.[17] Acknowledgment is a life-giving gift. God's first "avowal" (which is a form of acknowledgment) makes the case: "Let there be!"

Augustine returns God's generosity with his "confessions." He is open to God so that he can come to terms with God's truth and share it with others in a rhetorically competent manner. He has faith that he will succeed, although he worries about making sure that all he has to say is completely true. Achieving perfection takes time; making known the truth in an understandable and convincing way to others takes rhetorical competence. But how, exactly, is one to grasp and know the truth? The task calls for the behavior of acknowledgment, for a specific way of being open to the presence of otherness such that the truth of whatever form this otherness takes, how it discloses itself as what it *is*, can be appreciated as fully as possible. Acknowledging otherness prepares the way for formulating as completely as possible a correct interpretive understanding of the matter at hand. This specific task is that of hermeneutics.

THE HERMENEUTICS OF TRUTH

Hermeneutics refers to the essential capacity of human beings to understand and give expression to the world in meaningful ways. The term also refers to the study of the methodological principles and rules that govern acts of interpretive understanding and the "compositions" they produce, from texts and works of art to the intersubjective domains of meaning that inform and guide the interpersonal dynamics of a given culture. This second understanding of hermeneutics, of course, presupposes its first and more existential and rhetorical function. One cannot study a composition unless it already exists in some form. Indeed, as the anthropologist Clifford Geertz notes, "A good interpretation of anything—a poem, a person, a history, a ritual, an institution, a society—takes us into the heart of that of which it is the interpretation."[18] To speak of the "heart" of some matter is to refer to the essential or most vital part(s) of this matter: that which enables it to be what it is. A hermeneutical investigation of a given composition, in other words, is directed toward getting at the "truth" of the composition. The oldest and perhaps best-known application of hermeneutics—biblical interpretation or the exegesis of Scripture—provides a classic example of what this task entails.

The "simple" truth in question here is that of God's word, which, of course, was uttered "in the beginning" when God "created the heaven and the earth" (Gen 1:1). However, one of Judaism's holiest texts, the Zohar, teaches that the common translation of the first line of Genesis is, in fact, a mistranslation, for the actual words in Hebrew can be read another way. The first word of the sentence, *Be-Reshit*, may be translated as "with beginning," since the Hebrew preposition *be* means "with" as well as "in." When the rest of the sentence is read in the exact order in which the other words appear in Hebrew, "God" is thus transformed from the subject of the sentence into its object. As the Hebrew scholar Daniel Matt notes, this hermeneutic reading "erases the subject, which bolsters the Zohar's interpretation that the true subject of divine emanation" is beyond human comprehension and description. The Zohar's way of coming to terms with the enigma is to employ an oxymoronic phrase that points to this emanation: "A spark of impenetrable darkness flashed within the concealed of the concealed from the head of Infinity." We are dealing with an "ineffable source" of creation. Matt thus points out that "for the Zohar . . . the opening words of Genesis mean: 'With beginning, the ineffable source created God.'"[19]

The "truth" of God is more than the story that unfolds throughout the Old and New Testaments. Rabbi Abraham Joshua Heschel writes, "His is the call, ours the paraphrase."[20] And with this Word—the source from which the potential to begin was first created—we are given something that can be understood (paraphrased) symbolically as "God" but whose truth transcends, as an ongoing process, even the richest and most reverent meaning of this word. "Infinity" is the term commonly associated with the "meaning" of this process. For the Zohar, however, the process, referred to as *Ein Sof* ("limitless light"), is not restricted by infinity; rather, It created it. Commenting on the hermeneutical problem involved here, Rabbi David Cooper remarks, "Indeed, we have suddenly run out of words because the idea of 'trans-infinite' is a logical absurdity. What can go beyond infinity? . . . This is *Ein Sof.*"[21] Perfection exists, but it is beyond our symbolic grasp.

With this example of biblical hermeneutics, one sees how the activity of interpretative understanding may also be conceived as a matter of "translating," "explaining," and "asserting" or "saying." These specific functions of hermeneutic analysis have their etymological roots in the Greek verb *hermeneuein* ("to interpret") and the noun *hermeneia* ("interpretation"). In ancient Greek mythology, it is the wing-footed messenger god Hermes who is credited with the initial enactment of these functions whereby the words of the gods are communicated in a form that human intelligence can comprehend. Commenting on this "Hermes process," the philosopher Richard Palmer further clarifies the nature of hermeneutics when he notes that "something foreign, strange, separated in time, space, or experience is made familiar, present, comprehensible; something requiring representation, explanation, or translation is somehow 'brought to understanding'—is 'interpreted.' "[22]

Especially in the case of biblical hermeneutics, one receives instruction in how the process of interpretation is made possible by the human capacity for awe. I noted earlier that awe is the cardinal attitude stressed in the Old Testament, for with this particular way of experiencing the world, a person is *drawn toward* the "heart" of some matter of concern. Awe is acknowledgment being stretched to its limits. In a moment of awe, one's relationship to the world is that of respecting beings by letting them be what they are. The moment marks a time of wonder, of finding oneself in a place for acquiring wisdom. According to Heschel, "There is . . . only one way to wisdom: awe. Forfeit your sense of awe, let your conceit diminish your ability to revere, and the universe becomes a market place for you. The loss of awe is the great block to insight."[23] Caught up in wonder and awe, we are in the state of being asked by otherness to remain open to some disclosure of truth.

Biblical hermeneutics stresses the moral quality of its actions as it translates, expresses, and explains the awesome and wondrous nature of the Word. This quality of interpretive understanding is related to the heart, that gift from God that equips us with moral consciousness or "conscience" and that enables us to be receptive to God's teachings and the various emotions (e.g., fear, guilt, joy, love) they are meant to inspire. In returning God's favor of acknowledgment, we ought to be, at the very least, conscientious as we try to know together with God and others all that is right, true, good, and just.

Notice, then, that with biblical hermeneutics, the interpretive challenge of getting to the "heart of the matter" (hearing and responding to Its call) is essentially a "matter of the heart" (or conscience)—that gift of moral consciousness that enables us to remain open to, such that we can acknowledge and judge fairly, the goodness of all that stands before us. But the heart is not infallible; it is in constant need of care and instruction. Wisdom is something that must be cultivated time and again. With its classic interpretation of the story of Adam, Eve, and the serpent, Christianity makes clear that it is wise, indeed, to know the Devil's work. In the kabbalistic tradition, however, the serpent means more than that. The kabbalistic teaching is that Satan is not merely the lowly and horrible creature who rules the underworld but is instead "the force of fragmentation" that operates in the physical universe as a crucial element required for creation. According to Cooper, this does not mean, however, "that the splintering force of Satan is separate from the unity of God, but, paradoxically, that it is contained within the oneness of the Divine." Whenever the force of fragmentation (the serpent's bite) makes itself known in our lives by way of some conflict (e.g, a serious illness), we are given the chance to develop "messianic consciousness" and thus an awesome sense of what life and death are all about. "Without the serpent," writes Cooper, "without the energizing of creation, we would never have the opportunity to follow a path returning us to our Divine Source."[24]

Which of these two interpretations displays the most wholeheartedness (perfection) is, of course, a matter of debate. Influenced by Pythagoras' theory of mathematics, kabbalists do, however, have the rationality of number theory on their side. Hebrew writing consists of twenty-two letters, all of them consonants. Each letter has a corresponding number. Each Hebrew word, which is read from right to left, can thus be given a numerical value, calculated by summing the numbers represented in its letters. The process is called *gematria*, or the hermeneutical art of "making numbers speak."[25] The five books of Moses (the Torah) not only tell a story, their words also present series of numbers that are believed to offer "deeper" clues to God's truth, which lies beyond the words. For example, the numbers that make up the words "serpent" (*nahash*, נ ח ש: 300 + 8 + 50) and "messiah" (*meshiach*), מ ש י ח: 8 + 10 + 300 + 40) in both cases add up to 358. The kabbalist sees this fact as more than mere coincidence. The serpent and the Messiah are not simply opposing forces; rather, "the serpent biting at our heels indicates that we are moving closer to the realization of messianic consciousness."[26] The dynamism of conflict can be an invaluable source of wisdom. With his *Confessions*, Augustine offers himself as living proof of this fact and its application to Christianity. Having eventually seen the light that revealed the shortcomings of his pagan ways, he rejoiced in "the birthpangs of conversion" and in the challenge of answering God's call to spread the Word. In being born again, Augustine demonstrates the positive effects of conflict as he progresses toward perfection—practicing acknowledgment, hermeneutics, and rhetorical competence along the way.

THE NECESSITY OF CONFLICT

The relationship between conflict and perfection, and the practices that keep the relationship going, are fundamental to the Judeo-Christian tradition and its concern for disclosing the truth that is needed to inform and guide moral consciousness. Interpreting the serpent as an aspect of God's dynamism is, however, only part of the story. Kabbalists offer a more developed hermeneutic reading of the matter. One of their most influential and innovative teachers, the sixteenth-century rabbi Isaac Luria, is a classic case in point. Luria's interpretations of the five books of Moses and the Zohar give rise to a cosmological myth intended to clarify the workings of the self-manifestation of divinity and how human beings come to play a fundamental role in sustaining this holy happening. The myth calls into question a fundamental belief of older rabbinic theology. This belief emphasizes that God's own well-being is not contingent on human action. Luria insists, on the contrary, that the Creator does need our help. With his reading of the matter, Luria redefines the traditional understanding of God's perfection and, at the same time, addresses a crucial social, political, and rhetorical exigence related to the ongoing exile of the Jewish people.[27]

Luria's myth consists of three basic concepts: *tsimtsum* ("reduction" or "withdrawal"), *shevira* ("breakage"), and *tikkun* ("repair"). According to the myth, the Creator's first act ("with beginning") was not "revelation" but rather withdrawal, the creation of an opening, a "void" or empty place within Its infinite presence and perfection. *Ein Sof*, the "endless light" of the Creator, withdrew "from Itself into Itself" in order to make room in the midst of Itself for the entire cosmos to come into being. The action is the ultimate act of self-effacement. Otherness is granted priority in God's workings, a giving way to a place, an infinite dimension of space-time, which allows for life and its development. The essential nature of the Creator is that of sharing and compassion, a desire to give of Itself. Kabbalists also associate this desire with God's intention to "purge" and cleanse Itself of the "powers of stern Judgment" in order to be as merciful as possible. Stern judgment without mercy can often be too severe and thus unjust.

These holy actions take place before God's avowal, "Let there be light!" The creation of the cosmos presupposes a more primordial creation: "with beginning," there arises an absence, a "nothingness," a vacated place where something other than God can flourish under God's care (compassion and judgment). The grand metaphysical question of Western philosophy is, "Why is there something rather than nothing?" Kabbalistic teachings put it another way: "Why is there nothing, rather than something?"[28]

From out of nothing, the cosmos is destined to appear. Now it can be said, "Let there be light!" God reintroduces a "ray of light" back into the void in order to arrange its structure with a degree of divine illumination. The structure takes a circular form, an area that is "perfectly equidistant" from its centermost point and that thus reflects in a certain way the perfectly symmetrical nature of *Ein Sof.*[29] The light that illuminates this circle becomes matter in the form of ten receptacles or "vessels" (*seifirot*) that come into being so as to receive God's gift of sharing. No gift can be given without both a giver and a receiver being present. "Vessel" is an appropriate metaphor for the reception at work here because of the everyday use of this piece of equipment. The story of Adam and Eve is not so much about two "people" as it, too, is a metaphor for (a way to come to terms with) this primordial process of giving and receiving and what can go wrong when the acknowledgment that facilitates the process is not taken seriously. Indeed, in Luria's story of the creation of the cosmos, the process proves to be defective, resulting in an unforeseen consequence. Referring to the vessels in the singular ("Vessel"), Rabbi P. S. Berg identifies the defect when he writes, "The creation of the Vessel was by no means the end, however. It was not even the beginning, or the beginning of the beginning. A dialectical process had started, one whose continuation was implied by a fundamental duality in the Vessel's nature. Although the Vessel was created only to receive, because it was formed of God's sharing energy, which was heretofore ubiquitous, the Vessel also contained an x-factor of sharing, like a gene buried deep within its biological programming."[30]

The duality in the Vessel's nature made it unstable, and it eventually shattered, not having the full strength of God. With the shattering of the Vessel, most of the light it contained returned to the light's original source. A certain number of holy sparks, however, remained attached to the Vessel's broken shards and were dispersed throughout the opening that was first made possible by God's initial withdrawal into Itself. These sparks and the shards that concealed them became the basis for our material reality. That all of this happened because of what is described as a "contradiction in [the Vessel's] nature" raises an interesting problem.[31] If God made the Vessel, it should have been perfect, not breakable, unless God intended otherwise. Was that God's intention? Discussing what went wrong here, the Hebrew scholar Lawrence Fine notes,

> The paradox, of course, is that the processes of *tsimtsum* and the subsequent emanation of divine light were set in motion in the first place for a reason, namely, to bring forth Creation. But it turned out that

these processes were inherently flawed, that the lower vessels lacked the strength with which to conduct the light properly, or that the light itself was defective in some manner, and thus the creative process resulted in unforeseen consequences. . . . In Lurianic thinking . . . the original crisis that occurred within the realm of the divine was not dependent on the misdeeds of humanity but had to do with qualities of being and dynamic processes intrinsic to divinity itself. . . . [The] radical nature [of Lurianic myth] consists significantly in the potentially subversive proposition . . . that the world as we know it is a product of flaw and error, that "the world came about through a mistake."[32]

In short, God's perfection entails imperfection—a holy conflict, to be sure.

This conclusion, at first, may seem too shocking, too awesome, to be true. The shock and awe are less frightening, however, if one understands that God did, indeed, intend (will) the Vessel to break under the strain of its desire to both receive and share God's light. This holy intention is central to God's stated plan to make humankind in Its "image" (Gen 1:26). In kabbalistic and Lurianic thought, such image making is essential for the presence and utility (practicality) of God's truth. As Rabbi Alon Goshen-Gottstein notes, "creation" is "a way for God to realize aspects of [Itself] that could not otherwise be realized. Creation is the arena through which [God's] glory, greatness, and kinship can be made known. . . . [C]reation is an extension of God's inner life, which turns back in order to face and recognize [Itself]." The purpose of creation is "for God to realize and bring to expression aspects of [Itself] that could not otherwise be known and made manifest."[33] God's creation, the embodiment of God's image, thus has a fundamental role to play in the process—one that gives, but also needs, acknowledgment. The process was at work as Moses first stood in God's light and was told that the Jewish people had a future. When Moses asked for God's "Name," he was told, "*Ehyeh-asher-ehyeh*." English renders this reply in a static way: "I *am* who I *am*." In Hebrew, however, the dynamic of being open to the future is unequivocal: "I *will be* who I *will be*." According to Rabbi Lawrence Kushner, "Here is a Name (and a God), who is neither completed nor finished. This God is literally *not yet*."[34] This giving God needs acknowledgment and help in materializing the future. God will not give up as long as we do not give up.

We have a responsibility to hear and answer the call, "Where art thou?" "Here I am!" This exchange defines an ongoing process. We need God and God needs us, creatures who can perform necessary hermeneutical and rhetorical tasks, raise holy sparks, spread the truth to and for One and all. The perfection of this process *is* its "ongoingness," its continuous dialectic of the act of reciprocity: receiving in order to share. People and things can break when the process is interrupted by particular doings and sayings (e.g., those of racism or sexism) that close us off to others. The process demands openness, for it *is* openness, not some static entity or closed system. The process unfolds as a working out of conflict, or what was referred to earlier as the "force of fragmentation," the "energizing of creation," the "serpent biting at our heels," and the action that is thereby needed to survive, progress, and better our lives. By way of such action, we can raise holy sparks and thereby help "repair" whatever is broken in the world. The breaking of vessels is a part of life. An evolutionary metaphyics is at work. That's the "perfect" plan for constantly directing humankind in its appointed task of coming to terms with the truth. Encouragement comes with the "gift" of our ability to feel good when we offer others the life-giving gift of genuine acknowledgment—God's original gift to us. God certainly speaks of "goodness" when it all began with the first light (Gen 1:4). In describing the "history" that followed, Rabbi Marc-Alain Ouaknin remarks, "It could be said that the history of [humankind] is the history of *tikkun* [repair], that is to say the history of the failure of *tikkun*. Without this failure, history itself would not exist, and [every human being] would be a complete being, that is to say, dead. The impossibility of succeeding in making the *tikkun*, this attempt at repair, defines man as a being 'about to become' whose ethic is no longer that of perfection but of perfectability."[35]

The completeness of perfection lies in its being what it is: an ongoing process of disclosure, of being open to all that is (otherness). Perfection is, by definition, a paradox: its completeness *is* its incompleteness. This is the way the world is *meant* to be, at least as far as we can tell at the present time. Kabbalists are true to this paradox in word and deed. Recall how it is described in the Zohar: "A spark of impenetrable darkness flashed within the concealed of

the concealed from the head of Infinity." Moreover, Jewish orthodoxy insists on the daily action of prayer, study, and rhetorical
interaction with one's peers dedicated to coming to terms with the
holiness of the truth. *Tikkun* is always "in progress."

The followers of Luria saw their teacher as being unsurpassed
in his ability to perform *tikkun*. He was considered to be a "physician of the soul" and a "healer of the Cosmos."[36] His teachings
appropriated old and incorporated new ways of coming to terms
with God's truth and Its purpose: we *are* creatures who, at the
very least, have a responsibility to raise holy sparks for the benefit of ourselves and others, including our Creator, who is forever
at work doing the same. Sometimes the results go unnoticed; at
other times, they are too awesome to miss. The revelation of the
Torah to Moses on Mount Sinai over three thousand years ago
is a case in point.

Unfortunately, worshipping a golden calf got in the way of
people acknowledging the revelation. Breakage occurred and
could have gotten much worse if not for Moses' rhetorical skill
to persuade God that punishing the Jewish people with annihilation would not serve God's ultimate purpose: "The entire project
of existence, even the creation of the universe itself," writes Berg,
"consists in resolving [a particular] duality through the unification of 'getting' and 'giving' into a single desire to 'receive in
order to share.' "[37] Perfection, in the truest and holiest sense of
the word, leads not toward the self but toward the other. It is an
ongoing process of creation, of opening places where people and
things can live and know together in peace and in the light of the
truth that shows itself with the raising of holy sparks.

The design of the cosmos ensures that we will hear God's call
of and for perfection. God needs our help, and thus, as Heschel
puts it, "God is in search of [humankind]."[38] The meaning and
significance of all that happens in our lives are matters that are
in *our* hands, even as we exist in "God's hands." Does God, in
fact, have hands? How appropriate, perfect, is this metaphor of
flesh? Do we have it right when it comes to witnessing and being
true to God's ways?

These questions emphasize the importance of a relationship
that we are presently considering: the one between perfection,
truth, hermeneutics, and rhetoric. Luria's cosmology not only

presupposes this relationship but grants it a specific narrative form that addresses what was earlier described as a "rhetorical exigence": some imperfection in reality that may at least be partially remedied by reasoned and artful discourse. In his particular way of coming to terms with God's creation, Luria constructs an ideology that offers his people an explanation (a specific hermeneutic understanding) of why at the present time they continue to suffer the pain of exile from their homeland and what they can do about it. Their exile was in the cards all along: God's withdrawal defines the *original* exile. The breaking of the vessels and the dispersion of shards explains the resulting Diaspora. The call for repair directs Israel's destiny as a nation and gives its people hope: a most fundamental reason for withstanding and overcoming the evils that present themselves with the ever-recurring threats and actions of marginalization and extermination. The plight of the Jewish people displays cosmic meaning and significance. They are "the chosen" people, which is to say that their existence will serve as a gauge for assessing the good, the bad, and the ugly of human behavior. Being named the chosen people was a blessing and a curse.[39]

Luria's narrative is a holy spark that sheds light on his people's fundamental relationship with and responsibility to God's truth, God's perfection. This particular spark is central to the livelihood of present-day Jewish orthodoxy. With its light, we learn of what Berg defines as "an axiom of Kabbalah":

> [T]he Bible is an encrypted document—a code in which much is hidden and hinted at but little is explicitly revealed. Again and again the Zohar asserts the foolishness of a literal interpretation of the scriptures. We must read between the lines. We must extrapolate great truths from seemingly insignificant details. We must learn from the book's every word, just as in the world we must learn from every person. This is the task of the oral tradition of Kabbalah's biblical commentaries on the Bible. These should not be understood as appendages to the Bible, but as revelations of what is hidden within it. Like an X-ray of the text, they bring to light the underlying conditions from which the biblical narrative arises.[40]

These revelations (holy sparks) define disclosures of truth that, for the kabbalist, admit awesome life-changing potential. "If we think of electric light," writes Berg, "we can understand the sudden transformation" that is possible here. "A mere flip of the light switch transforms a dark room, whether it be a tiny closet or an immense auditorium. This event of transformation, so central to Kabbalah, is recognized in all spiritual teachings. All religions have their kabbalist."[41] Berg's analogy is intended to help the contemporary reader turn on the light with respect to understanding and appreciating the meaning and significance of Kabbalah for everyday existence. Berg is engaged in an act of hermeneutical and rhetorical competence that is meant to sustain the well-being of a tradition more than three thousand years old that is dedicated to coming to terms with the perfection of God's truth. We are called to interpret the truth, to find a way of helping others to understand it, and to remain open to the possibility that we have yet to get it right. Perfection is never without imperfection. Life is filled with breakage.

Luria shared his teachings only through the spoken word. His wisdom comes to us from the books of his students and from the books of rabbis and scholars who, over the ages, kept the light shining with their particular readings and teachings about the Kabbalah. Importantly, Luria instructed his followers that the wisdom of Kabbalah is not to be shared with "outsiders" who have not devoted their lives to the study of the Torah, the Zohar, and related material and who, perhaps, may contribute insights that strengthen and advance the cause. The hermeneutical and rhetorical ways of Judaism and its pedagogical practices are more insular than those of Christianity, with its imperative to spread the word as far and as wide as possible. Thousands of years of persecution have encouraged this defensive way of being. Still, the wisdom of the Kabbalah has found its way to a more public presentation as its teachers and students have allowed for greater flexibility in their understanding of what it means to receive in order to share. Scholem would thus have us remember that the true source of the divine light "does not reveal itself in a way that makes knowledge of its nature possible, and it is not accessible even to the innermost thought . . . of the contemplative. Only through the finite nature of every existing thing, through the actual existence of creation itself, is it possible to deduce the existence of *Ein Sof* as the first infinite cause."[42] Indeed, interpreting God's call and sharing what is believed to be at least part of its truth with others is a never-ending challenge that demands rhetorical competence. To receive in order to share: it's a matter of perfection.

Scholem's classic historical account of the Kabbalah encouraged many others to join the conversation meant to clarify and extend the outreach of the tradition's wisdom and applicability. Today, one can even learn about these holy matters in such books as *The Complete Idiot's Guide to Jewish Spirituality and Mysticism*, written by the biblical and Talmudic scholar Michael Levin, who certainly realizes that his book raises a serious question for any number of experts and devoted souls: have we gone too far in "dumbing down" the awesome mysteries and revelations found in the tradition of the Kabbalah? When does "simplification" of the truth become more of a covering up than a disclosing of all that it has to say?

Consider, for example, what Levin says about the issue of "recognizing" God's perfection:

> How do you know that a glass is completely full? You know it's completely full when a little bit of it spills over. Until you see at least a few drops of liquid spilling over, you cannot be absolutely sure. Perfection, similarly, requires a little bit of itself to spill over for it to be recognized. When Jews hear good news, they often say the following blessing: "Blessed is God, who is good and does good." The kabbalistic understanding of this blessing is as follows: When we say that God *is* good, we are referring to the perfection of God. When we say that God *does* good, we are saying that God, as it were, "spills over" and creates something in the universe that is at once God and at the same time separate. According to this approach to creation, it was necessary for God to create human beings, who are the "spill over" perfection. The definition of perfection requires some sort of imperfection to compare it against. . . . The Kabbalah is simply trying to find ways to express word pictures that are virtually impossible to grasp without some sort of metaphor or analogy.[43]

Indeed, coming to terms with perfection confronts us with a difficult hermeneutical and rhetorical challenge.

I am taken with Levin's work. As demonstrated in the above quotation, he is skilled in offering simple yet compelling analogies that are true to the spirit of Kabbalah and its acknowledgment of *Ein Sof*. Levin takes this matter seriously, even though he is not presently engaged in the arduous task of doing what Torah scholars rightfully pride themselves on: reading, interpreting, and arguing with other experts about the true meaning of Scripture.

Levin is writing for an audience that is basically uneducated in his topic. Are his efforts not a legitimate form of sharing? Is he offering no worthwhile instruction that might start others on a path for learning more about the mysterious, awesome, and demanding matters under consideration?

Watching what Levin is doing brings to mind the earlier quoted words of Augustine: "Of what use is a gold key if it will not open what we wish? Or what objection is there to a wooden one which will, when we seek nothing except to open what is closed?" Recall that these words are made in defense of rhetoric and its capacity to serve the truth. Serving the truth, receiving and sharing its revelation in an effective manner, requires a respect for otherness: both God's and that of the members of one's audience who also require acknowledgment if they are to come to terms in a meaningful way with the truth. Perfection happens in the midst of otherness. There is no way around it. Otherness is a phenomenon that warrants inclusion in the relationship between perfection, truth, hermeneutics, and rhetoric that concerns us here. In the next chapter, my treatment of this phenomenon directs our attention away from the metaphysics of God and toward material existence.

CHAPTER FOUR

THE OTHERNESS ALL AROUND US

In both Judaism and Christianity, the issue of otherness is central to the hermeneutical, rhetorical, and moral enterprise of casuistry, which is specifically concerned with *casus conscientiae* or "cases of conscience." These cases bring together the otherness of God's truth, as expressed primarily in the Scriptures, and the otherness of people's everyday lives in an attempt to see how some particular institutionalized way of interpreting and understanding this truth may be applied, enlightened, and perhaps transformed and advanced by the particular circumstances at hand. In their classic treatment of the topic, the philosophers Albert Jonsen and Stephen Toulmin note that the goal of casuistry is "to set out descriptions of moral behavior in which moral precepts and the details of action [are] looked at together" in order to determine how people, "concerned to act rightly," should "make a judgment of conscience in a specific kind of situation."[1] Cases of conscience call on our ability to be rhetorically competent such that we can engage others in collaborative deliberation about the meaning of the moral precepts found in a text and those precepts' relationship to everyday existence.

For the philologist and founder of modern hermeneutic theory, Friedrich Schleiermacher, the key to getting at the truth of any text is to "grasp the thinking that underlies" its composition. In order to gain the fullest access to the intended meaning in a given text, the reader must attempt to reconstruct and reexperience the distinctive mental processes that were at work as the author brought the text into being. Schleiermacher points to the rhetorical competence displayed in an author's particular style as a major source of evidence for comprehending these processes. He writes, "Thoughts and language are intertwined, and an author's distinctive way of treating the subject is manifested by his organization of his material and by his use of language."[2] An appreciation of the rhetorical competence that informs the text is therefore needed by the interpreter.

In the case of God, of course, we have yet to generate a definitive assessment of what exactly this competence entails. In his Pulitzer Prize–winning book, *God: A Biography*, Jack Miles speaks to this lack of knowledge on our part. Part of the problem is that there is not enough to go on here in what is known as "the greatest story ever told." God, notes Miles, is a

> living question mark, a wholly prospective character. [God] has no history, no genealogy, no past that in the usual way of literature might be progressively introduced into [God's] story to explain [God's] behavior and induce some kind of catharsis in the reader. No human character could be so fully without a past and still be human, yet we may see that by giving this inhuman character words to speak in human language and deeds to do in interaction with human beings, the writers of the Bible have created a new literary possibility. God frustrates our ordinary literary expectations, shaped as they are by the expectation that we have of other human beings when we meet them. We expect to learn who they are by learning how their past has led to their present. This is, almost by definition, what makes any human character interesting and coherent. God is not interesting or coherent in this way.[3]

Indeed, what makes God interesting and coherent is Its unknowable presence, which supplies a ray of light and hope for the future—be it here on earth or in the hereafter. It seems that God's rhetorical competence entails, at the very least, the ability to make us optimistic, whereby we are more willing and able to engage in the hermeneutical and rhetorical process of receiving in order to share. The otherness of God's perfection directs us not only toward Itself but also to the related matter of the otherness of other people and their particular circumstances. Rabbi Isaac Luria's cosmological myth and its applicability to the Jewish experience of exile is a case in point. Recall that the myth emphasizes how God needs our help in repairing the wrongs of the world. A call of conscience is uttered. The challenge of acting in an ethically responsible way is before us: "Walk before me and be thou perfect" (Gen 17:1). The hermeneutic rhetoric of Luria's myth grants hope and guidance to a suffering people; it brings God to these souls and these souls to God. An impulse for perfection drives the process.

The related enterprises of hermeneutics and rhetoric, of course, are not concerned only with helping us come to terms with the otherness of God. The otherness of everyday material existence also demands the workings of the process as we attempt to interpret and understand in meaningful ways other people, places, and things. What I have to say below about this particular domain of otherness will lead to a discussion of how the ontological structure of human being is itself informed by an empirically verifiable dimension of otherness that is other than a human creation, stimulates our metaphysical impulse for perfection, and thereby invites us once again to think about perfection in holy terms.

OTHER PEOPLE, PLACES, AND THINGS

The whole enterprise of hermeneutics—from the interpretive understanding that is needed to compose and present a work of art to the interpretive understanding that is needed to compose and present a critical response to the work—is a rhetorical process of meaning formation that would be unthinkable without the active participation of audiences. The literary theorist Hans Robert Jauss emphasizes this point when he notes that "in the triangle of author, work, and public the last is no passive part, no chain of mere reactions, but rather itself an energy formative of history. . . . For it is only through the process of its mediation that the work enters into the changing horizon-of-experience of a continuity in which the perpetual inversion occurs from simple reception to critical understanding, from passive to active reception, from recognized aesthetic norms to a new production that surpasses them."[4] Indeed, the otherness of people is "itself an energy formative of history."

Implied in Jauss' assessment here—especially as it emphasizes the phenomenon of "perpetual inversion"—is a requirement of hermeneutical and rhetorical competence on the part of those audience members who are attempting to form a critical understanding of a work of art and who, of course, may find help in the expertise of professional critics. According to the literary theorist Barbara Herrnstein Smith, such competence provides a way for works "to endure as something other than vivid historical artifacts" in that it enables one to comprehend how works "serve as metaphors and parables of an independent future"—that is, how they "continue to have meanings which would inevitably include meanings that the author did not intend and could not have intended to convey."[5] Furthermore, the competence emphasized here would be at work whenever an audience was engaged in the critical task of determining whether or not a new production had surpassed recognized and accepted norms and, in turn, whether or not the aesthetic and sociopolitical implications of the new production warranted any respect or allegiance.

The specific factor in the hermeneutical and rhetorical process of meaning formation that keeps a work alive is the otherness of the hearer, the reader, and the audience, and their particular circumstances. With the lessons of biblical exegesis in mind, one might think of the interaction here as having something of a "spiritual" nature. Seeking the life-giving gift of acknowledgment, the author's work calls out "Where art thou?" and awaits a response ("Here I am!") from those who are interested and competent enough to keep the conversation going about the meaning and significance of the pertinent issue(s) at hand. A work without a receptive audience is a work whose truth remains mute.

Abraham Lincoln's Gettysburg Address (1863) provides a classic example of this point. With this Address, delivered as it was within a situation fraught with social, political, and economic problems and filled with immense heartbreak over the loss of life, Lincoln initially emerged as a rhetorical "failure" in the pragmatic and immediate sense. In the long run, however, we have come to know better. With this masterpiece of rhetorical competence that, according to historian Gary Wills, "remade America" as it set forth a "revolution" in thought and speech, we witness a work of art whose distinctive and appropriate use of grammar, syntax, signs, tempo, topics, figures, tropes, emotion, narrative, and argument itself creates a dwelling place or character (ethos) of eulogized time and space.[6] Here an opening is created in the midst of immense suffering in which there is still hope to be found as we acknowledge the devotion and courage not of individuals dressed in blue or gray but, as Lincoln tells us, of those "brave men, living and dead, who struggled here" and who would have us realize "that this nation, under God, shall have a new birth of freedom, and that government of the people, by the people, and for the people, shall not perish from the earth."

The form and content of Lincoln's Address are inextricably bound together in a rhetorical disclosure of conscience that calls for assistance in the building of ethos—dwelling place, character, ethics—for the nation. The Gettysburg Address is rationally designed and arranged so to have us acknowledge and know together something of the truth of being with and for others, of feeling at home in their company and of treating them in a just and moral way. In short, to dwell with Lincoln at Gettysburg is to learn how important it is to have a heart that is open to the world and, hence, to the experience of wonder and awe that shows itself in acts of commitment, courage, and sacrifice.

With such an interpretive reading of the Gettysburg Address, it might be said that we are getting at the heart of its being, its truth, its genuine meaning and significance. This might also explain why the Address has become a "rhetorical touchstone": in speaking as it does about a time and place wherein wounded humanity begged for relief and such relief called for the medicaments of a variety of healing emotions and virtues that are known to make human beings feel and do "good," the Address offers a "fitting response" to a situation of crisis (war and its many horrible consequences). Perhaps the Gettysburg Address remains alive today because its hermeneutical, rhetorical, moral message is essential to the well-being of a public that, in being able to understand its teachings and rejoice in putting them into practice, continues to be receptive to the message's appeal and, hence, to its meaning and significance. As the rhetorical theorist and critic Edwin Black notes, there is something "perfect" about how Lincoln gets us to come to terms with his topic.[7]

MEANING AND SIGNIFICANCE

In speaking about the relationship that exists between the author's work and present and forthcoming audiences (otherness), I have continued to employ the phrase "meaning and significance" as a way of explaining how it is that the work's truth is able to endure over time. The literary theorist E. D. Hirsch Jr. makes much of the difference between those two major terms. "Meaning," writes Hirsch, "is that which is represented by a text; it is what the author meant by his use of a particular sign sequence. . . . Significance, on the other hand, names a relationship between that meaning and a person, or a conception, or a situation, or indeed anything imaginable."[8] Only by keeping this distinction in mind, argues Hirsch, can one hope to offer a "valid" interpretation of a given text. "Validity requires a norm—meaning that is stable and determinate no matter how broad its range of implication and application. A stable and determinate meaning requires an author's determining will . . . All valid interpretation of every sort is founded on the re-cognition of what an author meant."[9] Or to put it another way, "If an interpreter did not conceive of a text's meaning to be there as an occasion for contemplation or application, he would have nothing to think or talk about. Its thereness, its self-identity from one moment to the next allows it to be contemplated. Thus, while meaning is a principle of stability in an interpretation, significance embraces a principle of change."[10]

Clearly, Hirsch is not an advocate of what I had to say in the last chapter about casuistry, the Kabbalah, and its interpretation of God's process of creation. What I said above about the meaning and significance of Lincoln's Gettysburg Address, however, is consistent with Hirsch's directive. Rhetorical critics generally agree that this short but robust and revolutionary Address was intended to be a call of conscience directed toward uniting of the nation and encouraging its moral integrity and growth. The "obviousness" of this meaning required temporal distance from a blood-soaked and haunting battlefield in order to rise above the blinding prejudices of the day such that Lincoln's "determining will" could be properly identified. Lincoln addressed a particular situation with a rhetorical strategy that accommodated cultural differences and directed people to think about humankind in more universal terms. He spoke not only to the actual consciousness of his immediate audience but also to the potential consciousness of forthcoming generations who, with continuing experience and education, could develop the practical wisdom and interpretive competence needed to prevent, or at least heal, the horrible wounds of war. Hence the applicability (significance) of the meaning of Lincoln's Address: it continues to *speak* and thus to have something to *say* to people who have yet to overcome completely their violent tendencies but who nevertheless have the hermeneutical, rhetorical, and moral capacities to understand and develop a feeling for the importance of cultivating unity and peace.

Although the Gettysburg Address is a text that can help illustrate Hirsch's take on the relationship between meaning, significance, and the validity of interpretation, I suspect that he nevertheless would object to the way I phrased the last point. For, according to Hirsch, "it is natural to speak *not of what a text says*, but of what an author means, and this more natural locution is the more accurate one."[11] This claim reflects Hirsch's opposition to the program of philosophical hermeneutics that is rooted in the works of such twentieth-century philosophers as Martin Heidegger, Hans-Georg Gadamer, and Paul Ricoeur. This program advocates a theory of meaning that is not confined to the intentions of an author and that stresses how any act of interpretive understanding unfolds within a "hermeneutical situation" in which texts do, in fact, "speak" to those who are willing to remain open to what these texts have "to say."[12]

Unlike Hirsch, whose appreciation of hermeneutics reflects the philologist's methodological interest in "validity," Heidegger emphasizes the term's more primordial and existential association with the essential capacity of human beings to understand and give expression to the world in meaningful ways. Heidegger's phenomenological assessment of this capacity is credited as being a hallmark of twentieth-century philosophy. I referred to this assessment in chapter 1. Recall that phenomenology is a way of thinking devoted to interpreting, analyzing, and describing how

the immediate content of experience and the otherness that necessarily comes with it actually present themselves to human consciousness. The discourse of phenomenology assumes the task of
disclosing a phenomenon's own disclosure, *its* being and truth.
Truth happens first and foremost as a disclosing of the world, as
a revealing or uncovering of the "givenness" of something that is
perceived *to be.*[13]

Heidegger's assessment of truth is not restricted to what facts
may be disclosed in some verbal judgment ("the sky is blue")—
some epistemic correspondence of some reified proposition with
some equally reified state of affairs. The truth of such a disclosure
presupposes a more original happening of truth, a more original
instance of disclosing: the actual presencing of that which shows
itself and thus gives itself for thought and understanding. This is
the fundamental truth of human existence that Heidegger is after;
his phenomenology is directed toward a hermeneutic assessment
of how this primordial showing and giving take place. Heidegger
describes this task as requiring one to "listen" to "the call of
Being."[14] This notion of "the call" is reminiscent of biblical hermeneutics' passion for interpreting "the call of God." For Heidegger,
however, the question of God is one that must be bracketed in an
attempt to be as empirically oriented to the matter at hand. As he
puts it, "only from the truth of Being can the essence of the holy
be thought. Only from the essence of the holy is the essence of
divinity to be thought. Only in the light of the essence of divinity
can it be thought or said what the world 'God' is to signify. . . .
How can man at the present stage of world history ask at all seriously and rigorously whether the god nears or withdraws, when
he has above all neglected to think into the dimension in which
alone that question can be asked?"[15] If human beings were made
in God's image, then studying the ontological intricacies of this
image in action should provide valuable data for assessing what
God's truth may, in fact, be. With its empirical orientation, however, phenomenology is devoted to avoiding what cosmologists
term "God-of-the-gaps" thinking.[16]

Phenomenology goes about telling the truth by "letting something be seen" with its discourse. Heidegger identifies such a
disclosing or evocative use of discourse with what he defines as
the "essential being of language" (*logos*): its "saying" power, its

capacity to "speak" by pointing to and showing us something, its perfectionist impulse. "Language speaks," insists Heidegger, and it does so especially in those discourses that warrant praise for being revelatory and perhaps even awe inspiring because of the way in which they call forth and disclose their subject matter, thereby enabling us to better our understanding and appreciation of what is being discussed.

So, for example, in order to understand and appreciate what Lincoln is trying to tell us with his Gettysburg Address (a most evocative discourse, to be sure), we must listen not only to his voice (which of course we can no longer do) but also to the power of his language as it displays a capacity for making manifest certain matters of importance, for saying something to us by showing us what this something is thought to be. If the Gettysburg Address is to speak to us in a truthful manner, this, at the very least, is what it must do: through an act of saying, of showing, it must give us something to understand. Heidegger reminds us that the "oldest word" for "saying" is *logos*: "saying which, in showing, lets beings appear in their 'it is.'"[17] The saying power of language is what enables any discourse to give expression to things that call for attention. Heidegger further reminds us that the word for "saying" is also the word for Being (*logos*). Indeed, Being is constantly disclosing and showing itself in how things exist, in the presencing of all that lies before us, in the circumstances of life that call for thought. The truth of Being is a saying, a showing, a phenomenon that gives itself for understanding. This is what Heidegger is referring to when he speaks of the "call of Being": that primordial "saying" whose showing provokes thought. And this is why Heidegger tells us that if we are to "listen" attentively to this call, we must "follow the movement of showing" so as to let whatever concerns us speak for itself. Phenomenology admits a "scientific" impulse by dedicating itself "to the things themselves."

Heidegger hears and answers the call differently than does Hirsch, who, as noted above, restricts hermeneutics to the issue of validity: determining the original and stable (perfect) verbal meaning intended by an author. For Heidegger, however, the "hermeneutical situation" that is present whenever one tries to uncover such willed meaning is more complex than acknowledged by defenders of objectivity and validity. As it emerges and takes form in the world of everyday concerns, meaning is not something that is simply willed and intended by an author; rather, any speech act operates in an already established realm of intersubjective understanding that speaks of what things are according to the established points of view and prejudices that constitute the tradition of the author's culture. Again, Luria's cosmological myth is a case in point.

Moreover, as Ricoeur points out, with any speech act there emerges a dialectical process that refers to the meaning or truth of something that may have yet to be articulated and comprehended by the majority of the culture's members. This dialectic is borne in the ways in which "discourse refers back to its speaker at the same time it refers to the world. This correlation is not fortuitous, since it is ultimately the speaker who refers to the world in speaking. Discourse in action and in use refers backwards and forwards, to a speaker and a world."[18] Ricoeur thus argues that the meaning of a text is not simply "behind" the text but rather, and more importantly, "in front of it." Meaning "is not something hidden, but something disclosed" as an author makes use of tradition and his or her own creative abilities to "project a world." Philosophical hermeneutics "has less then ever to do with the author and situation. It seeks to grasp the world-propositions opened up by the reference to the text. To understand a text is to follow its movement [its saying and showing] from sense to reference: from what it says, to what it talks about."[19] Texts speak and thereby show us a world. The ongoing debate over whether the Constitution of the United States supports a woman's right to abortion, for example, is based in part on how legal scholars interpret the way this text speaks of a world wherein such matters as "freedom of choice" and "privacy" are deemed essential to humankind.

With his emphasis on the intention of an author, Hirsch fails to account for this process of world disclosure. Hence, although his theory is instructive in alerting us to how, for example, the Gettysburg Address is steeped in the hermeneutic and rhetorical capacities of its author, his theory marginalizes the fact that Lincoln offers only an interpretation of a world whose "true" meaning may still lie beyond what Lincoln was able to put into words. Although I have suggested above that the acknowledged significance of the Address supports the wisdom of Lincoln's interpretation of the meaning of the world in question, the fact still remains that without this world the issue of Lincoln's intended meaning would not arise. Of course, an author's intended meaning gives critics something to think and write about, but this meaning is only one factor in a hermeneutical situation whose enduring nature is dependent on the receptivity of potential interpreters who, with additional time and experience, may be able to correct and extend an author's assessment of the meaning of a world that, for whatever reason, continues to warrant attention with all that it has to say.

Hirsch contends that this understanding of the hermeneutical situation exposes interpretation theory to the problem of "relativism," since it collapses the distinction between meaning and significance by insisting that the meaning of some matter can evolve and thus change over time. But such relativism, one should realize, would not merely be a game of throwing the truth up for grabs. On the contrary, the project of philosophical hermeneutics at issue here is dedicated to getting to the heart, and thus to the truth, of some matter—be it God's truth or the truth that unfolds in the discourse of the Gettysburg Address. With time and changing circumstance, this truth may disclose itself to people who are better prepared to receive, understand, and express it in a rhetorically competent manner such that others, too, can put its meaning to good use. The project of philosophical hermeneutics, in other words, is more aligned with what was described earlier as the rhetorical enterprise of casuistry than with the "anything goes" attitude of relativism—an enterprise that pays homage to the relationship of otherness that exists between God and God's creations, and between the creations themselves. With this latter form of the phenomenon, we are immersed in the practical workings of everyday life in which notions of perfection are continually succeeding and failing in the openness of existence and its way of subjecting us to the uncertainty of the future. This uncertainty is constantly calling us into question, constantly challenging us to test out the meaning and significance of our claimed truths.

We Are Otherness

Human being is structured ontologically as an evocation and a provocation, or what Heidegger describes as the most original and empirical instance of "the call of conscience": as it discloses itself to us, the openness of existence calls for the responsiveness of concerned thought and action, for that which enables us, even in the most distressful situations, to take charge of our lives as we assume the ethical responsibility of affirming our freedom through resolute choice and thereby become personally involved in the creation of a meaningful existence. This is how systems of morality (e.g., institutionalized religion) come into being in the first place. The perfectionist-driven language of morality is the language of responsiveness and responsibility that is called for by the ontological workings of human being.

Notice, however, that this ontological structure and function of the call of conscience are always already operating before the specific ethical prescriptions and prohibitions of language are created by human beings. The call of conscience is *not* a human invention; we did not create the ontological (spatial and temporal) structure of existence—the way it opens us to the contingency of the future and thereby, within this openness, gives us a place to perceive whatever presents itself to us. Heidegger thus tells us that human being, owing to its cognitive and symbolic capacity, should be understood ontologically as "the region" that Being requires in order to disclose itself. Human being is "the site" of openness, "the there," "the dwelling place" within all of existence where Being finds a "clearing," where it can be observed with care and then shared in language that is remarkable for its disclosive (truth-telling) capacity.[20] One must not forget, however, that this place of human being has something about its nature that is *more* and thus *other than* its own making—something whose objective uncertainty is the basis of "mystery." What will happen tomorrow? Who can say for sure? Otherness lies at the heart of human existence; it makes its presence known even when we are all alone. Existence brings with it the task of wondering about the source of this otherness that discloses itself in our lives but is not of our own making.

The most common name given to this mystery is, of course, "God." Heidegger neither denies nor affirms the "correctness" of this name. He is more interested in being true to the empirical demands of phenomenological inquiry and thus does not deviate from the task of advancing a description of the ontological workings of this "otherness." How exactly does this phenomenon work itself out in our lives? Both in his early and later philosophies, Heidegger addresses this question by examining how human beings *embody* some aspect of otherness in the way we exist as a "being-toward death." We *are* finite creatures. Life carries its own negation. As soon as we are born (or conceived), we are old enough to die. The otherness ("nothingness") of death names "a presence of absence" at play in the midst of existence that can make its nullifying move into our everyday lives at any moment and that is well known for inciting the "dread" of anxiety. Individuals who suffer from "communication apprehension" (the "stage fright" of speaking in public before an audience), for example, are well acquainted with this emotion. What will people think of them as they express themselves to others? Some of these reticence-prone souls are even known to say that they "felt like they were dying" while in the situation.[21]

For Heidegger, however, this example points to something of "greater" ontological significance. When trying to come to *complete* terms with the experience—terms that grapple with how it is that Being can be so disturbing, disruptive, and overpowering—we eventually find ourselves at a loss for words. Being (its presence *and* absence) is! That's life! Short of the word "God," the play going on here "gives" only itself to go on. As Heidegger puts it, the revealing or presencing of Being is at the same time a concealing, for the play of Being is also that which "holds itself back and withdraws" whenever we attempt to grasp *the* reason for its happening, for its Being the way it is. "The play is without 'why,'" writes Heidegger. "It plays since it plays. It simply remains a play: the most elevated and the most profound."[22] Following Heidegger, it may thus be said that the play of Being—which gives itself to us by way of the presencing of all that lies before us—is itself a "mystery," for it is never without an element of "absence."

Recall that, for Heidegger, Being is not God, but is rather that empirical event that has to be acknowledged and carefully described and understood as perfectly as possible in order to think truly or say "what the word 'God' is to signify." Notice, however, how closely Heidegger's description of the workings of Being resembles the rhetoric used in kabbalistic thought and Luria's cosmological myth to describe the workings of God. I alluded to this fact earlier when noting that "the call of Being" is reminiscent of "the call of God" and that the rhetoric of Luria's myth functions in accordance with Heidegger's understanding more than four hundred years later of the hermeneutical and rhetorical process of meaning formation. When Heidegger speaks about how the play of Being "holds itself back and withdraws," he again describes an event that, according to the myth, took form originally when God, in the ultimate act of self-effacement, chose to "withdraw" unto Itself and thereby create an opening for the entire cosmos to come into being. The "gift" of Being comes from the presence of an absence, the play of an ongoing process (*Ein Sof*) that makes possible all of life and calls for our acknowledgment.

What I am saying here about the analogs that exist between Heidegger and the kabbalistic tradition is not meant to suggest that Heidegger offers himself as a voice for this tradition's livelihood. Heidegger certainly never acknowledges this tradition, and his tragic association with National Socialism, or Nazism, in 1933 stands in the way of crediting him with having a heart for the plight of the Jewish people.[23] Still, I find the deep structural similarities striking. For, if nothing else, they exist as a reminder of Heidegger's political failings. As a Jew, I do not hesitate to say, "Never forget!" And Heidegger continues to fuel the fire of this demand. He describes the absence characterizing the play of Being as the void of "nothingness," the "Nothing" out of which the presence of all beings appears. The philosophical tradition of metaphysics, with its concern over the issue of why there is something rather than nothing, has it wrong. The "Nothing of Being" is real; it exists as the "nihilating" nature of Being itself, the way in which Being holds itself back and slips away from our grasp, refusing to be known completely, perfectly.[24] Indeed, the "withdrawal" is an actual event. For the sake of humanity, Heidegger should have been more caring to a people who saw the event long before he did. There is more to "otherness" than Being. Otherness does not lead necessarily to the otherness of

God. But what about the "otherness" of other people and the acknowledgment of their circumstances? This Heidegger fails to consider in a careful way.

Using one of Kenneth Burke's favorite terms to describe the event of withdrawal, or what he describes as the resistance of material reality to be perfectly disclosed by acts of interpretation, one might say that the truth of Being, or what Burke refers to as "the eternally unsolvable Enigma," is exceptionally "recalcitrant." Burke puts matters this way:

> We in cities rightly grow shrewd at appraising man-made institutions—but beyond these tiny concentration points of rhetoric and traffic, there lies the eternally unsolvable Enigma, the preposterous fact that both existence and nothingness are equally unthinkable. Our speculations may run the whole qualitative gamut, from play, through reverence, even to an occasional shiver of cold metaphysical dread—for always the Eternal Enigma is there, right on the edges of our metropolitan bickerings, stretching outward to interstellar infinity and inward to the depths of the mind. And in this staggering disproportion between man and no-man, there is no place for purely human boasts of grandeur, or for forgetting that men build their cultures by huddling together, nervously loquacious, at the edge of an abyss.[25]

This abyss grants us a view of the otherness of Being, that primordial way of being open to the future that we did not create and that makes itself known when some conflict or crisis interrupts our everyday habits and routines, challenging us to think ahead and rebuild our worlds of meaning. The challenge defines the ontological workings of the call of conscience that lies at the heart of human existence. The call is existence disclosing itself to the one who is living it and who can (and must) respond to its challenge. Here, at this ontological level of existence, language is not understood first and foremost as a capacity of communication but rather as the original and silent manifestation, the "showing," of what is: "The call dispenses with any kind of utterance. It does not put itself into words at all; . . . [c]onscience discourses solely and constantly in the mode of keeping silent."[26]

Heidegger speaks to us of a discourse, a silent "voice," that is more original than anything he or anyone else has to say about it.[27] He describes what he is doing when he notes, "To speak means to say, which means to show and to let [something] be seen. It means to communicate and, correspondingly, to listen, to submit oneself to a claim addressed to oneself and to comply and respond to it."[28] Conscience calls and Heidegger, listening attentively, phenomenologically, responds with a discourse meant to communicate to us (to come to terms with) the ontological workings of this call, its way of saying and showing itself to that particular being who has the linguistic ability to put into words the call's disclosive workings. Heidegger is engaged in a hermeneutical and rhetorical task in which, according to Gadamer, rhetoric is not primarily a theory of forms, speeches, and persuasion, but instead is the "practical mastery" or know-how for making known to others that which is understood. To put it in more Heideggerian terms: rhetoric serves as a basis for "the everydayness of Being with one another," or what Heidegger also designates as "publicness."[29]

Although Heidegger associates this realm of common sense and common practice with the breeding ground for the evils of conformism, he also sees it as providing the necessary background for coming to terms with who we are first and foremost as social beings and for determining whether or not our extant ways of seeing, interpreting, and becoming involved with things and with others might be changed "for the better." Influenced particularly by his reading of Aristotle's *Rhetoric*, Heidegger admits that this discursive art plays a valuable role in rousing the emotionally attuned interests and guiding people "in a right and just manner" (*"in der rechten Weise"*).[30] This is how rhetoric helps to promote civic engagement and civic virtue and how it thereby lends itself to the task of perfecting the moral character of a people's communal existence by encouraging collaborative deliberation about contested matters.

In Aristotle's case, this last claim presupposes the acceptance of the metaphysical notion of "entelechy," which emphasizes how any entity—be it a stone, a tree, a bird, or a human being—comes about and develops toward *the perfection or completeness natural to its kind*: the essence of what it *is*. According to Aristotle, the perfection of human beings is related to our ability to contemplate God's divine presence in our lives and, by way of everyday deliberation and social interaction, to develop a moral character that is as perfect as it can be. The "good life" entails thinking about the truth of things and participating in activities that ensure the moral well-being of communal life. Here, for example, is how Aristotle states it in his *Politics*:

> There is this to be said for the Many. Each of them by himself may not be a good quality; but when they all come together it is possible that they may surpass—collectively and as a body, although not individually—the quality of the few best. . . . When there are many [who contribute to the process of deliberation], each can bring this share of goodness and moral prudence; and when all meet together the people may thus become something in the nature of a single person, who— as he has many feet, many hands, and many senses—may also have many qualities of character and intelligence.[31]

Aristotle's point is crucial. Our concern for truth, for developing a perfect understanding of whatever calls for our attention, emerges in the midst of otherness. Situated between the otherness of mystery (the future, death, God) and the otherness of other people and things, rhetoric offers itself as something more than an art given over to manipulation, deception, and selfishness. Perfection, truth, conscience, acknowledgment, hermeneutics, rhetoric, and otherness go hand in hand.

With this chapter, my story about perfection has shifted a bit: we have moved from the otherness of God to the otherness of human being and this being's involvement with other people and things. Otherness is a fact of life displaying vertical and horizontal dimensions. The vertical dimension is best known for directing us toward the stars, the heavens, and the Almighty. This upward movement, however, is grounded existentially and phenomenologically in the horizontal dimension: the temporality of human existence that we did not create, that pushes forward to the objective uncertainty of the future, to the not yet and the unknown, to our own "passing away," and that along the way involves us with the earthly otherness of our everyday lives— and, thus, with others. Here, situated among all of this otherness, is the place where we demonstrate our purposefulness, our goal-directed behavior, our reasons for being whatever we are at the time. We typically do not give much careful thought to this place as we navigate successfully through life with the help of our many habits and routines. Yet, when something happens to disrupt these everyday and instrumental ways of being, our placement in the world can become all too (e.g., frighteningly) apparent and imperfect.

For example, who enjoys "feeling out of place" wherever he or she goes? Being the social creatures that we are, not having a place where we can feel at home with others is cause for serious concern. The loneliness of being "all dressed up with no place to go" is known to foster frustration and despair as we seek some degree of acknowledgment. Our outlook may improve as we look upward and pray for hope and relief. Acknowledgment can come as a life-giving gift from God. Others, too, can grant us this gift. If the gift is perceived to be way overdue or nonexistent, however, then a final purposive event may occur: the pull of a trigger, an overdose, or some other suicidal act.

The Old Testament calls on us to "choose" life over death (Deut 30:19). Luria's cosmological myth heeds this call of conscience. God's work must be done. Some might see this work going on in Lincoln's Gettysburg Address as he moves from the topics of suffering and death to that of how our "nation, under God, shall have a new birth of freedom, and that government of the people, by the people, and for the people, shall not perish from the earth." Both Luria and Lincoln are engaged in the hermeneutical and rhetorical process of creating a dwelling place where others, suffering from crises, may find some comfort and confidence in their future. Luria and Lincoln are "homemakers."[32] We need the place of home in order to deal with the otherness of existence, to receive and share acknowledgment, and, if possible, to "live life to the fullest," at least within reason.

CHAPTER FIVE

REASON

L ive life to the fullest! This well-known expression typically comes from people—parents, spouses, teachers, close friends, lovers—who care about our well-being. The expression speaks to the possibility and joy of reaching our full potential before it is too late. When something is "full," *Webster's Dictionary* tells us, a state of perfection is at hand. How does one live life to the fullest? "Discovering and heeding God's word" is one of the best-known and most humble and respected answers to this question. Yet all too often bad things still happen to good people. Life can be "hell on earth." The Great Physician does not always answer our call. Poor health is not conducive to perfection, to living life to the fullest.

I noted earlier how Hippocratic physicians began to remedy this situation by emphasizing the crucial difference between science and opinion: "the former begets knowledge, the latter ignorance." Science is reason at its best. From the time of the Hippocratics until the sixteenth century, the full effect of this teaching on the science of medicine was inhibited in great part by the religious and social prohibitions against dissecting human corpses. Beginning in the sixteenth century, however, the rhetoric that informed these prohibitions, and thereby restricted the teaching's scientific calling, was dismantled as anatomists, true to their calling's allegiance to rationality and reason, opened the human body to the gaze of the physician. These anatomists thus revealed through careful observation physiological structures and happenings that had been greatly misjudged by the Hippocratics and by those medievalists who knew only how to respond to the letter and not the scientific spirit of their Hippocratic texts.[1]

Praising the progressive nature of this spirit as it showed itself in the seventeenth century, the philosopher and mathematician Rene Descartes stressed that "we might rid ourselves of an infinity of maladies, both of the body and mind, and even perhaps also the enfeeblement brought on by old age, were one to have a sufficient [scientific] knowledge of their causes and of all the remedies that nature has provided us."[2] Extending into the eighteenth century, medical science's innovative experiments in dissection enabled physicians to behold a wealth of information about illness. Physicians could now understand their patients and their bodies from the inside out; they could now correlate illness with places in the body and could begin telling the "true" story of disease, its pathophysiology. The Great Physician's counterparts on earth were hard at work while God, for whatever reason, was delayed (or at least was content to let others construct the story). Moreover, by the early eighteenth century, the achievements in mathematics, astronomy, and physics, which culminated in Isaac Newton's *Principia* (1687), had spread widely through the public mind of the West. The Age of Reason, the Enlightenment, was at hand—a time when scientists, philosophers, and other intellectuals stressed the importance of developing "a science of freedom" that would enable people to improve their physical, mental, social, political, and moral well-being as they lived their lives to the fullest in the midst of otherness.[3] The mathematician and social philosopher A. N. de Condorcet speaks with great enthusiasm about the spirit and ambitious goals of the age when he writes, "The real advantages that should result from [its] progress, of which we can entertain a hope that is almost certainty, can have no other term than that of the absolute perfection of the human race.[4]

THE ENLIGHTENMENT

Was the Enlightenment's agenda for progress and human perfectibility God's intention, a product of the snake biting at our heels, a way for human beings to enact their moral duty to perfect themselves, "to receive in order to share" the magnificence of God's gifts, especially the proper (i.e., scientific) use of reason? Speaking of this ultimate use of reason for achieving the absolute perfection of the human race, Condorcet tells us,

> The time will . . . come when the sun will shine only on free men who know no other master but their reason; when tyrants and slaves, priests and their stupid or hypocritical instruments, will exist only in works of history and on the stage; and when we shall think of them only to pity their victims and their dupes; to maintain ourselves in a state of vigilance by thinking on their excesses; and to learn how to recognize and so to destroy, by force of reason, the first seeds of tyranny and superstition, should they ever dare to reappear amongst us.[5]

Notice that it is the institution of the church ("priests and their stupid or hypocritical instruments"), not God per se, that is criticized here. The Enlightenment did not do away with God; rather, its representatives sought to clarify methodically, scientifically, the laws of nature and the nature of humankind that came after this ultimate source of reason. We are the ticking of the clock that was designed by the greatest "watchmaker" that ever was and that will ever be.[6]

The original title Descartes proposed for his influential *Discourse on Method*, which along with his *Meditations* certainly admitted the necessity of God's presence, was *The Prospect of a Universal Science which Can Elevate Our Nature to Its Highest Perfection*. Gottfried Wilhelm Leibniz—inventor of calculus, doctor of law, founder of the Prussian academy of science, and moral philosopher—would have us believe the metaphysical "fact" that reaching this goal is an ongoing, evolutionary process: to understand completely "the general beauty and perfection of the works of God, we must recognize a certain perpetual and very free progress of the whole universe, such that it advances always to still greater refinement. It is thus that even now a great part of our earth has received cultivation [culture] and will receive more and more." Responding to the possible objection that, if this were so, "the world ought long ago to have become a paradise," Leibniz offered his "Law of Continuity," which emphasized how nothing happens all at once in nature, but only in degrees. Nature never makes leaps. Thus, for Leibniz, "there always remain in the depths of things slumbering parts which must yet be awakened, and become greater and better, and, in a word, attain a better culture. And hence progress never comes to an end."[7]

In making this last statement, however, Leibniz nevertheless maintains that "the supreme perfection of God" results in God's choosing "the best possible plan, in which there is the greatest variety along with the greatest order; ground, place, [and] time being as well arranged as possible; the greatest effect produced by the simplest ways; the most power, knowledge, happiness and goodness in created things that the universe allowed. For as all possible things in the understanding of God claim evidence in proportion to their perfections, the result of all these claims must be the most perfect actual world that is possible."[8] This is not to say that Leibniz denies the presence of evil existing in the world at any given moment. His evolutionary metaphysics accepts the fact that "imperfections" are ever present in various forms, but these imperfections are not without value in helping people to ascertain the moral principles of right and justice that are given by divine nature. Leibniz employs an aesthetic analogy to make his point: "It's a bit like what happens in music and painting, for shadows and dissonances truly enhance the other parts, and the wise author of such works derives such a great benefit for the total perfection of the work from these particular imperfections that it is much better to make a place for them than to attempt to do without them. Thus, we must believe that God would not have allowed sin nor would he have created things he knows will sin, if he could not derive from them a good incomparably greater than the resulting evil."[9]

Morality presupposes God's presence. Scientific reasoning helps to disclose with the greatest accuracy something of this presence as it shows itself in the decipherable laws of nature, the essential aspects of human being, and the immense otherness that marks this being's existence with all kinds of people and things. Leibniz associated God's presence with the attainment of world peace and with our ability to create a scientific language that is unfettered by the rhetoric of religious myth and superstition and that can serve as a common instrument of communication in the discovery of truth. Scientific reasoning is more of a genuine and honest friend to God than is the mythic, habitual, and ritualized language of the church.[10] Immanuel Kant's development of this claim helps secure its status in the rationalist tradition of philosophy.

According to Kant, "Morality does not need religion at all . . . ; by virtue of pure practical reason it is self-sufficient."[11] For Kant, humans are rational and dutiful creatures by nature; "the law of morality" is incorporated into our very beings as a "categorical imperative": "Act only according to that maxim [or principle of conduct] whereby you can at the same time will that it should become a universal law."[12] Kant makes much of how this "supreme principle of morality" is imposed and legislated by reason itself; it is not derived from our existentially conditioned needs, inclinations, desires, aversions, sensibilities, emotions, and the otherness all around us. He thus maintains that our actions ought to be guided first and foremost by the dictates of pure practical reason. Here, for example, is Kant's formulation of the dictate "concerning the foremost command of all duties to oneself":

> . . . know (search, fathom) yourself, not for the sake of your physical perfection (fitness or unfitness for all kinds of ends whether of your own liking or ordered of you), but for your moral perfection regarding your duty; test your heart—whether it be good or bad, whether the source of your actions be pure or impure, whether the source of your actions be such as can be imputed to yourself and belong to your moral condition, either as part of the original essence of man, or as something derivative (acquired or developed). . . . Only descent into the hell of self-knowledge prepares the way for godliness.[13]

Kant was a Christian, but his passion for rational insight showed the utmost allegiance to the power of reason that had not yet been misled or dulled by the rhetoric of religion. His descent into the hell of self-knowledge led him to clarify, for example, what he considered to be the "true" nature of conscience, unfettered by ideological temperaments.

CONSCIENCE

According to Kant, conscience comes into play when reason assumes its role of judging whether an action is really right or wrong. Kant emphasizes that it is reason, not conscience, that performs such a judgment. "But," he says, "concerning the act which I propose to perform I must not only judge and form an opinion, but I must be sure that it is not wrong." Conscience, for Kant, is the enactment of this requirement: "It is the moral faculty of judgment, passing judgment upon itself"; it is reason judging itself "as to whether it has really undertaken that appraisal of actions (as to whether they are right or wrong) with all diligence, and it calls the man himself to witness for or against himself whether this diligent appraisal did or did not take place."[14] It thus makes no sense to Kant to speak of a misinformed conscience. Conscience is innate; it does what it does, "involuntarily and inevitably." As rational beings, we have an obligation "to cultivate our conscience, to sharpen our attention to the voice of this internal judge, and to use every means to get it a hearing." To hear and obey the voice of conscience is to be extremely and unconditionally conscientious about one's effort to act dutifully. Conscience calls for neither more nor less than this.[15]

Conscience is infallible; its workings are free of all influences (otherness) from empirical, contingent grounds, argues Kant. The Judeo-Christian interpretation of the matter has no basis in pure practical reason, although Kant does allow for a rational understanding of conscience as the basis for serious speculation about an "intelligent cause," an "all-powerful original being" that may be the first cause of all the otherness that exists in the cosmos. Kant made no apologies for his critique of institutionalized religion and was forever demanding about the need to abide by the "spirit" of his "Age": "Enlightenment is man's release from his self-incurred tutelage. Tutelage is man's inability to make use of his understanding without direction from another. Self-incurred is this tutelage when its cause lies not in lack of reason but in lack of resolution and courage to use it without direction from another. *Sapere aude!* 'Have courage to use your own reason!'— that is the motto of enlightenment."[16] Going on to suggest how this courage could lose out to the "laziness and cowardice" of human beings, Kant notes, "It is so easy not to be of age. If I have a book which understands for me, a pastor who has a conscience for me, a physician who decides my diet, and so forth, I need not trouble myself. I need not think, if I can only pay—others will readily undertake the irksome work for me."[17]

The courage called for by Kant presupposes freedom: one's ability to assume the personal and ethical responsibility of making a rational and resolute choice without necessarily being told exactly what to do by others. The importance of human freedom to Kant's entire philosophical program is clearly announced in his lecture "The Ultimate Destiny of the Human Race":

> The ultimate destiny of the human race is the greatest moral perfection, provided that it is achieved through human freedom, whereby alone man is capable of the greatest happiness. God might have made men perfect and given to each his portion of happiness. But happiness would not then have been derived from the inner principle of the world, for the inner principle of the world is freedom. The end, therefore, for which man is destined is to achieve his fullest perfection through his own freedom. God's will is not merely that we should be happy, but that we should make ourselves happy, and this is the true morality. . . . If we all so order our conduct that it should be in harmony with the universal end of mankind, the highest perfection would be attained. We must each of us, therefore, endeavour to guide our conduct to this end; each of us must make such a contribution of his own that if all contributed similarly the result would be perfection.

Kant ends his lecture by equating "the universal end of mankind" with "the kingdom of God on earth. Justice and equity, the authority, not of governments [and religious institutions], but of conscience within us, will then rule the world. This is the destined final end, the highest moral perfection, to which the human race can attain; but the hope of it is still distant; it will be many centuries before it can be realized."[18]

Kant keeps the otherness of God in his equation for perfection, but only after pure practical reason allows him to talk about this otherness in a rational way. Deists, like Voltaire, did the same. God is credited with creating the universe. But then God stood back to watch the show with no intention of ever demonstrating divine intervention. God leaves us to our own devices and to our freedom to create a future in which sound reason prevails and the universe runs according to its own natural and scientifically predictable laws. Reason, and the happiness it can produce, come and go with the "man-made" development of *human* nature. Progress is a "god term" for Enlightenment thinkers. Believing that this phenomenon of improvement was *the* way to achieve the "highest moral perfection," Kant insists that the reasoning that directed progress should be as rigorously "scholastic" as possible. When it comes to perfecting our *rational* understanding of moral perfection, "popularity (vernacular) is unthinkable."[19] Kant demands discipline, expertise, and specialization in the use of our faculty of reason to critique whatever human nature has become under the influence of governmental, social, and religious institutions.

Although he thought that the achievement of the highest moral perfection was centuries away, Kant was optimistic about humankind eventually reaching this end. Science embodied right reason, and science was advancing like never before. The "scientists' talent," writes Kant, "lies in continuing to increase the perfection of our cognitions and of all the benefits that depend on [these], *as well as imparting that same knowledge to others.*"[20] Indeed, interpersonal communication has an important role to play in helping others to appropriate, understand, and enact the findings of reason. I will have more to say about this matter shortly. A few additional observations announced by Enlightenment thinkers about the related workings of reason and conscience will further prepare us for appreciating the matter.

Moral Sentiment Theory

Theories of "moral sentiment," such as those advanced by David Hume, Adam Smith, and Charles Darwin, would have us question Kant's assessment of pure reason (and reason alone) and its role in achieving "the highest moral perfection." For Hume, Smith, and Darwin advance the argument that conscience does arise from the contingency and the otherness that are necessarily a part of social relationships, especially as these relationships are based on the natural disposition of human beings to have certain emotions. "Reason," says Hume, "can never be the source of so active a principle as conscience, or a sense of morals"; rather, "morality . . . is more properly felt than judg'd of."[21]

Hume points to "sympathy" as the central emotion inspiring moral consciousness. Indeed, conscience—from the Latin *conscientia* (*con*, with; *scientia*, knowledge)—is a "knowing-with" others. Religion emphasizes how God is our true counterpart to knowing. God is in our hearts and beyond all that can be known. Kant reduces the legislative process of conscience to the innate workings of reason judging the rightfulness and wrongfulness of its ongoing assessments of the matters at hand. For Kant, the knowing-with of conscience is strictly an internal happening in which we are in dialogue with nothing other than our own innate reasoning capacities. The marvel of this happening may be an indication of the existence of a Being that is far greater than us. Hume, on the other hand, situates the knowing-with process of conscience in the otherness of our everyday and emotional experiences with things and with others. Hence, for Hume, the true place of reason is not so much in the head as it is in the heart. We first and foremost feel for the world's presence; reason aids in our understanding of this emotional connection between the environment and ourselves.

Adam Smith affirms and extends Hume's treatment by discussing how our sympathetic orientation toward others, which promotes our sociability, enables us to develop a sense of what pleases or offends people. We thereby acquire an understanding of what constitutes "appropriate" modes of conduct. Standards of moral judgment arise from the reciprocity of this ongoing process. We feel for and judge others, and they feel for and judge us. Based on the process, we also learn to judge the "praiseworthiness" of our own behavior. Human beings desire "not only to be loved," says Smith, "but to be lovely."[22] That is, we are creatures who want to feel that the approval (or disapproval) of others is truly warranted. "The love of praise is the desire of obtaining the favourable sentiments of our brethren. The love of praise-worthiness is the desire of rendering ourselves the proper objects of those sentiments."[23] Smith emphasizes, however, that when genuinely attending to this love of praiseworthiness, our judgments are directed not merely by the drift of current "public opinion" but rather by "the eyes" of those people whose character and conduct admit "excellence" and who thereby inspire in us a habit for acquiring a "real love of virtue." For Smith, conscience (or what he also terms "the man within the breast") develops in accordance with our ability to sympathize with and appropriate the moral sentiments of such people. The love of praiseworthiness and the call of conscience inform each other.[24]

Kant would have us regard this understanding of conscience as being "lax" and "superficial" because it is not grounded *solely* in the a priori workings of reason.[25] Charles Darwin, on the other hand, approaching the matter "exclusively from the side of natural history," is much more supportive of the teachings of moral sentiment theory. Like both Hume and Smith, he emphasizes how the development of conscience is made possible by our "instinctive sympathy" for others.[26] He also makes much of three additional factors that inform the evolution of this "most noble of all the attributes of man." First, conscience, Darwin maintains, presupposes the intellectual ability of comparing past and future actions or motives and, as a consequence, feeling "dissatisfied" with how one has heretofore attended to his or her "social sympathies." Second, our moral sense also requires "the power of language" so that "the wishes of the members of the same community . . . [can] be distinctly expressed," thereby allowing a "common opinion" to form regarding "how each member ought to act for the public good."[27] And finally, if the call of conscience is to maintain a strong influence in our lives, we must, with the help of others, develop habits of recollection, reasoning, and instruction that promote and strengthen our "social affections and sympathies."[28]

There is definitely something "progressive" about Darwin's evolutionary view of conscience. He associates the development, the perfecting, of our moral sense with the "very idea of humanity," with "our sympathies becoming more tender and more widely diffused until they are extended to all sentient beings."[29] For Darwin, the evolution of conscience is an emotional and communal endeavor requiring some degree of communication competence on the part of the people involved.

COMMUNICATION

We are back now to where we left off with Kant: the need to "impart" knowledge to others for the well-being and moral perfection of our communal life. The ancient Greeks attended to this need by creating "the Western rhetorical tradition"—a tradition that begins to take form as the democratic inclinations of ancient Greek society require its citizens to be schooled in the practical art of public address.[30] Kant indicates his particular and misguided understanding of this tradition when he speaks, for example, of how "rhetorical power and excellence of speech (which together constitute rhetoric) belong to fine art."[31]

This particular understanding of the rhetorical tradition is misguided, since, beginning with the ancient Greeks, rhetoric is associated first and foremost with the "practical art" of "speaking well" in public, especially in situations in which convincing arguments are needed to inspire right judgment. Aristotle provides the first systematic analysis of the matter in his *Rhetoric*, in which he answers Plato's call for an intellectual assessment of emotion and its relationship to truth and the orator's art. We learn here that (1) the emotional character of human beings plays an important role in their development; it constitutes a person's spirited potential for coming to judge what is true, just, and virtuous; (2) a moving of the passions is the sine qua non of persuasion; truth alone is not sufficient to guide the thoughtful actions of human beings; and (3) rhetoric, conceived as the art of persuasion, is a faculty or power (*dynamis*) in its nascent state, a potential for acting and doing; when actualized in discourse, this potential not only moves people to take an interest in the truth but encourages them to act in accordance with this truth. "Rhetoric," in other words, "is the counterpart of Dialectic."[32] Knowing how to stir the soul rhetorically is essential because existential questions concerning the livelihood of society are not usually decided with the equations of demonstration or the syllogistic reasoning of dialectic. Existence is a gamble based on probabilities, and the emotional outlook of people influences their judgment at the time the bet is placed. If rhetoric is to perform its most worthy function of trying to move people toward "the good," it must cast a concerned and knowing eye on the emotional character of those whom it wishes to move. The moral sentiment theories of Hume, Smith, and Darwin support Aristotle's assessment of the relationship between reason, emotion, rhetoric, oratory, and truth.

Kant, on the other hand, confuses the matter with his understanding of rhetoric as a fine art. This confusion allows him to condemn the orator's skill as he praises that particular fine art that he maintains "holds the highest rank": poetry. This fine art, according to Kant, "owes its origin almost entirely to genius"; it "expands" and "fortifies the mind; for it lets the mind feel its ability—free, spontaneous, and independent of natural determination—to contemplate and judge phenomenal nature as having . . . aspects that nature does not on its own offer in experience either to sense or to the understanding." Poetry "lets the mind feel its ability to use nature on behalf of . . . the supersensible." In so doing, poetry "plays with illusion, which it produces at will, and yet without using illusion to deceive us, for poetry tells us itself that its pursuit is mere play, though this play can still be used purposively by the understanding for its business."

Now comes the condemnation of a specific form of communication:

> Oratory [on the other hand], insofar as this is taken to mean the art of persuasion (*ars oratoria*), i.e., of deceiving by means of a beautiful illusion, rather than mere excellence of speech (eloquence and style), is a dialectic that borrows from poetry only as much as the speaker needs in order to win over people's minds for his own advantage before they judge for themselves, and so make their judgment unfree. Hence it cannot be recommended either for the bar or for the pulpit. For when civil laws or the rights of individual persons are at issue, or the enduring instruction and determination of minds to a correct knowledge and a conscientious observance of their duty are at issue, then it is beneath the dignity of so important a task to display even a trace of extravagant wit and imagination, let alone any trace of the art of persuading people and of biasing them for the advantage of someone or other.[33]

Oratory, in short, is a communicative practice that is all too willing to sacrifice the disciplined ways of reason as it concerns itself with the contingency and otherness of everyday existence. Here, with the help of the "fine art" of rhetoric, claims Kant, oratory takes unfair advantage of our emotional attachments to things and to others. It thus "is unworthy of any *respect* whatsoever."[34] The scholastic precision of scientific reasoning, even if it burdens common sense with meticulous discourse, must lead the way toward humankind's highest moral perfection.

I think it is fair to say that, like Leibniz before him, Kant was passionate in his never-ending insistence on this last point. Kant loved reason; he was emotional about its promise of progress. His scholastically disciplined and meticulous discourse functions rhetorically to conceal his emotional attachment to his topic. But the emotion had to be there. As Aristotle and many other scholars throughout history remind us, emotions make possible our "taking an interest" in the world.[35] Kant had to have some emotional attachment with his many related concerns (e.g., reason, conscience, moral perfection) in order to find them interesting enough to think, talk, and write about. Emotion is an essential (ontological) feature of human existence that enables us "to feel" the disclosing of the world's presence (otherness). Emotions take form in the interaction between a person and the world as the world is perceived by the person through an act of consciousness. The act allows for a disclosing of the world whereby, for example, a person is awed by the beauty of nature. Any form of cognitive determining owes at least something to the disclosing capabilities of emotion. Reason itself poses no exception here. Even when reason is couched in the most positivistic and dispassionate language (such that it can be "objective" in its registration of "facts"), its announcements will always be rooted in what emotion makes possible—that is, an interpretation of some matter of interest, a concern for being and whatever truths it has to share.

In the last chapter, I emphasized how the happening of any truth takes place first and foremost as a disclosing of the world, a revealing or uncovering of the "givenness" of something that is perceived to be. Emotion enables us to take an interest in how things and people disclose themselves. Emotion has a fundamental relationship with the perception of truth. Recall, for example, that human existence discloses something of its truth as a call of conscience, a call that can register itself in both joyful and dreadful ways and that beckons us to assume the ethical responsibility of affirming our freedom of choice in the midst of otherness. Kant's view of conscience (reason judging itself) omits any consideration of this ontological matter. For him, conscience is in the head, not the heart, of our everyday existence, with all of its contingency and passion for things like the orator's art. The truth of the highest moral perfection demands more than this practically oriented art is willing to give, at least as Kant (mis)understands it: reason unfettered by emotion. Kant returns us to Hippocrates,

Socrates, and Plato and their views on the relationship between scientific medicine and rhetoric. The lesson is clear: "There are in fact two things, science and opinion; the former begets knowledge, the latter ignorance."[36]

The Enlightenment associates this habitat of ignorance with the everyday existence of the masses, informed as it is by habits, rituals, and ideological dogma that direct the emotional outlook of people. The project of the Enlightenment was to deconstruct and then reconstruct this habitat in conformity with the dictates of scientific reasoning, dedicated as they are to progress and the achievement of human perfection. Such ancient ancestors of the Enlightenment as Hippocrates, Socrates, and Plato were willing to employ the orator's art up to a point in their respective scientific and philosophical projects. Aristotle's *Rhetoric*, especially when read together with his *Politics* and *Nicomachean Ethics*, further enlightens us about the pragmatic and moral importance of the orator's art. Hume, Smith, and Darwin do the same. Kant, however, with his confusion about the rhetorical tradition, sees only how the orator's art stands in the way of and contaminates the project at hand. The goal of this project, as Kant puts it, was noted above: increasing "the perfection of our cognitions and of all the benefits that depend on [these], as well as imparting that same knowledge to others." We must come to know the imperative that is innate to reason and that speaks of the importance of our moral duty to ourselves and others. This duty thus necessitates forming an interpersonal relationship with others in order to communicate to them what we maintain we know about our moral duty.

I noted earlier how Kant stressed that such an imparting of knowledge should be steeped in the scholastic precision of scientific reasoning rather than in the popular vernacular of the public. Yet, when offering more-specific advice about this communicative task, Kant suggests that the most effective way to clarify and vivify the motive of duty may be to take advantage of our natural liking for examples conveyed in stories, cases, and other modes of demonstration and argumentation. The "vivid presentation of the moral disposition in examples" is, for Kant, an invaluable pedagogical tool. "Examples are the go-cart of judgment; and those who are lacking in the natural talent can never dispense with them."[37]

What Kant emphasizes here is a commonplace of the rhetorical tradition. Eloquence facilitates vividness and its attendant emotions and moods. The philosopher Raphael Demos offers a perceptive description of this "evocative" process. Evocation, he writes,

> is the process by which vividness is conveyed; it is the presentation of a viewpoint in such a manner that it comes real for the public. It is said that argument is a way by which an individual experience is made common property; in fact, an argument has much less persuasive force than the [eloquent and] vivid evocation of an experience. The enumeration of all the relevant points in favor of a theory and against its opposite can never be completed; far more effective is it to state a viewpoint in all its concreteness and in all its significant implication, and then stop; the arguments become relevant only after this state has been concluded.[38]

Stating a viewpoint in all its concreteness and all its significant implication helps to stimulate the emotional dispositions of an audience that must be called into play if the members of the audience are to take an interest in the matter at hand. Kant, however, argues that emotional appeals should be avoided when using stories or cases for illustrative and argumentative purposes because they have no lasting "genuine [moral] effect." Instead, such appeals contaminate "the dry and earnest idea of duty." So, for example, Kant maintains that appeals to "so-called noble (super-meritorious) actions" are injurious because they encourage people to think too highly of themselves. Our moral duty should not be based on our becoming delighted about receiving acclaim for personal heroics. Emotion gets in the way of a genuine appreciation and enactment of the innate moral directive that informs the dutiful nature of our being and that might very well be an indication of God's presence in our lives.[39]

In teaching us about our moral duty, Kant wants us to avoid the very thing that not only makes his recommendations about the use of stories, cases, and examples attractive and effective, but that he also employs in certain dramatic, "casuistical" examples meant to instruct us about achieving our highest moral perfection. The examples are found in his "The Metaphysics of Morals" and include such emotional matters as hurling "oneself to certain death . . . in order to save one's country."[40] Perhaps Kant would have us resolve this contradiction regarding his assessment of the discursive use of emotion by realizing that his instructions have nothing to do with the orator's art. He is not enticing us with "beautiful illusions" designed to deceive. The orator's art, however, certainly entails more than this limited aesthetic and unethical exercise in public communication.

RHETORIC AS A "PERFECT CHEAT"

In *An Essay Concerning Human Understanding*, the philosopher and political theorist John Locke, who to a certain extent influenced Kant's appreciation of the rhetorical tradition, discusses the communication predicament that confronted those dedicated to advancing the project of the Enlightenment. He writes, "Since wit and fancy find easier entertainment in the world than dry truth and real knowledge, figurative speeches and allusion in language will hardly be admitted as an imperfection or abuse of it. I confess, in discourses where we seek rather pleasure and delight than information and improvement, such ornaments as are borrowed from them can scarce pass for faults." Locke expands on this confession when he notes, "It is evident how much men love to deceive and be deceived, since rhetoric, that powerful instrument of error and deceit, has its established professors, is publicly taught, and has always been had in great reputation: and I doubt not but it will be thought great boldness, if not brutality, in me to have said this much against it. Eloquence, like the fair sex, has too prevailing beauties in it to suffer itself ever to be spoken against. And it is vain to find fault with those arts of deceiving, wherein men find pleasure to be deceived."[41]

Locke's confession is a concession to our everyday existence, with all of its emotional attachments. The confession is structured rhetorically such that it performs the clever move of "damning with faint praise." A habitat of ignorance necessarily comes with the rhetorical territory of daily life. Here, according to Locke, the "civil use" of communication is at work: the sharing "of thoughts and ideas by words, as may serve for upholding common conversation and commerce, about the ordinary affairs and conveniences of civil life." Locke nevertheless insists that the communication practice of oratory that serves civil life be disciplined as much as possible when using words "to convey the precise notions of things, and to express in general propositions certain and undoubted truths, which the mind may rest upon and be satisfied with in its search after true knowledge." Locke thus maintains that

> . . . if we would speak of things as they are, we must allow that all the art of rhetoric, beside order and clearness; all the artificial and figurative application of words eloquence hath invented, are for nothing else but to insinuate wrong ideas, move the passions, and thereby mislead the judgment; and so indeed are perfect cheats: and therefore, however laudable or allowable oratory may render them in harangues and popular addresses, they are certainly, in all discourses that pretend to inform or instruct, wholly to be avoided; and where truth and knowledge are concerned, cannot but be thought a great fault, either of the language or person that makes use of them.[42]

Locke's solution to the communication predicament of his age begins with "God," who, "having designed man for a sociable creature, made him not only with an inclination, and under a necessity to have fellowship with those of his own kind, but furnished him also with language, which was to be the great instrument and common tie to society." Focusing more closely on the earthly process at issue here, Locke emphasizes, "To make words serviceable to the end of communication, it is necessary . . . that they excite in the hearer exactly the same idea they stand for in the mind of the speaker. Without this, men fill one another's heads with noise and sounds; but convey not thereby their thoughts, and lay not before one another their ideas, which is the end of discourse and language." For Locke, this end of communication applies to both the "civil" and the more rigorous "philosophical" and scientific use of words.[43]

Locke's and Kant's overall assessments of the orator's art are, to be sure, unflattering. With Locke, however, we have a crucial admission: if one's use of words is to serve "the end of communication," they must "excite" in an audience "exactly the same idea they stand for in the mind of the speaker." An earlier version of the admission is offered by Francis Bacon, the founding spokesman for modern science, when he defines what he considers to be the proper role of rhetoric: the "duty and office of Rhetoric, if it be deeply looked into, is no other than to apply and recommend the dictates of reason to imagination, in order to excite the appetite and will."[44] Such excitement, by definition, presupposes the workings of emotion. Excitement helps the audience to take an interest in the matter at hand and to become passionate about whatever truth is being disclosed in the situation. Notice, however, that Locke thus confronts us with a contradiction. His critique of the art of rhetoric is associated with its inclination for moving the passions. The art of rhetoric, along with its "words of eloquence," are "perfect cheats."

This last *pointedly foolish* phrase is an "oxymoron" (from the ancient Greek, *oxys*, "sharp, keen," plus *moros*, "foolish"), a rhetorical figure that combines contradictory or incongruous words for the purpose of making a particular point in a creative and thought-provoking manner. Depending on how well it is used, an oxymoron can be a tool of eloquence: having a way with words that makes the truth memorable as it *moves* us to better understand a given reference. Locke uses eloquence to excite his readers to condemn its presence; he is willing to contradict himself through his rhetorical actions in order to incite his readers to criticize and rid themselves of their dependency on such actions as much as possible. This rhetorical strategy is as old as the teachings of Hippocrates, Socrates, and Plato.[45] Nothing less than a finely tuned scientific rhetoric can aid us in our coming to terms with perfection. Locke's theory of communication serves this end: words, for him, are "voluntary signs" of "ideas" or "internal conceptions" that take form by way of our everyday sense perceptions of the environmental world. Words enable us to share with others the meaning and significance of our individual ideas in order to form a communal understanding of the truth of any given matter. Such is "the end" or goal of communication, so prized by the Enlightenment.

More with Locke than with Kant, we find an acknowledgment of how emotion and the rhetoric that can evoke it have a genuine role to play in humankind's quest for achieving the highest moral perfection. The presence of emotion and its exciting ways must, however, serve the rule of reason and its dedication to the discovery of truth. The communication theorist John Durham Peters sums up what he terms the "legacy" of Locke's theory of communication: it "lives when we bemoan the inadequacy of words for catching our inner feelings, fear the tyrannical power of words, or praise the scientific method as a way to ensure reasonable human intercourse."[46]

Guided by his theory of moral sentiments and his appreciation of how rhetorical eloquence serves humankind's communal
nature, Hume grouped Locke with authors who "knew too little
of the rules of . . . [rhetorical eloquence] to be esteemed elegant
writers."[47] Still, Locke's theory of communication proved significant for rhetorical theorists who were interested in showing how
a science of rhetoric could be developed in a more robust manner
than that provided by Locke with his confession regarding the
civil use of words and his admission about the role of emotion
in achieving the end of communication. The public needs to be
enlightened, excited, and moved by well-reasoned discourse that
imparts knowledge in clear and distinct ways and that thereby
provides others with a model for doing the same.

RHETORIC AS A MEANS OF TRUTH

Three of the best-known and most influential works of the
Enlightenment that attend to the task for both secular and religious reasons are George Campbell's *The Philosophy of Rhetoric*
(1776), Hugh Blair's *Lectures on Rhetoric and Belles Lettres*
(1783), and Richard Whately's *Elements of Rhetoric* (1828). With
these works we find an appropriation and expansion of numerous directives from the classical rhetorical tradition that lend
themselves to a rational assessment of the orator's art—an assessment grounded in the ever-developing scientific understanding of
human nature, especially its mental/psychological faculties (e.g.,
logic, imagination, sympathy, taste, eloquence). In instructing
readers on how to improve their faculty for eloquence, Blair, for
example, emphasizes how rhetorical competence "is a great exer-
tion of human powers" directed not at "pleasing the fancy merely,
but of speaking both to the understanding and to the heart; of
interesting the hearers in such a degree, as to seize and carry
them along with us; and to leave them with a deep and strong
impression of what they have heard." Blair asks, "How many
talents, natural and acquired, must concur for carrying this to
perfection?" His summary of the answer he develops throughout
his work is worth noting: "A strong, lively, and warm imagination; quick sensibility of heart, joined with solid judgment,
good sense, and presence of mind; all improved by great and
long attention to style and composition; and supported also by

the exterior, yet important qualifications of a graceful manner, a presence not ungainly, and a full and tunable voice. How little reason to wonder that a perfect and accomplished orator should be one of the characters that is most rarely to be found?"[48]

Indeed, Blair speaks of a person whose presence might bring to mind the saying "God on a good day." The practice of rhetoric is a noble art that helps people come to terms with and develop a "taste" for the truth. Taste is an essential topic in Blair's theory of rhetoric. It is the "power of receiving pleasure from the beauties of nature and art," "a faculty common in some degree to all men." Taste manifests itself in "the relish of beauty of one kind or other; of what is orderly, proportioned, grand, harmonious, new, or sprightly. . . . It is no less essential to man to have some discernment of beauty, than it is to possess the attributes of reason and of speech." Language "improved by science and philosophy" so that its particular use demonstrates its well-reasoned character is necessary in order to cultivate and perfect the faculty of taste.[49] But such language still must be fitted appropriately to the concerns and interests of the orator's audience to help ensure that they will be open to, acknowledge, and understand what they are hearing or reading. The art of rhetoric is essential to the perfecting of this process.

Campbell makes much of this fact when he notes,

> In order to evince the truth considered by itself, conclusive arguments alone are requisite; but in order to convince me by these arguments, it is moreover requisite that they be understood, that they be attended to, that they be remembered by me; and in order to persuade me by them to any particular action or conduct, it is further requisite, that by interesting me in the subject, they may, as it were, be felt. It is not therefore the understanding alone that is here concerned. If the orator would prove successful, it is necessary that he engage in his service all these different powers of the mind, the imagination, the memory, and the passions. These are not the supplanters of reason, or even rivals in her sway; they are her handmaids, by whose ministry she is enabled to usher truth into the heart, and procure it there a favourable reception.[50]

Socrates said the same thing two thousand years earlier. Guided by a love of truth, the ultimate goal of science, rhetoric offers itself as a valuable tool of reason. Drawing from such sources as Cicero, Bacon, Locke, and Hume, Campbell emphasizes that by way of the art of rhetoric the orator demonstrates sympathy, sincerity, and good will toward an audience, thereby building trust between the parties. Without the ingredient of trust, the truth of well-reasoned discourse is forever at risk of not being given a fair hearing, especially when this truth calls into question the accumulated common sense of a given audience. Whately puts it this way: "There is a 'Presumption' against any thing *paradoxical*, i.e. contrary to the prevailing opinion: it may be true; but the Burden of proof lies with him who maintains it; since men are not to be expected to abandon the prevailing belief till some reason is shown."[51]

Whately's major contribution to the rhetorical tradition comes with his pioneering analysis of presumption and burden of proof, whereby he develops a logic-based theory of "Argumentative Composition." For Whately, "the only province that Rhetoric can claim entirely and exclusively is 'the art of inventing and arranging arguments' " (eloquence) that, with respect to any given topic, can advance our "knowledge, intelligence, and intellectual cultivation" to "the highest pitch of perfection."[52]

With Blair, Campbell, and Whately, rhetoric becomes an audience-oriented art that is less concerned with the investigation and discovery of truth than with the "management" of the reasoned discourse that is offered to communicate the truth to others. The art of rhetoric is associated more with *how* a discourse means than with *what* it means: with how, for example, a story is *best* arranged and told such that its teachings, what it has to say, will be acknowledged, remembered, and perhaps advanced by later generations. Rhetoric is a technology, a tool, a means to an end; its goal of perfection includes helping us to live our lives to the fullest, within reason. The process unfolds amidst the otherness of everyday existence. Rhetoric assists reason in its consideration of and dealings with other people, places, and things; it is a competency of having a way with words that facilitates the communication process of "receiving in order to share."

Cicero long ago spoke of the importance of such assistance when, emphasizing how philosophy and rhetoric must complement each other for the moral benefit of communal life, he accused philosophy, with its fondness for abstract reasoning, of bringing about "the undoubtedly absurd and unprofitable and reprehensible severance between the tongue and the brain, leading to our having one set of professors to teach us to think and another to teach us to speak."[53] Remember, says Cicero, "to be drawn by study away from active life is contrary to moral duty."[54]

Active life, with all of its otherness, calls on our capacity for being rhetorically competent souls. In chapter 4, I briefly discussed the ontological nature of this "call of conscience": how it discloses a truth about the temporal and spatial structure of human existence. I expand on this matter in the next chapter when discussing how this call is a source of beauty. Now, however, in bringing the present chapter to a close, I want to offer a reading of one additional nineteenth-century text that is especially noteworthy in coming to terms with the topic of reason as it has been discussed here so far. The text is Mary Shelley's 1818 classic: *Frankenstein; Or, the Modern Prometheus*. This text establishes the literary genre of science fiction as it tells a story about how the progressive impulse that marks the Enlightenment's program of scientific reasoning, discovery, and practical application (especially as demonstrated in the industrial revolution of the late eighteenth and early nineteenth centuries) can turn rotten with perfection. The practice of rhetoric warrants consideration in assessing this problem, especially as the art helps to remedy a serious consequence of the problem: the inhibiting of the life-giving gift of acknowledgment. Critical theorists from the Frankfurt School of philosophy have written much about how the problem became a reality throughout the twentieth century, leading to what Max Horkheimer famously termed an "eclipse of reason."[55] Shelley prophesized this reality. Some brief background material on Shelley's life helps to contextualize my reading of her work.

FRANKENSTEIN'S PROBLEM

Shelley's tale reflects various existential concerns that arose as she was exposed to her famous father's (the minister-turned-atheist and radical philosopher William Godwin) and her famous husband's (the Romantic poet Percy Shelley) enthusiasm for the scientific spirit of the Enlightenment. Recommended reading included a book by the chemist Humphry Davy, who insisted that

Science has . . . bestowed upon [man] powers which may be called almost creative; which have enabled him to change and modify the beings surrounding him, and by his experiments to interrogate nature with power, not simply as a scholar, passive and seeking only to understand her operations, but rather as a master, active with his own instruments . . . who would not be ambitious of becoming acquainted with the most profound secrets of nature; of ascertaining her hidden operations; and of exhibiting to man that system of knowledge which related too intimately to their own physical and moral constitution.[56]

Influenced by her deceased and famous mother's (Mary Wollstonecraft) feminist writings, as well as by her own lack of confidence in the unbridled and unrelenting enthusiasm of scientific progress, Shelley questioned the masculine, power-oriented attitude of science espoused by Davy. What guarantee is there that things will not go wrong even with this attitude securely in place? Is science, in fact, the favorite child of God? Does God really have anything to do with this child's gifts? What moral obligations come with science's proper use of these gifts? Science must seek the truth, to be sure, but this capacity, as echoed in Davy's book, presupposes the valuing of a certain form of power, mastery, and domination over nature. According to the literary critic Maurice Hindle, Shelley's story cautions against the potential dangers of this specific valuation, especially as it is found in "those who find an endless thrill of excitement in scientifically 'penetrating' the 'secrets of nature,' taking little or no responsible account of the damaging implications 'theory' might have for 'practice.'[57] Indeed, Shelley's work is well known as a touchstone for cultural critics who are interested in "the making of the modern consciousness" and who would have us realize the possible evils of playing God through science and technology. My reading of *Frankenstein* complements and expands on this haunting theme. Shelley's work addresses the importance of acknowledgment and the way rhetoric serves this favored act of reason.

Dr. Frankenstein constructed his "creature" as a result of a scientific calling that requires its practitioners, in the spirit of perfectionism, to acknowledge and aid others: "Wealth was an inferior object, but what glory would attend the discovery if I could banish disease from the human frame and render man invulnerable to any but a violent death!"[58] Thinking about the "glory" of such a being for others was especially intoxicating: "A new species would bless me as its creator and source; many happy and excellent natures would owe their being to me. No father could claim the gratitude of his child so completely as I should deserve theirs. Pursuing these reflections, I thought that if I could bestow animation upon lifeless matter, I might in the process of time . . . renew life where death had apparently devoted the body to corruption."[59] Driven more by the potential glory than by the altruism of his self-appointed and compulsive task, however, Frankenstein turned selfish when his creation came alive and showed itself to be a physical monstrosity: "How can I describe my emotions at this catastrophe, or how delineate the wretch who with such infinite pains and care I have endeavored to form. His limbs were in proportion, and I had selected his features as beautiful. Beautiful! Great God! His yellow skin scarcely covered the work of muscles and arteries beneath." The doctor's success was also a failure. The creature was far from perfect. Frankenstein wanted nothing to do with such a "hideous wretch"—"a thing such as even Dante could not have conceived."[60]

The creature's imperfection brought out an even uglier imperfection in his creator: extreme selfishness in the face of the other. The situation is not without a bit of irony, since it was first made possible by one who, *as a scientist*, is obligated to remain open to what is other than oneself in order to acknowledge the truth of the specific matter at hand and thereby to provide, at the very least, better care for beings in need. The creature's physical appearance was grotesque, but that fact should not get in the way of the scientist who is devoted to acknowledging the essence of things, the real beauty of their truth. And, to be sure, there was an inner beauty to behold with the creature's being. As becomes clear as the story unfolds, the creature was exceptionally intelligent and caring. In his attempt to be accepted by others, he learned to appreciate and employ with eloquence the "godlike science" and technology of language. Recall that the perfectionist impulse of this most low-tech of tools—its *defining* of what is—serves our metaphysical desire for developing a complete understanding of matters of importance.

The creature mastered the technology of language as he secretly listened to the rule-governed speech of others and as he taught himself to read such books as Milton's *Paradise Lost*, a volume of Plutarch's *Lives*, and Goethe's *Sorrows of Young Werther*. The creature sought only the life-giving gifts of acknowledgment and companionship. He "hoped to meet with beings who, pardoning my outward form, would love me for the excellent qualities which I was capable of unfolding. I was nourished with high thoughts of honor and devotion."[61] The creature valued "praiseworthiness"; he lived for the day that he could offer certain life-giving gifts to others and receive some degree of appreciation for his efforts. But this never happened. He remained an outcast, a victim of an ongoing social death, and his virtues eventually turned evil.

The tragedy of this transformation is especially painful to the reader as he or she recalls the desperate words that were spoken to Frankenstein by his "monster" when he was eventually given the opportunity to recall his first moment of self-awareness and some related subsequent thoughts:

> My person was hideous and my stature gigantic. What did this mean? Who was I? What was I? Whence did I come? . . . Hateful day when I received life. . . . Accursed creator! Why did you form a monster so hideous that even *you* turned from me in disgust? God, in pity, made man beautiful and alluring, after his own image; but my form is a filthy type of yours, more horrid even from the very resemblance. Satan had his companions, fellow devils, to admire and encourage him, but I am solitary and abhorred. . . . I cherished hope, it is true, but it vanished when I beheld my person reflected in water or my shadow in the moonshine, even as that frail image and that inconstant shade. . . . [S]ometimes I allowed my thoughts, unchecked by reason, to ramble in the fields of Paradise, and dared to fancy amiable and lovely creatures sympathizing with my feelings and cheering my gloom; the angelic countenances breathed smiles of consolation. But it was all a dream; no Eve soothed my sorrows nor shared my thoughts; I was alone. I remembered Adam's supplication to his Creator. But where was mine? He had abandoned me . . . Oh! My creator, make me happy; let me feel gratitude towards you for one benefit! Let me see that I excite the sympathy of some existing thing; do not deny me my request![62]

There is eloquence at work here. The discourse is expressed to establish the truth and to arouse a love for it in the hearts of human beings. Things which strike and arouse the heart—eloquence is just that. Eloquence is beauty in the making: the art of enhancing the perfectionist capacity of language, especially as this capacity is employed in order to share one's views with others such that they will genuinely care about the matters at hand. The creature involves himself in and promotes the rhetorical process of receiving in order to share.

From ugliness can come beauty. Frankenstein's monster speaks the truth eloquently as he raises key questions regarding the "why" and "how" of his life and as he makes demands associated with as-yet-articulated, honest answers to these questions. His discourse pleads for a sense of "beginning," an understanding of his reason for being and how his existence might and must be improved. Like his "human" counterparts, the creature wants to feel some sense of being at home with himself and others. Religious references help to make clear his pained state of mind. What would life be like if people did not care enough to take the time to make a place for you in their lives by acknowledging your existence and whatever goodness it has to offer? Far from perfect, to be sure.

Frankenstein created a being that embodied a metaphysical desire for some degree of perfection in his life. The perfectibility of the human species requires nothing less than the activation of this desire. Such activation is always ready to go, grounded as it is in the openness of the spatial and temporal structure of human existence, with its silent call of conscience. The call discloses a fundamental challenge of existence: the need to assume the ethical responsibility of affirming one's freedom through resolute choice. The creature's way of answering this call involves the belief that sometimes it is better to die on your feet than to live on your knees. The doctor refused to respect the metaphysical desire in his "wretched" creation; he thereby closed himself off to a being whose imperfection was only skin deep but who was nevertheless perceived by the doctor to be an impediment to his own quest for perfectibility. Not wanting to assume any responsibility for what he had created, the selfish Frankenstein thus exhibited a capacity for being "rotten with perfection." Burke maintains that the capacity is "revealed most perfectly in our tendency to conceive of a 'perfect enemy'. . . . The Nazi version of the Jew, as developed in Hitler's *Mein Kampf,* is the most thoroughgoing instance of such ironic 'perfection' in recent times, though strongly similar trends keep manifesting themselves in current controversies between East and West."[63]

Frankenstein carried the disease, for he created his own perfect enemy—a being who, despite his outward appearance, was capable of perfecting himself to be a good neighbor, a dear friend, and an overall man of virtue. Shelley's *Frankenstein* tells a story about the honorific and ironic ways of perfection. Scientific reasoning and know-how can go wrong. The "dispassionate," albeit still emotional, ways of science can turn unpleasant and coldhearted, if not threatening and murderous. Human emotion can get out of control, forsaking its role to aid reason in opening others to the truth. The problem here, however, is not simply the fault of science. Rather, it is the fault of *a man* of science who, for selfish reasons, refuses to remain open to the central matter at hand: the truth and well-being of the creature's existence.

A spiritually informed eloquence fails to remedy the disease of closed-mindedness at work in Shelley's story. The doctor is too rotten with perfection to engage in the rhetorical process of receiving in order to share. Perhaps the creature would have been better off employing the meticulous language of science, rather than the metaphysical discourse of religion, in arguing his case. Still, abiding by an ethic of acknowledgment, of being and remaining open to its subject matter, scientific reasoning is supposed to care for what something is as this something shows itself in how it exists. The creature existed religiously, lovingly, for a part of its life. Frankenstein's refusal to remain open to this specific truth suggests that, as the literary critic Marilyn Butler puts it, the doctor knew "too little science rather than too much."[64]

As was made clear during the Enlightenment, science can flourish without denying what Leibniz described as "the universal beauty and perfection of the works of God." The scientist is in the business of acknowledging the truth of these works: how they attest to the empirically verifiable laws of nature. Discovering these laws displays a form of human perfection at work providing invaluable evidence of what may be indications of an even greater perfection at work in and beyond the cosmos. Science is not in the business of engaging in metaphysical speculation about the matter. It leaves that to the saving-grace rhetoric of religion. Frankenstein's monster was denied such grace by his creator. "Frankenstein is [thus] himself a monster," writes Butler. "He will not acknowledge his only child, the Being he chooses to call Monster, Fiend and Demon, though no human father ever played so thorough-going a role in any birth."[65]

The powerful and dominating ways of science must not close themselves off to arguments (be they religious or otherwise) that, although not based in science, are nevertheless important because they raise questions of morality that science must address in its quest for progress and perfection. The arguments sound a call of conscience; their rhetoric emphasizes the importance of acknowledging what is truthful, good, and beautiful in even the ugliest of things. Scientific reasoning prides itself on its enactment of such acknowledgment, which is fated to take place in the midst of otherness. An act of acknowledgment opens us to what is. Rhetoric can facilitate the endeavor.

CONCLUSION

Throughout his many works, the twentieth-century philosopher and critical theorist Jürgen Habermas develops a "theory of communicative action" that is meant to remedy the problem of closed-mindedness being noted here. Habermas is true to the goals of the Enlightenment. He develops his theory, in great part, to extend and thereby remedy Kant's limited understanding of the workings of "public communication." Unlike Kant, Habermas aligns reason with what he discovers to be the "validity conditions" of "the ideal [democratic] community of communication." The conditions are the basis of "communicative rationality." They include choosing a comprehensible expression of one's interpretation of some matter of interest, intending to communicate a true proposition regarding this matter, expressing intentions truthfully, and choosing an appropriate expression with respect to the communication situation at hand. Habermas argues that these conditions "are already built into [the communicative] action" of people who are "oriented toward reaching an understanding" of contested matters, whether this understanding confirms or calls into question existing opinions and truth claims. For Habermas, the conditions thus define, a priori, the genuine moral basis and nature of language, its true beauty. The conditions must be operative in communicative interactions in order to ensure that these interactions function to reveal the truth and provide "equal opportunity for participation in argumentation" by members of the public.[66]

Habermas' theory emphasizes the importance of keeping reason at work in the world of otherness as "perfectly" as possible. It thereby serves the interests of critics who would expose the ideological element of authority that, as seen in Shelley's *Frankenstein*, inhibits acknowledgment of others and collaborative deliberation. By refusing to remain open to the arguments that his only child offered to explain and defend his humanity, Frankenstein acted immorally. What Habermas fails to attend to carefully, however, is a major concern of the rhetorical critic: *how* discourse is invented and arranged in order to be expressed in an appropriate, truthful, and effective manner. Remember, the rhetorical critic is concerned not only with what a text means but also with how it means. A specific form of eloquence proved unsuccessful in opening Frankenstein to the truth. But this same eloquence proves successful in moving readers to acknowledge and care about the life of an unfortunate soul. The closest Habermas comes to appreciating the existential and phenomenological significance of such a movement is when he identifies the particular validity condition of choosing an appropriate expression for communicating one's arguments to others. At this level of what Habermas admits is a "quasi-transcendental" conception of the validity condition, the intricacy and the beauty of the everyday workings of rhetoric fade from view and are too easily dismissed by reason as mere "ornamentation" that aids in the manipulating use of language. Habermas speaks too abstractly of a "positive" function of rhetoric that makes possible collaborative deliberation as it contributes to the eloquence of one's discourse, to its ability to establish the truth and to arouse a love for it in the hearts of human beings. Eloquence serves humankind's passion for perfection—a passion that certainly informs Habermas' theory of communicative action.[67]

With this chapter, we continue to build a relationship of terms that speak to us of perfection. Reason belongs to the relationship, along with truth, conscience, acknowledgment, hermeneutics (interpretation), otherness, and rhetoric. In my discussion of reason, I have had a number of occasions to mention the phenomenon of beauty, especially when considering the way reason and rhetorical eloquence work together to open people to the truth. For the sake of my project, more needs to be said about the phenomenon. Beauty and perfection have long been recognized by philosophers, theologians, scientists, and artists as complementary phenomena. Beauty is a sign of perfection.

CHAPTER SIX

BEAUTY

Professor of civil engineering and historian Henry Petroski tells the story of a person who shared with him on a public radio show her enthusiasm for an object "that she was not sure anyone else would appreciate but which she marveled at when she had a hot pizza delivered: the 'thingy' that keeps the top of the box from sagging and getting stuck to the melted cheese." Petroski admits that he, too, admires the white plastic tripod for its ingenuity and simplicity. Another listener (an artist) emailed him and also declared her admiration. Moreover, she "described shortening [the tripods'] legs and using them as spacers between staked palettes in her paint-storage box. She had also used them for a different purpose, turning them upside down to support, like little Atlases, spherical objects for display." Another person used the tripod "for holding eggs, to which she applies sequins, beads, and other festive trim to make Christmas-tree decorations."[1] Petroski notes, "That the pizza-box tripod can also serve, albeit unintentionally, for holding round and ovoid objects for display and decoration . . . makes its design all the more satisfying. Indeed, though it may never garner awards for aesthetic excellence, admirers see it as a thing of beauty."[2]

The beauty of the tripod shows itself in its "technical perfection": an invention doing exactly what it was designed to do with the maximum efficiency. The tripod's beauty is further enhanced as it lends itself to the inventiveness of its users. Beauty, in other words, has a genuine relationship with the purposive function of our creations and their successful employment. Petroski expands on this point:

> Beauty is ultimately in the eye of the beholder, of course. We tend to develop an affection and a fit for our familiar tools and furniture, no matter what they look like. Our favorite hammer or chair is often the one that we have grown so accustomed to that any other feels awkward or uncomfortable to use. Our favorite things get old and worn, but they become so molded to our shape that we do not care that they are dirty and deformed and possibly even offensive to the senses of others. By absolute aesthetic standards, they may be downright ugly. But judged by personal aesthetics, they may belong in a museum.[3]

Indeed, we are metaphysical creatures: we have a longing for security and completeness, for feeling comfortable and at home with others and our surroundings. Petroski emphasizes that our designs are always "works in progress," an ongoing process of betterment: "There can never be an end to the quest for the perfect design."[4] Still, there are moments throughout the quest that warrant the response, "Beautiful!" Beauty and perfection can, and do, go together in our everyday, purposeful lives. Beauty is found in things that suit our purposes in particularly pleasing and satisfying ways.

I am associating beauty with the utility or instrumental function (technical perfection) of some tool, what Immanuel Kant terms its "objective purposiveness."[5] Pizza-box tripods, our favorite hammers and chairs, and any other number of useful devices exhibit such purposiveness. The same can be said of language. Language is a tool, a means to an end: making things meaningful such that what these things are perceived to be, their "truth," can be communicated to others in an understandable way. Recall that this most basic and fundamental use of language is what defines its "perfectionist" capacity. Kenneth Burke's observation of the matter noted in the introduction is worth repeating: "The mere desire to name something by its 'proper' name, or to speak a language in its distinctive ways, is intrinsically 'perfectionist.'

What is more 'perfectionist' in essence than the impulse, when one is in dire need of something, to so state this need that one in effect 'defines' the situation?" Also recall that the art of rhetorical eloquence enhances the perfectionist capacity of language. The objective purposiveness of such eloquence is to help a given discourse establish the truth of a particular matter and to arouse a love for it in the hearts of others. Rhetorical eloquence functions to cultivate the faculty of "taste," which, as Hugh Blair reminds us, manifests itself in "the relish of beauty of one kind or other; of what is orderly, proportioned, grand, harmonious, new, or sprightly."[6]

I will have more to say about rhetorical eloquence later in this chapter. Now, however, I want to clarify further how beauty and perfection are related to the notion of purpose. Insights from philosophy, religion, science, and art continue to inform my story.

THE PURPOSE OF BEAUTY

"A natural beauty is a beautiful thing," writes Kant; "artistic beauty," on the other hand, "is a beautiful presentation of a thing."[7] Kant's clarification of this distinction is worth noting:

> In order to judge a natural beauty to be that, I need not have a prior concept of what kind of thing the object is [meant] to be; i.e. I do not have to know its [objective purposiveness]. Rather, I [simply] like the mere form of the object when I judge it, on its own account and without knowing the purpose. But if the object is given as a product of art, and as such is to be declared beautiful, then we must first base it on a concept of what the thing is [meant] to be, since art always presupposes a purpose in the cause (and its causality). And since the harmony of a thing's manifold [its various constitutive elements] . . . with its purpose . . . is the thing's perfection, it follows that when we judge artistic beauty we shall have to assess the thing's perfection as well, whereas perfection is not at all at issue when we judge natural beauty (to be that). . . . Thus if we say, e.g., That is a beautiful woman, we do in fact think nothing other than that nature offers us in the woman's figure a beautiful presentation of the purposes [inherent] in the female build.[8]

For Kant, "natural beauty" has no purpose other than what we conceive it to be: "the purposiveness of nature is a special a priori concept that has its origin solely in reflective judgment. For we cannot attribute to natural products anything like nature's referring them to purposes, but can only use this concept in order to reflect on nature as it regards that connection among nature's appearances which is given to us in terms of empirical laws."[9]

Kant favors a scientific understanding of nature and beauty. Reason serves this goal by allowing us to stick to the facts as we figure out on strictly empirical grounds the physical laws of nature that define its essence and thus make it what it is. The beauty associated with discovering this truth lies in our liking and being pleased by the form that these laws take in nature's exhibition of itself to us. The orderly, well-proportioned, grand, and harmonious character of the exhibition may be particularly lovely and striking. The resulting awe and wonder, however, do not offer definitive evidence of some underlying purpose that informs and guides the entire process. Natural beauty is judged "on the basis of a merely formal purposiveness, i.e., a purposiveness without a purpose."[10] For Kant, we have to transcend the limits of reason and engage in metaphysical speculation if we are to understand the physical laws of nature as being the product of a greater intelligence that designed the cosmos with a specific end (purpose) in mind. Science cautions against this "leap of faith" in acquiring genuine knowledge about the empirical workings and beauty of nature. Religion, of course, makes the leap every day. God is perfection, purpose, and beauty in their most complete, related, and unified forms.

We demonstrate what the intellectual historian John Passmore terms "obedientiary perfection" when our deeds are done in response to a higher calling: absolute obedience to the will of God.[11] The creation of a pizza-box tripod is not the most stunning piece of technical evidence for the presence of such perfection. On the other hand, however, the so-called "miracles" of modern medical science and technology *are* technical accomplishments that are oftentimes associated with the good that should and must be done in God's name. Physicians, in fact, declared as much before the one known as the "the Greatest Physician," Jesus Christ, was born. As noted in the Hippocratic treatise *Decorum*, the wisdom that these healers possess and that they must constantly seek as their first priority makes them "the equal of a god. Between wisdom and medicine there is no gulf fixed."[12] With medicine, something of the "beauty" of God's creation—human being—can sometimes be cured of what ails it. Medicine serves the goal of "teleological perfection" that God designed for humankind and that is heard in the command "walk before me, and be thou perfect" (Gen 17:1-2). As one of God's tools, human beings are fated to struggle constantly to live "the purposeful and good life." That is how we show our most genuine beauty, what it is that we were truly designed to be and to do.

We take our metaphysical capacity to its limit in believing that God intentionally created the cosmos and endowed it with purposefulness. This belief need not, however, lead to a misguided dismissal of the wonders of science. Influenced by both Pythagorean and Hippocratic doctrines, Plato long ago championed the excellence and beauty of mathematics and a scientific understanding of the body and its environment. But, as explained throughout his *Timaeus*, he also spoke highly of God in his account of the creation of the "fitting" and "beautiful arrangement" (*cosmos*) of the universe's geometric nature. According to Plato, the person "who should attempt to verify all this by experiment would forget the difference of the human and divine nature. For God only has the knowledge and also the power which are able to combine many things into one and again resolve the one into many." Plato thus contends that "God created in each thing in relation to itself, and in all things in relation to each other, all the measures and harmonies which they could possibly receive." In concluding his account, Plato writes, "The world has received animals, mortal and immortal, and is fulfilled with them, and has become a visible animal containing the visible—the sensible God who is the image of the intellectual, the greatest, best, fairest, most perfect—the one only begotten heaven."[13]

For Plato, God is truth, an eternal now, unchangeable and forever inexpressible. God created the "essential forms" (truths) of all things. We represent these forms with our creations, be they as concrete as a "couch" or as abstract as a "sense of justice." For example, in the *Republic*, Plato tells us that the specific design for and manufacturing of a couch presupposes "the Form or essential nature of couch." Couches serve the purpose of a thing designed to sit on. This purpose, however, is itself made possible by God's design for us: our ability to conceive of the form or idea of "couchness," the unique and unvarying transcendental reality that must be, however imperfectly, embodied in any couch.[14] Thanks to God, we are given a way of resting our bodies with some degree of comfort. The greater the comfort, the greater the beauty of the experience. Comfort is also afforded people who have succeeded in instituting a sense of justice in their communities. Following Socrates, Plato develops this point throughout his philosophy as he advances the metaphysical and idealistic belief that to know the good is necessarily to do the good. A more famous and updated version of this belief is found in the New Testament: "And ye shall know the truth, and the truth shall make you free" (John 8:32). Knowing the truth is a beautiful thing to do.

God is the ground, the originating source of perfection and its related elements: purpose, truth, and beauty. Although the ultimate Form of this relationship is beyond the grasp of scientific reasoning, Plato regards such reasoning as the one and only true way of revealing some of the essentials of the form's being. Science is a gift given to us by God so that we may understand something of God's reasoning. Science is a tool that enables us to demonstrate our "godlike" possibilities of being purposive, truthful, and beautiful creatures.

In his nearly seven-hundred-page reading of the book of Genesis, the physician and medical ethicist Leon Kass maintains that the central question of the text is this: "Is it possible to *find*, *institute*, and *preserve* a way of life, responsive to both the promise and the peril of the human creature, that *accords with man's true understanding in the world* and that serves to *perfect his god-like possibilities*?"[15] For Kass, an answer to the question lies in a close reading of the text in order to determine "what God is like." Kass writes,

> In the course of recounting His creation, Genesis 1 introduces us to God's *activities and powers*: (1) God speaks, commands, blesses, and hallows; (2) God makes, and makes freely; (3) God looks at and beholds the world; (4) God is concerned with the goodness or perfection of things; (5) God addresses solicitously other living creatures and provides for their sustenance.

"In short," Kass notes, "God exercises speech and reason, freedom in doing and making, and the powers of contemplation, judgment, and care."[16] Human beings are capable of doing the same, hence, according to Kass, our "god-like possibilities."

Although Kass omits any discussion of how the doing of science belongs in this category, he does make much of how science is all too easily blinded by its own prejudices regarding an appreciation of these possibilities. According to Kass, nature as understood by science "is not teleological or purposive," and "it has nothing to teach us about human good," nor do "the descriptive laws of nature . . . issue normative Natural Law or Natural Right. In this respect above all, nature by herself does not provide us with a home. As subject to the flux as is everything else, we human beings have no fixed nature or special dignity."[17] Kass takes strong exception to this last point. Genesis, for him, is more telling than science when it comes to revealing our godlike possibilities. Kass points to certain rhetorical features, or what he terms "formal features of the text," that "are responsible for its enduring vitality and the success of its timeless pedagogical power." These features include "sparseness, lacunae, ambiguity, reticence, and lack of editorial judgment that both permit and require the engagement of the reader." With all that it has (and does not have) to say about the "beginning," Genesis takes on an "open form" that calls into question any claim for a definitive interpretation of the text. This fact, for Kass, is key: "The open form of the text and its recalcitrance to final and indubitable interpretation are absolutely perfect instruments for cultivating the openness, thoughtfulness, and modesty about one's own understanding that is the hallmark of the pursuit of wisdom."[18]

Still, Kass feels certain about the godlike possibilities that he finds inscribed in the text, possibilities that he maintains provide evidence that, indeed, human beings were created in the "image of God." An image of something, however, is not the thing itself. God is good. And as Kass points out, after "nearly every act of creation, God looked at the creature and 'saw that it was good.'" But Kass is quick to add that neither the creation of "the firmament (or heavens), on Day Two, nor man, on Day Six, is said to be good." Commenting on this specific omission, Kass writes, "Now, one might say that there is no need to see or say that man is good; after all, he is made in God's image and that might make man 'better' than good. Moreover, once human beings are present, the whole is said to be *very* good: does this not imply that each part—man especially included—is good? Perhaps. But what if the omission were intended and meaningful? What if it were very good that the creation contain a creature that is himself *not*—or not *yet*—good?"[19]

Kass offers a close reading of the text; he takes seriously the presence of a specific omission or absence in the discourse that opens inquiry into the relationship between the "image of God," its beauty and goodness, and the beauty and goodness of human beings. "A being is good insofar as it is fully formed and fully fit to do its proper work," writes Kass. Yet a "moment's reflection shows that man as he comes into the world is not yet good. Precisely because he is the free being, he is also the incomplete or indeterminate being; what he becomes depends always (in part) on what he freely will choose to be." God, at one and the same time, gives and takes away, reveals and conceals the presence, perfection, purpose, truth, and beauty of what God is. Directed by the rhetorical and metaphysical logic at work here, Kass emphasizes that "precisely in the sense that man is in the image of God, man is not good—not determinate, finished, complete, or perfect. It remains to be seen whether man will *become* good, whether he will be able to complete himself (or to be completed)."[20]

Kass' reading of Genesis is steeped in a Judaic theory of hermeneutics that, as discussed in chapter 3, cannot emphasize enough the importance of being open to the world of experience, with all of its contingency, uncertainty, ambiguity, and conflict. We are here on earth to answer a call—"Where art thou?"—that is neverending in its request for acknowledgment: "Here I am!" The request is for a life-giving gift that, when originally given by God, created the universe.[21] Recall that acknowledgment is more than simple recognition; it is *the way* that human beings open themselves to life's otherness. "Good science," like "good religion," is dependent on how well its practitioners perform the activity when searching for the particular truths that concern them. Both science and religion thrive on revelations. But, of course, there is a mighty difference between the two.

Religion is interested first and foremost in *divine* revelation, what the prophets of the Old Testament spoke of and shared with others. The prophets did not engage in "self-revelation"; they did not speak in the name of personal experience. Rather, as Rabbi Abraham Joshua Heschel explains, the "prophetic event impresses itself on the prophet as a happening that springs exclusively from the will and initiative of God. He cannot himself control or call forth inspiration; it must proceed from God and therefore depends utterly on God's willing it. He is unable to conjure it up by human means, not even prayer."[22]

Prayer is, however, a holy version of acknowledgment that opens us to God and the hope that this opening provides. Prayer, if done with all of one's heart, attunes our consciousness to a mystery that, literally, is all about perfection, purpose, truth, and beauty. Prayer is the most powerful and humble way we know to communicate with God, to catch, if only for a brief moment, God's attention. "Where art thou?" "Here I am!" "Where art *thou?*" The Old Testament makes clear that God, likewise, wants the acknowledgment that comes with an answer to the question. In the best of all possible worlds, it is supposed to be a reciprocal relationship. Human beings are known to get mad at God when prayers are not answered and things do not go right. God's reaction to being unacknowledged is recorded in Isaiah 50:2, 65:1-2, and 66:4:

> Why, when I came, was there no man? When I called, was there no one to answer? . . . I was ready to be sought by those who did not ask for Me; I was ready to be found by those who did not seek Me. I said: Here am I, here am I, to a nation that did not call on my name. I spread My hands all the day to a rebellious people, who walk in a way that is not good, following their own devices. . . . I will choose affliction for them, and bring their fears upon them; because, when I called, no one answered, when I spoke they did not listen.

What are we supposed to hear when listening to God with the most devout attention? At their best, prophets provide a hint, a clue with their revelations of a divine revelation. Such revelation, writes Heschel, "is not a voice crying in the wilderness, but an act of received communication. It is not simply an act of disclosing, but an act of disclosing *to* someone, the bestowal of a content."[23] In the Judeo-Christian tradition, this content has been interpreted and expressed poetically and rhetorically in the narratives of the Bible. The stories told of God, Abraham, Moses,

Israel, Christ, and the church reflect the extent to which the content of God's word can be put into words that human beings can understand and that can move them in awesome ways.

The question of just how true these words are to "the truth" of the original content continues to be a highly debatable and heated issue.[24] Talmudic and biblical scholars, as well as a great number of the laity, devote much of their lives trying to figure out whether or not we have gotten it right so far. The Scriptures demand as much: "walk before me, and be thou perfect" (Gen 17:1). In the New Testament, the command is repeated in Christ's Sermon on the Mount: "Be ye therefore perfect, even as your Father which is in heaven is perfect" (Matt 5:48). The command is voiced immediately after Christ provides a specific example of the type of behavior that is being called for here:

> Love your enemies, bless them that curse you, do good to them that hate you, and pray for them which despitefully use you, and persecute you; That ye may be the children of your Father which is in heaven: for he maketh his sun to rise on the evil and the good, and sendeth rain on the just and on the unjust. For if ye love them which love you, what reward have ye? Do not even the publicans the same? And if ye salute your brethren only, what do ye more *than others*? Do not even the publicans so? (Matt 5:44-47)

Following Christ, we must engage in paradoxical behavior; that is, we must go beyond (*para*) the received opinion (*doxa*) of the common folk (publicans) and expand our understanding of the limits of love by employing the emotion to bind ourselves with our enemies. Perfection entails love, no matter the cost. It also entails things like mercy: "Be you therefore merciful, as your Father also is merciful" (Luke 6:36). Mercy draws on our capacity to be as charitable as possible. Perfection requires a lot; it is beauty in the making—so much so, in fact, that acts of compassion can sometimes bring us to shed tears of joy as we witness their results.

A demonstration of perfection is also known to happen with the experience of epiphanies. What we perceive at the moment of these instantaneous manifestations of reality may be God's word in the form of something "miraculous" (e.g., the birth of a child), "everyday" (e.g, feeling good about opening a door for another person), or "dreadful" (e.g, the loss of a loved one). Neither the prophet nor anyone else knows when the moment will come that is especially, if not overwhelmingly, awesome in getting them to see something of the light. Prayer is preparation for the moment; it opens us to otherness but offers no immediate guarantee that all or anything will be well. Our brains have yet to develop enough for us to comprehend completely the total beauty of God's perfection, purpose, and truth.

GET REAL!

Confronted with musings and sermons that expound on these related topics, nonbelievers are known to request, if not demand, "Get real!" The much-esteemed twentieth-century mathematician and philosopher Bertrand Russell was such a person. Having given considerable thought to the question of whether there is a "purpose" to the cosmos and whether the "good intentions" of this purpose are substantiated by the fact "that the universe has produced US," Russell had a number of provocative things to say about the matter. He noted, for example, that

> Before the Copernican revolution, it was natural to suppose that God's purposes were specially concerned with the earth, but now this has become an unplausible hypothesis. If it is the purpose of the Cosmos to evolve mind, we must regard it as rather incompetent in having produced so little in such a long time. It is, of course, *possible* that there will be more mind later on somewhere else, but of this we have no jot of scientific evidence. It may seem odd that life should occur by accident, but in such a large universe accidents will happen.[25]

Responding to those who still might maintain that, despite the billions of years that it took to come into being, our presence on earth is far more than a fortuitous event, Russell offered this lengthy but noteworthy rejoinder:

> But are we really so splendid as to justify such a long prologue? The philosophers lay stress on values: they say that we think certain things good, and that since these things are good, we must be very good to think them so. But this is a circular argument. A being with other values might think ours so atrocious as to be proof that we were inspired by Satan. Is there not something a trifle absurd in the spectacle of human beings holding a mirror before themselves, and thinking what they behold so excellent as to prove that a Cosmic Purpose must have been aiming at it all along? Why, in any case, this glorification of Man? How about lions and tigers? They destroy fewer animal or

human lives than we do, and they are much more beautiful than we are. How about ants? They manage the Corporate State much better than any Fascist. Would not a world of nightingales and larks and deer be better than our human world of cruelty and injustice and war? The believers in Cosmic Purpose make much of our supposed intelligence, but their writings make one doubt it. If I were granted omnipotence, and millions of years to experiment in, I should not think Man much to boast of as the final result of all my efforts.

Man, as a curious accident in a backwater, is intelligible: his mixture of virtues and vices is such as might be expected to result from a fortuitous origin. But only abysmal self-complacency can see in Man a reason which Omniscience could consider adequate as a motive for the Creator. The Copernican revolution will not have done its work until it has taught men more modesty than is to be found among those who think Man sufficient evidence of Cosmic Purpose.[26]

Russell's argument is directed against what in cosmology is termed the "anthropic principle," especially as this principle is used as an argument for the existence of God. Put briefly, the principle states that the universe must have those finely (beautifully) tuned properties (the constants and laws of nature) that allowed life to develop, at least on planet Earth. With advanced stages of life (human being), the complex structure of consciousness emerged whereby the universe exhibited a capacity of self-awareness. We are those creatures who can be awed by and acknowledge the wonders of the universe; who care about why, what, and how we are; and who display an appreciation for progress and the pursuit of perfection. We thus find in our own existence evidence for believing that the universe was designed to evolve an intelligence that could and would struggle to come to terms with its truth, its reason for being. The anthropic principle, in other words, allows for the possibility of there being an original Designer (God) of the universe whose cosmic purpose necessarily includes human being. What a beautiful, self-fulfilling arrangement![27]

Russell scoffs at such nonsense. God (if It exists) is "incompetent." The "glorification" of humankind is unwarranted. The two claims go together. God has taken too long of a time to bring "mind" (human intelligence) into existence. As evidenced in its tendency for "abysmal self-complacency," this mind, too, is flawed. For it fails to admit how human existence, as the purported end product of some cosmic purpose, says more about the deficiencies of this purpose than it does about the greatness of the purpose. We think too much of ourselves. As it currently functions in our evolutionary history, our metaphysical desire for perfection blinds us to the fact that we are but "a curious accident in a backwater" region of the universe. As a way of helping it evolve successfully, Russell would thus place certain limits on the unruly tendencies and reach of this desire. Indeed, we can and must have a hand in evolution, in honing our talents and cultivating the knowledge that is needed to secure our social and political welfare. Russell was clear about the task at hand: "Whatever knowledge is attainable, must be attained by scientific methods; and what science cannot discover mankind cannot know."[28] Get real!

Science's quest for knowledge brackets out any consideration of God's role in the creation of reality. What is not eliminated from this quest, however, is the scientist's dependence on the metaphysical desire that stimulates the quest in the first place. Science situates the source of this desire in the workings of the brain. As the neuroscientist Michael Gazzaniga puts it, "We are wired to form beliefs."[29] Neuroscientists Andrew Newberg and Eugene D'Aquili expand on this point in an especially enlightening way:

> If God does exist . . ., and if He appeared to you in some incarnation, you would have no way of experiencing His presence, except as part of a neurologically generated rendition of reality. You would need auditory processing to hear His voice, visual processing to see His face, and cognitive processing to make sense of His message. Even if He spoke to you mystically, without words, you would need cognitive functions to comprehend His meaning, and input from the brain's emotional centers to fill you with rapture and awe. Neurology makes it clear: There's no other way for God to get into your head except through the brain's neural pathways.[30]

Religion teaches us that our capacity to strive for perfection, know the truth, and experience the beauty of it all is made possible by God's power to get into our heads and our hearts. Science has no need for this hypothesis. As the physicist Leonard Susskind maintains, the "compelling human need to believe—to be comforted" arises from those "mindful" aspects of the brain that get "pleasure from being proved right" and that, according to Susskind, are "especially well developed in theoretical physicists. To make a theory of some phenomenon followed by a clever calculation and then finally to have the result confirmed by an experiment provides a tremendous source of satisfaction." Such satisfaction is made possible by the ability of scientists to train, condition, and control their metaphysical desire for perfection, to keep it aimed squarely at empirical reality. In this way, writes Susskind, scientists "resist, to the death, all explanations of the world based on anything but the Laws of Physics, mathematics, and probability" and, of course, the scientific evidence that we accumulate from the natural ("hard") sciences.[31]

Scientists reduce the reach of their perfectionist tendencies from the transcendental heights of God to the real world. As noted by the theoretical physicist Paul Davies, however, such reductionism need not be read as a complete and final dismissal of God: "Our ignorance of the origin of life [and the universe] leaves plenty of scope for divine explanations, but that is a purely negative attitude, invoking 'the God-of-the-gaps' only to risk retreat at a later date in the face of scientific advance." Hence, "to invoke God as a blanket explanation of the unexplained is to invite eventual falsification, and make God the friend of ignorance. If God is to be found, it must surely be through what we discover about the world, not what we fail to discover."[32]

Notice that with this way of thinking, scientists do God a favor by acknowledging the possibility of the Creator while, at the same time, saying that the best way to do this is not to acknowledge this possibility because it gets in the way of and undercuts the scientific endeavor. Commenting on this paradoxical way of accounting for God's presence and/or absence, the Nobel Laureate and theoretical physicist Steven Weinberg writes, "One of the great achievements of science has been, if not to make it impossible for intelligent people to be religious, than at least to make it possible for them not to be religious. We should not retreat from this accomplishment."[33]

The accomplishment, especially as it pertains to understanding the development of our purposeful and metaphysical nature, owes much to Charles Darwin's evolutionary theory of natural selection. The following passage from his *The Origin of Species* warrants consideration:

As natural selection acts by competition [in "the constantly recur-
rent Struggle for Existence"], it adapts the inhabitants of each country only in relation to the degree of perfection of their associates; so
that we need feel no surprise at the inhabitants of any one country,
although on the ordinary view supposed to have been specially created and adapted for that country, being beaten and supplanted by
the naturalized productions of another land. Nor ought we to marvel if all the contrivances in nature be not, as far as we can judge,
absolutely perfect; and if some of them be abhorrent to our ideas of
fitness. We need not marvel at the sting of the bee causing the bee's
own death; at drones being produced in such vast numbers for one
single act, and being then slaughtered by their sterile sisters; at the
astonishing waste of pollen by our fir-trees; at the instinctive hatred
of the queen bee for her own fertile daughters; at ichneumonidae
feeding within the live bodies of caterpillars; and at other such cases.
The wonder indeed is, on the theory of natural selection, that more
cases of the want of absolute perfection have not been observed.[34]

Evolutionary science teaches that brute existence, with its
"law" of "survival of the fittest," is purpose enough to keep life
going. Our metaphysical desire for perfection evolves from this
most basic purpose and "power" of life. Darwin asks, "What
limit can be put to this power, acting during long ages and rig-
idly scrutinizing the whole constitution, structure, and habits of
each creature,—favoring the good and rejecting the bad?" And
he answers. "I can see no limit to this power, in slowly and beautifully adapting each form to the most complex relations of life.
. . . When I view all beings not as special creations [of God], but
as the lineal descendants of some few beings which lived long
before the first bed of the Silurian system was developed, they
seem to me to become ennobled."[35] The successful evolution of
life, although not always absolutely perfect in the virtuous sense
that pleases human beings, nevertheless warrants the description
of being beautiful. Indeed, as Darwin makes clear in the much-
quoted last sentence of his work, "There is grandeur in this view
of life, with its several powers, having been originally breathed
into a few forms or into one; and that, whilst this planet has gone
cycling on according to the most fixed laws of gravity, from so
simple a beginning endless forms most beautiful and most wonderful have been, and are being, evolved."[36]

In the second and subsequent editions of *The Origin*, Darwin
revised this concluding sentence to read ". . . having been originally

breathed by the Creator. . . ." This addition is consistent with a statement he makes in the preceding paragraph: "Authors of the highest eminence seem to be fully satisfied with the view that each species has been independently created. To my mind it accords better with what we know of the laws impressed on matter by the Creator, that production and extinction of the past and present inhabitants of the world should have been due to secondary causes, like those determining the birth and death of the individual."[37] Here, Darwin is crediting the Creator with at least impressing the laws of nature on material existence. Did Darwin believe in God? The evolutionary biologist, atheist, and disciple of Darwin Richard Dawkins argues that Darwin's inclusion of "the Creator" in *The Origin*'s last sentence served as but "a sop to religious sensibilities."[38] Dawkins, however, omits any mention of Darwin's earlier use of the holy term; he thus promotes the impression that, beginning with his second edition, Darwin, at the conclusion of his work, was sacrificing his scientific commitment to the theory of natural selection in order to appease the superstitious inclinations of his audience. Weinberg associates such appeasement with what he describes as the employment of the term "Creator" as "a form of protective coloration."[39] This phrase is intended as a pejorative description of rhetorical eloquence understood as a tool for ornamenting and thus beautifying discourse. Recall that this disparaging assessment of the orator's art can at least be traced back to the first men of Western scientific medicine, the Hippocratics, and becomes especially forceful with the Enlightenment.

For religious souls, "the Creator" is certainly a term of beauty, an instance of eloquence meant to open the minds and hearts of an audience to a speaker's or author's message. Darwin's message, to be sure, is scientifically oriented. If there is a Creator, It does not play a role in our evolutionary history. Rather, it is all a matter of the "secondary causes" of natural selection, which "works solely by and for the good of each being" such that "all corporeal and mental endowments will tend to progress towards perfection."[40] We need not look any further than the evolutionary struggle for existence in order to identify the purpose, beauty, and truth of all living beings. But to repeat a point I made in chapter 5, Darwin emphasizes that, in the case of human beings, "the power of language" must be cultivated "so that the wishes of the members of the same community can be distinctly expressed," a "common opinion" can form regarding "how each member ought to act for the public good," and our social affections and sympathies can become "more tender and more widely diffused until they are extended to all sentient beings." Darwin is an advocate of rhetorical competence when it comes to moving ideas to people and people to ideas.[41] Did Darwin believe in God? Does it really matter?

Influenced by the thinking of Darwin and like-minded evolutionary biologists, Weinberg does not believe that science will find an interested God in the final laws of nature, for all "our experience throughout the history of science has tended in the opposite direction, toward a chilling impersonality in these laws." Moreover, writes Weinberg, "Remembrance of the Holocaust leaves me unsympathetic to attempts to justify the ways of God to man. If there is a God that has special plans for humans, then He has taken very great pains to hide His concern for us. To me it would seem impolite if not impious to bother such a God with our prayers."[42] Such cynicism is commonplace in the rhetoric of atheism and agnosticism. Certainly Weinberg wields the power of rhetorical competence.

Nevertheless, Weinberg argues that science does not need rhetoric (e.g., God) in order to describe and explain the fitting, appropriate, and beautiful arrangement of the cosmos. The *real* beauty lies in the physical laws of nature and in our ability to reveal them in the truthful language of mathematics. "God" is but a "metaphor" for the "mystery" that is found in nature, a mystery that science continues to expose and rationally explain with symbols that, as far as we know, are as near to perfect as can be in revealing the truth of what is. "Today for real mystery one has to look to cosmology and elementary particle physics. For those who see no conflict between science and religion, the retreat of religion from the ground occupied by science is nearly complete."[43] What has yet to be conquered by science is most likely to inspire "an almost irresistible temptation" to believe in a Creator intent on making us feel at home in the universe. For Weinberg, however, there is "honor" to be found in resisting this temptation, which he acknowledges "is only a thin substitute for the consolations of religion" but "is not entirely without satisfactions of its own."[44] These satisfactions include the sheer "excitement" and "enjoyment" of practicing science, making "aesthetic judgments" about the beauty of some theory (its "simplicity" and "inevitability"). The "kind of beauty we are looking for," writes Weinberg, is "like the beauty of a piano sonata . . . in the specific sense that the theories we find beautiful are theories which give us a sense that nothing could be changed. Just as, listening to a piano sonata, we feel that one note must follow from the preceding note—and it could not have been another note—in the theories we are trying to formulate, we are looking for a sense of uniqueness, for a sense that when we understand the final answer, we will see that it could not have been any other way."[45]

A comment made by Weinberg elsewhere in his writings further clarifies the point:

> It is when we study truly fundamental problems that we expect to find beautiful answers. We believe that, if we ask why the world is the way it is and then ask why that answer is the way it is, at the end of this chain of explanations we shall find a few simple principles of compelling beauty. We think this in part because our historical experience teaches us that as we look beneath the surface of things, we find more and more beauty. Plato and the neo-Platonists taught that the beauty we see in nature is a reflection of the beauty of the ultimate, the *nous*. For us, too, the beauty of present theories is an anticipation, a premonition, of the beauty of the final theory [that can explain the existence of "everything" in mathematical terms]. And in any case, we would not accept any theory as final unless it were beautiful.[46]

Weinberg grants the appropriateness of beauty a transcendental status; it is something "that is built into the structure of the universe at a very deep level." Discovering the beauty and truth of the ultimate laws of nature does not require divine guidance. Human intelligence, commitment, state-of-the-art technology, and mathematics are enough. These things have long served and will continue to serve in that "demystification of the heavens" that has led those like Weinberg to believe that beyond the order, symmetry, and harmony—a.k.a. the appropriateness of beauty— of the cosmos there is "nothing." Or, as Weinberg also likes to put it, "the more the universe seems comprehensible the more it seems pointless"—which is not to say "that science teaches us that the universe is pointless, but rather that the universe itself suggests no point."[47] God has nothing to do with the beauty of the universe. Whatever attractive aspects of nature we perceive go no further back than the big bang. We should just consider ourselves lucky that we have evolved into creatures who can be dazzled by the intricate and deep nature of our surroundings, ourselves, and our place in the universe and who can act accordingly in sharing the wealth of knowledge and know-how that we discover through our assessments of the matters at hand.

Science, practiced in a knowledgeable, rigorous, and honest way, defines an expression of beauty. It serves our metaphysical desire for completeness. Listen, though, to what Weinberg says regarding a limitation of his profession: "Science can't . . . justify science; the decision to explore the world as it is shown to us by reason and experiment is a moral one, not a scientific one."[48] The beauty of science unfolds as a doing of the good, as an uncovering of truth. Without any allegiance to or dependence on the existence of God, science knows itself to be doing the right thing with its various reductionistic ways of thinking and exploring nature's ways. The work of the evolutionary biologist Richard Dawkins is a case in point.

SELFISH GENES

Dawkins argues that human being is a self-replicating genetic entity whose genes are "selfish" to the core: their basic function is to survive and to propagate their own kind. Dawkins thus speaks to us of "the fundamental law" of "gene selfishness." Dawkins emphasizes, however, that selfish genes "have no foresight. They are unconscious, blind, replicators" that "come into existence, in the first place, by chance, by the random jostling of smaller particles" whose origins originated with the big bang.[49] These replicators "behave . . . as if they were purposeful," writes Dawkins, but he stresses "that we must not think of genes as conscious, purposeful agents." Rather, their behavior is only the result of "blind natural selection."[50]

For Dawkins, the planned action of purposefulness enters the evolutionary scene only with the chance occurrence of creatures eventually becoming intelligent enough to enact this way of being. Intelligence makes way for well-reasoned action and the development of moral consciousness—which, as the atheist Dawkins reminds us, may be thought of (albeit erroneously) as a "gift" given to us by a purposeful God who has our ultimate welfare in mind. Hence, for example, that fundamental directive offered in the Old Testament: "See, I have set before thee this day life and good, and death and evil; In that I command this day to love the Lord thy God, to walk in his ways, and to keep his commandments and his statutes and his judgments, that you may live and multiply. . . . I have set before you life and death, blessing and cursing: therefore *choose life*, that both thou and thy seed may live" (Deut 30:15-19; emphasis added). Dawkins, of course, dismisses such metaphysical musings, preferring instead Darwin's take on the matter that, as Dawkins summarizes it, still allows for hope even without God's security: "Stand tall, Bipedal Ape. The shark may outswim you, the cheetah outrun you, the swift outfly you, the capuchin outclimb you, the elephant outpower you, the redwood outlast you. But you have the biggest gifts of all: the gift of understanding the ruthlessly cruel process that gave us all existence; the gift of revulsion against its implication; the gift of foresight—something utterly foreign to the blundering short-term ways of natural selection—and the gift of internalizing the very cosmos."[51]

Darwin, recall, wrote that these gifts, or what he describes as "powers," were "originally breathed into" our existence. Dawkins claims that the wise and moral use of these beautiful and wonderful powers is first and foremost up to us. "God" supplies only "a warm comfortable lie." We "can no longer suck at the pacifier of faith in immortality." Yes, admits Dawkins, there are "risks" (e.g., psychological distress) that come with this fundamental change of mind, but the risks are worth the effort and rewards, for we "stand to gain 'growth and happiness'; the joy of knowing that [we] have grown up, faced up to what existence means; to the fact that it is temporary and all the more precious for it."[52]

Dawkins would have us recondition our brains and the metaphysical desire for perfection that this awesome organ makes possible. This reconditioning is as much an art as it is a science. Brains are housed in bodies that dwell in the material conditions of everyday existence. Scientists readily admit that the development of our brains and bodies is inextricably tied to these conditions and their influence on our bodies' biological and chemical composition. Dawkins speaks of these influences as constituting a "cultural transmission" of "memes" or social practices that—like their gene counterparts operating in a "selfish," albeit necessary, way to ensure nature's law of "survival of the fittest"—function to secure the survival of a community's body politic.[53] Importantly, Dawkins also admits that we have the "power" to deconstruct and reconstruct our memes in order to free ourselves from harmful deterministic influences operating in culture: "We are built as gene machines and cultured as meme machines, but we have the power to turn against our creators. We, alone on earth, can rebel against the tyranny of the selfish replicators."[54] This rebellion is a moral action on our part, a decision-making process that, according to Dawkins, is informed and cultivated by our linguistic and communicative abilities. Morality is dependent on using language and other symbolic devices (e.g., works of art) to generate and refine the goodness of our memes.

Scientists like Dawkins tend to speak only in generalities when discussing the existentially based, intricate, and aesthetic workings of the civic-minded discourse that exhibits this power and that is essential to the vibrancy of democratic politics. Aristotle provided the first systematic assessment of the matter with his related works: *Politics*, *Rhetoric*, and *Nicomachean Ethics*. The over two-thousand-year-old rhetorical tradition testifies to the importance of keeping the inquiry alive as a way of ensuring the moral nature of our communal existence. This tradition also stresses that much of the *real* communication and rhetorical action takes place outside the brain, in the muck and mire of our everyday material existence. Here arguments and their related memes are advanced and critiqued publicly for audiences that await proper acknowledgment from those who want to be heard. Democracy demands as much: an ongoing dialogue of questions ("Where art thou?") and answers ("Here I am!"). Human evolution is served by rhetorical competence.

A case in point (on which I elaborate in chapter 9) is found in the recent report by the President's Council on Bioethics, *Beyond Therapy: Biotechnology and the Pursuit of Happiness*.[55] The authors emphasize that the book was written for members of the general public who are rightly concerned about how the technological achievements of medical science (e.g., genetic engineering) are outstripping the discursive boundaries of medical ethics. By way of their own respective efforts in rhetorical competence, the authors call for cultivation of this competence in the public domain in order to ensure that all will have a voice in determining how far we should allow science and technology to dictate the future of what it means to be a human being. The question before us is urgent, argue the authors: do biotechnical "enhancements" of our minds and bodies necessarily translate into our becoming morally better people? The question sounds a call of conscience. When answering the call, people want to be acknowledged for demonstrating some logical and aesthetic skill in speaking their minds in a rhetorically competent and worthwhile manner. The status of our memes is at stake. Science is not the only way to "get real!" about matters of perfection, truth, and beauty.

AESTHETICS

"The Universe we live in is beautiful," writes physicist Lee Smolin, and "it is so at least partly for the same reason a beautiful landscape or a beautiful city is, because a multitude of phenomena are taking place on a vast array of scales. . . . Indeed, in our universe we not only find structure on a variety of scales, we find structure on every scale we have so far explored"—from the subatomic quantum world of quarks, electrons, and neutrinos to the logarithmic spiral wave of the whole galaxy.[56] A fundamental property unique to this spiral is its "self-similarity": it does not alter its shape as its size increases (see figure 1).

"Nature loves logarithmic spirals," writes astrophysicist and cosmologist Mario Livio. "From sunflowers, seashells, and whirlpools, to hurricanes and giant spiral galaxies, it seems that nature chose this marvelous shape as its favorite 'ornament.'"[57] Put this way, one might wonder whether nature is, itself, skilled in rhetorical competence. Rhetorical competence presupposes some agent, a speaker or a writer, using discourse in an intentional, purposive, and appropriate way. The discourse makes manifest the author's aesthetic sense of "style." Does nature have style? Did nature intend to create logarithmic spirals? The petals of a rose—the most famous being perhaps the one named American

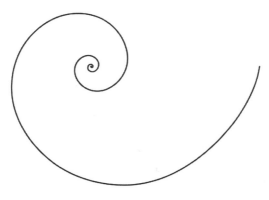

Figure 1

Beauty—display this geometric form. A rose is often taken as a symbol of natural symmetry, harmony, love, and fragility. Did nature design this specific floral display on purpose and with the best of intentions? Does nature have a mind, a consciousness that is conscious of itself? The evolution of the human brain makes possible the power of pattern recognition. Along with spirals, we thus can see, for example, circles in nature. Is this seeing a meeting of minds?

Fascination with the circle's completeness (perfection) dates back to ancient Egyptian culture (1650 B.C.E.). Dividing a circle's circumference by its diameter in order to dissect and better understand the geometry of its perfection gives us the ratio 3.141592653 . . . , more commonly known as pi (π) (see figure 2).

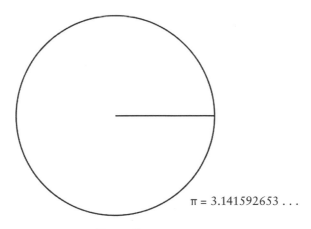

$\pi = 3.141592653 \ldots$

Figure 2

With the help of computers, the value of pi has been calculated to over 51 billion digits. There appears to be no end to the number, no exact value. Pi is "transcendental." The mathematician Peter Borwein speaks of this nature of the number when he writes, "There's a beauty to pi that keeps us looking at it. . . . The digits of pi are extremely random. They really have no pattern, and in mathematics that's really the same as saying they have every pattern."[58] The beautiful pattern of pi is "infinite." Is nature trying to tell us something about perfection with the beauty of its circles? The computer analyst David Blatner points out that "no measurement realistically requires even 100 digits of pi. In fact, even the most obsessive engineer would never need more than 7 digits of pi, and a physicist wouldn't use more than 15 or 20." So why, asks Blatner, are mathematicians "so driven" to complete the count? His answer: "The search for pi is deeply rooted in the human spirit of exploration—of both our minds and our world—and in our irrepressible drive to test our limits."[59]

Indeed, we are metaphysical creatures: we are drawn by infinity to find some sense of completeness, a sense of who we really are and how far we can go in life with the physical and cognitive abilities that we have. Is all of this nature's doing? For what reason? It will be helpful to examine some additional and related material before addressing these questions.

Around 300 B.C.E, the founder of geometry, Euclid of Alexandria, defined a proportion derived from a simple division of a line into what he called its "extreme and mean ratio" (see figure 3).

A   C   B

Figure 3

The proportion appears when the ratio of a longer segment of a line (AC) to the shorter and remaining segment (CB) is the same as the ratio of the entire line (AB) to the larger segment (AC). This specific proportion is commonly referred to as the golden ratio (phi or ϕ), which, like pi, speaks to us of infinity. Computed mathematically, the golden ratio is the never-ending, never-repeating number 1.6180339887. . . . Pi and phi are numbers that are neither whole nor fractions (i.e., "rational"); they are thus defined as "irrational numbers." There is reason to wonder: does the irrational have a role to play in nature's beauty?[60]

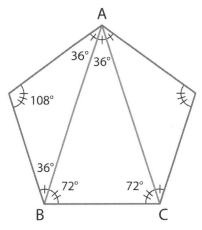

Figure 4a

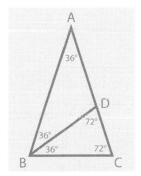

Figure 4b

Euclid found that the golden ratio was crucial for the construction of the pentagon. Every angle in a "regular" (perfect) pentagon is equal to 108 degrees. When diagonal lines are used to connect point A to point B and point C, we find that the ratio of the diagonal to the side is equal to phi (see figures 4a and 4b). The ability to construct a line divided in a golden ratio thus provides at the same time a simple means of constructing the regular pentagon. The triangle that forms with the diagonals in the pentagon has a ratio of side to base of phi. This "golden triangle" has a unique property: it can be dissected into smaller triangles that are also golden triangles. This same property is also manifest in a "golden rectangle," in which the lengths of the sides of the rectangle are in a golden ratio to each other. The golden rectangle is the only rectangle with the property by which cutting a square from it produces a similar rectangle (see figure 5).

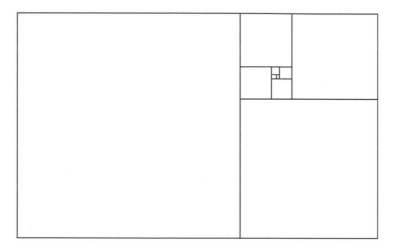

Figure 5

The resulting series of ever-smaller and never-ending golden rectangles unfolds in such a way that if we draw two diagonals of any "mother-daughter" pair of rectangles in the series, they will all intersect at the same point. If we connect the successive points where these "whirling squares" divide the sides in golden ratios, we obtain a logarithmic spiral that coils inward toward the point of infinity (sometimes referred to in mathematics as "the eye of God"; see figure 6).[61]

Thinking of nature as acting intentionally and having a purpose leads metaphysical creatures to attribute agency to nature and to imagine that something holy is going on: "the perfection of beauty" (Ps 50:2). God ever geometrizes, claims Plato.[62] Western religion maintains that the aesthetics of nature have been formed by the greatest designer, arranger, rhetorician, and mathematician that there ever was and ever will be. In the beginning was God's word, with all of its sights, sounds, and ornaments. Science, having disciplined and reduced its metaphysical desire

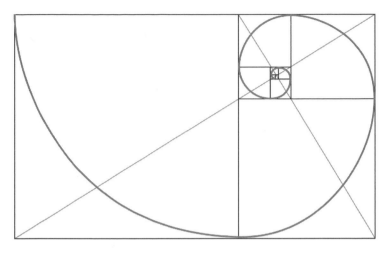

Figure 6

for perfection, favors the more mathematical of these ornaments. With mathematics in hand, science speaks to us of the possibility of constructing a "final theory"; a "theory of everything" (TOE); a theory that is truthful, elegant, perfect. The leading candidate for this theory at the present time is called "string theory." According to the physicist and leading string theorist Brian Greene, "the discovery of the TOE—the ultimate explanation of the universe at its most microscopic level, a theory that does not rely on any deeper explanation—would provide the firmest foundation on which to *build* our understanding of the world. Its discovery would mark a beginning, not an end. The ultimate theory would provide an unshakable pillar of coherence forever assuring us that the universe is a comprehensible place."[63] And with the mathematical findings presently supporting string theory, such a pillar is taking form. The theory emphasizes "that the 'stuff' of all matter and all forces is the *same*. Each elementary particle is composed of a single string—that is, each particle *is* a string— and all strings are absolutely identical. Differences between the particles arise because their respective strings undergo different resonant vibrational patterns. What appear to be different elementary particles are actually different 'notes' on a fundamental string. The universe—being composed of an enormous number of these strings—is akin to a cosmic symphony."[64]

Introduced by the big bang, this symphony gives substance, form, and function to life and brings into being the aesthetic "symmetries of nature." For physicists, the symmetries of nature speak of how "nature treats every moment in time and every location in space identically—symmetrically—by ensuring that the same fundamental laws are in operation. Much in the same manner that they affect art and music, such symmetries are deeply satisfying; they highlight an order and a coherence in the workings of nature"—which is rightly called "beautiful."[65] The complexity and beauty of this symphony and its symmetries are astonishing, awesome. "In fact," writes Greene, "the mathematics of string theory is so complicated that, to date, no one even knows the exact equations of the theory. Instead, physicists know only approximations to these equations, and even the approximate equations are so complicated that they as yet have been only partially solved."[66] Heraclitus said it over two thousand years ago: "Nature loves to hide."[67]

The evolution of human intelligence has a way to go before it can come to terms with and understand what "essentially" keeps the cosmos in tune and allows it to play on into the future. Greene is encouraged by a host of ongoing scientific findings and speaks of string theory as leading the scientific community in the direction of "unified-theory paradise."[68] Here would be the ultimate and thus most appropriate place for comprehending the aesthetics of nature's laws: what it *really* means to speak of what *is* right, fitting, and timely—the essence, the truth, of the appropriateness of beauty.

There is, however, something of a problem here. String theory is reductionistic to the "*n*th degree." Its mathematics reflect the world of quantum mechanics; it speaks to us of things happening (strings vibrating) in a space of 10^{-33} centimeters. To see the strings vibrating in the quantum world "would require a microscope that is one hundred thousand trillion times more powerful than the Tevatron, the current most powerful particle accelerator."[69] Without these vibrations, nothing would exist. Everything that is, is made possible by an immensely tiny cosmic symphony possessing mind-boggling power and influence. As a way of conveying the symmetrical beauty of this symphony, scientists sometimes refer to the musical genius of Johann Sebastian

Bach and the complex symmetries of his compositions. The theoretical physicist and Nobel Laureate Leon Lederman and his colleague Christopher Hill make the point in an exceptionally clear manner:

> Listeners often cannot grasp a Bach composition upon the first hearing; it requires patience, often several hearings, before we begin to comprehend the inner world of these majestic compositions, in which this complex hierarchical structure takes wings and soars. As we begin to comprehend, we feel as though we are experiencing a new and complex universe, with unfolding patterns upon patterns, a universe defined by underlying principles of logic and symmetry. The music transcends the instruments upon which it is played. Bach sounds as "right" on a kazoo or an electronic synthesizer as on a harpsichord or a massive pipe organ. It is ultimately not the particular instruments that define the structure of the music, but rather the deep internal symmetry structures themselves and the overall *Affekt* they produce.[70]

And these specific, magnificent, and awesome internal symmetry structures have their basis in the most original symphony of all time.

Bach's music is in tune with something much greater (and smaller) than itself. Its various arrangements echo cosmic happenings. Bach was moved by something beyond himself; his musical genius is an *Affekt*, a rational and emotional consequence, of a "first cause": vibrating strings. To enjoy and perhaps fall in love with Bach is to experience something of the beauty of these strings' workings. And here the problem of the reductionism of string theory is revealed. Favorable reactions to Bach's music cannot be carefully and genuinely explained by merely referring to the mathematical nature of vibrating strings. The beauty of Bach's music requires emotion, an aspect of animalistic life that, as far as we know, has nothing to do with why and how quantum strings do what they do. Reducing an understanding of Bach's music to its quantum components really misses a lot of the beauty of his specific arrangements of the original and ever-going cosmic symphony. These arrangements were designed to be heard, to have an *Affekt*, to move audiences to the point that their reactions would help sustain the life and message of the art at hand. Bach's music calls on its listeners to have a "lived experience" with its message. Musical genius and the beauty it reveals come about not without some degree of artistic and rhetorical competence.[71]

That Bach was a religious soul may suggest that behind his music are not just strings—nature at its most fundamental level—but also the One who originally made them to be played and heard in the most beautiful way possible. Here, of course, is where religion and science part ways on matters of aesthetics. Science stops at nature, that far-ranging environment in which, beginning with the big bang, chaos arises and is ordered with our help. Perhaps "for the first time in human history," writes the physicist Lee Smolin, "we know enough to imagine how a universe like ours might have come to be without the infinite intelligence and foresight of a god. For is it not conceivable that the universe is as we find it to be because it made itself; because the order, structure and beauty we see reflected at every scale [and represented in 'elegant' mathematical equations] are the manifestations of a continual process of self-organization, of self-tuning, that has acted over very long periods of time?"[72] Religion contests science's answer to this question. The resulting controversy, however, need not be as finalizing as some scientists and theologians suggest. I expand on this point with the help of another scientific and artistic genius: Leonardo da Vinci.

LEONARDO

In the preface to his unfinished treatise on the art and science of painting, Leonardo begins by noting "that many will say that this is a useless work, and these people will be those of whom Demetrius said that he took no more account of the wind from their mouths, which caused their words, than of the wind which issued from their lower regions. These men possess a desire only for material wealth and are entirely devoid of the desire for wisdom, which is the sustenance and truly dependable wealth of the mind."[73] The rhetorical competence should be obvious here. Leonardo has a humorous way of talking about people who he believes "talk crap." Their notion of "wealth" is derivative and crass compared to the genuine source of the derivation: wisdom, the wealth of the mind. Wisdom, for Leonardo, is a product of directly experiencing and assessing nature in as a precise of a way as possible. Leonardo's exemplar is science. He tells us that "true sciences are those which have penetrated through the senses as a result of experience and thus silencing the tongues of disputants, not feeding investigators on dreams but always proceeding successively towards the conclusion. This may be witnessed in the principles of mathematics, that is to say, number and measure—termed arithmetic and geometry—which deal with discontinuous and continuous quantities with the utmost truth."[74]

Leonardo is after the truth with his drawings and paintings of the human form in various settings and circumstances. Science led him to study dissected human corpses in order to better understand the anatomical basis of our everyday bodily presence and posture, be it at rest or in motion. Science, too, informed his understanding of geometric proportions and optics: how, for example, light falling on the sides of multifaceted polygons is instructive for learning about the dynamics of "shading" and how this particular phenomenon must be accurately captured in painting in order to bring the subject matter alive for spectators, thereby encouraging their emotional participation with the work of art. Whatever "there is in the universe through essence, presence, or imagination," writes Leonardo, "[the painter] has it first in his mind [by way of an intricate experiencing of nature] and then in his hands, and these are of such excellence that they can generate a proportional harmony in the time equivalent to a single glance, just as real things do."[75] Leonardo cannot say enough about the importance of painting: "O marvelous science, you keep alive the transient beauty of mortals and you have greater permanence than the works of nature, which continuously change over a period of time, leading remorselessly to old age. And, this science has the same relation to divine nature as its works have to the works of nature, and on this account is to be revered."[76] Regarding the specific role played by the "draughtsmanship" of the painter, Leonardo writes, this capacity "is of such excellence that it not only investigates the works of nature but also infinitely more than those made by nature. . . . On this account we should conclude that it is not only a science but a goddess which should be duly accorded that title. This deity repeats all the visible works of almighty God."[77]

Leonardo speaks of a higher calling in detailing his "science of painting." Attending carefully to the smallest detail in one's subject matter is an "ethical" requirement for the painter who seeks to answer the call. This requirement necessitates an appreciation of reductionism. So, for example, Leonardo pays scrupulous attention to the measurements of the human body: "If you open your legs so that you lower your head by one-fourteenth of your height, and open and raise your arms so that with your longest fingers you touch the level of the top of your head, you should know that the central point between the extremities of the outstretched limbs will be the navel, and the space which is described by the legs makes an equilateral triangle."[78] With his famous drawing the *Vitruvian Man*, Leonardo also associates the beauty of the human body with the square and the circle (see figure 7). The man's arm span equals his height, and these equal proportions can be inscribed in a square. When he does a spread

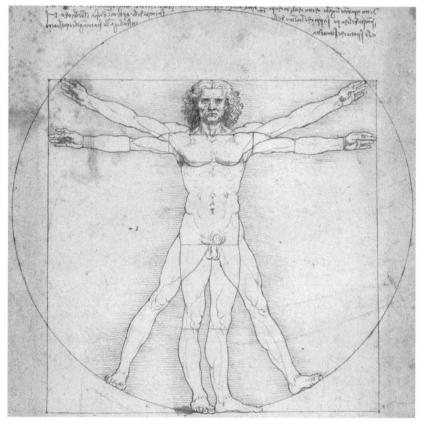

Figure 7

eagle with his arms and legs, he is inscribed in a circle. The center of the circle is located at the man's navel. The ratio of his height divided by the height of his navel is the golden ratio.

There is a link between the organic and the geometric basis of beauty. Consider Leonardo's *Mona Lisa* (see figure 8).

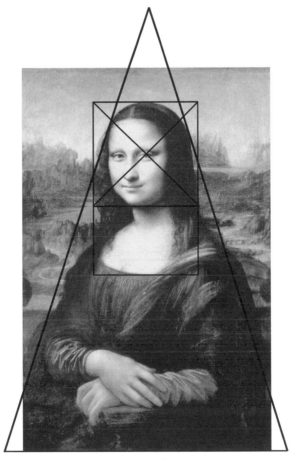

Figure 8

The torso of the woman is composed so that it can be inscribed by a golden triangle, her face by a golden rectangle. The enigmatic expression of this beauty's face takes form in a specific display of light and shading. Look at what she is wearing, its textures and folds: "The draperies that clothe figures must show that they are inhabited by these figures, enveloping them neatly to show the posture and motion of such figures."[79] Leonardo is interested in what phenomenologists term the "lived body": how its presentation is actually affected and conditioned not only by its physiological condition but also by the spatial, temporal, social, and psychological events of its everyday existence. This last category of events is especially important for Leonardo. He makes much of how the origin of movement is in the mind. Behavior reveals inner thoughts. "The [human] figure is most praiseworthy," insists Leonardo, "which best expresses through its actions the passion of its mind."[80] The Mona Lisa sits still, but the passion of her mind is present in her face, with its lighting, shading, specific geometric proportions, muscle tone, wondering eyes, and the ambiguous contour of her lips, all working together to convey a feeling of being alive. The *Mona Lisa* is not simply rendering an exact physiognomic or photographic likeness of its subject. Rather, she is a lived body; there is something on this woman's mind that we see in the geometric proportions and anatomic features of her smiling presence that captivates our attention and that is more than simply the sum of its parts—its physiological and mathematic features.

Leonardo challenges us to ponder the nature of a beautiful mind. As Sylvia Nasar makes clear in her award-winning story about the tragic yet hopeful life of the Nobel Laureate and severely schizophrenic John Forbes Nash Jr., such a mind needs more nourishment than what science and mathematics can provide. It also needs "a wider range of emotional experiences." Nash finds these experiences in the "daily effort to give others their due, and to recognize their right to ask this of him." The "disjunction of thought and emotion that characterized Nash's personality, not just when he was ill, but even before are much less evident today. In deed, if not always in word, Nash has come to a life in which thought and emotion are more closely entwined, where getting and giving are central, and relationships are more symmetrical."[81]

A beautiful mind needs to acknowledge and to be acknowledged by others. Acknowledgment is a life-giving gift. In the movie version of Nash's life story, the writers allow Nash to have the last word as he addresses the audience and his loving and lifesaving wife, Alicia, when accepting the Nobel Prize:

I have always believed in numbers and the equations and logics that lead to reason. But after a lifetime of such pursuits, I ask: What truly is logic? Who decides reason? My quest has taken me through the physical, the metaphysical, the delusional, and back. And I have made the most important discovery of my career, the most important discovery of my life. It is only in the mysterious equations of love that any logical reasons can be found. I am only here tonight because of you [camera pans to his smiling and tearful wife]. You are the reason I am. You are all of my reasons. Thank you.[82]

Nash displays a very sincere and humble demeanor as he speaks. His words admit rhetorical competence: they are appropriate, fitting, and beautiful. Nash's verbal and nonverbal communication is further enhanced as he pulls from the breast pocket of his tuxedo a small handkerchief that Alicia gave him when they were first falling in love. He kisses the handkerchief and gestures to her. The entire scene is exceptionally moving. It does what the *Mona Lisa* was designed to do: presents us with a lived body.

Like Nash, Leonardo's famous painting speaks to us through nonverbal communication, a necessary feature of the rhetorical competence that is needed and valued in guiding and regulating our everyday interpersonal relationships. Leonardo has such competence in mind when writing about "posture, expression, and decorum." An example he offers is especially fitting for my purposes: "Good orators, when they wish to persuade their listeners of something, use their hands and arms to accompany their words, although some senseless men do not care for such ornamentation and seem in court to be statues of wood, through the mouth of which passes as in a conduit the voice of another man who is concealed within the court."[83] Indeed, the ornamentation of nonverbal communication is a necessary feature of the lived body. Leonardo is thus always on the lookout for what he terms "masters of movements." Consider this piece of advice:

The good painter has to paint two principal things, that is to say, man and the intention of his mind. The first is easy and the second difficult, because the latter has to be represented through gestures and movements of the limbs—which can be learned from the dumb, who exhibit gestures better than any other kind of man. Do not laugh at me because I propose an instructor without speech, who is to teach you an art of which he is unaware, because he will teach you better through what he actually does than others can through their words.

> And do not despise such advice, because the dumb are the masters of movements and understand what one says from a distance when one accommodates the motions of the hands to the words.[84]

Leonardo is interested in the truth and beauty of being alive, with its various actions and states of consciousness. How do you look when thinking a loving or devious thought that you want others to perceive correctly and immediately? Is the *Mona Lisa* the portrayal of a soul thinking such thoughts? Would your judgment of the perfection of the painting be affected if you knew all there was to know about the true character of the beauty that is seen in this most famous work of art? Leonardo advocates reductionism, but only as a means to a much greater end. A more dramatic and historically relevant case is Leonardo's *The Last Supper* (see figure 9).

This monumental painting is composed to capture an important moment in an ongoing narrative. Christ has just announced, "Verily I say unto you that one of you shall betray me." The intensity and shock of the moment is registered on the faces, movements, and postures of the apostles as their minds, in a flash, react to the announcement. Leonardo knows what he is after:

Figure 9

That which is included in narrative painting ought to move those who behold and admire them in the same way as the protagonist of the narrative is moved. So if the narrative shows terror, fear or flight or, indeed, grief, weeping and lamentation, or pleasure, joy and laughter and similar states, the minds of the beholders should move their limbs in such a way as to make it seem that they are united in the same fate as those represented in the narrative painting. And if they do not do this, the painter's ability is useless. . . . Therefore, painter, decide broadly upon the position of the limbs of your figures and attend first to the movements appropriate to the mental attitudes of the creatures in narrative rather than to the beauty and quality of their limbs. You should understand that if such a rough composition turns out to be right for your intention, it will all the more satisfy in subsequently being adorned with the perfection suitable to all its parts. I have in the past seen in clouds and walls stains which have inspired me to beautiful inventions of many things. These stains, while wholly in themselves deprived of perfection in any part, did not lack perfection in regard to their movements or other actions.[85]

Displaying the perfection of lighted and shaded movements and actions as they actually occur brings a painting to life. Here, for example, is some of what Leonardo admits he is trying to capture in *The Last Supper*: "One who was drinking has left his glass in its place and turned his head towards the speaker. Another wrings the fingers of his hands and turns with a frown to his companion. Another with hands spread open to show the palms shrugs his shoulders up to his ears and mouths astonishment."[86] Leonardo was as scientific (reductionistic) as he could be in studying all that goes into the production of such nonverbal communication and its attending rhetorical competence.

What would you say about an apostle who was not shaken by Christ's announcement? The specific situation at hand calls for appropriate and fitting behavior (which, of course, can be faked). With what he makes of *The Last Supper* in his blockbuster work of fiction *The Da Vinci Code*, Dan Brown commends Leonardo's advice: Look closely at the nature of those who you wish to portray in a painting! What truths do you see? Is anyone lying?[87] Rhetorical competence is not always put to good (moral) use, but it nevertheless remains a necessity for maintaining the well-being of our interpersonal relationships. *Lived bodies are perfect rhetorical beings.* Leonardo, however, does caution us against the dangers of being too extravagant with our rhetorical talents: "Do you not see that among the beauties of mankind it is a very beautiful face which arrests passers-by and not their rich adornments? And I say to you as you adorn your figures with costly gold and other expensive decorations, do you not see the resplendent beauty of youth lose its excellence through excessive devotion to ornament? Have you not seen the women who dwell among the mountains wrapped in their poor rude draperies acquiring greater beauty than women who are decked in ornament?"[88]

The beauty of rhetoric lies in its capacity to serve the truth without getting in its own way with, for example, excessive ornamentation. Based on his or her best judgment, the rhetor does only what is deemed necessary to produce what is arguably a true understanding of nature that will help motivate people to judge and act in a moral manner. Rhetoric must not be deaf to the teachings of those who advocate the importance of reductionism. The disclosing of a truth can sometimes best be served by the economy of simplicity. Such reductionism makes the point with its use of a rhetorical figure: the oxymoron "less is more."

The rhetorical tradition is well aware of the importance of having a way with words when it comes to disclosing some truth in a manner that captivates others. Recall that an oxymoron combines contradictory or incongruous words for the purpose of making a particular point in a creative and thought-provoking manner. The tension inherent in an oxymoron is meant to catch our attention and tantalize our thinking. An oxymoron can be a tool of eloquence: a way with words that makes the truth memorable as it *moves* us to better understand a given reference. This movement happens as we experience the surprise of something being false at a superficial level yet true at a deeper one. The reader is supposed to be so moved, for example, by Burke's notion of the disease of being "rotten with perfection." The oxymoron encourages an interruption of, and thus a momentary change in, our everyday consciousness. *Perfection can be rotten?* An oxymoron is a type of rhetorical interruption. The interruption and change define what is commonly known as a "double take," whereby our simple recognition of something inspires us to ponder its presence once again, but this time more carefully.

In his discussion of rhetorical interruptions in general, Thomas B. Farrell writes, "Rhetoric, despite its traditional and quite justifiable association with the preservation of cultural truism, may also perform an act of *critical interruption* where the taken-for-granted practices of culture are concerned. . . . The phenomenon of rhetorical interruption juxtaposes the assumptions, norms, and practices of a people so as to prompt a reappraisal of where they are culturally, what they are doing, and where they are going."[89] What Farrell fails to acknowledge, however, is that the phenomenon of interruption that concerns him and that defines the dynamics of an oxymoron is always already at work before the orator steps in with his or her discourse (wherein some oxymoron might be employed for whatever reason). I referred to this primordial instance of interruption when I discussed how the call of conscience embedded in the spatial and temporal structure of human existence calls us into question with its open-endedness, its objective uncertainty. The call of conscience reveals to us how we exist (ontologically) in a constant state of *complete incompleteness*. We *are* an oxymoron. Thought of this way, one can say that the call of conscience that comes from the heart of human existence is a rhetorical interruption in its purest form. If one is religious, the thinking here can move one step further—from ontology to metaphysics: rhetoric has its roots in the workings of the greatest orator there is. God is truth, eloquence, the perfect epideictic (showing-forth) discourse. In the beginning was the Word and the call of conscience that would eventually be interpreted, for example, by the writers of the Holy Scriptures. The First Author, however, made sure that the characters created had an awesome essence: a complete incompleteness.

An eloquent and reasonable use of an oxymoron calls on us to stretch our minds and *acknowledge* the true meaning and significance of a given matter that remains concealed by the humdrum of everyday existence. A good, truth-telling, and effective oxymoron teaches us a lesson that is "simply" put by the scientist, engineer, and metaphysician R. Buckminster Fuller in his consideration of our human beginnings:

> And consciousness begins
> As an awareness of otherness,
> Which otherness awareness requires time.
> And all statements by consciousness
> Are in the comparative terms
> Of prior observations of consciousness
> ("It's warmer, it's quicker, it's bigger

Than the other or others").
Minimal consciousness evokes time,
As a nonsimultaneous sequence of experiences.
Consciousness dawns
With the second experience,
This is why consciousness
Identified the basic increment of time
As being a *second*.
Not until the second experience
Did time and consciousness
Combine as human life.[90]

An oxymoron encourages an awareness of otherness, a dawning of consciousness, by using contradiction to instigate a second and more respectful experience of this otherness. I will have more to say about such a dawning of consciousness in the next chapter.

Conclusion

Does nature have a mind? Is it God's consciousness? Human beings have minds that can sense that something is going on in nature. But what, exactly, is this something? "What is it that breathes fire into the equations and makes a universe for them to describe?" asks the physicist and cosmologist Stephen Hawking. "Why does the Universe go to all the bother of existing?"[91] And I would add, Why does it allow for creatures who can be awed by and acknowledge its wonders and beauty? Does the universe itself really call for such acknowledgment? Is that truly part of its logic and laws? Is there an Intelligent Designer behind all the chaos and order that appears before us, or is it all merely chance and accident?

If God is the answer, then the rhetorical tradition is granted a very long history: "In the beginning was the Word" that was intentionally designed and arranged to move people toward the truth and the truth toward people. Science, on the other hand, maintains that it all starts with the empirical displays of nature that first began appearing and evolving with the big bang. The genius of Leonardo is more generous: he offers a theory of aesthetics that speaks of the importance of bringing together science, religion, and art in order to perfect our understanding and appreciation of the truth and appropriateness of nature's ways and eloquence. The generosity found in Leonardo's works is itself a thing of beauty. As with the other great names referred to in this chapter, Leonardo, it seems, is destined to be remembered for a long time by metaphysical creatures who value efforts in the struggle to come to terms with perfection.

In the next chapter, I further investigate the nature of this struggle by extending Leonardo's concern with the phenomenon of the lived body. There is an element of reductionism present in my analysis, although, unlike Leonardo's, its parameters are not dictated by mathematics, geometry, optics, and a scientific understanding of human anatomy. Rather, I am interested in identifying and clarifying the ontological structures of existence that inform the lived body's struggle with the chaos and order of existence. These structures, most of which have already warranted some attention, include space, time, place, purpose, freedom, otherness, conscience, emotion, truth, acknowledgment, hermeneutics, salvation, heroism, beauty, rhetoric, reason, and justice. With the workings of these structures, human beings are caught up in the process of coming to terms with perfection. The significance of this happening is undeniable, as perhaps is its insignificance in the great scheme of things.

CHAPTER SEVEN

THE LIVED BODY

In his meditations on beauty and how its presence is related to the order and chaos of life, Crispin Sartwell offers the following observation:

> Perfectly ordered systems are boring and perfectly chaotic systems are merely bewildering. But combined systems are arenas of desire in which one might intervene to impose order or attack it, in which one might introduce organizations or contribute to their disintegration. Such systems, we might say, are political: they can yield to transformations. In systems of extreme order, we long for disintegration, while in systems of extreme disorder we long for organization. Thus the sort of systems in which longing can arise and be satisfied are systems of mixed order and disorder. . . . We love unity and rationality, yearn for it. But we also focus obsessively on the possibility of a release from it.[1]

Science's interest in the relationship between ordered systems and chaotic systems has led to what scientist and MacArthur Fellow Stuart Kauffman terms the "theory of emergence": the mathematical and cosmological "search for the laws of self-organization and complexity."[2] The working hypothesis of the theory "is that on many fronts, life evolves toward a regime that is poised between order and chaos. The evocative phrase that points to this working hypothesis is this: life exists at the edge of chaos."[3]

The theory of evolution advocated by emergence theorists is not simply rooted in Darwin's theory of natural selection; rather, it emphasizes that "the order in organisms may not be the result of selection at all, but of the spontaneous order of self-organized systems. Order, vast and generative, not fought for against the entropic tides but freely available, undergirds all subsequent biological evolution. The order of organisms is natural, not merely the unexpected triumph of natural selection." In short, the theory of emergence seeks to "account for the creation of the stunning order out our windows as a natural expression of some underlying laws." The theory wants to show how we "are at home in the universe, expected in it, rather than present despite overwhelming odds."[4] We are an amazing moment of ever-evolving order in the midst of a process that also admits chaos. What Kauffman describes as the "deep and beautiful" laws of emerging life define a dialectical process of chaos and order, order and chaos, that natural selection "has further molded." Life is fundamentally a living on the edge of a forever-opening system of space and time. "In such a poised world," writes Kauffman,

> we must give up the pretense of long-term prediction. We cannot know the true consequences of our own best actions. All we players can do is be locally wise, not globally wise. All we can do, all anyone can do, is hitch up our pants, put on our galoshes, and get on with it the best we can. Only God has the wisdom to understand the final law, the throws of the quantum dice. Only God can foretell the future. We, myopic after 3.45 billion years of design, cannot. We, with all the others, cannot foretell the avalanches and their intertwinings that we jointly generate. We can only do our local, level best. We can get on with it.[5]

The theory of emergence leaves room for the existence of God: the One who does not intervene beyond having already created the laws of emerging life, but who in Its "grace and simplicity . . . should welcome our struggles to find [Its] laws" as we attempt to improve and perfect our existence with, for example, the discovery of "promising new drugs, vaccines, and medical miracles."[6] God is a loving spectator who appreciates being acknowledged and approached, without ever making it perfectly clear why this is so. Are we really that significant to warrant God's favor?

Perhaps our insignificance in God's entire (perfect) order is reason enough for God's reticence. Kauffman neither explains nor justifies this awesome silence. At least for the time being, the laws of self-organization and complexity, the ultimate dialectic of chaos and order, remain the first and final saying, the last and perhaps most revealing and instructive clue for determining the source and fundamental nature of human being.

Kauffman's charge—to get on with doing our level best—returns us to the existential realm of the dialectic that attracts Sartwell's attention. Everyday existence marks out the grounds, or what I describe as the "dwelling place," where the lived body must face the challenge of chaos and order posed by the circumstances of life. We show our moral character (ethos) when meeting this challenge. Please note that the term "ethos" additionally translates in ancient Greek as "abode," "habitat," or "dwelling place." It can thus also be said that when meeting the challenge, we show how we are empirically situated in this particular place of lived space and time, especially as it shows itself when chaos takes the lead in its dialectical relationship with order and rocks the very foundations of our personal and social existence. The ontological assessment of these matters offered in this chapter supports the feasibility of the theory of emergence. It does not, however, make any claim that confirms or denies the existence of God. For the time being, I am only interested in coming to terms with the perfection of the lived body. My discussion begins with a consideration of a specific mood that Sartwell refers to in the chapter's opening quotation and that is easily recognized by human beings as they feel its presence: boredom. The effect that this mood can have on the lived body is extraordinary. As boredom intensifies, it can transform itself into other emotional states—melancholy and anxiety—that are especially powerful in disclosing the ontological nature of our dwelling place here on earth.

BOREDOM, MELANCHOLY, AND ANXIETY

I do not know any scientists who do what they do as scientists because it is boring. Nor do I know any devout religious souls who admit that their faith suffers this fate. The Holocaust survivor and Nobel Prize–winning author Elie Wiesel does, however, make an interesting case for the role played by boredom in the biblical story of Genesis.

Before the fall, Adam, "the prototype of perfect man," was "wise, intelligent, erudite, understanding, generous [and] endowed with a flawless soul. Incapable of wrong-doing, of thinking ill; closed to weakness, to doubts." Moreoever, Wiesel notes, Adam "was humble, shy, grateful. Some sources refer to him as *Hasid*. Others call him the luminary, the 'candle of the world.' Some go as far as seeing in him the future Messiah. So glorious was he that the angels, dazzled by his perfection, confused him with his Creator and began to sing him their praises. God responded by making him fall asleep and the frightened angels recognized their error." Wiesel immediately adds this parenthetical comment: "(As for me, I'd rather think that Adam fell asleep not because of God but because of the angels: nothing bores a perfect man more than excessive praise.)" Clarification follows:

> For Adam was indeed bored in paradise; all the texts point to it. Since he had the whole universe to himself, he desired nothing, thought of nothing and nobody. Happy, content, he seems singularly uninteresting before his downfall. No cloud, no shadow to mar his person. No indifference to the world extended to his own person. No trace of foreboding or concern. He was intoxicated with God, brimming over with God, joined to God in God: no need for him to seek God, to serve Him, understand Him, woo Him. So total was God's presence, he did not feel it. Nor did he think of it; he didn't need to, for the very source and cradle of his mind were occupied by God.[7]

Wiesel's rhetorical way of telling the story impresses upon readers that, indeed, it is *a story* that *his story* is about: stories that are meant to disclose the truth of great matters of importance but that nevertheless are limited in all they can say about these matters. Wiesel's version of the story is designed to accommodate a modern sensibility that does not believe that one needs to quote Scripture and verse in order to hear and learn about God's ways. Other entertaining, thought-provoking manners of expression exist. But with the specific way that Wiesel tells the story, we are forced to come to terms with the possibility that perfection is boring. Based on what experiencing this mood can do to us, the possibility is chilling. I offer the following consideration of the matter to make the point.

Existential occurrences (e.g., sickness) that disrupt our purposive nature prompt us to think about this essential but often taken-for-granted fact of life. The disruption, however, need not be catastrophic; rather, it can come about with something as simple as finding ourselves bored with whatever we are doing at the time. Caught up in the influence of this mood, we make ourselves susceptible to experiencing two other and more dreadful moods: melancholy and anxiety. Boredom sets us on a path that, as we tread its course, places us before a stark reality: ourselves, stripped of pretensions and faced with a most ancient question regarding perfection—what does it mean *to be*?

Boredom is not known for its pleasantness. Boring jobs and relationships are a "drag," weighing down our dreams as we wait for better things to come. In order to avoid being bored, we will engage ourselves, if only half-heartedly (at best), in any number of diversions and distractions (e.g., reading a magazine, surfing the Web, watching television, overeating) that might protect us from this lifeless mood. Indeed, boredom puts us on the alert for things to do. I suspect that the radical Christian philosopher Søren Kierkegaard had this benefit of boredom in mind when, as Wiesel would do many years later, he offered the following brief history of the mood: "The gods were bored, and so they created man. Adam was bored because he was alone, and so Eve was created. Thus boredom entered the world, and increased in proportion to the increase of population. Adam was bored alone; then Adam and Eve were bored together; then Adam and Eve and Cain and Abel were bored *en famille*; then the population of the world increased and the peoples were bored *en masse*."[8] Kierkegaard's entertaining way of recalling history, however, is meant to serve a greater purpose than mere amusement. Boredom—especially as it reaches the state in which we find ourselves "bored to death" with things, others, and perhaps ourselves—discloses and reveals a fundamental aspect of human existence: how our being is structured spatially and temporally so as to open us to the future, its possibilities, its freedom, whereby the option of finding things to do is made possible. Freedom is an ontological structure of existence; its presence forms the backdrop of all resolute thought and action. Any specific act of freedom presupposes that we are already situated in the world in such a way that we are faced with the choice of making a decision about what to do. We not only *have* freedom, the ontological structure of our existence *is* freedom. The openness of existence allows for choice, hence the options to relieve our boredom immediately with distractions and diversions that add a little bit of purpose to our lives, at least for the moment.

Being bored is not a perfect way to be. Better to be busy; better yet, creative. Failing this second option, busy will do. Being constantly busy, however, can become tedious; thus, a remedy for boredom can itself become boring. Boredom is capable of growing in intensity. Fueled by the tedium of life's everyday tasks, this disquieting state of mind can fester, stimulating a feeling of "emptiness" in which all meaningful contexts of life begin losing their significance. When this feeling totally (perfectly) overtakes our lives, we suffer from the disease of melancholia: an existential condition characterized by extreme depression, bodily complaints, and sometimes even hallucinations and delusions. People can become so bored to death with their everyday lives that they, in fact, will admit that they occasionally "feel like dying."

Getting out of bed in the morning can be a chore for these people. They feel so unmotivated, useless, unacknowledged, achy, and alone. Nothing matters. If you have ever been in bed this way, you know how depressing it can be. Your mood closes you off to the possibility of doing anything other than staying in bed, feeling bad for yourself. Losing yourself in other, more pleasurable activities is a hope fading fast. You are beyond the point of being able to ease your boredom by, excuse the expression, "doing fucking anything!" that might enable you to forget about your pitiful existence and the "nothingness" that it has in store for you.

"What's it matter, anyway?" The question is asked by a purposive creature who no longer feels that he or she has a purpose in life. In this particular case, human being is crippling itself, unable to shoulder the burden of freedom of choice and responsibility that comes with this being's existence and the fundamental way it opens us to the future, to possibilities that still can be enacted if we don't give up. Death is inevitable, but it need not necessarily happen right *now*. The choice is ours.

The anxiety of the moment can be overwhelming. "What is anxiety? It is the next day," writes Kierkegaard.[9] Anxiety functions by directing our attention to how the future orientation of existence is always calling us into question with its openness and uncertainty. Anxiety is order losing out to chaos. Anxiety brings us face-to-face with this uncertainty of existence and the challenge that comes with it: having to assume the responsibility of affirming our freedom through resolute choice. Anxiety opens wide boredom's capacity to disclose our purposive nature. We are creatures who need to do things in order to avoid being bored, and even then the mood can affect us. What is required to prevent the situation from getting worse is the very thing that gave rise to the habits and routines of everyday existence that have now become dull, mindless, worthless, boring. If any degree of optimism remains, we might utter the famous plea—"There must be *more* to life than this!"—and then act in one way or another in order to make it so. With what it begins to uncover about our existence, boredom indicates what it takes to remedy its ill effects: action, our responding to what has been referred to in my story as the call of conscience that comes from the very heart of our purposive existence and that challenges us with the benefit and burden of freedom, of being open to the possibility and uncertainty of the future and choosing to do something about it.

Is perfection boring? We seek release from this mood and its momentum. For example, some people might turn (pray) to God with a question that supposedly was first asked by God: "Where art thou?" We await an answer (and possibly, at the same time, confront the guilt of not having responded responsibly enough in the past): "Here I am!" Kierkegaard and Wiesel put us through a lot with their rather simple and direct ways of relating the story of Adam. Indeed, understanding the mystery behind the story is not meant to be a snap. To become a teacher of what the mystery is about is to take on the challenging rhetorical task of being "true to the Word" (respecting its mysterious nature) while at the same time finding a way to make its meaning understandable and interesting to others, hence Kierkegaard's and Wiesel's observations about boredom. To have us think about the possibility of heaven's perfection being boring is to have us think again about what we think we know about perfection and its relationship to the purposive nature of our everyday existence. The matter of the lived body is once again before us. What is our true purpose on earth? Consciousness dawns with the second experience.

BACKED UP AGAINST LIFE AND BEING

The spatial and temporal structure of human existence defines a dwelling place where this question of what it means to be is always at issue as we live out our daily lives, just trying to make it from day to day without giving up, staying in bed, and suffering. The philosopher Emmanuel Levinas writes of this suffering in its most abject state. Here "there is an absence of all refuge." Suffering "is the fact of being directly exposed to being. It is made up of the impossibility of fleeing or retreating. The whole acuity of suffering lies in the impossibility of retreat. It is the fact of being backed up against life and being."[10] But where exactly are we when we are "backed up against life and being"?

I started to develop an answer to this question with the above discussion of how boredom and related moods bring us face-to-face with the challenging call of our own purposeful existence: a primordial call of conscience that is always at work to promote the dawning of consciousness. Levinas expresses this fact of life with the help of his Hebraic heritage. He writes about how the fundamental way we are positioned in life guarantees our continual involvement in an ontological and metaphysical process whereby the question "Where art thou?" is always being asked and always must be answered: "Here I am!" In living out the openness of our existence, we are necessarily exposed to "alterity": the "otherness" of people, things, the "not yet" of the future, and whatever we might imagine transcends these earthly forms of some assumed spiritual presence. Otherness calls for attention (the dawning of consciousness) and an appropriate response. We are creatures of accountability and responsibility: creatures who owe it to others and to ourselves to be good and just. This fundamental state of indebtedness is where we find ourselves when we are "backed up against life and being" and the chaos that accompanies this bottom-line place of lived existence.

According to Levinas, the response that is called for here constitutes "salvation" in its most primordial form (*before* it is made to accommodate any institutionalized character of religion). "Everyday life," claims Levinas, "is a preoccupation with salvation": we are forever caught up in the dynamics of the spatial and temporal functioning of existence that is always at work to call us into question and to call us to responsible action.[11] The history of human being is literally a narrative about hearing and responding to this call. That this narrative continues to be written today testifies to what Levinas describes as our "love for life." Although he does not admit it, this love shows itself on a physiological level, in the evolution of our immune and autonomic nervous systems.[12] Levinas does emphasize, however, that such love is at work in our desire "to make something" of ourselves, to remedy chaos by recreating a sense of order in our lives, no matter how bad off we may be at the time. The call of conscience, a love of life, and salvation all function together in the ontological workings of human being.

A less philosophical and religious way of conceiving and expressing the matter is offered in the lyrics of a song that I first heard when listening to the bluegrass maestro Ricky Skaggs and his awesome band, Kentucky Thunder:

> I would have given anything to make you want my love.
> Only to see you walk away and leave me in the dust.
> But for who I blame these bitter tears, girl you're not the one,
> Cause you can't break a heart when it's already been done.
> And darling, I'm still paralyzed by the sound of her goodbye.
> Nothing to lose this time, I'm too far down to fall.
> Running on wounded pride,
> No need to sympathize,
> Cause you didn't make me cry,
> I was too far down to fall, too far down to fall.[13]

When, for whatever reason, we are backed up against life and being, we are at that fundamental place of existence in which we are too far down to fall: the primordial spatial and temporal structure of human being that opens us to the future, is the source of anxiety, and calls for the concerned thought and action that is needed in order to create and sustain a meaningful existence. Empirically speaking, we can't fall any further "down" than we are when physiologically, socially, and emotionally spent—alone with ourselves, with the existence that *we are* first and foremost as human beings. A love of life helps us to withstand the posed challenge and the suffering that it can bring. An act of salvation on our part, however, is needed to take the next step toward recovery.

For both philosophical and bluegrass purists, the juxtaposition of Levinas and Skaggs might seem, at best, strange. For my purposes, however, the juxtaposition is appropriate. When reading, teaching, and discussing Levinas with colleagues and students, I know that something worthwhile is happening when they understand how the simple and earthy expression "too far down to fall" captures a large amount of hard-fought philosophical discourse meant to disclose the truth about how we are backed up against life and being and the moral obligations that follow from this situation. That's the beauty of the expression: with its rhetorically competent use of alliteration, it condenses the essential meaning of a very involved argument into a few memorable words that have a ring of truth about them.

"Too far down to fall": we are talking about a place of unquestionable ontological significance, a place that founds everyday existence and that is verifiable to anyone who has had a memorable bout with boredom, sadness, suffering, and anxiety (perhaps because, as in Skagg's case, he or she lost a *true* love). Levinas' discourse is designed to reveal the phenomenological and ontological intricacies of this dwelling place so that we might be in a better position to answer a two-part question that our own existence raises every nanosecond of the day: what does it mean *to be*, and what are our moral obligations to others?

Although Levinas' prose throughout his many works is couched in philosophical and religious rhetoric that is quite cryptic to the untrained ear, this discourse, too, warrants consideration as a thing of beauty. Its rhetoric is designed to disclose and express the truth and goodness of something that is essential to the very existence and well-being of our species: a dynamic and beautiful event that, as suggested so far, involves space, time, purpose, freedom, the call of conscience, emotion, otherness, acknowledgment, interpretation, responsibility, and salvation in a most fundamental way. We stand face-to-face with the ontological features of this event when we are "too far down to fall," when, owing to some existential disruption, we find ourselves in a place that lies at the very heart of our being and that is always calling us to task, to an act of salvation for the love of life. We exist in such a way that we are forever being challenged to assume the ethical responsibility of affirming our freedom through resolute choice. The challenge is a call for concerned thought and action—a call well known for its ability to incite anxiety in its hearers as it directs their concern to the uncertainties of "the next day."

We are fated to hear a most primordial call of conscience. This call and all that comes with it defines who, what, and how we are, ontologically speaking. Our desire for completeness (perfectibility) is inextricably tied to a process of evocation and provocation, a process of chaos calling for some degree of order, and order (especially if it is stifling) calling for some degree of chaos. The American Revolution, for example, is a case of a stifling order (British rule) instigating a state of chaos that seeks a better order (more freedom) in the world. Stressing the ethical importance of this dialectical process of "deconstruction and reconstruction" is a hallmark of much "postmodern" scholarship and art.[14] Recalling Sartwell's and Kauffman's observations of this process noted at the beginning of the chapter, we can further describe it as an unfolding display of the "deep and beautiful" laws of emerging life that natural selection has further molded and that takes on additional design with the everyday behaviors of our lived bodies. The space and time of the lived body marks out a dwelling place in which perfection becomes a major issue: a place that is structured perfectly (as an openness) for continuing to raise the issue of the origin and eventual outcome of human perfectibility. Dr. Frankenstein's monster (chapter 5) came face-to-face with the issue, hence the creature's plea to his creator for a sense of "beginning," an understanding of his reason for being and how his existence might and must be improved. Like his human counterpart, the creature longed to feel some sense of being at home with himself and others. Loneliness, boredom, melancholy, and anxiety became too much to bear. The creature was backed up against life and being—too far down to fall any further. As a lived body possessing a metaphysical desire for perfection, he was back to the beginning of his body's existence. The creature had a love for life. He sought salvation from his creator. "In the beginning," life is needful of assistance.

THE BEGINNING

"It is so difficult to find the beginning," writes Ludwig Wittgenstein in his book *On Certainty*. "Or, better," he continues, "it is difficult to begin at the beginning. And not try to go further back."[15] The lived body's metaphysical desire for perfection inspires us to want to know the true source and grounds of our being, especially when we are too far down to fall. Religion has the longest and most popular history in dealing with this desire. Its assessment, however, also serves to complicate the issue. Religion tells us that the beginning, in its perfect state, "once was" but no longer "is"—at least here on planet Earth. "In the beginning was the Word, and the Word was with God, and the Word was God" (John 1:1). The beginning and God go hand in hand. A perfect relationship—so perfect, in fact, that it defies complete comprehension. To speak about "the beginning" is to speak of a "starting point" that comes "before" it "all began" and that thus only appears to human consciousness as something that has already begun to happen. Moses, for example, was only allowed to see the "back parts" of God as this power and glory, no longer representing Itself as a burning bush, passed by Moses' eyes as he stood "in a cleft of [a] rock," knowing full well that "Thou canst not see my face: for there shall no man see me, and live" (Gen 33:20-23).

Experiencing and knowing absolute perfection, the most perfect form of perfection that there is, is beyond our grasp. Recall: the beginning makes possible the begun; it thus is *other* than the happening in question. God, we are told, is the ultimate Other, the (w)hol(l)y Other—otherness in its most complete and purest form: perfection, right from the start, in the beginning *and* before it, too. In attempting to put the entire matter into words without appealing to God, the philosopher Martin Heidegger writes,

> The beginning does not at first allow itself to emerge as beginning but instead retains in its own inwardness its beginning character. The beginning then first shows itself in the begun, but even there never immediately and as such. Even if the begun appears as the begun, its beginning and ultimately the entire "essence" of the beginning can still remain veiled. Therefore the beginning first unveils itself in what has already come forth from it. As it begins, the beginning leaves behind the proximity of its beginning essence and in that way conceals itself. Therefore an experience of what is at the beginning by

no means guarantees the possibility of thinking the beginning itself in its essence. The first beginning is, to be sure, what is decisive for everything; still, it is not the primordial beginning, i.e., the beginning that simultaneously illuminates itself and its essential domain and in that way begins.[16]

Coming to terms completely with perfection is no easy matter, but it is in our nature to keep on trying. Religion tells us that the struggle is worth it. When they die, truly religious souls supposedly "go home to their Maker"—back to the beginning, a place called heaven. The home of heaven is another word for perfection: that way of being that allows itself to be thought about and symbolized but never totally comprehended. The heavenly home known as the garden of Eden is only a metaphor, a representation of a place that defies complete understanding. Words are not "the thing itself." A leap of faith is required. We leap over the distance that separates words from things as metaphysical animals. Religion shouts encouragement: "Be ye therefore perfect, even as your Father which is in heaven is perfect" (Matt 5:48). But what exactly does this mean? The encouragement challenges us *to perfect* and thus improve ourselves so that we can eventually attain the very state of perfection that, by definition, is forever beyond the grasp of mortal beings. This paradoxical fact of life, however, need not bother creatures who, persuaded and guided by the rhetoric of religion, "know" that if they are "pure in heart," in "the end" they will be blessed and "shall see God" (Matt 5:8). Indeed, it takes death to see God face-to-face, to be in the full presence of the perfection that we cannot know totally while we live and breathe.

Still, before we die we can travel a long way in coming to know something of the awesome nature and scope of what this presence may very well be. Religion's famous counterpart, science, admits as much. Like religion, science, too, has a substantial investment in working its way back to "the beginning" and thereby coming to terms with perfection. Cosmology takes the lead here in its study of the entire observable universe, treated as a single entity. With powerful technologies (e.g., telescopes, computers) and highly sophisticated mathematical theory at hand, cosmologists look to the sky to study "fossils" (e.g., old stars, synthesized chemical elements) that tell of how the universe is expanding. To speak of an expanding universe is to admit the possibility that the process had a starting point, a beginning that was there before the process itself began with what is now commonly referred to as the big bang. "Using well-established physics," writes astronomer Martin Rees, "we can extrapolate cosmic evolution back to the stage when the universe was a millisecond old (10^{-3} seconds); the most powerful particle accelerators can generate the conditions that prevailed at 10^{-14} seconds; earlier than that, energies would have been higher still."[17] The awesomeness of such calculations is clear when one realizes that they also allow cosmologists to claim with mathematical "certainty" that the big bang took place "approximately" 15 billion years ago and that the entire universe is at least 10 billion light-years across and growing. We are talking about a lot of space here. Light travels at 186,000 miles per second. With science as our guide, we must realize that from "the beginning" to the "sixth day," when God supposedly created man, marks a period of billions of years.

Moreover, cosmologists have much to tell us about what immediately preceded the big bang. Before this awesome happening blasted into being everything in the universe (space, matter, time), there existed what cosmologists term a "singularity." According to Paul Davies, "A singularity is the nearest thing that science has found to a supernatural agent."[18] At a singularity, one finds a state of infinite temperature, infinite density, and infinite energy, all condensed into a point the size of an infinitesimal speck of dust and where space-time as we know it does not exist. A singularity exists outside of space-time, or what cosmologists sometimes describe as a state of "nothingness." Before the big bang, there *was* something that *was* nothing, a presence of absence that exploded and thereby set forth (created) all the material of the universe that will ever exist. The big bang was not an explosion *in* space, but an explosion of *all* space, an explosion whose echo is still detectable as long-wavelength radiation or what is also called the cosmic microwave background.

Without this particular beginning, we would not exist as lived bodies. But the everyday existence of the lived body also has its own ever-happening beginning, which takes place in the openness of being: the way in which the no longer (the past), the not yet (the future), and the here and now (the present) interpenetrate each other such that human existence is always in the "ecstatic" state of "standing outside and beyond itself" (Greek, *ek-stasis*), at every moment opening toward the future, toward the world of possibilities, and thus toward the realm of objective uncertainty in which the finality of death will eventually also take place, yet we know not when. Commenting on the fundamental and truthful nature of this process—how it serves as a basis for understanding, knowing, and making public the truth of *anything* else— Heidegger emphasizes that "truth" happens first and foremost as "an act of disclosure," a revealing or uncovering of something that presents itself to us. "To be certain of an entity means to *hold* it for true as something true. But 'truth' signifies the uncoveredness [the disclosure] of some entity, and all uncoveredness is grounded ontologically in the most primordial truth, the disclosedness of [the lived body's existence]." Heidegger thus maintains that with the relationship that we hold with this disclosedness, with our own existence, we are constantly and "essentially 'in the truth.'"[19] In other words, we are necessarily involved with a revelatory process that defines a "good" (an essential ingredient of life); sustains everyday existence; and can be thought of, spoken about, and otherwise represented by we who are living it.

Following Heidegger, we have associated this process with the lived body's original call of conscience. Recall that the act of disclosure happening here comes before any symbolic act that attempts to disclose whatever truth is at issue at the time. The call of conscience that calls for concerned thought and action "dispenses with any kind of utterance," writes Heidegger. "It does not put itself into words at all; . . . *Conscience discourses solely and constantly in the mode of keeping silent.*"[20] This discourse operates as what Heidegger terms a "Saying as Showing": "*The essential being of language is Saying as Showing. Its showing* character is not based on signs of any kind; rather, all signs arise from a showing within whose realm and for whose purposes they can be signs. . . . Even when Showing is accomplished by our human saying, even then this showing, this pointer, is preceded by an indication that it will let itself be shown."[21]

This last point was briefly introduced in chapter 4 when discussing how the perfectionist impulse of language is defined by its "saying" power, its capacity to "speak" by pointing to and showing us something. Lincoln's Gettysburg Address served as an illustration. The philosopher and novelist Umberto Eco offers the example of the unprecedented morality play of Adam and Eve: "We are not told in what language God spoke to Adam. Tradition has pictured it as a sort of language of interior illumination, in which God, as in other episodes of the Bible, expresses himself by thunderclaps and lightning. If we are to understand it this way, we must think of a language which, although not translatable into any known idiom, is still, through special grace or dispensation, comprehensible to its hearer."[22] Eco emphasizes here an ontological appreciation of the function of language: he associates its essence with the original presenting ("saying") of all that lies before us (e.g., thunderclaps and lightning). At this ontological level of existence, language is not understood first and foremost as a capacity for interpersonal communication but rather as the original and silent manifestation, the saying and "showing-forth" (*epi-deixis*), of *what is*. The saying and showing of human existence manifests itself as a call of conscience to that particular being who has the capacity for acknowledgment and the ability to represent symbolically what is perceived to be: the truth of our being, its primordial language, its saying/showing of itself in the dwelling place of the lived body.[23]

The reductionism of science does not include such an ontological appreciation of language and the lived body, for the mechanics of the brain are thought to be what really counts in understanding our linguistic and symbolic nature. "Yes, science is, in a sense, 'reducing' us to the physiological processes of a not-very-attractive three-pound organ," writes the cognitive scientist Steven Pinker. "But what an organ!"[24] Religion balks at such reductionism because it limits our metaphysical desire for perfection. The brain without God, insists religion, makes no sense. The ontological appreciation of the lived body and its language being offered here lies somewhere between science and religion: human beings are capable of being awed by the beauty of their own existence and having something "truthful" to say about it. Any truth claim *is what it is* because it works to disclose the "real" existence of some matter of concern. Truth begins with a primordial event of disclosure—one that needs us to witness its happening and to grant it meaning and significance by bringing it into some symbolic form. This original happening of truth is displayed in the lived body's being, the dwelling place of its spatial and temporal existence where is heard the original saying of the call of conscience and all that this call entails.

BEING OPEN

Are we witnessing God here? The laws of nature? We certainly stand face-to-face with the beginnings of the lived body, with the spatial and temporal structure of existence and the challenge that it poses with its openness. Heidegger speaks of this primordial event as marking out a "clearing" in the midst of "all that there is" (Being), the place where as much of this "all" as possible can be brought into language by our symbolic efforts and thereby understood to some degree. In evolutionary and cosmological terms, the birth of this place marks the moment when "the universe first became conscious of itself."[25] Although typically measured with such technologies as clocks, calendars, maps, and computers, the specific ontological structure and function of this place is itself not a human creation. The openness of our existence is a happening that is always already at work disclosing itself before we decide to notice and to calculate its presence. Human existence, in other words, has something about its nature—a primordial dimension of time and space—that, in truth, is more and thus other than its own making. It is a fact of life that we owe our very being to something other than ourselves.

Religion speaks "in good faith" of the "holiness" of this otherness. In its constant struggle to avoid such "God-of-the-gaps" thinking, science, on the other hand, with the essential aid of physics, mathematics, and technology, speaks of a "singularity" that came "before the beginning," was as small as a speck of dust, and delivered its contents (*everything* that exists in the cosmos) with a big bang that occurred approximately 15 billion years ago. The beautiful laws of emerging life came into being: chaos and order, order and chaos. Is it possible that "God" is behind all of these deconstructive and reconstructive happenings? With scientists like Kauffman, the question is not totally dismissed out of hand. Forming an ontological appreciation of the lived body also requires that we enact such generosity. Indeed, human being, with its own revelation—the truthful process of disclosure that it is—speaks to us of the value of being "open-minded" when dealing with uncertainty. There is an undeniable openness to the spatial and temporal structure of human existence. Contingency is a fact of life. Religion deals with this fact by creating doctrines of faith that employ contingency to their own advantage. Contingency is part of God's design for stimulating our metaphysical desire for perfection beyond the empirical boundaries of existence and toward some absolute other. As detailed in chapter 3 when discussing certain features of kabbalistic doctrine that inform Judaic, Christian, and Islamic thought, God, too, desires acknowledgment.

Although science doesn't go this far with its teachings, it nevertheless prides itself on holding a healthy respect for the related phenomena of contingency and uncertainty. Listen, for example, to what the Nobel Prize–winning physicist Richard Feynman has to say about the scientist's acknowledgment of these matters: "Every scientific law, every scientific principle, every statement of the results of an observation is some kind of a summary which leaves out details, because nothing can be stated precisely." Feynman thus maintains that

> All scientific knowledge is uncertain. This experience with doubt and uncertainty is important. I believe that it is of very great value, and one that extends beyond science. I believe that to solve any problem that has never been solved before, you have to leave the door to the unknown ajar. You have to permit the possibility that you do not have it exactly right. Otherwise, if you have made up your mind already, you might not solve it. . . . Scientists are used to this. We know that it is consistent to be able to live and not know. Some people say, "How can you *live* without knowing?" I do not know what they mean. I always live without knowledge. That is easy. How you get to know is what I want to know.[26]

Feynman goes on to stress how this "freedom to doubt" allows science to thrive and how he feels a responsibility as a "citizen-scientist" to "proclaim the value of this freedom and to teach that doubt is not to be feared, but that it is to be welcomed as the possibility of a new potential for human beings. If you know that you are not sure, you have a chance to improve the situation. I want to demand this freedom for future generations."[27]

What Feynman is arguing for is nothing more and nothing less than what comes with the temporality of human existence and its openness to the future: the ethical responsibility of answering a call that challenges people to affirm their freedom of choice. Indeed, argues Feynman, "openness of possibility is an opportunity. Doubt and discussion are essential to progress."[28] As a way of justifying the moral urgency of their art, rhetoricians have been making the same argument for over two thousand years. Feynman's continuation of his argument is worth noting:

> Why do we grapple with problems? We are only in the beginning. We have plenty of time to solve the problems. The only way that we will make a mistake is that in the impetuous youth of humanity we will decide we know the answer. This is it. No one else can think of anything else. And we will jam. We will confine man to the limited imagination of today's human beings.
>
> We are not smart. We are dumb. We are ignorant. We must maintain an open channel.[29]

To maintain an open channel is to remain true to the openness and objective uncertainty of our temporal existence. The lived body comes with an ethic already inscribed in its being, in the dwelling place of its existence and the otherness that is always a part of this place, this existential clearing in the midst of Being. Here is where we respond to the call of conscience, where we enact our freedom and responsibility, where we seek salvation, and where we put our symbolic capacities to use in order to understand reality, with all of its chaos and order.

THE SYMBOL-USING BEING

Such capacities serve our purposeful nature. Kenneth Burke's consideration of this matter is worth noting. Burke admits that

> Insofar as men are animals, they derive purposes from their physical nature. For instance, bodily hunger is enough to move them in search of food. Also, they can invent machines with "built-in" purposes, for instance missiles that will pursue a moving target with the persistence of a maniac, and that are responsible to no other kinds of signal.

But Burke then emphasizes that, as symbol-using creatures, human beings are not merely

> content with sheer *bodily* purpose. And insofar as men "cannot live by bread alone," they are moved by doctrine, which is to say, they derive purposes from language, which [with its perfectionist impulse] tells them what they "ought" to want to do, tells them how to do it,

and in the telling goads them with great threats and promises, even unto the gates of heaven and hell.

For Burke, it is from the lived body and the workings of language that "a whole new realm of purpose arises, endless in scope."[30] The realm of religion, according to Burke, is a perfect case in point. He notes that "without regard for the ontological truth or falsity of the case, there are sheerly technical reasons, intrinsic to the nature of language, for belief in God and the Devil. Insofar as language is intrinsically hortatory (a medium by which men can obtain the cooperation of one another), God perfectly embodies the petition. Similarly, insofar as vituperation is a 'natural' resource of speech, the Devil provides a perfect butt for invective. Heaven and Hell together provide the ultimate, or perfect, grounding for sanctions."[31]

Burke grounds his understanding of the genesis of religion in the perfectionist impulse of language to "define" situations. For Burke, such almighty notions as "God" are a product of the lived body's symbolic capacities. Being primarily interested in more materialistic concerns than the transcendental nature of some deity, Burke is not particularly bothered by how his way of dealing with matters calls into question God's true (definitional) status. Rather, he focuses on the definitional process itself and its effects on human behavior. In the following assessment, Burke uses science as his case study.

> A given terminology contains various *implications*, and there is a corresponding "perfectionist" tendency for men to attempt carrying out those implications. Thus, each of our scientific nomenclatures suggests its own special range of possible developments, with specialists vowed to carry out these terministic possibilities to the extent of their personal ability and technical resources. Each such specialty is like the situation of an author who has an idea for a novel, and now will never rest until he has completely embodied it in a book. Insofar as any of these terminologies happen also to contain the risks of destroying the world, that's just too bad; but the fact remains that, so far as the sheer principles of investigation are concerned, they are no different from those of the writer who strives to complete his novel. There is a kind of "terministic compulsion" to carry out the implications of one's terminology, quite as, if the astronomer discovered by his observations and computations that a certain wandering body was likely to hit the earth and destroy us, he would nonetheless feel compelled to argue for the correctness of his computations, despite

the ominousness of the outcome. Similarly, of course, men will so draw out the implications of their terminologies that new expectations are aroused (promises that are now largely interwoven with the state of Big Technology, and that may prove to be true or false, but that can have revolutionary effects upon persons who agree with such terministic "extrapolations").[32]

Burke's concluding parenthetical remark reflects his interest in what he describes as "the master psychosis" of the twentieth (and presumably the twenty-first) century: "the technological."[33] Although this description is not particularly flattering, Burke emphasizes that he does not use the word "psychosis" in the traditional psychiatric sense; rather, he employs it primarily to signify "a pronounced character of mind" that both reflects and informs one's interests and occupations (40). Being itself a technology—that is, a tool (or means) invented and employed primarily for the specific purpose (or end) of creating a common world of meaning among people—language necessarily carries the psychosis with it. The "terministic compulsion" registers itself in everything from the "objective" nomenclatures of science, to the "subjective" prose of the novelist "who will never rest until he has completely embodied . . . [his idea] in a book," to the rhetoric of religion that promises us redemption as we follow God's teachings.

There is no more central and foundational point to Burke's work than this: human beings (lived bodies) are motivated and conditioned by language (and the meanings and values it registers) to think and act in certain predefined ways. Language, in other words, exerts a deterministic influence on those who appropriate its workings. The writer (e.g., novelist) makes use of this influence to establish some common ground of understanding or "identification" with his or her readership and their particular interests. "Without the assistance of this factor," writes Burke, "the entire paraphernalia of appeal—comprehensiveness, conciseness, cogency, construction, pliancy, and all the rest *ad lib*—are wasted. The dullest sentences, exchanged between young lovers or between employee and employer, may be vibrant, whereas the results of many years' effort and engrossment may seem insipid. We interest a man by dealing with his interests."[34] Moreover, without the assistance of this factor, the author would, at best, be on shaky grounds in trying to express fully, perfectly, his or her own "novel" ideas that, by definition, are "paradoxical"—that is, "beyond" (*para*) the currently established "received opinion" (*doxa*) or status quo—and thus can only flourish by transcending and extending the deterministic constraints of a readership's typical linguistic repertoire.

We see this rhetorical process at work, for example, in the writings of the critical theorist Max Horkheimer as he attempts to educate his readers in the mid-1940s about the horrors of the Holocaust and what these horrors teach us about "the profoundly human resistance to irrationality—a resistance that is always the core of true individuality":

> The real individuals of our time are the martyrs who have gone through infernos of suffering and degradation in their resistance to conquest and oppression, not the inflated personalities of popular culture, the conventional dignitaries. These unsung heroes consciously exposed their existence as individuals to the terroristic annihilation that others undergo unconsciously through the social process [of everyday life]. The anonymous martyrs of the concentration camps are the symbols of the humanity that is striving to be born. The task of philosophy is to translate what they have done into language that will be heard, even though their finite voices have been silenced by tyranny.[35]

This task is a representing of a "saying" into a said, a speaking about the presence of "anonymous martyrs of the concentration camps [who] are the symbols of the humanity that is striving to be born" whenever people seek a remedy to the evils of some tyrannical rule. With his rhetoric, Horkheimer would have us acknowledge "unsung heroes," not only the more well-known and lumped-together mass of "millions of people" who died in the camps. Horkheimer is making use of his rhetorical competence to come to terms with and open others to the truth of some reality. Frankenstein's monster did the same thing. He spoke eloquently about a matter of life and death: the importance of receiving the life-giving gift of genuine acknowledgment. Eloquence facilitates the process of helping others understand and gain a feel for, as perfectly as possible, some matter at hand. Remember, things which strike and arouse the heart—eloquence is just that. Eloquence is beauty in the making: the art of enhancing the perfectionist capacity of language to define and make known the truth of something to others. To speak of the beauty of some discourse is to have been affected by its eloquence: its most fitting and timely way of disclosing the truth of something that warrants thoughtful and careful consideration.

Horkheimer has in mind the truth of heroes who are rightly remembered for why and how they lost their lives during a time when perfection turned rotten. He involves himself in and promotes the rhetorical process of receiving in order to share—of hearing, interpreting, and sounding a call of conscience whose eloquence is directed toward helping others acknowledge and become receptive to an instructive, albeit horrific, fact of life. Consciousness dawns with the second experience. Horkheimer ends his book by reminding us of the overall purpose that directs his eloquence—a purpose dedicated to the perfection of reason: "When called upon to act independently, we cry for patterns, systems, and authorities. If by enlightenment and intellectual progress we mean the freeing of man from superstitious belief in evil forces, in demons and fairies, in blind fate—in short, the emancipation from fear—then denunciation of what is currently called reason is the greatest service reason can render."[36] Reason, with the help of rhetoric, promotes the happening of acknowledgment, of our being open to the truth, especially when "superstitious belief in evil forces," masquerading as reason, would have it otherwise. Being open to the truth is heroic. Horkheimer is a hero writing about heroes whose lives ended too soon and too violently.

HEROISM

We are creatures whose existence can become so death defying that, not being able to take it anymore, we might act to end it way before its time. As the "postmodern" saying goes, "life is a bitch and then you die." The saying reflects the "downside" of existence. Indeed, "shit happens!" But there is also an upside to our being. The openness of human existence allows not only for worst-case scenarios but also for the possibility of better things to come, of people having the character, commitment, and courage to improve and thus perfect their lives.

In his Pulitzer Prize–winning book, *The Denial of Death*, Ernest Becker associates this possibility with what he terms "our central calling, our main task on this planet": to be "heroic." Becker turns to psychoanalytic theory to justify his claim. The issue of heroics, writes Becker, "goes deeper into human nature than anything else because it is based on organismic narcissism and on the child's need for self-esteem as *the* condition for his life." Becker's clarification of this point is worth noting:

> In childhood we see the struggle for self-esteem at its least disguised. The child is unashamed about what he needs and wants most. His whole organism shouts the claims of his natural narcissism. And this claim can make childhood hellish for the adults concerned, especially when there are several children competing at once for the prerogatives of limitless self-extension, what we might call "cosmic significance." The term is not meant to be taken lightly. . . . We like to speak casually about "sibling rivalry," as though it were some kind of by-product of growing up, a bit of competitiveness and selfishness of children who have been spoiled, who haven't yet grown into a generous social nature. But it is too all-absorbing and relentless to be an aberration, it expresses the heart of the creature: the desire to stand out, to be *the* one in creation.[37]

Indeed, heroes "stand out" from the crowd as they exhibit greatness in some achievement and are admired for doing so. Heroes provide the material that directs a culture's moral compass and offers instructions for understanding what human greatness is. Each "cultural system is a dramatization of earthly heroics; each system cuts out rules for performances of various degrees of heroism: from the 'high' heroism of a Churchill, a Mao, or a Buddha, to the 'low' heroism of the coal miner, the peasant, the simple priest; the plain, everyday, earthy heroism wrought by gnarled working hands guiding a family through hunger and disease."[38] What heroism represents for a culture informs its members about what it takes for a finite being to live on after death in the hearts and minds of others. Becker thus emphasizes that the esteemed values celebrated in a given culture's symbolic "hero system" speak of the possibility of being immortal and thus "godlike," hence its great metaphysical attraction to humankind. The symbolism of heroism admits a call of conscience: a call that incites moral consciousness and beckons us to be upstanding and outstanding citizens in all that we say and do.

Let us keep in mind, however, that *this* call and our attraction to the "outstanding" achievements of those who answer it are rooted in *a more primordial call.* The actions of heroes answering a culturally informed call of conscience are themselves made possible by the outstanding (ecstatic) function of our spatial and temporal existence. We *are* creatures whose truth is situated in the openness of Being, in an event of disclosure, a fundamental truth, that is other than a human creation and that *itself* calls on us to do what any hero does: show courage in assuming the ethical responsibility of affirming our freedom through resolute choice. The ontological structure of human existence admits its own ethic, its own call of conscience; with its ecstatic nature, its way of having us stand out into the future, it has something fundamentally heroic (godlike) about it. The potential is there in our very being for all of us to be heroes. Is this to suggest that the heroic structure of existence is *meant* to have us think about and remember the work of God? Who can say for sure? I simply take the matter as a given, something that an ontological appreciation of the lived body reveals: we *are* beings of heroic potential who must face the fact that our fate is to be open and to listen to a constant calling that challenges us with the ethical and moral struggle of coming to know and to speak the good, the just, and the truth.

The purposive actions of heroes head us in the direction of perfection—a direction that begins in the clearing of our spatial and temporal existence, the freedom it provides, and the courage and responsibility it calls for. Heroes do what existence would have us all do with its ongoing call of conscience. This most original call announces its presence in a place where we seem to end up when we are "too far down to fall." But this place is certainly not all bad. How could it be? It is our *own* existence, along with its otherness—which is not of our own making. When we are "backed up against life and being," "too far down to fall," and perhaps staring death in the face, we are at that place in our lives that also makes possible and sustains our ability to change things for the better. "The irony of man's condition," writes Becker, "is that the deepest need is to be free of the anxiety of death and annihilation; but it is life itself which awakens it, and so we must shrink from being fully alive."[39] Unless, of course, one is a hero, a person who is willing to risk it all for the good of others. Indeed, the call of conscience that comes from our existence speaks to us of the importance of otherness, of something that is not of our own making, something that always shows a bit extra, like heroes do with their actions.

Heroes respond to the call of conscience. Responding to this call is humankind's most original vocation. The philosopher Joan Stambaugh makes the point this way: "Response is nothing passive or reactive; it is the essential human deed. People with severe depression are in what is perhaps the most unbearable state there is, because they are utterly unable to respond to anything at all. Even pain or suffering can be preferable to that since they are, after all, some sort of response. Without some kind of response, no poet would write a poem, no composer would write a symphony, nobody would fall in love, no one would find a friend."[40]

Be it in the sciences, the arts, or religion, the genuineness of the response lies in how open we are to the presentation, the disclosing, the saying of whatever is under consideration at the time. Openness, we have seen, is the ground of truth; it allows for the act of disclosure, the showing-forth of what is. The term "acknowledgment" names the process: with our willingness to acknowledge otherness, we attune ourselves most carefully, truthfully, to, for example, the intricate physics of the universe, the pathophysiology of a disease, the genius of a symphony, the meaning and significance of a remarkable book, the situation of people who need our help. Acknowledgment is a life-giving gift.

Notice that my remarks about acknowledgment do not contain the word "recognition." People oftentimes speak of these two phenomena as if they were synonymous. For the purpose of this book, however, their difference must be kept in mind. As Calvin Schrag reminds us, "The blurring of the grammar of acknowledgment with the grammar of recognition is one of the more glaring misdirections of modern epistemology."[41] The definition of "recognition" found in the *Oxford English Dictionary* reads, "The action or fact of perceiving that some thing, person, etc., is the same as one previously known; the mental process of identifying what has been known before; the fact of being thus known or identified." The phenomenon of acknowledgment, however, entails more than the mental process of identifying what has been known before.

For example, I can recognize a person walking toward me as an old acquaintance. Once we meet, some ritualistic behavior might be enough to satisfy the demands of proper decorum: "Hey! Long time no see. How've you been doing? What's going on?" A few more seconds of "conversation" and we are off once again on our separate ways. But what if the acquaintance was hoping for more than the recognition that I had given him? What if he was looking forward to the added space and time, the openness, that comes with my genuine acknowledgment of his presence and that provides a dwelling place for developing a more caring conversation? This ethos of acknowledgment establishes an environment in which people can take the time to know together some topic of interest and, in the process, perhaps gain a more authentic understanding of, and feel more at home with, those who are willing to contribute to its development. *Recognition is only a preliminary step in this process of attuning one's consciousness toward another and his or her expression of a topic in order to facilitate the development of such existential knowledge and personal understanding.* Acknowledgment makes possible the moral development of recognition by enabling us to remain open to the world of people, places, and things even if, at times, matters become boring or troublesome. Perhaps such openness was what my acquaintance wanted and was willing to give. I, on the other hand, opted to keep the relationship in a state of simple recognition—a state that may give the impression that one is being noticed and that genuine acknowledgment is thus a possibility. People can become quite skilled at faking acknowledgment.

Remaining unacknowledged is a slight to one's being. The damage done disrupts a person's sense of self-worth. Depending on how seriously they are taken to heart, such disruptions can move a person into a state of anxious wonder about his or her existence: "What am I, what am I failing to do, what should I do?" The disruption exposes an imperfection in our being and thus triggers a metaphysical impulse. We are creatures whose longing or nostalgia for security and completeness makes us susceptible to the ailment of becoming homesick for familiar and welcoming surroundings where others show heartfelt concern for our well-being.

Acknowledgment must transpire in order to initiate and sustain moral action. Recall that acknowledgment is that way of being toward "otherness" that accomplishes and cultivates the moral character of human society as it promotes "the miracle of moving out of oneself," of egoism becoming altruism. Also recall that "hope" can arise from this transformation of self-centeredness as people, in a "heroic" gesture, opt to go out of their way to make us feel wanted and needed. Heroes "stand out" from the indifference of the crowd; they are thus true to the ecstatic (outstanding) nature of human being: the way our existence is at every moment opening out toward the "otherness" of the future, that awesome place of uncertainty, anxiety, hope, and joy. The ontological structure of human being is structured as a heroic event.

JUSTICE

In coming to the aid of another, a hero enacts acknowledgment. This act functions to transform space and time as it makes room in our lives for others. People literally save lives by performing the deed. And even if another's life is not on the line, the workings of acknowledgment still establish an environment or dwelling place in which people can take the time to deliberate and know together some topic of interest and, in the process, perhaps gain a more authentic understanding of, and feel more at home with, those who are willing to contribute to its development. Only by way of acknowledging others, by staying open to all that they have to offer, can we make sure that we avoid the dreadful error of Frankenstein, who, in failing to remain open to the "eloquence" and to see the "inner beauty" of his "monstrous" creation, refused the creature's urgent request for compassion and companionship. Unlike the egotistical and selfish Frankenstein, people with "big hearts" are known to be heroes; they are open to and do "beautiful" things that "truly" speak of the perfectibility of human nature and the "justice" that it can produce.

Elaine Scarry's provocative and insightful assessment of beauty stresses this very point. Something deemed beautiful, argues Scarry, creates "the aspiration for enduring certitude [perfection]." It "calls" for the "perceptual acuity" (acknowledgment) that enables us to appreciate as perfectly as possible some object's disclosure, its truth, and thereby appropriate and cultivate the knowledge and wisdom made possible by this revelation. Scarry offers a wonderful example for the rhetorician in developing her point.

> [T]here is no way to be in a high state of alert toward injustices—to subjects that, because they entail injuries, will bring distress—without simultaneously demanding of oneself precisely the level of perceptual acuity that will forever be opening one to the arrival of beautiful sights and sounds. How will one even notice, let alone become concerned about, the inclusion in a political assembly of only one economic point of view unless one has also attended, with full acuity, to a debate that is itself a beautiful object, full of arguments, counterarguments, wit, spirit, ripostes, ironies, testing, contesting; and how in turn will one hear the nuances of even this debate unless one also makes oneself available to the songs of birds or poets?[42]

Scarry emphasizes that acknowledgment is attuned to the "aliveness" of a person or object, an aliveness that makes the object's "abrasive handling seem unthinkable. The mind recoils—as from a wound cut into living flesh." The recoil gives us pause for concerned thought. Beauty "incites deliberation." What is brought to mind here "is not the level of aliveness, which is already absolute, but one's own access to the already existing level of aliveness, bringing about, if not a perfect match, at least a less inadequate match between the actual aliveness of others and the level with which we daily credit them." Scarry thus maintains that beauty places "requirements on us for attending to the aliveness . . . of our world, and for entering into its protection.[43] Meeting these requirements helps to establish the "justice" that is needed if we intend to treat other people and other things with heartfelt concern and respect.

Justice has an ontological ring to its nature, which is heard in a rhetoric of perfection: justice develops with the primordial relationship between the self and otherness, with the epideictic call of conscience that is announced by this relationship, with the acknowledgment that keeps us open to the interruptive function of this call and to the disclosure of truth that happens in the midst of this openness, with the salvation that transpires as we act heroically to respect and cultivate the truth in question and the beauty of which this truth speaks. Justice requires that we, in turn, attempt to speak the truth as perfectly as possible, especially in those rhetorical situations in which some exigence or "imperfection"—something "which is other than it should be"—sounds a call of conscience and urgently awaits acknowledgment and resolution.[44]

We have now covered the key terms associated with perfection that I promised to integrate with my discussion of the lived body. The discussion was ontologically and thus empirically oriented. The lived body speaks to us of space, time, place, purpose, freedom, otherness, conscience, emotion, truth, interpretation, acknowledgment, salvation, heroism, beauty, reason, rhetoric, and justice. I made much of how the relationship of these terms (a rhetoric of perfection) is particularly striking in those dire circumstances in which, for whatever reason, we find ourselves backed up against life and being, too far down to fall, and are thereby immediately challenged to do something about our potentially dead-end situation. "What if this is as good as it gets?" The thought can become so discomforting that, as the saying goes, we might "feel like we are dying." The saying makes sense. When we are backed up against life and being, we find ourselves in a primordial dwelling place known for making us anxious by the way it opens us to the objective uncertainty of our existence and thus to that fact of life that is "not yet now" but that is bound to come sooner or later: death. Indeed, as soon as we are conceived and ready to be born, we are old enough to die. Life and death are inextricably bound together. The lived body must know itself in light of its eventual demise.

For many (if not most) people, such knowledge is discomforting. Death is termed an "enemy," an "evil," a "grammatical error" in a personal narrative, something that a rhetoric of perfection is meant to counter. But death can also be thought otherwise. The physician Timothy Quill reminds us, for example, that when a patient's medical condition becomes "a meaningless existence with no escape . . . death can be a welcome friend," a savior.[45] With Quill, we are alerted to how a rhetoric of perfection is also present in the discourse of those who take issue with their right-to-life counterparts and who argue for a patient's "right to die." In the debate over the morality of euthanasia and physician-assisted suicide, one thus finds a rhetoric of perfection at odds with itself. I offer a case study of this predicament in the next chapter. The study is meant to clarify not only how a rhetoric of perfection actually works, but also how it does so in a situation that makes it particularly difficult for this rhetoric to achieve its goal. Putting a rhetoric of perfection to such a test is called for by such a project as the present one.

CHAPTER EIGHT

THE GOOD LIFE, THE GOOD DEATH

Despite our many excellences, human beings are still animals, fallible creatures: at our best, we live lives that, at one and the same time, advance and forever fall short of the metaphysical goal of ever having it all together before we pass away. As noted in the introduction of this book, there appears to be a significant insignificance to our being. Recall how David Hume makes the point: "the life of man is of no greater importance to the universe than that of an oyster."[1]

Hume offers this declaration when discussing how "suicide is no transgression of our duty to God," the One who supposedly is so *completely* perfect that It guides "all the causes" in the universe. "[N]othing happens . . . without [God's] consent and co-operation." And this being the case, "then neither does my death, however voluntary, happen without [God's] consent; and whenever pain and sorrow so far overcome my patience as to make me tired of life, I may conclude, that I am recalled from my station, in the clearest and most express terms."[2] Responding to those religious souls who would still insist that suicide is a "sin," Hume again uses their holy notion of perfection to further *his* case: "Were the disposal of human life so much reserved as the peculiar province of the almighty that it were an encroachment on his right for men to dispose of their own lives; it would be equally criminal to act for the preservation of life as for its destruction. If I turn aside a stone, which is falling upon my head, I disturb the course of nature, and I invade the peculiar province of the almighty, by lengthening out my life, beyond the period, which, by the general laws of matter and motion, he had assigned to it."[3]

Hume's considerations of the perfectibility of human nature, God, and the morality of suicide not only have precedent dating as far back as Socrates but also live on in the current rhetoric of the euthanasia debate.[4] The case study offered below is a famous reference point in this debate, what the bioethics scholar Bruce Jennings describes as a story about life and death that is "unprecedented in the annals of American end of life care," a "perfect storm of controversy" of medical ethics.[5] The case is that of Ms. Terri Schiavo, a young woman who lived in a persistent vegetative state for fifteen years before she was allowed to die the "dignified" death that she supposedly wanted all along. With the Schiavo case, we see the medical profession, the courts, Congress, religious institutions, the media, a grieving and quarrelsome family, and an outraged American public all struggling to express the morally best solution for remedying a heartbreaking situation. The Schiavo case is very much about coming to terms with perfection when questions of the "good life" and the "good death" are right in our face, begging for acknowledgment.

A rhetoric of perfection lies at the heart of the case—a rhetoric that addresses what medical ethicists agree is a major and growing problem in the ongoing euthanasia debate and in health care in general: "the need to encourage people . . . to do what is always so difficult to do in our culture, and that is *to communicate better* with their families, with their physicians, perhaps even with themselves—in that internal dialogue, in their minds and in their hearts—about the inevitability of our eventual death" and the related issue of "how we [want to] die."[6] The Schiavo case exemplifies this problem of the lived body. Fueled by the rhetorics of both the right-to-life and the right-to-die movements, the case illustrates how perfection can be both a benefit and a burden, something that makes human beings appear significant and admirable as it simultaneously humbles them with the realization of their incompleteness and, perhaps, insignificance. The specific rhetorical artifacts that I examine here were chosen not only on the basis of their being representative examples of the discursive exchanges that inform and direct the Schiavo case, but also because they offer vivid illustrations of how sincere efforts in the moral practice of rhetoric can still lead to the "pathology" of matters becoming rotten with perfection. The Schiavo case provides a rigorous test for the worthiness of any rhetoric of perfection. A brief history of the circumstances of the case is presented first. Following this history, I analyze the case in terms of the rhetoric of perfection described above.

THE RHETORICAL SITUATION OF TERRI SCHIAVO

Case History

In 1990 Terri Schiavo, then twenty-six, experienced cardiac arrest and sustained severe brain damage to her cerebral cortex due to what doctors said was a "potassium imbalance," possibly due to the fact that she was bulimic. The binging and purging of that eating disorder could have caused the imbalance. Regardless, the medical diagnosis of Ms. Schiavo's brain damage identified her as being in a "persistent vegetative state" (PVS). Her EEG was flat. She was incapable of emotion, memory, or thought. In the hospital, a percutaneous endoscopic gastrostomy (PEG) tube was inserted for administering nourishment and hydration. Michael Schiavo (Terri's husband) was appointed legal guardian, without objection from Ms. Schiavo's parents (Mr. and Mrs. Schindler).

In 1992 a Florida jury awarded Michael Schiavo $300,000 for loss of consortium as part of the medical malpractice suit he filed against her physician for not diagnosing the potassium imbalance associated with her bulimia. The jurors also awarded $725,000 to Ms. Schiavo, which her husband placed in a trust for her medical care and legal expenses. The original ruling was for two million dollars. Over one million dollars of that money had to be used for attorney's fees and related costs. No money was awarded to the Schindlers, who argued vigorously that they, too, deserved compensation because Terri was their daughter. The total amount of damages and their distribution were determined, in part, by the jury's decision that Terri's bulimia was 70 percent her fault, and only 30 percent the fault of the doctor. Recalling his father-in-law's "selfish" reaction to the situation, Michael Schiavo writes, "Here's a man who was disappointed beyond belief when he learned that he and Terri's mom had no standing to file their own malpractice suit against Terri's doctors. I could never be certain whether he was more interested in punishing the doctors, or in getting money to help bail him out of the desperate financial condition they were in as a result of his futon business going bust and their subsequent bankruptcy in 1989." Mr. Schindler threatened to sue Michael if he did not get some of the money awarded to his daughter. The only way the Schindlers could receive damages was if they, not Michael, were appointed by the court to be her legal guardians.[7]

In February 1993 the Schindlers and Mr. Schiavo had a disagreement over the "proper" care of Terri and the management of the malpractice settlement. The Schindlers believed that Michael was not showing proper compassion for Terri and that a primary motive for his doing this was to "torture" them.[8] Michael's story is radically different than his in-laws'.

During the first year and a half after her collapse, still hoping that Terri could recognize and communicate with him, Michael was diligent in caring for his wife. He instructed Terri's healthcare providers, the Palm Gardens nursing home, "that she was to be up, out of bed, dressed nicely with her hair done. I learned by then how to apply the makeup she used and I'd go shopping . . . for her clothes." He did such things based on advice from one of Terri's doctors. He was given hope that having her dressed the way she used to dress and allowing her to wear and smell perfume might trigger a response. Moreover, Michael admitted that if "Terri came out of [the coma] one day, I wanted her to see that I'd made sure she was taken care of, that she hadn't been abandoned. The makeup and clothes were a part of that." The demands he made on the nursing home staff resulted in his being described as a nursing home director's "worst nightmare." Michael also admitted that "eventually, however, after years of no progress and doctors telling us that 'this is all there is,' I had to believe them. Perhaps if the Schindlers had gotten some help dealing with the grief and loss, they might have come to accept it, too."[9] In conversations with Michael before she collapsed, Terri had been adamant about her right to die a dignified death: "I would never want to live like that, I would want to just die. . . . Don't ever keep me alive on anything artificial."[10]

In July 1993 the Schindlers initiated their twelve-year legal attempt to remove Mr. Schiavo as Terri's guardian. In this role, and under Florida law, Mr. Schiavo had full power of attorney for his wife's medical decisions. He announced publicly that his wife, who did not leave a living will, had told him that she would rather die than be forced to exist in a PVS. Mr. Schiavo's parents, brother, and sister-in-law also testified to this fact.

Mr. Schiavo promised that he would carry out his wife's decision. Throughout the years of litigation, Mr. and Mrs. Schindler argued, to the contrary, that their daughter, given her Catholic upbringing and her allegiance to the church, would never have said this, and even if she had, they would still keep her alive and take care of her. Mr. Schindler also admitted in a deposition and in open court that in order to keep Terri alive and respect her wishes as a good Catholic (i.e., uphold her right to life), he would "absolutely" amputate Terri's legs if she developed gangrene. He also admitted that he would amputate an arm "if necessary." Terri's brother testified that "it is not speculative to say if Terri knew that it was bringing my parents an ounce of joy in her [sic] life she would want to be like this."[11] Mr. Schiavo's reaction to these admissions is worth noting:

> I know the girl I married. I know that she valued her dignity. But I also know that she understood the concept of quality of life. We've already presented testimony . . . that Terri would not want to be kept alive by artificial means. If you accept that, can you imagine Terri saying to her parents, "If I'm in a vegetative state, and you need to lop off my arms and legs so I don't die of gangrene, and if keeping me alive in that condition will give you joy, then do it."
>
> It's absurd. If they thought it was a demonstration of their love for Terri, it was a sick kind of love. And the fact that they were willing to say it, whether or not they believed it, was enough reason for me to never even consider giving them guardianship of my wife. Would you do that to the person you loved the most in the entire world?[12]

Mr. Schiavo attributed this absurd and ghastly situation to how the Schindlers were firmly caught "in the clutches of the moral troglodytes of the religious right" who argued "that [his] wife's death came as a result of the forces of the euthanasia. [The Schindlers] dishonor their own daughter's memory by allowing her to be used by those waging a culture war on America."[13]

In May 1998 Mr. Schiavo filed a petition to remove his wife's PEG tube. His rationale, supported by testimony over the years from court-appointed physicians who verified her condition of being in a PVS with no chance of improvement, was accepted by the county circuit court: Terri Schiavo wanted, and had the legal right, to end her life "with dignity." The Schindlers disagreed. Their daughter wanted to live. In the preface to their book, they write,

> . . . our girl was lost to us. The outpouring of support couldn't save her; the condolence letters, cards, and notes cannot bring her back. We lost. Terri lost. America lost. In upholding Michael Schiavo's petition to have his wife's life terminated, the courts ruled for death over life, and we are individually and collectively diminished by their decision. . . . We believe that Terri was nothing less than the victim of judicial murder. And if by revealing ourselves as we really are, and Terri as she really was, means that no one else shares Terri's fate, then our story will be the one memorial Terri would have wanted.[14]

The Schindlers sought review by the Florida Supreme Court four times. There were several proceedings in the federal counts. The U.S. Supreme Court declined to hear the case on four separate occasions, having already dealt with the issue in the 1990 case of Nancy Cruzan.[15] During all of this litigation, the PEG tube was removed and reinserted two times. The Schindlers argued that Mr. Schiavo committed perjury; physically abused Ms. Schiavo, causing her PVS; did not attend properly to the physical therapy that was available for his wife; and grew so unloving toward Terri in the months before her collapse that she told her sister and brother that she wanted a divorce but "didn't have the courage or the guts." As a "devout Catholic," she "wasn't *supposed* to get divorced."[16] Right-wing Florida Governor Jeb Bush and national advocacy groups favoring the right to life intervened, claiming that the removal of the tube represented abuse and neglect. On October 21, 2003, the Florida legislature enacted "Terri's Law," which allowed Governor Bush to issue a "one-time stay" to prevent the withholding of nutrition and hydration. The PEG tube was reinserted on that day. On March 18, 2005, the tube was removed for the third time by court order. Pressured especially by the religious Right, the U.S. House Committee on Government Reform reacted immediately. Congress enacted a private bill for Ms. Schiavo, with the Senate delaying the Easter recess and the house suspending its rules. President Bush signed the bill on March 21, 2005. This bill effectively reversed a lawful order of the courts, violating separation of powers and encroaching on the authority of an independent judiciary.

Advocacy groups supporting the Schindlers maintained that Ms. Schiavo was not in a PVS and that she could improve with proper therapy. At a Web site (http://terrisfight.org) constructed in support of the Schindler family, visitors could watch an edited video clip that read "Terri Big Eyes" across the top of a scene featuring Terri opening her eyes, supposedly on command, and following her parents' movements with what looks like a smile on her face. Although a person in a PVS would be incapable of having any meaningful interaction with others, the Schindlers and two of her nurses at the Palm Gardens nursing home maintained that Terri recognized and communicated with each of them. She smiled in their presence and was "heard" to say things like "mommy" and "I want to live." According to nurse Heidi Law, Terri also displayed displeasure toward her husband who, having been encouraged by the Schindlers to see other women, had done just that and currently lived with a woman and their two biological children. "When she was upset," Law stated, "which was usually the case after Michael was there, she would withdraw for hours. We were convinced that he was abusing her, and probably saying cruel, terrible things to her because she would be so upset when he left."[17] Nurse Carla Iyer emphasized that throughout her time at Palm Gardens:

> Michael Schiavo was focused on Terri's death. Michael would say "When is she going to die?" "Has she died yet?" and "When is the bitch going to die?" . . . Any time Terri was sick, like with a UTI or fluid buildup in her lungs, colds, pneumonia, Michael would be visibly excited, thrilled even, hoping she would die. . . . He would blurt out, "I'm going to be rich!" and would talk about all the things he would buy when Terri died, like a new car, a new boat, and going to Europe, among other things. . . .[18]

This account, I think it is fair to say, sounds too dark to be true. Perhaps this is the kind of thing that happens when one's opposition is described as a group of "moral troglodytes."

Additional support for the Schindlers came from such high-ranking Republican officials as the Harvard-trained heart surgeon and Senate majority leader Dr. Bill Frist, who pressed hard for federal intervention in the case even though he never conducted an "in-person" examination of Ms. Schiavo. Referring to the years of bedside medical diagnoses of Ms. Schiavo's condition, however, the U.S. Court of Appeals for the Eleventh Circuit dismissed these efforts. The PEG tube was not reinserted.

Terri Schiavo died on the morning of March 31, 2005. An autopsy confirmed the diagnosis of PVS and showed no evidence that Ms. Schiavo had been abused or neglected by her husband. In fact, in order to care for her during her years of crisis, Michael Schiavo became an emergency medical technician (EMT), then a registered respiratory therapist, and finally a registered nurse. He was described by the Sabal Palms Health Care Center administration as being the "nursing home administrator's worst nightmare" not because of what nurses Law and Iyer claimed he did, but because, as he maintained, he demanded "perfection" in Terri's care and was at times overly harsh with the staff when such care was lacking.[19] The bronze plaque on his wife's granite gravestone reads:

SCHIAVO
THERESA MARIE
BELOVED WIFE
BORN DECEMBER 3, 1963
DEPARTED THIS EARTH
FEBRUARY 25, 1990
AT PEACE MARCH 31, 2005
I KEPT MY PROMISE[20]

The Schindlers phrased it another way: "Terri did not die from atrophy of the brain. She died from atrophy of compassion."[21] The Schindlers' lawyer, David Gibbs, added this: "The Terri Schiavo case is to our generation what *Roe v. Wade* was to our parents' generation. Life itself was on trial."[22]

A Rhetoric of Perfection

The radical Christian philosopher Søren Kierkegaard writes that "the magnitude of anxiety is a prophecy of how wonderful perfection is."[23] Kierkegaard measures this magnitude in terms of how open we become to the otherness of the "unknown" when, for whatever reason, the call of conscience presents itself to us. For Kierkegaard, the unknown is a sign of God's unfathomable perfection, hence his praise for that emotion that exposes us in the most direct way to this ultimate source of truth—a source that discloses something of itself in the ontological structure of our spatial and temporal existence.

The Schiavo case was a source of heartbreak and anxiety for all concerned parties, especially her immediate family. A serious illness is a powerful catalyst for the call of conscience and the moment of truth that comes with it. The event is a "showing-forth," an epideictic display, of wounded humanity—a rhetorical interruption par excellence, giving evidence of an "imperfection" urgently in need of some remedy. Thoughtful action and good judgment are immediately required. Bulimia embodies such an imperfection. At the risk of endangering her health, Terri was trying to look better, more attractive, before she collapsed. Many other rhetorical interruptions were to follow.

The Schindlers tell how "Terri was a chunky child, not a fat one." When she "went to high school, for some reason she just kept gaining every year, eventually reaching upwards of two hundred pounds (she was five foot five), to the point that we worried about it." Terri's weight kept her and her other "overweight" friends "out of the mainstream social life of their high school class." As soon as she graduated high school, Terri told her parents that she was "ready to lose weight." A family physician "put her on a Nutri-System diet . . . and slowly, gradually, the pounds came off." At no time in her life did Terri admit to her parents that she was bulimic, and her parents admitted that they therefore did not consider the possibility.[24]

Michael Schiavo tells a different and more detailed story about Terri's condition:

> If you want to trace the cause of Terri's collapse, you begin with an eating disorder, bulimia, and work backward. When Terri collapsed, she weighed about 115 pounds. When we married, she was

approximately 130 pounds. She was losing weight so quickly before our wedding that between the second fitting of her gown and our ceremony, the dress had to be pinned into place. When we met, she was approximately 160 pounds. When she was in high school, she had ballooned to nearly 250 pounds. The questions that have to be asked are why did she lose all that weight? And *how* did she lose all that weight?

There's no doubt in my mind that Terri was suffering from bulimia nervosa. The experts don't know the causes of the disorder with any degree of certainty, but they do know that if an individual is vulnerable to the disease, environmental factors such as verbal abuse can trigger it.

Terri told me from the time she was in seventh or eighth grade through high school, her father ridiculed her about her weight [e.g., "she got fat jokes and offers of money to slim down"]. The older she got, the worse the ridicule. It was so intense, she often ran to her room in tears and cried herself to sleep.

Daughters want to hear expressions of unconditioned love and support from their fathers, not put-downs because of the way they look. The damage done is long-term.

Mr. Schiavo also recalled Terri telling him how her brother Bobby

managed to get hold of her driver's license with its photo of her as an overweight teenager, and when visitors would come to the house, he and her father got big laughs out of showing it around. Terri told me that while her mom would yell at Bobby and even whack him with a broomstick for doing it, she never put a stop to it: She never stepped in to protect her daughter from the ridicule of her father, and she never took the damned photo away from them.[25]

Although bulimia and its personal history in Terri's life may have been the primary causes of her collapse, the central issue in the case was the severity of her brain damage. Short of a "miracle," a person in a PVS has no hope of regaining the consciousness that is needed to hear and respond to the call of conscience. Nor is this person capable of acknowledging others and of knowing that he or she is being acknowledged. Indeed, the person "is a vegetable" and thus requires others to speak on their behalf.[26]

Having "faith in God," however, can trump this discouraging reality. Miracles can happen; science does not necessarily have the final say. The power of Western religion is made possible in great part by the belief that when the call of conscience exposes us to the anxiety of the unknown, God is always there to grant us the life-giving gift of acknowledgment when no one else cares to do so. One need not ever be alone in the midst of the unknown. The rhetorical act of "prayer" is thought to help. God, too, is known to say "Here I am!" when the question is asked, "Where art thou?" As noted in chapter 2, the concept of "god" without the life-giving gift of acknowledgment is rather vacuous.[27]

The world most likely never would have heard about the Terri Schiavo case if her parents did not decide to go public with their perception of their daughter's circumstances and to beg that she not be "murdered." The Schindlers were determined to set the record straight, especially given their perception of how the media unfairly depicted them as "unreasonable people, even fanatics," people rotten with perfection. A rhetorical interruption was called for. Recall that in the preface to their book on the "legacy" of their daughter, they write, "We believe that Terri was nothing less than the victim of judicial murder. And if by revealing ourselves as we really are, and Terri as she really was, means that no one else shares Terri's fate, then our story will be the one memorial Terri would have wanted."[28]

Michael Schiavo, too, was primarily interested in revealing the truth about the horrible situation. His book offers his "personal account of the lengthy battle that [he] fought to see that Terri's wishes were fulfilled. . . . The book is [his] opportunity to introduce the real Terri Schiavo" to readers and to show them that, contrary to what the Schindlers and their supporters maintained about his character, he was not rotten with perfection.[29] Michael Schiavo, too, believed that a rhetorical interruption was desperately needed.

Terri collapsed. A call of conscience was sounded. The call may have come earlier given Terri's eating habits and physical condition, but nobody gave it enough careful thought. Such a call is a catalyst for anxiety and summons us to think and act in a caring and resolute way. For Terri and her family, a moment of truth was at hand, a moment whose duration would last fifteen years. After that, according to the Schindlers and their supporters, Terri was murdered. But was this in fact the case when her PEG tube was removed the third and final time? The act certainly constitutes a form of "passive euthanasia": the legal withholding or withdrawing of life-prolonging and life-sustaining technologies.

Anything more "active" than that (injecting a patient with potassium chloride, for example) does constitute murder.

The different stories told by the Schindlers, Michael Schiavo, and their respective supporters illustrate how rhetorical competence is employed to respond to a call of conscience and to acknowledge and reveal as honestly and effectively as possible the truth about Terri—the source of the call. "Where art thou?" "Here I am!"

The Schindlers and their supporters had no doubt that God was on their side as they accused others of murder. Terri's brother Bobby made it perfectly clear: Terri "touched millions of people around the world. Christ works through the most vulnerable and the most sick. And I think this is a perfect example of Him using Terri—being the most vulnerable and sick—and how she's been able to change the world from a position of complete vulnerability. As evil as her killing was, we can also look at the good that's eventually going to come from it."[30] The Schindlers and their supporters had a moral obligation to put forth this "truth claim" and to be the agents heeding God's call to acknowledge a loved one in desperate need of help.

Why God had yet to perform the task never became an issue in the fifteen-year debate over Ms. Schiavo's physiological status and "quality of life." The rhetoric of the right to life excuses such inaction by emphasizing the more serious and sinful actions encouraged by the rhetoric of the right to die. This rhetoric, for example, is criticized for showing utter disrespect for the teachings of Pope John Paul II, which emphasized the need to sustain a "culture of life," especially regarding such matters as abortion and euthanasia. President Bush, Senator Frist, and many like-minded souls made much of this point in their support of the Schindlers' request not to kill their daughter. They thereby sided with the view, as articulated by the pope in a 2004 proclamation, that "the administration of food and water, even when provided by artificial means, *always* represents a *natural means* of preserving life, *not a medical act*."[31] The Schindlers considered this statement to be "a blessing from God." They "felt humbled, thankful, awed, and wildly excited." The statement offered "new evidence" supporting their position. "The legal system failed [them]. A higher court lifted [them] up."[32] In a full-page advertisement

("The Truth about Terri Schiavo") in *USA Today*, the Life Legal Defense Foundation emphasized how "true" the Pope's assessment was and then went on to belittle the courts who didn't see the light: the courts constantly refer to Terri's "gastric feeding tube as 'life support'—as if she's hooked up to a machine that is keeping her alive. If food and water is 'life support,' we're *all* on 'life-support'!"[33]

. The reasoning here is faulty, at least on empirical grounds. Ms. Schiavo's PEG tube *is*, in fact, a medical technology, a life-support device that artificially sustains the existence of patients who cannot swallow food and water or who would sustain further life-threatening injury if they tried. Ms. Schiavo was such a patient. Believing in miracles, of course, makes it easier to accept that, with the food and water that run through it, a PEG tube is transformed right before our eyes from a "medical act" to a "natural means." As seen in an editorial in the Catholic magazine *Commonweal*, however, this entire line of argument was not considered by all Catholics to be a morally sound act:

> For generations, Catholic moral teaching has attempted to balance the need to safeguard life with the need to allow for families and doctors to discontinue futile and burdensome treatment. Sound medical ethics tells us that the ultimate purpose of any medical treatment—including artificial hydration and nutrition—is to help the patient recover. If treatment fails to achieve this, at some point it must be judged unsuccessful and, when appropriate, abandoned. When a feeding tube is removed in such cases, the cause of death is rightly understood to be the underlying condition that made it impossible for the patient to swallow food and water in the first place. It is this kind of rigorous yet compassionate thinking that has earned Catholic moral principles an honored place in the public debate about end-of-life care. That Catholic voice must not be silenced or diminished.[34]

Here is stated the classic rationale for the "merciful morality" of passive euthanasia. Notice that the author's argument favors moving in the direction of the *particular* case, rather than emphasizing the abstraction of a "culture of life." The social critic Anna Quindlen makes the move with eloquence in her response to the Schiavo case. The culture of life, writes Quindlen,

> is an empty suit of a phrase, absent an individual to give it shape. There is no culture of life. There is the culture of our life, and the culture of mine. There is what each of us considers bearable, and

what we will not bear. There are those of us who believe that under certain conditions the cruelest thing you can do to people you love is to force them to live. There are those of us who define living not by whether the heart beats and the lungs lift but whether the spirit is there, whether the music box plays.[35]

Indeed, a music box that does not play music is just a box.

Quindlen speaks the rhetoric of the right to die—a rhetoric that is better known for emphasizing the existential, rather than the "holy," spirit of human being. In giving voice to the call of conscience, this rhetoric seeks to acknowledge and grant priority to the "personhood" of the patient (which may or may not entail some religious belief). The right-to-die movement insists that such acknowledgment must never be morally depleted in treating patients. This heartfelt way of attending to a person defines an ontologically oriented act of salvation that, as discussed above, requires that we answer the call of conscience by assuming the personal and ethical responsibility of making choices for ourselves and helping others, especially when the concerned parties are "backed up against life and being." The rhetoric of the right to die has something "religious" about it—something that no institutionalized religion can be without—even though this rhetoric makes little explicit use of God in formulating and expressing its arguments.

Indeed, salvation is not the exclusive right of religious doctrine. As any decent dictionary will confirm, the act occurs when someone or something is "saved" from destruction, failure, danger, or serious difficulty. The right-to-die movement supports salvation. It is dedicated to the above-noted belief "that under certain conditions the cruelest thing you can do to people you love is to force them to live" (especially when, in a living will, for example, they make clear their personal opposition to this "unmerciful" and "immoral" act of being forced by others to suffer a "living death").[36] Although Terri Schiavo left no living will, she did leave a husband who promised to save her from the abject pain and suffering that can accompany the lived body's miseries, inevitable decline, and eventual death. Michael Schiavo admitted that he "was very angry at God" for all that happened to his wife, but he also was willing to give God the benefit of the doubt: "if God had a purpose for Terri's illness and death, perhaps it was to make more people aware of the types of eating disorders such as the one from which she suffered. Going the next step, perhaps that awareness could result in interventions that might save lives."[37] Michael Schiavo's book about his wife's life and death is intended to be a story of and for salvation.

The euthanasia debate is filled with rhetoric that turns the linguistic tables on its participants. More often than not, however, it is the right-to-life movement that claims that God is most certainly on *its* side: Read your Bible! "Choose life"! Although it can be nearly at its end when a patient is experiencing the pain and suffering of a *living* death, life itself—an essential ingredient of perfection—is still on hand. The Schindlers and their supporters emphasized that

> Terri was NOT dying. She has *no* terminal disease or illness, and her brain injury is *not* lethal. She is merely disabled. And like millions of disabled Americans, she simply needs appropriate medical care. . . . Terri is NOT in pain or agony. She is *not* "suffering." Removing her feeding tube would *not* "put her out of her misery" or "let her die peacefully." It wouldn't even be "mercy killing." It would, in our opinion, be a cold-blooded *homicide*.[38]

Granted, Terri was not dying, and she was certainly disabled (a point that I will deal with in greater depth later). But who can say for sure that she was not suffering from a living death that, as she supposedly had already told her husband, she in no way would want to experience, and would have confirmed as much if she could have communicated with others? Terri was in desperate need of salvation. The call of conscience sounded by her physical condition is heard differently depending on the secular or religious definition of salvation one chooses to accept as being most truthful.

Arguments over determining correct definitions necessarily involve us with the phenomenon of perfection. Recall Kenneth Burke's insight: "The mere desire to name something by its 'proper' name, or to speak a language in its distinctive ways is intrinsically 'perfectionist.' What is more 'perfectionist' in essence than the impulse, when one is in dire need for something, to so state this need that one in effect 'defines' the situation?"[39] I certainly am being perfectionist with the rhetoric of perfection being discussed and applied here. There *is* something going on with the temporal and spatial structure of human existence that can be identified with the meaningful phrase "the call of conscience." "Salvation" *is* an especially fitting word to describe an act directed toward saving someone or something from a tortuous death. "Acknowledgment," too, speaks the truth for me as a term that names the process of consciousness whereby a person is being as open-minded as possible to any given matter of concern. In the Schiavo case, this specific process was continually at work as the various parties pleaded and argued for Terri's salvation. As seen in this case, however, the process is more involved than described so far.

Consider, for example, how psychologist Eugene Kennedy—"a longtime observer of the Roman Catholic Church"—directed the process in his syndicated article, "Mystery: Terri's Eyes Inflame our Questioning."[40] The article appeared five days before Ms. Schiavo died; it asks readers to recall the much-publicized edited Web video that the Schindlers made of their bedridden daughter with her wide-opened eyes.

Kennedy begins by noting that "Terri is our spring moon, silent and pale, fragile but not barren, circling us as we circle around her bedside. Her eyes hold us even when we want to lower our heads and look away." According to Kennedy, "we cannot look away from Terri's eyes because in their depths we glimpse a truth that makes us uneasy, that—as St. John of the Cross wrote on the Mount of Perfection—there is no way here, no certainty possible for us here either." Terri's eyes speak "silently of the intrinsic uncertainty of the human condition. . . . We cannot break away from Terri's eyes because their depths reflect the mystery of being human, the mystery that by its very nature cannot be solved but can only be entered and lived." Kennedy considers this "boundless mystery of existence" as being "the common ground of both religion and science." The mystery, argues Kennedy, is what is forgotten by "the classic American impulse for pragmatic solutions built on certainty, on solving the problem in can-do fashion so that we can shake Terri's image out of our heads and move on." Kennedy, however, would have us remember as he ends his article, "We cannot look away from this woman's eyes for we find our own image reflected in them, the mystery we share with her and with each other, the great spiritual mystery expressed by Joseph Campbell to all religious insight: *Tat tuam asi*—This is you."

This "oneness" of the self and the other—a phenomenon long praised for its "goodness" and "beauty," especially as it signals a connection with "Almighty Being"—presents itself when we look at Terri and she looks at us.[41] Kennedy could turn to Elaine Scarry for support of his thesis. Recall that, for Scarry, that otherness of something deemed beautiful "calls" for the interpretive workings of acknowledgment, for our being open to the "aliveness" of a person or object, an aliveness that makes the person's or object's "abrasive handling seem unthinkable. The mind recoils—as from a wound cut into living flesh." The recoil, however, "incites deliberation" with oneself and others as a way of ensuring long-lasting respect for the goodness, beauty, and truth of something *that is*. Kennedy facilitates the process as he writes of Terri's presence—the heavenly spirit of her eyes that shine like a "spring moon."

Neurological science tells us that patients in a PVS can open their eyes, turn their heads, and display facial expressions, but they have no awareness of their surroundings. Facial expressions occur randomly and are "thought to be reflexes" that are not connected with any thought or emotion.[42] Kennedy takes advantage of the doubt (i.e., ". . . thought to be . . .") that is sometimes expressed by the medical profession when it comes to knowing all there is to know about a patient in Terri's condition. A few physicians employed by the Schindlers' lawyers maintained that Terri was actually in a state of "minimal consciousness" and that she thus was "perhaps" capable of responding with emotion to others.[43] Kennedy does not explicitly side with this view; rather, he emphasizes the uncertainty that informs its possibility—an uncertainty grounded in the openness (the ecstatic, outstanding, and thus heroic) character of human existence itself, wherefrom is heard the call of conscience. Kennedy's response to this call is to have us remain open to and acknowledge the openness of Terri's eyes, an openness well known for being a window not merely to the brain but, most importantly, to the soul and to the beauty of God's loving-kindness. Such beauty is acknowledged by believers as establishing the standard for treating others, especially those who are in need of help, like the "orphan," the "widow," and the "stranger" of the Old Testament.[44] Terri's eyes speak silently of ontological and metaphysical matters. This primordial discourse, along with Kennedy's rhetoric, admits an epideictic quality. The two function together to disclose and show forth a specific "truth": "the great spiritual mystery" of human being that continues to live on in Terri and that enables us to appreciate her circumstances in a most heartfelt manner. Terri's eyes are a synecdoche for her whole person, for the whole of humanity, and for the whole right-to-life movement, with its connection to God.

Kennedy sees "life" in Terri's severely diminished, but still beautiful and heroic, presence. His rhetoric encourages readers to identify with this "fact." But is the life at hand one that we would want to live? Although Kennedy makes much of uncertainty, there is little doubt, in my opinion, about the answer he is trying to encourage: in Terri's eyes/face, we see the "Other" (ourselves and God) calling for respect, reverence, and the hope allowed for by the objective uncertainty of existence. The "classic American impulse for pragmatic solutions built on certainty, on solving the problem in can-do fashion," should not apply here. Better to err on the side of life and the hope that comes with it. Hope makes room for salvation. The saving of life is a beautiful and heroic thing. Kennedy is acting heroically as he writes of a particular human being who is, herself, heroic in both an ontological and a metaphysical (religious) sense.[45]

Like its counterpart, the right-to-life movement knows the importance of paying homage to the particular, especially since it is the individual case that helps to inspire an understanding and acceptance of a higher truth. God calls to us through Terri, a human being with a particularly severe disability. In his critique of those who "pulled the plug" on Terri's life, the physician and neuroscientist Paul McHugh describes this disability when he emphasizes that "[b]y definition . . . PVS is not death hidden by machinery. It is human life under altered neurological circumstances."[46] This specific state of disability should not be confused with the state of "brain death." McHugh stresses the importance of this distinction by sharing a life-changing experience he had early in his career when attending to a patient "who, after a botched brain operation, had been left in an apathetic state not too different from Terri Schiavo."

The patient, a famous physician, "gave little evidence of awareness, responding mostly with groans and grimaces and moving little if at all." He remained in that state for thirteen years. Yet during this time there was that one moment when McHugh, in an act of desperation, shook the patient by the shoulder and asked him in a sharp voice, " 'Dr. A., what's the serum calcium in pseudopseudohypoparathyroidism?' For the first time in my experience with him, he glanced up at me and, loudly enough for all the interns to hear, said: 'It's just about normal.' " McHugh's conclusion of this specific story is worth noting:

> A full and complete sentence had emerged from a man whom none of us had ever heard speak before. His answer was correct—as he should know, having discovered and named the condition I asked him about. Subsequently, in all the months we cared for him, he would never utter another word. But what a difference that moment had made to all of us. We matured that day not only in matters of the mind but in matters of the heart. Somehow, deep inside that body and damaged brain, he was there—and our job was to help him. If we had ever had misgivings before, we would never again doubt the value of caring for people like him. And we didn't give a fig that his EEG was grossly abnormal.[47]

Like Kennedy, McHugh employs epideictic rhetoric to make his point. He praises the life of a severely disabled person and its educational potential. "To praise a [person]," writes Aristotle, "is in one respect akin to urging a course of action."[48] Kennedy has a more spiritual orientation in mind with his particular urging to respect Terri's life and *all* that it represents. There is something holy about Terri's existence. Rather than making this metaphysical move, McHugh adheres to a more empirical orientation and concentrates on the physiological nature of her disability. He offers precedent for understanding and treating this disability in a certain way. Such precedent is crucial for McHugh's argument. As he notes, "As soon as Terri Schiavo's case moved into the law courts of Florida, the concept of 'life under altered [neurological] circumstances' went by the boards—and so, necessarily, did any consideration of how to serve such life. Both have been trumped by the concept of 'life unworthy of life,' and how to end it."[49]

McHugh notes how this concept played a fundamental role in Nazi Germany's "culture of death." The comparison is a commonplace in the euthanasia debate. But is it legitimate in the

Schiavo case? I know of no instance in which right-to-die advocates assumed a fascist state of mind and described Terri's life
as being *unworthy* of life. On the contrary, the rhetoric of the
right to die, as noted above, acknowledges and compassionately
addresses the problem of being backed up against life and being
and the pain and suffering that turns this state of existence into
an "undignified" living death. The rhetoric of the right to die
also speaks of salvation and heroism. Hence exists the argument
that helping one to die with dignity does not merely put an end to
dignity; rather, it also may help both to demonstrate and to serve
as a reminder of this virtue's essential worth. Being the ultimate
sacrifice, dying with dignity can define a holy act (*sacer facere*,
"to make holy")—one that not only allows a patient a last chance
for taking some control over the final chapter of his or her life
story before it is too late, but also one that pays homage to the
well-being of others and their need for narratives that, as much
as possible, have a good ending. Self-respecting human beings
who hold a loving concern for others have an interest in the kind
of memories that will survive after death. When they call out,
"Where art thou?" and request release, we owe it to them to say
"Here I am!" It is a matter of mercy, not murder; a matter that
calls for the life-giving gift of acknowledgment as a way of being
for others who want to be remembered for the way they lived
and died with dignity rather then for the way they ended up suffering in a prolonged and abject state of "living death." Human
beings have a desire to *live on* in the *fond* memories of others; it
is a mark of having done something right, good, if not perfect,
during our earthly existence.[50]

McHugh sees this argument as lying at the heart of "contemporary bioethics." In the last paragraph of his article, he notes
that this particular field of study "has become a natural ally of
the culture of death, but the culture of death itself is a perennial human temptation; for onlookers in particular, it offers a
reassuring answer ('this is how X would have wanted it') to otherwise excruciating dilemmas, and it can be rationalized every
which way till Sunday." He concludes by emphasizing the point:
"The more this culture continues to influence our thinking, the
deeper are likely to become the divisions within our society and
within our families, the more hardened our hatreds, and the more

manifold our fears. More of us will die prematurely; some of us will even be persuaded that we want to."[51]

Advocates of the right to life do not accept their counterparts' tendency to associate themselves with acts of salvation and heroism. The "sin" here is a "misuse" of terms that puts us on a slippery slope where people with severe disabilities are encouraged to understand that they have an "obligation" eventually to end their lives for the benefit of others. Such reasoning could easily be dismissed as an unethical fear appeal if not for evidence that, as it showed itself in the Schiavo case, suggested that the appeal has some purchase. The evidence came from disability civil rights groups like "Not Dead Yet!" (NDY)—an organization that opposes the rhetoric of the right to die and whose presence in the Schiavo case provided additional empirical (in your face) substance to her circumstances.

The members of NDY are persons whose physical disabilities might encourage others to think and say, "I wouldn't want to exist that way," but whose desire to live on enables them to cope with these disabilities. One of the added burdens that goes with these disabilities is having to deal with the way advocates of the right to die often advance arguments by telling stories of pain and suffering that the disabled know all too well but that now are being employed for the specific purpose of having people realize that they have the right *not* to live that way. This added burden is ethically and rhetorically significant. The disabled who want to live on are made to listen to discourse that uses the material of their lives to justify why people who suffer as they do need not, and should not be forced to, live on. The disabled thus find themselves in a situation in which their own existence, which has already been marginalized by society, is now actually being turned against them by people whose stories and arguments, ironically, are meant to ease the pain and suffering of disabled individuals.[52]

In discussing the Schiavo case, Stephen Drake, the head research analyst for NDY, stressed that "thousands of people with disabilities across the United States are watching the [Schiavo] case anxiously. . . . Obviously, we want to know how all those commenting in this case feel about the lives of people with Down's syndrome, autism, Alzheimer's and other disabilities. Are they next for death through starvation? It's not so farfetched." Drake cites a few cases from the 1970s and 1980s to support his perception of the slippery slope and its consequences. He stresses that "medical professionals" are known to "grossly underestimate the quality of life of people with disabilities compared with what we ourselves [people with disabilities] report. The same professionals are also more likely to regard certain disabilities as 'worse than death' than are the public or families of people with severe disabilities." Adding to the problem, Drake insists, is how the issues at hand are "inaccurately portrayed as a battle between 'progressives' and 'religious conservatives.' People with disabilities end up as 'collateral damage' in that kind of extension of the 'culture war.'" Drake notes that he was spared this fate: "I was born brain-damaged as a result of a forceps delivery. The doctor told my parents I would be a 'vegetable' for the rest of my life—the same word now being used for Schiavo—and that the best thing would be for nature to take its course. They refused. Although I had a lot of health problems, surgeries and pain as a child, I went on to lead a happy life."[53]

The NDY once called its proactive campaign against the right to die "The National Heroes Campaign." Disabled individuals *stand out* from the crowd not only because of their particular bodily presence, but also because they have the courage to face the physical, psychological, social, and political problems that accompany their existence. NDY members are not yet ready to die, but reactions to their presence can often make them feel that their life "is not worth living." Moreover, according to Drake, people like him are often made to think that they are too much of a drain on the health-care economy. "There are probably even more bioethicists and [right-to-die] advocates," he claims, "who feel the same but aren't willing to be honest about it. We feel that if people want to use economic considerations to end the lives of people like Terri Schiavo, let them be frank about it instead of hiding the motivation behind terms like 'compassion,' 'dignity,' and 'choice.'"[54]

Drake and his NDY colleagues want justice, for, despite their disabilities, they "still have rights." These rights have an ontological status: as is the case with all human beings, the presence of people with severe disabilities sounds a call of conscience. They want to be acknowledged for who they are: human beings whose existence, in truth, stands out in a heroic and beautiful way and warrants respect. Although their mere presence may make *us* feel uncomfortable because it offers a stunning display of difference, otherness, our own finitude and fallibility, our inevitable fate of decline, decay, and unattractiveness, it nevertheless is a presence that clearly admits a love of life. The disabled seek salvation from the social death of discrimination. They want to feel at home with others in their everyday existence. In short, they desire to live lives that are as perfect as they can be. Who can blame them? Human beings are metaphysical creatures: we *are* perfection in the making, in search of a "dwelling place" (ethos) where we feel comfortable with others.[55]

The Schiavo case provided a rhetorical situation in which the voice of the disabled and their supporters could be heard loud and clear, even as the person at the center of the controversy remained mute. From the right-to-life movement comes a rhetoric of perfection that is meant to tell the truth and that calls for justice. The call is oftentimes startling: "Well, Terri Schiavo has finally died from starvation. The American Civil Liberties Union and the Humane Society would never have allowed a mass-murderer or an animal to slowly starve to death. Terri's problem was that she was innocent and human."[56]

Right-to-die advocates counter such claims with their own rhetoric of perfection. Although this rhetoric presents problems for the disabled, it does not deny justice for any patient whose love of life encourages them to maintain a heroic stance in their continuing quest for genuine acknowledgment. What this rhetoric does insist on, however, is that heroism be understood to include certain acts of sacrifice on the parts of a particular class of patients and their caregivers. For right-to-die advocates, when the dying are able to demonstrate whatever is left of their dignity (for example, freedom of choice), they may help combat the "endless" suffering that their loved ones are often sentenced to after the dying process. Wanting to die with dignity out of respect for oneself and others can be a heroic and holy act. What Martin Foss said about the matter forty years ago still holds true for the right-to-die movement:

> Sacrifice, even if it is a sacrificial death, is not an end but a transition to a new beginning. It is an offering which in its passing way

is somehow preserved because it integrates and intensifies that for which it was an offering. In the sacrificial deed, that which is seemingly destroyed is made to live on and is thus not only preserved but— more than that—is elevated [*dignitas*] and plays a role in a higher sphere of meaning. Here is a destruction which turns into a creation, it is an end which converts into a beginning and has meaning beyond mere destruction.[57]

Sacrifice is a mighty act of justice.

The courts allowed for such justice in the Schiavo case. They did it by remaining true to the letter of the law: *stare decisis*. Here is how it is stated in the majority opinion of the United States Court of Appeals for the Eleventh Circuit:

> There is no denying the absolute tragedy that has befallen Mrs. Schiavo. We all have our own family, our own loved ones, and our own children. However, we are called upon to make a collective, objective decision concerning a question of law. In the end, and no matter how much we wish Mrs. Schiavo had never suffered such a horrible accident, we are a nation of laws, and if we are to continue to be so, the pre-existing and well established federal law governing injunctions . . . must be applied to her case. While the position of our dissenting colleague has emotional appeal, we as judges must decide this case on the law.[58]

The Court adheres to a "standard of perfection" found in our legal system: be objective, nonemotional, true to established precedent in order to ensure that one "interprets" the law rather than "constructs" it. In the Schiavo case, granting an injunction against removing her PEG tube required, among other things, that "a substantial likelihood of success on the merits" was established such that it was reasonable to believe that Terri would awaken from her PVS and that rehabilitation was possible. Time and again the courts maintained that the plaintiffs failed to make this case.

Ironically, the standard of perfection at work here is a staple of conservative legal thought that is commonly associated with such Supreme Court justices as Antonin Scalia and Clarence Thomas, informs the worldview of right-to-life advocates, and pays homage to the priority of states' rights. The irony was especially vivid as conservative political leaders (e.g., Republican Tom DeLay) threatened the courts with retribution if they failed to relax their grip on the law in order to be more humane toward

Terri and her parents. The legal judgments of the state of Florida and the federal courts were wrong, according to DeLay and like-minded politicians: a long-trusted standard of perfection should not be made to call itself into question when an "innocent" life is at stake.[59]

Innocence and justice are supposed to go together. The right-to-die movement has long objected to how this relationship can be manipulated by right-to-life advocates. James Rachels speaks to the problem when he notes, "it is simply irrelevant to urge, as a reason against euthanasia, that the one to be killed is innocent. The fact that he is not an aggressor has nothing to do with the issue; what is relevant is that he is dying wretchedly."[60] The rhetoric of innocence gets in the way of remedying this horrible situation. Although the actions of the courts in the Schiavo case gave the impression that such manipulation should not be tolerated by the judiciary, the courts consistently stayed clear of this emotional and rhetorical issue. Perfection demanded as much.

Once the PEG tube was removed for the last time, polls showed that the majority of Americans believed that Terri should be allowed to die as much of a dignified death as was now possible. Quindlen comments on this specific fact: those who sided with Michael Schiavo did so "probably because they've been there. They are the true judges and lawmakers and priests. They've been at the bedside, watching someone they love in agony as cancer nipped at the spine, as the chest rose and fell with the cruel mimicry of the respirator, as the music of personality dwindled to a single note and then fell silent. They know life when they see it, and they know it when it is gone."[61] The Schindlers and their supporters, however, knew no such thing. A legal standard of perfection was perceived as being terribly deficient when compared to another standard of perfection informed and motivated by a rhetoric of conscience, acknowledgment, truth, salvation, heroism, beauty, and justice. As employed by advocates of the right to life, this rhetoric voiced great displeasure and hatred toward Michael Schiavo. He was selfish and cruel; he was a cause of Terri's bulimia; he wanted his wife to die not for *her* benefit but for *his*; he wanted to be saved from further psychological and economic costs that came with the holy act of saving Terri's life. Such accusations were ever apparent in the media "feeding frenzy" that accompanied the Schiavo case, especially in the last six months of Terri's life.[62]

Michael Schiavo believed he was engaging in an act of salvation by ordering the removal of the medical technology that sustained his wife's living death. Standing at her bedside after her PEG tube was removed for the final time, he said that he felt that "peace was happening" for her: "And I felt like she was finally going to get what she wants, and be at peace . . . with the Lord."[63] Attaining this peace would not bring on the suffering of starvation because, as physicians pointed out, the part of the brain that allows a person to suffer was not functioning in Terri's case.[64]

Michael Schiavo was steadfast in keeping his "promise" to his wife. For right-to-die advocates, the action, although tragic, was still heroic, beautiful, and just. Indeed, as Georges Gusdorf notes, "to give one's word" not only grants others genuine acknowledgment, it also "shows the human capacity of self-affirmation despite all material restrictions. It is the disclosure of a human being as he really is, the projection of value into existence. . . . He who breaks his word is dishonored not only in the eyes of others, but in his own eyes as well."[65] Michael Schiavo refused to break his word. The Christian value of "perfect suffering" (Heb 2:10) no longer applied. The suffering had lasted fifteen years. All this time there sounded a call of conscience, a plea for acknowledgment, a desire for salvation and justice. This desire says something beautiful about human being, something that stands out in this being's character but that is not made by human hands. We are metaphysical creatures. We have a nostalgia for completeness in our lives. We are fated to exist as perfection in the making, a process operating in a deconstructive and reconstructive manner. God may be *the* cause of this process. God certainly is one of its persistent *outcomes*.

This process was no longer present in Terri's being. Michael Schiavo believed he did the right thing in helping his wife to die a dignified death. A rhetoric of perfection informed and aired his rationale. The phenomenological components of this rhetoric are the same ones found in the rhetoric of those who condemned Mr. Schiavo and his supporters. Perfection is a matter of conscience, acknowledgment, truth, salvation, heroism, beauty, reason, and justice. The controversy that marked the Schiavo case had much to do with how concerned parties chose to interpret and act out their understanding of these phenomena. The controversy continues as I write. Coming to terms with perfection is no easy matter for beings whose existence is ontologically structured such that it is constantly calling itself into question.

CONCLUSION

The life and death of Terri Schiavo was a catalyst for displaying the scope and function of these terms. Did the Schindlers and their supporters tell the whole truth? Did they engage in exaggeration and hyperbole in making their case as perfect as possible? How about Michael Schiavo and his supporters? Each side saw the other as being rotten with perfection. Each side employed the same rhetoric of perfection to make their case. Both sides, however, at least agreed on one thing: Terri Schiavo offered this country a "gift": yet another opportunity to debate publicly and to come to terms with what the "good life" and the "good death" are all about.[66] The beauty of this gift is associated with, among other things, its way of inciting deliberation and public moral argument in the name of reason and justice. Hence, the rhetoric of perfection showed itself in the Schiavo case, a rhetoric that tells how perfection can be both a benefit and a burden to beings who have it in their nature to desire its completeness. Sincere efforts in the moral practice of rhetoric can nevertheless lead to the pathology of matters becoming rotten with perfection.

This pathology breeds closed-mindedness, which by definition is not attuned to the spatial and temporal workings of human being and the way they open us to the objective uncertainty of our existence. The happening of human being calls for open-mindedness and a genuine acknowledgment of otherness. Ontologically speaking, we are being most true to ourselves when answering this call of conscience. Life-and-death situations like the Schiavo case bring us face-to-face with these and related matters regarding our perfectibility, our complete incompleteness. We employ our rhetorical competence in order to help adjudicate these matters in a reasonable and just way. Failing the task is always a possibility, and when this happens, the rhetoric being employed can certainly cause dissatisfaction, disappointment, disdain, and even outright loathing for the art and its practitioners. The public moral argument informing the Schiavo controversy is a case in point.

Despite its failings in any given situation, however, the art of rhetoric still warrants respect as a practice that serves our ethical and moral responsibility of being open to, acknowledging, and caring for otherness and that thus has a role to play in administering to our desire for perfection. At the present moment of our evolutionary history, it can be no other way. We remain what Hans Blumenberg terms "creatures of deficiency"—creatures whose "human nature" is not perfectly one with the otherness of nature itself and who must therefore use language in a rhetorically competent way to understand the circumstances at hand and to produce the "mutual understanding, agreement, or toleration on which the actor depends." Such action "compensates for the 'indeterminateness' [the objective uncertainty] of the creature man, and the place of the 'substantial' base of regulatory processes in order to make action possible." The dialogical intent of rhetoric "implies the renunciation of force." In short, Blumenberg emphasizes that "rhetoric is a system not only of soliciting mandates for action but also of putting into effect and defending, both with oneself and before others, a self-conception that is in the process of formation or has been formed" with some degree of perfection in mind.[67]

This process was at work as both sides in the Schiavo controversy attempted to reveal "the real Terri" along with their "true selves." A rhetoric of perfection served one side better than the other. The "true" meanings of various terms composing this rhetoric remain contested, however. The situation poses a question: how much more robust, lucid, and persuasive will the rhetoric have to become in the euthanasia debate before this debate is, if at all possible, brought to a perfect ending in which all can live and die in peace? Having reached this goal, rhetoric would no longer be needed.

I have already noted how the fathers of scientific medicine, the Hippocratics, saw rhetoric as a sign of failure. Recall: "There are in fact two things, science and opinion; the former begets knowledge, the latter ignorance." A perfect ending for medical science is finding a cure for diseases. This achievement helps relieve medicine from the burdens of rhetoric. Science and technology, not the orator's art, are what protect and prolong life. There would have been no need for rhetoric in the Schiavo case if medicine had the biotechnological know-how to treat and reverse Terri Schiavo's physiological condition.

Although medical science has yet to accomplish such a "miraculous" achievement, its present-day biotechnology revolution is certainly aimed in that direction. Medicine is currently and quickly enhancing and perfecting its health-care calling with such things as DNA diagnostic tools, gene-discovery software applications, embryonic cloning procedures, stem cell research, regenerative medicine, psychotherapeutic drugs, organ harvesting and transplantation, and plastic surgery techniques. Biotechnology offers itself as *the* scientific way of enhancing and extending the lived body's existence; it makes us less the slaves to illness, pain, disability, and premature death. Commenting on this development in his book *Enhancing Evolution: The Ethical Case for Making Better People*, John Harris writes,

> It is significant that we have reached a point in human history at which further attempts to make the world a better place will have to include not only changes in the world, but also changes to humanity, perhaps with the consequence that we, or our descendants, will cease to be human in the sense in which we now understand this idea. The possibility of a new phase of evolution in which Darwinian evolution, by natural selection, will be replaced by a deliberately chosen process of selection, the results of which, instead of having to wait the millions of years over which Darwinian evolutionary change has taken place, will be seen and felt almost immediately. This new process of evolutionary change will replace *natural selection* with *deliberate selection*, *Darwinian evolution* with *"enhanced evolution."*[68]

As witnessed on the Web site of the Cato Institute, the growing reality of enhanced evolution has even led bioethics scholars to debate the topic, "Do We Need Death? The Consequences of Radical Life Extension."[69]

Those who have been termed "the new conservatives in bioethics," critics like Francis Fukuyama, for example, would, however, have us respond with caution to biotechnological progress and what they argue is its "significant threat": namely "that it will alter human nature and thereby move us into a 'posthuman' stage of history" in which a genuine understanding and appreciation of

"human dignity" is likely to become tragically confused and mis-
leading.[70] Dismayed by what they perceive to be a lack of normative moral standards in today's "postmodern culture," Fukuyama
and his fellow conservatives in the biotechnology debate warn
against the possibility of humankind becoming rotten with perfection. The rebuttal to this warning can be phrased in terms of
my project: although too much perfection can lead to disaster, not
having enough of this specific *pharmakon* can also be dangerous
to our health. Along with the ailment of being rotten with perfection, we must also take seriously the disease of being "rotten
with imperfection," of not doing enough to tap the full potential of human being. This disease, too, is an assault on our dignity. Remember, we are metaphysical creatures who have a desire
for the fullness and completeness of perfection. Cases like Terri
Schiavo's pose an impasse to this desire. But they also serve as a
catalyst for the desire's drive to overcome any such impasse.

In the next chapter, I turn my attention to the current U.S.
debate over the benefits and burdens of developing biotechnologies to perfect our lives. The debate returns medical science to
the challenges of rhetoric and to such related issues as the good
life, the good death, and the lived body's perfectibility. A rhetoric
of perfection is present in the debate; it is anchored to two related
and contested terms that lie at the heart of the controversy: "the
giftedness of life" and "human dignity." My assessment of the
debate centers on the controversy over the use of these terms, especially as this controversy was incited and continues to be fueled
by various publications of the President's Council on Bioethics
(PCB) and the personal viewpoints of the noted physician, conservative bioethics scholar, and past chairman and present member of the PCB Leon Kass. Although these specific sources define
but a small portion of a very robust and sometimes mean-spirited
debate, they nevertheless are required readings for anyone who is
interested in the perfectionism that stimulates public moral argument over the benefits and burdens of biotechnology.*

* On June 10, 2009, when this book was already in the production stage at the press, President
Barack Obama notified the members of the PCB that their work as a "philosphically" oriented
group of experts responsible for encouraging public moral argument about the potential consequences of biotechnological progress would end on June 11. Organized by the Bush administration,
the PCB was seen by the Obama administration as having a neo-conservative slant that was not
conducive to Obama's views on health care. Obama's current intention is to appoint a new bioethics
body whose mandate will call for "practical policy options." The views I advance in the next chapter on the importance of public moral argument encourage me to disagree with Obama's decision.
My assessment of the council's discourse, however, remains unaffected by this decision.

CHAPTER NINE

THE BIOTECHNOLOGY DEBATE

In his award-winning book *Redesigning Humans: Choosing Our Genes, Changing Our Future*, Gregory Stock speaks to us of what in the literatures of computer science and biotechnology is termed a "transhumanist" or "posthumanist":

> We know that *Homo sapiens* is not the final word in primate evolution, but few have yet grasped that we are on the cusp of profound biological change, poised to transcend our current form and character on a journey to destinations of new imagination. . . . Some imagine we will see the perils, come to our senses, and turn away from such possibilities. But when we imagine Prometheus stealing fire from the gods, we are not incredulous or shocked by his act. It is too characteristically human. To forgo the powerful technologies that genomics and molecular biology are bringing would be as out of character for humanity as it would be to use them without concern for the dangers they pose. We will do neither. The question is no longer whether we will manipulate embryos, but when, where, and how. . . . Well before this new millennium's close, we will almost certainly change ourselves enough to become much more than simply human.[1]

The change referred to here is championed by posthumanists who appreciate the vision of what was earlier termed "postmodern wisdom": a wisdom directed by the call of conscience that lies at the heart of human existence and that encourages us to stay *wide* open to the future, to its possibilities, and to how we might improve the human condition with, for example, the help of science and technology. The transformation, of course, is already underway. There was, for example, the Enlightenment. Eventually came the computer revolution. No technology in the history of humankind (with the exception of language itself) allows for and facilitates an experimenting with self-identity and acknowledging others more than the personal computer. Cyberspace offers itself as a postmodern dream become reality: an awesome transformation of space and time, an immense and easily accessible dwelling place for people to meet, possibly feel at home with others, and thereby know together what is going on in their lives. Sherry Turkle thus sees cyberspace as exhibiting "a postmodern ethos."[2] Indeed, here is a habitat made possible by the wonders of science and technology and where the challenge-response (deconstructive-reconstructive) logic of human being is constantly being demonstrated in calls and responses. With these calls and responses, one might even feel that there is something holy going on here: "Where art thou?" "Here I am!" The call of conscience and the call of technology go hand in hand.[3]

The ways and means of cyberspace speak to us not so much of our being *totally* posthuman as they do of our heading in that direction. Actually becoming God, of course, would be the ultimate posthuman event. Artificial intelligence scientists like Hans Moravec and Ray Kurzweil head us in this awesome direction when discussing how humans will eventually be capable of downloading the cognitive self into computers so that they can outlive their bodies. The goal here is to transcend biology. Immortality awaits us.[4]

Taken with the call of technology, the scientist as posthumanist not only has a postmodern attitude toward the openness and possibilities of the future, but also revives the Enlightenment's zeal for scientific and technological progress as the ultimate means for perfecting humankind. Key principles for conducting this work include "perpetual progress," "self-transformation," "practical optimism," "intelligent technology," "open society," "self-direction," and "rational thinking."[5] Such zeal is a source of criticism for many postmodernist critics who are concerned, for example, with the relationship between "patriarchal capitalism" and the "business" of developing biotechnologies.[6] The scientist as posthumanist answers these critics by making much of how his or her work is dedicated not only to improving the self's existence but also the existence of others as biotechnology continues developing its tools (e.g., stem cell research, regenerative medicine, human embryonic cloning procedures) for the betterment of humankind. Having such tools at hand, the scientist as posthumanist is committed to fighting the disease of being rotten with imperfection.

With all of these postmodernist and posthumanist thoughts and developments in mind, the newly formed President's Council on Bioethics (PCB) was charged on November 28, 2001, with deliberating about the benefits and burdens of biotechnology and then publishing these deliberations as a way to "spark and inform public debate" about the matter throughout the nation. President Bush appointed the noted physician and conservative bioethics scholar Leon Kass to chair the PCB, which consisted of sixteen additional members from the fields of medicine, law, political economy, biochemistry and biophysics, psychology, cognitive science, biology, psychiatry, philosophy, political science, philosophy, and business management. Here is an example of how this distinguished, but not always agreeing, group of experts phrased the issue:

> Seemingly from the beginning, human beings have been alive to the many ways in which what we have been given falls short of what we can envision and what we desire. We are human, but can imagine gods. We die, but can imagine immortality. . . . Although [human beings] are far from omnipotent, we have extraordinary powers, unique among the earth's creatures, to shape our environment and even ourselves according to our wills. It is perhaps not surprising, therefore, that also from the beginning human beings have struggled with two opposing responses to our lot. Should we try to mold the imperfection we have been given into something closer to our ideal? Or should we content ourselves with beholding and enjoying it as it is? And what about our own natures? Does our ability to flourish as human beings depend on our ability to improve upon the human form or function? Or might the contrary be true: does our flourishing depend on accepting—or even celebrating—our natural limitations?[7]

The PCB readily and repeatedly admits that our "extraordinary powers" have enabled medical science to develop a vast number of life-saving ("therapeutic") and life-bettering ("enhancing") technologies. The PCB, however, is especially concerned with how these powers, their medical successes, and the consequences of these successes might condition us to undervalue our "natural limitations" and thus to perceive them only as imperfections that must be remedied if at all possible. The fear of being rotten with imperfection might result in our becoming rotten with perfection. Here is how the PCB frames the problem:

> We want better children—but not only by turning procreations into manufacture or by altering their brains to gain them an edge over their peers. We want to perform better in the activities of life—but not by becoming mere creatures of our chemists or by turning ourselves into bionic tools designed to win and achieve in inhuman ways. We want longer lives—but not at the cost of living carelessly or shallowly with diminished aspiration for living well, and not by becoming people so obsessed with our own longevity that we care little about the next generations. We want to be happy—but not by means of a drug that gives us happy feelings without the real loves, attachments, and achievements that are essential for true human flourishing.[8]

Where are we to draw the line between being rotten with perfection and being rotten with imperfection? As noted above, the PCB admits that "we have been given" "extraordinary powers" and "natural limitations" that both promote and inhibit our ability to provide a definitive answer to the question. Who or what is the "giver" here? Where did the gift of life and all that it brings about come from? Might answers to these questions help in our deliberations and recommendations about the proper use of biotechnology for perfecting our lives?

These and many other questions raised by the PCB are meant to stimulate the interruptive and educational workings of public moral argument and the rhetoric that necessarily informs it. The PCB is aware of how rhetoric will play a role in its deliberations and in public reaction to its published report. In its first report, *Human Cloning and Human Dignity* (2002), the PCB makes much of its use of "fair and accurate terminology"—"especially because the choice of terms can decisively affect the way questions are posed, and hence how answers are given. We have sought terminology that most accurately conveys the descriptive reality of the matter, in order that the moral arguments can then proceed on the merits." The PCB also emphasizes that "we have resisted the temptation to solve the moral questions by artful redefinition or by denying to some morally crucial element a name that makes clear that there is a moral question to be faced."[9]

This attitude toward the mandatory use of fair and accurate terminology is a crucial feature of Enlightenment philosophy. Recall Immanuel Kant's argument that, when considering how humankind might achieve the "highest moral perfection," "popularity (vernacular) is unthinkable." Rather, "scholastic precision . . . even if such precision is denounced as meticulosity," must be granted priority in order to guard against rhetoric's ways of manipulating and deceiving others about the truth of some matter of interest. Rhetoric, of course, need not serve such an inauthentic end. The very existence of the PCB and its goal of encouraging public moral argument presupposes as much.[10]

Vivid illustrations of this point emerge with the PCB's use of the ontological notions "the giftedness of life" and "human dignity" to ground and direct its questioning of biotechnology's ever-developing ability to improve our lives. A detailed examination of these related rhetorical endeavors is offered below.

THE GIFTEDNESS OF LIFE AND HUMAN DIGNITY

The PCB considers the giftedness of life a "given"—an empirical and a priori fact of life. The PCB's fair and accurate definition of this given reads, "Acknowledging the giftedness of life means recognizing that our talents and powers are not wholly our own doing, nor even fully ours, despite the efforts we expend to develop and to exercise them. It also means recognizing that not everything in the world is open to any use we may desire or devise. Such an appreciation of the giftedness of life would constrain the Promethean project and conduce to a much-needed humility. Although it is in part a religious sensibility, its resonance reaches beyond religion."[11]

The PCB speaks to us of the giftedness of life like postmodern philosophers speak to us of the lived body and the "otherness" that characterizes human existence. We did not create the spatial and temporal structure, the openness, of our being and its inherent call of conscience. We "are not wholly our own doing." Certain questions come to mind: Who or what else is at work here? How is it that its call of conscience requires us to recognize "that not everything in the world is open to any use we may desire or devise" and that "humility" is thus called for? What else is called for—all of the virtues that display the dignity of human being? Indeed, there seems to be a "religious sensibility" associated with the giftedness of life. But this gift "reaches beyond religion." To whom, what, where? Are there normative standards for perfect behavior to be found at the gift's source? Religion makes much of how what is beyond itself is the basis of its existence: God. Science, on the other hand, is content with the otherness of nature in its search for truth. Who or what is the ultimate giver of the giftedness of life?

With its discussion of the benefits and possible burdens of biotechnology, the PCB neither affirms nor denies that God is on its side with its understanding of the giftedness of life. Rather, the PCB typically refers to "nature" and writes in ways that are designed to stimulate discussion and debate about the matter, hence the questions that, as suggested above, can be raised about the PCB's definition of the phenomenon under consideration. Such questions expose the ambiguity that is at work in the PCB's fair and accurate definition of a normative standard that lies at the heart of their discussion. Yet, when matters are ambiguous, as they are in the biotechnology debate, is it not fair and accurate to employ a rhetorical maneuver that is as old as rhetorical theory itself and that is well known for its ability to stimulate public moral argument?

Kass defends the use of this rhetorical maneuver in his study of the book of Genesis. Kass reads this text as being concerned with a question that I first noted in chapter 6 and that is easily related to the biotechnology debate: "Is it possible to *find, institute, and preserve* a way of life, responsive to both the promise and the peril of the human creature, that *accords with man's true standing in the world* and that serves to *perfect his god-like possibilities*?" Recall that in his assessment of the book's discourse, Kass maintains that it "is precisely the text's sparseness, lacunae, ambiguity, reticence, and lack of editorial judgment that both permit and require the engagement of the reader." With these rhetorical qualities in mind, Kass stresses that the "open form of the text and its recalcitrance to final and indubitable interpretation are absolutely perfect instruments for cultivating the openness, thoughtfulness, and modesty about one's own understanding that is the hallmark of the pursuit of wisdom."[12] The book of Genesis is filled with the deconstructive workings of rhetorical interruptions.

Whether intentionally or not, the PCB uses a perfect instrument of rhetoric (i.e., ambiguity) to define in a fair and accurate way its essential notion of the giftedness of life. Postmodernist writers are known for their appreciation and use of such instruments to open others to possibilities for thought and action that presently are lost, marginalized, or going completely unnoticed in the cultural routines and rhetoric of the day.[13] With its notion of the giftedness of life, the PCB is cultivating postmodern wisdom. In the biotechnology debate, however, this deed tends to go unrecognized because of the ideological influences that are known to motivate the individual PCB members and that thereby attract their critics. Chairman Kass is, by far, the PCB member who appears most often in the crosshairs of these critics.

Kass, to be sure, is no deconstructionist, and he loathes the type of postmodern philosophy that such a critical stance supports.[14] Rather, his appreciation for ambiguity, especially as it can be used to stimulate our moral growth, is rooted in what is described by one of his defenders as "a natural law position colored by [the] religious revelation" of Judaism.[15] Indeed, throughout his writings, Kass speaks of the empirically based giftedness of life as something that is best interpreted with the help of a biblical cipher: the "image of God." We supposedly were created in this image. We are "godlike." Kass emphasizes both in his reading of Genesis and in his later, more secular-oriented *Life, Liberty, and the Defense of Dignity* that, being like God, we are blessed with "speech and reason, freedom in doing and making, and the powers of contemplation, judgment, and care"—the very qualities that enable human beings to imagine and be awed by God's presence and to spread the Word that said it all "in the beginning."[16]

Kass associates the dignity of human being with its "divine-like status," or what he also terms "human godliness." Interestingly, he also asks us to keep in mind that "the *truth* of the Bible's assertion [about humankind and God's image] does *not* rest on biblical authority: Man's more-than-animal status [his being godlike] is in fact performatively proved whenever human beings quit the state of nature and set up life under . . . a law . . . which exacts just punishment for shedding human (that is, more-than-animal) blood."[17] This last point places aside the question of whether or not the giftedness of life has a deeper source than itself. Past PCB members Francis Fukuyama and Michael Sandel, for example, would have us do just that.[18] The philosopher Jürgen Habermas also recommends as much in his critique of eugenic parenting.[19] But the natural law theology at work in Kass' rhetoric should not be missed, especially when it comes from one who would have us believe that "we stand most upright when we gladly bow our heads."[20]

Please keep in mind that I am discussing Kass as a way of clarifying a position that is often associated by critics with the PCB's "own" ideological worldview.[21] The PCB denies this assessment.[22] There is no argument in the PCB's reports suggesting that God directs its presentation of materials regarding the benefits and burdens of biotechnology. As used by the PCB, the giftedness of life is not necessarily associated with the workings of God. Rather, it is more a question of human nature. In the end, it might all be nothing more than the dynamics of logarithmic spirals and physical forces that bring about such perfection.

Still, I can understand why the assessment is made. Given his conservative religious bent, his appointment by a right-wing president, and the admired (even by critics) eloquence of his writing, Kass is *the* lightning rod of the PCB. He is well known for warning us about "a posthuman future" driven by our excitement over the "transforming powers" of biotechnology, some of which are already here: "The Pill. *In vitro* fertilization. Bottled embryos. Surrogate wombs. Cloning. Genetic screening. Genetic manipulation. Organ harvesting. Mechanical spare parts. Chimeras. Brain implants. Ritalin for the young. Viagra for the old. Prozac for everyone. And, to leave this vale of tears, a little extra morphine accompanied by Muzak."[23] Skepticism, cynicism, and some gentle humor are characteristic of Kass' writings. He does not hesitate to speak his mind: "[O]ur views of the meaning of humanity have been so transformed by the scientific-technological approach to the world and to life that we are in danger of forgetting what we have to lose, humanly speaking."[24]

The nature and dignity of human being reflects "the image of God"—an image that Kass terms a "miracle" that suspends the laws of nature and the reductionistic ways of science.[25]

Kass makes much of how the giftedness of life warrants more respect than biotechnology is oftentimes known to give it: "No friend of humanity cheers for a posthuman future." Kass reminds us of Aldous Huxley's *Brave New World* to help make his point: "At long last, mankind has succeeded in eliminating disease, aggression, war, anxiety, suffering, guilt, envy and grief. But this victory comes at the heavy price of homogenization, medical mediocrity, trivial pursuits, shallow attachments, debased tastes, spurious contentment and souls without loves or longings. The Brave New World has achieved prosperity, community, stability and near universal contentment, only to be inhabited by creatures of human shape but stunted humanity."[26] For Kass, stunted humanity cripples the giftedness of life and the "human godliness," the dignity, that the Giver of the gift makes possible.

This potential disaster is a central concern of the PCB, although it brackets out consideration of the ultimate source of the giftedness of life. Consider, for example, the PCB's chapter on creating "better children." Here the PCB discusses such issues as the ever-developing biotechnological practice of prenatal screening and its effect on the parent-child relationship. This practice

> establishes the principle that parents may choose the qualities of their children, and choose them on the basis of genetic knowledge. This new principle, in conjunction with the cultural norm [that encourages parents "to abort any abnormal fetus"], may already be shifting parental and societal attitudes toward prospective children: from simple acceptance to judgment and control, from seeing a child as an unconditionally welcome gift to seeing him as a conditionally acceptable project. If so, these changes in attitude might well carry over beyond choices confined to the presence or absence of genetic diseases, to the presence or absence of other desired qualities. Far from producing contentment and gratitude in the parents, such changes might feed the desire for better—and *still* better—children.[27]

We have here, of course, the construction of a slippery slope argument that suggests the danger of our becoming rotten with perfection: of our "extraordinary powers" going too far in transforming our "natural limitations." Recall that when the PCB framed the problem of being rotten with perfection versus being rotten with imperfection, it favored the directive of these limitations. Conservatives make much of the slippery slope argument being considered here. Developments in biotechnology can, for example, change "the traditional structure of the family."[28] What does it mean to be a good parent, a good child? Is it the case that attitudes toward prospective children are moving from simple acceptance to judgment and control, from seeing a child as an unconditionally welcome gift to seeing him or her as a conditionally acceptable product whose potential can be further enhanced by an ever-growing market of pharmaceutical medicaments? Conservative religious writers have "good reason" to speak of the child as a gift: "The Spirit itself beareth witness with our spirit, that we are the children of God" (Rom 8:16). "Every good gift and every perfect gift is from above, and cometh down from the Father of lights, with whom is no variableness, neither shadow of turning" (Jas 1:17). Adam and Eve forgot about the "no variableness." The sin of humankind begins with the fall.

Writing in the Hastings Center Report, Ruth Macklin tells of how Kass, "during a presentation on genetic selection and enhancement, emphasized that it is wrong for parents to be able to choose the traits of their children." His claim was based simply on the position that "children are a gift." Macklin's response is noteworthy: "Kass's answer may have been understood and accepted by members of a homogenous, religious audience, especially if he had made reference to the giver of the gift (is it even meaningful to speak of a 'giverless gift'?). But as a response to a question at a secular conference, and without further explication, Kass's reply was a conversation stopper, not a stimulant to dialogue."[29]

To speak of the child as a gift presupposes the giftedness of life. The PCB refers to both phenomena: the first is conceived in an ambiguous way, and thus the second, too, is not without an element of uncertainty in its meaning. Remember, the ultimate goal of the PCB's report is to stimulate public moral argument. The ambiguity fades, however, when someone with Kass' inclinations and reputation adds his voice to the debate. The giftedness of life harkens back to God. The child as gift has holy underpinnings, at least until science claims that all of this has nothing to do with almighty happenings and everything to do with the evolution of cosmological, chemical, and biological processes. Much like intellectuals guided by postmodern wisdom, Kass takes offense to such reductionism—aligning his response specifically with Martin Heidegger's critique of science and technology and the potentially ill effects that they have on the actual nature and dignity of human being.[30] But Kass is also a severe critic of this wisdom and what he perceives to be its nihilistic and relativistic tendencies. Why, for example, must we accept Nietzsche's ranting that "God is dead"? Instead, Kass pleads, "Let us cleave to our ancient wisdom and lift our voice and properly toast *L'chaim*, to life beyond our own, to the life of our grandchildren and their grandchildren. May they, God willing, know health and long life, but especially so that they may also know the pursuit of truth and righteousness and holiness. And may they hand down and perpetuate this pursuit of what is humanly finest to succeeding generations for all time to come."[31]

Setting aside the question of holiness, the PCB takes great interest in this pursuit. How might biotechnological advances affect our understanding "of what is humanly finest" and our related "expectations of perfection"?[32] Throughout the PCB's publications, the notion of what is humanly finest is directly associated with the topic of human dignity—put simply, that which is made possible by the giftedness of life and that displays the worthiness of this gift in and through our most noble thoughts, judgments, and actions. Thus, for the PCB, the matter of human dignity arises with the issue of using biotechnology to create better children. The PCB aligns human dignity with "human procreation in its natural context." The "salient fact" about this specific matter

> is that children are not *made* but *begotten*. By this we mean that children are the issue of our love, not the product of our wills. A man and a woman do not produce or choose a *particular* child, as they might buy a particular brand of soap; rather, they stand in relation to their child as recipients of a gift. Gifts and blessings we learn to accept as gratefully as we can; products of our wills we try to shape in accordance with our wants and desires. Procreation as traditionally understood invites acceptance, not reshaping or engineering. It encourages us to see that we do not own our children and that our children exist not simply for our fulfillment. Of course, parents seek to shape and nurture their children in a variety of ways; but being a parent also means being open to the *unbidden* and *unelected* in life.[33]

Some of the rhetoric here, I think it is fair to say, sounds a bit religious: the child is "begotten," a "gift," and a "blessing." The PCB, remember, would have us understand this rhetoric as being fair and accurate regarding the situation at hand. Connected as they are to the PCB's ambiguous account of the giftedness of life, however, the terms need not be associated with religion. Notice, for example, that the PCB's definition of a parent also includes "being open to the unbidden and unelected in life." One need not turn to God for this instruction. The lived body, with its openness to the future's objective uncertainty, is enough to teach parents that "chance" always has a role to play in human activities. With this uncertainty comes the ability to answer an ontologically based call of conscience, to assume the ethical burden of freedom of choice, and to do so with the welfare of others in mind (e.g., a child). Why get religious over the matter? The giftedness of life enables us to perceive emotionally, aesthetically, and mathematically nature's symmetry, its beauty, and the infinity that speaks so awesomely to we finite and metaphysical creatures. The otherness of the call of conscience is forever happening in the presence of other things and other people. The giftedness of life brings together the finite and the infinite. Human being is perfect in its incompleteness. At the present stage of human evolution, natural limitations are a part of life. For someone like Kass, God would have it no other way.

Our extraordinary powers, however, have long been evolving to deal with and overcome our natural limitations. Is such progress a sign of God's plan? What is the ultimate goal of this plan? Is it possible that its course is toward a "dignified" posthuman future? The future remains open to grand achievements, hence, for example, the evolution of biotechnology and its capacity to tell would-be parents of East European Jewish ancestry that genetic screening has exposed the possibility of giving birth to a child who suffers from Tay-Sachs disease. The disease's pathophysiology is brutal and fatal: sometime during the first year after birth, the child's central nervous system will begin to degenerate, the child will become noticeably lethargic, and his or her motor skills will decline. Then, during the following year, the child will become blind, experience petit mal seizures lasting for several seconds, be unable to eat because of the deterioration of his or her respiratory and digestive systems, and suffer mental retardation and complete paralysis. The cost of caring for the child will be substantial. If a physician failed to ask about the parents' heritage, run the proper medical tests, and then explain all of this to the parents, and if the parents ended up unknowingly giving birth to a child with Tay-Sachs disease—a child they admit they would have aborted if they would have had full knowledge of their situation—they could legally sue the doctor for the child's "wrongful life."[34] Indeed, medical authorities have long acknowledged that "for Tay-Sachs, with its well-demonstrated early mortality, the decision to terminate pregnancy is a relatively easy one."[35]

Would it be easy for you? Would you bring such a child into the world? At least for a few months, perhaps, the child could experience the love of his or her parents without interference from the effects of the disease. Would this wonderful parent-child relationship be worth the pain and suffering that would eventually occur? The PCB does not raise this question; it does, however, consider the instructive nature of suffering and the "sorrow" and "sadness" that it brings. The PCB tells us, for example, that

> We cannot ignore the truth that life's hardships often make us better—more attuned to the hardships of others, more appreciative of life's everyday blessings, more aware of the things and the people that matter most in our lives. Sadness in the recollection of a loss or a national tragedy (for example, September 11) keeps alive and pays tribute to the blessing we once enjoyed or still enjoy, gratuitiously and vulnerably. Anxiety in the face of a crucial meeting or big decision registers the importance of the undertaking and prods us to rise to the occasion. Shame at our own irresponsible or duplicitous conduct exhibits knowledge of proper conduct and provides a spur to achieving it. These emotional stings not only reflect the truth. If they do not crush us, they may make us better.[36]

All of this makes good sense to me. With the exception of the use of the word "blessing," the discourse is sound with respect to the ontological workings of the lived body.[37] Would the PCB recommend giving birth to a child with Tay-Sachs disease? Its report does not say beyond telling us such things as this: "When nature dispenses her gifts, some receive only at the end of the line."[38] Kass agrees and adds, "Humanity is owed humanity." It "is owed the bolstering of the human, even or especially in its dying moments, in resistance to the temptation to ignore its presence in the sight of suffering." Kass thus goes on to emphasize that "what humanity needs most in the face of evils is courage, the ability to stand against fear and pain and thoughts of nothingness."[39] Suffering calls for courage, not surrender. Courage helps us face death with dignity to the very end—when the least bit of the will to live operating in our physiology vanishes. Suffering has much to teach us about human dignity and human godliness. Read your Bible! Kass emphasizes this point in his siding with the right-to-life movement in the euthanasia debate.[40] Certainly, even a child fated to die from Tay-Sachs disease has such a right. One year of life is better than nothing. Is it still better if this life is fated to bring with it another year of abject suffering with no possibility of hope? Does enduring such suffering perfect the nature and dignity of human being?

I do not know what Kass would say about the specific issue being raised here. He sees the blastocyst, the early human embryo, as a beginning of life and thus as something that warrants the highest respect. He is against abortion. He would have us reply "No" to even "the most heart-rending cases" of patients whose diseases and bodily injuries have brought about a "living death" and who beg others to help them "die with dignity."[41] He believes that our flourishing depends on accepting and celebrating our natural limitations. He thus questions his religion's unrestricted, orthodox promotion of *L'chaim*, whereby one might conclude, for example, that "if cloning human beings is intended to advance medical research or cure infertility, it has a proper place in God's scheme of things."[42] Kass maintains, however, that those who toast "to life" must acknowledge and respect humankind's natural limitations. Suffering can make us better. The Bible and everyday existence teach as much. The giftedness of life is sacred. Kass is against the development and use of biotechnology that threatens this sacredness and the dignity it makes possible. As is seen throughout his writings, he employs slippery slope arguments to make his point. One, in fact, can hear his voice when the PCB considers the matter: "We should not be self-deceived about our ability to set limits on the exploitation of nascent life. What disturbs us today we quickly or eventually get used to it; yesterday's repugnance gives way to tomorrow's endorsement. A society that already tolerates the destruction of fetuses in the second and third trimesters will hardly be horrified by embryo and fetus farming (including in animal wombs), if this should turn out to be helpful in the cure of dreaded diseases."[43]

What is especially telling here of Kass' influence on the PCB is its use of the term "repugnance." Kass is (in)famous in the biotechnology debate for crediting this emotion with the "wisdom" that it takes to know where to draw the line between our being rotten with imperfection and our being rotten with perfection. Repugnance, writes Kass, is "the emotional expression of deep wisdom, beyond reason's power completely to articulate it." Kass goes on to ask, "Can anyone really give an argument fully adequate to the horror that is father-daughter incest (even with consent), or bestiality, or the mutilation of a corpse, or the eating of human flesh, or the rape or murder of another human being? Would anybody's failure to give full rationale justification for his revulsion at those practices make that revulsion ethically suspect? Not at all."[44] Within the biotechnology debate, the "wisdom of repugnance" is, for Kass, best understood with the case of human cloning in mind: "We are repelled by the prospect of cloning human beings not because of the strangeness or the novelty of the undertaking, but because we intuit and we feel, immediately and without argument, the violation of things that we rightfully hold dear. We sense that cloning represents a profound defilement of our given nature as procreative beings, and of the social relations built on this natural ground. We also sense that cloning is a radical form of child abuse. . . . Shallow are the souls that have forgotten how to shudder."[45]

Kass would have us shudder whenever biotechnological progress demeans the giftedness of life and the "unalterable human nature" that this gift and its Giver make possible. Remember, "no variableness"! The claims of the "bioprophet" about progress and our posthuman future, argues Kass, encourage a worldview "whose moral boundaries are seemingly up for grabs" and where we hear such erroneous claims that it is "unwise today to ground" our biotechnological aspirations "on dogmas about souls endowed by God." Kass laments, "We are all—or almost all—postmodernists now." We thus fail to realize that as human embryonic cloning and such related biotechnological developments as genetic and pharmaceutical enhancements continue to advance in medical practice, "standards of health, wholeness or fitness will be needed more than ever, but just then is when all pretense of standards will go out the window."[46] As Kass sees it, posthumanists and postmodernists are prone to dismiss any appreciation that we are souls endowed by God; these scientists and philosophers make us insensitive to the wisdom of repugnance and thus to things that ought to make us shudder. Shuddering displays human dignity at work.[47]

Critics of Kass' notion of the wisdom of repugnance point out that it too easily substitutes emotional responses or "yuck reactions" for rational argument; it commends the thesis that "because X disgusts me, X must therefore be wrong."[48] With this type of reasoning at work, bigots would have a field day, as would those who are repulsed by such closed-minded creatures. The wisdom of repugnance as a standard of judgment has its burdens and benefits. Kass acknowledges that repugnance "is not an argument," but that, he maintains, is no reason to keep it from informing our arguments: repugnance "need not stand naked before the bar of reason"; its emotional wisdom "can be partially articulated" even in "those instances about which the heart has its reasons that reason cannot entirely know."[49] Remember, we must not forget how to shudder. The lived body's emotional attachment to the world of everyday experience grounds this reaction and its call of conscience. As Aristotle long ago discussed in his *Rhetoric*, the validity of pathos can be sustained and critiqued within a rational framework of public moral argument. Kass points to our "holiness" as the true foundation of this entire process.

The PCB invites the possibility of shuddering with the many slippery slope arguments that it presents in its report. Consider, for example, how the PCB elaborates on its earlier noted observation about prenatal screening and its affect on the parent-child relationship:

> With genetic screening, procreation begins to take on certain aspects of the *idea*—if not the practice—of manufacture, the making of a product to a specified standard. The parent—in partnership with the IVF [in vitro fertilization] doctor or genetic counselor—becomes in some measure the master's of the child's fate, in ways that are without precedent.... Today, parents using [IVF and] PGD [preimplantation genetic diagnosis] take responsibility for picking and choosing which "advantages" their children shall enjoy. Such an enlarged degree

of parental control over the genetic endowments of their children cannot fail to alter the parent-child relationship. . . . [S]electing for desired traits inevitably plants specific hopes and expectations as to how their child might excel. More than any child does now, the "better" child may bear the burden of living up to the standards he was "designed" to meet.[50]

Considering the wider social effects of an increased use of genetic screening and selection, the PCB warns against

the prospect of diminished tolerance for the "imperfect," especially those born with genetic disorders that could have been screened out. It is offensive to think that children, suffering from "preventable" genetic diseases, should be directly asked, "Why were you born?" (or their parents asked, "Why did you let him live?"). Yet it is almost as troubling to contemplate that "defective" children and their parents may be treated contemptuously and unfairly in light of such prejudices, even if they go unspoken.[51]

When considering the rationality and fairness of slippery slope arguments and the way they are rhetorically designed to make us shudder and to stimulate public moral argument, it is important to keep in mind the difference between paranoia and logical fearfulness. The PCB, of course, would certainly maintain that they favor and practice the second option. Their construction of the slippery slope argument here is to ensure that the public is given the chance to shudder. With Kass, however, chance becomes fate. Not shuddering is not an option. "One of the most worrisome but least appreciated aspects of the godlike power of the new genetics," writes Kass, "is its tendency to 'redefine' a human being in terms of his genes. Once a person is decisively characterized by his genotype, it is but a short step to justifying death solely for genetic sins." Kass continues:

Make no mistake: the price to be paid for producing optimum or even only genetically sound babies will be the transfer of procreation from the home to the laboratory. Increasing control over the product can only be purchased by the increasing depersonalization of the entire process and its coincident transformation into manufacture. Such an arrangement will be profoundly dehumanizing, no matter how genetically good or healthy the resultant children. And let us not forget the powerful economic interests that will surely operate in this area; with their advent, the commodification of nascent human life will be unstoppable.

And then there is Kass returning to the specific topic of human embryonic cloning:

> Is cloning a fulfillment of human begetting and belonging? Or is cloning rather, as I contend, their pollution and perversion? To pollution and perversion, the fitting response can only be horror and revulsion; and conversely, generalized horror and revulsion are *prima facie* evidence of foulness and violation. The burden of moral argument must fall entirely on those who want to declare the widespread distastes of humankind to be mere timidity and superstition.[52]

Kass' positions here support and are supported by the stated "mission" of "conservative bioethics": "to prevent our transformation into a culture without awe filled with people without souls."[53] Without awe and souls, shuddering and the wisdom of repugnance are not possible, and the way from human dignity to the giftedness of life and then to God is dismissed as pure fiction. For Kass, this dismissal, too, warrants a shuddering response. He encourages us to be logically fearful of how developments in biotechnology and their attending postmodern and posthuman rhetoric expose us to the disease of becoming rotten with perfection. With God on his side, we might even become a bit paranoid. We are being watched from above—all of the time. Heaven help us.

THE STATUS OF PUBLIC MORAL ARGUMENT

In the introduction to its report on biotechnology, the PCB emphasizes that its "document is not a research report, but an ethical inquiry." The inquiry seeks "to identify exactly the sorts of questions and concerns to which researchers, policy makers, and the public at large should be paying attention." In raising these questions and concerns, the PCB did "not mean to be setting ourselves up as prophets."[54] Rather, as stated at the end of their report, the PCB's goal was to keep readers open to a host of pressing issues. They note, for example, that in "wanting to become more than we [human beings] are, and in sometimes acting as if we were already superhuman or divine, we risk despising what we are and neglecting what we have. . . . [W]e risk turning a blind eye to the objects of our natural loves and longings, the pursuit of which might be the truer road to a more genuine happiness."[55]

I have credited the PCB with being a producer of postmodern wisdom. A rhetoric of perfection is operative: the PCB's discourse instigates a call of conscience meant to interrupt the complacency of its readers. A dwelling place for public moral argument is provided by this interruption. Here people are invited to enact the ethical responsibility of their freedom of choice; to be open to, acknowledge, and become emotionally and reasonably involved with others; to interpret matters in a rhetorically competent and truthful manner; and thereby to promote the beauty and justice of a heroic communicative process that is a defining feature and a saving grace of democracy. We demonstrate human dignity as we involve ourselves with this process. We make good the giftedness of life. This act of making good speaks to who we are as metaphysical creatures who desire some degree of completeness in our lives. The giftedness of life admits a perfectionist impulse. The Council respects what is given and called for here: it opens itself to others and asks them to do the same. Such openness is an essential feature of the spatial and temporal nature of the giftedness of life.

Perhaps, however, this assessment of the PCB exhibits too much hermeneutic charity. With its slippery slope arguments and religious-sounding rhetoric, the PCB invites a less charitable response. But the ontological notions that lie at the heart of its discourse—the giftedness of life and human dignity—admit an ambiguity that grants the PCB a way out from simply being seen as an agency of conservative thought and religious-right tendencies. To those critics who brand the PCB as such—critics who include such distinguished scientists as Michael Gazzaniga (himself a member of the PCB when it published its report)—the PCB should admit that their published report is, for example, "full of unsubstantiated psychological speculations on the nature of sexual life and theories of moral agency."[56] The PCB could respond, however, that the sometimes-conservative slant of its rhetoric is intended only as a means for amplifying its call of conscience in order to ensure that its goal of stimulating public moral argument comes to fruition.

With the publication of its most-recent edited volume, *Human Dignity and Bioethics* (2008), the PCB continued to promote and advance this goal by responding to criticism over its perceived failure to be as clear as possible in defining the essential nature and function of human dignity and its necessary relationship with the giftedness of life. Macklin, who, as noted above, had earlier taken Kass to task with his discussion of the "child as gift," was identified by the PCB as being a major source of the criticism. In an editorial in the *British Medical Journal*, she argued that dignity "is a useless concept in medical ethics and can be eliminated without any loss of content" because it essentially is rooted in medicine's already well-established principle of respecting a patient's personal autonomy. This principle entails "the need to obtain voluntary, informed consent; the requirement to protect confidentiality; and the need to avoid discrimination and abusive practices." Macklin suspects that such religious sources as the Roman Catholic Church are responsible for people erroneously thinking that human dignity "means something over and above respect for persons or for their autonomy."[57]

Human Dignity and Bioethics contains twenty-eight essays and commentaries by PCB members and invited contributors. Some of these essays and commentaries pay homage to a tradition that insists on how the order of nature is divinely sanctioned. Other contributions favor a more scientific worldview. Still others emphasize how an understanding of human dignity evolved not only in theological thought but also in philosophical and political traditions that continue to inform our country's present-day postmodern culture, with its "pluralistic" perspective on any number of matters of importance. With this point in mind and in the final paragraph of his introduction to the volume, F. Daniel Davis, executive director of the PCB staff, offers "a prediction—and an acknowledgment of the partial truth of Ruth Macklin's complaint":

> Many of the essays in this volume do explore in depth the complex and divergent meanings of human dignity and thus fill a void left open by the published work of the President's Council—*until now*. I predict, however, that after careful reading and reflecting on these essays, most readers will reject Macklin's conclusion that human dignity is a "useless" concept and will, instead, find their understanding of questions and issues in contemporary bioethics deepened and enriched. That is the hope and aim of the President's Council in publishing this volume of essays on the bioethical significance of human dignity.[58]

In a scathing review of the volume, titled "The Stupidity of Dignity: Conservative Bioethics' Latest, Most Dangerous Ploy," the noted cognitive scientist Steven Pinker, who supports Macklin's position, finds little to justify Davis' prediction. Taken with what he perceives as a "theocon bioethics" permeating the volume, Pinker displays his disgust when he asks in amazement, "How did the United States, the world's scientific powerhouse, reach a point at which it grapples with the ethical challenges of twenty-first-century biomedicine using Bible stories, Catholic doctrine, and woolly rabbinical allegory?" Pinker points to "the outsize influence of Kass" as a major factor.[59]

Presumably, the PCB was adhering (now more than ever before) to its ethic of using "fair and accurate terminology" as it reviewed and organized the contributions to its most recent volume. The newly appointed chairman of the PCB, Edmund D. Pellegrino, admits that these contributions "make it clear that there is no universal agreement on the meaning of the term, human dignity." He still insists, however, that an "appreciation of the variety of these views is critical, if we are to understand the divergences in how we think and act in response to the challenges posed by contemporary bioethics."[60] Pinker doesn't buy it. The "general feeling" he gets from the volume is associated with what was noted earlier about the PCB's concern with the extraordinary powers of biotechnology going too far in transforming our "natural limitations." Pinker thus reads the overall collection of essays and commentaries—"three-quarters of the invited contributors [have] religious entanglements"—as promoting the view that "even if a new technology would improve life and health and decrease suffering and waste, it might have to be rejected, or even outlawed, if it affronted human dignity." For Pinker, what the volume reveals "should alarm anyone concerned with American biomedicine and its promise to improve human welfare. For this government-sponsored bioethics does not want medical practice to maximize health and flourishing; it considers that quest to be a bad thing, not a good thing."[61]

Pinker is a brilliant mind and an exceptionally productive researcher and scholar whom I much admire. I find his reading of *Human Dignity and Bioethics*, however, to be a bit unfair. The publication of the text is consistent with the PCB's original and specific charge to encourage public moral argument. The religious slant of various contributors, no matter how much critics may dislike the perceived bias, is not a sufficient reason to deny the worth of the overall text in meeting its assigned goal. Public moral argument presupposes capacities (e.g., being open to and acknowledging others) that demonstrate human dignity. In her contribution to the volume, PCB member Rebecca Dresser, who takes issue with Macklin's criticism but who in no way is a card-carrying theocon bioethicist, puts the matter this way: "Like any other moral arguments, appeals to dignity may be inappropriate or superficial, or they may mask inadequately supported claims. But it does not follow from this that bioethics should abandon appeals to dignity."[62]

Pinker credits Dresser with offering a "fine discussion" of "the avoidable humiliations that today's patients are often forced to endure (like those hideous hospital smocks that are open at the back). No one could object to valuing dignity in this sense." And that, argues Pinker, is exactly the point: "When the concept of dignity is precisely specified, it becomes a mundane matter of thoughtfulness pushing against callousness and bureaucratic inertia, not a contentious moral conundrum. And, because it amounts to treating people in the way that they wish to be treated, ultimately it's just another application of the principle of autonomy."[63] Dresser maintains, however, that such a reductionistic understanding of the matter displays "a lack of respect for the individuals and groups that see dignity as a significant bioethical concern. . . . A belief's popularity is not necessarily evidence of its validity, of course. But widespread popularity is a reason for critics to consider that belief carefully, instead of dismissing it outright."[64]

Pinker's rebuttal to such a charge unfolds as he centers his attention on Kass, pointing out, for example, that "after several members [of the PCB] opposed Kass [while he was still the chairperson] on embryonic stem-cell research, on therapeutic cloning (which Kass was in favor of criminalizing), and on the distortions of science that kept finding their way into Council reports, Kass fired two of them (biologist Elizabeth Blackburn and philosopher William May) and replaced them with Christian-affiliated scholars."[65] Kass' essay in the PCB's edited volume is consistent with the thrust of his earlier writings. It is no surprise, then, that he ends his piece with the following words: "Human beings must open their ears as well as their eyes, they must hearken to a calling . . . the transcendent voice. . . . The dignity of being human, rooted in the dignity of [the giftedness of] life itself and flourishing in a manner seemingly issuing only in human pride, completes itself and stands tallest when we bow our heads and lift our hearts in recognition of powers greater than our own. The fullest dignity of the god-like animal is realized in its acknowledgment and celebration of the divine."[66]

Kass' rhetoric has a prophetic ring to it: we are fated to encounter the perverted, polluted, and repulsive environment of a posthuman future if we fail to hear and respond to the call as he recommends.[67] Political philosopher and past PCB member Michael Sandel agrees when he writes that we should "view genetic engineering as the ultimate expression of our resolve to see ourselves astride the world, the masters of our nature. But that vision of freedom is flawed. It threatens to banish our appreciation of life as a gift, and to leave us with nothing to affirm or behold outside our own will."[68] Kass is more definitive: "[U]nless we mobilize the courage to look foursquare at the full human meaning of our new enterprise in biogenetic technology and engineering, we are doomed to become its creatures if not its slaves."[69] According to Kass, this outcome is already taking shape in our biotechnological quest to extend our "normal" life span and remain "forever young." Kass writes,

> [T]he desire to prolong youthfulness is not only a childish desire to eat one's life and keep it; it is also an expression of a childish and narcissistic wish incompatible with devotion to posterity. It seeks an endless present, isolated from any thing truly eternal, and severed from any true continuity with past and future. It is in principle hostile to children, because children, those who come after, are those who will take one's place; *they* are life's answer to mortality, and their presence in one's house is a constant reminder that one no longer belongs to the frontier generation. One cannot pursue agelessness for oneself and remain faithful to the spirit and meaning of perpetuation. . . . Indeed, the mitzvah to be fruitful and multiply (the Bible's first positive commandment), when rightly understood, celebrates not the life we have and selfishly would cling to, but the life that replaces us.

Kass insists "that the finitude of human life is a blessing for every human individual, whether he knows it or not." Our finitude, for example, makes possible "the peculiarly human beauty of character, *virtue and moral excellence*." Kass' clarification of this point is noteworthy:

> To be mortal means that it is possible to give one's life, not only in one moment, say, on the field of battle, but also in the many other ways in which we are able in action to rise above attachment to survival. Through moral courage, endurance, greatness of soul, generosity, devotion to justice—in acts great and small—we rise above our mere creatureliness, spending the precious coinage of the time of our lives for the sake of the noble and the good and the holy. We free ourselves from fear, from bodily pleasures, or from attachments to wealth—all largely connected with survival—and in doing virtuous deeds overcome the weight of our neediness; yet for this nobility, vulnerability and mortality are the necessary conditions. The immortals cannot be noble.[70]

Our finitude may make us shudder and suffer, but it also informs and encourages the godliness of human dignity. Shuddering, suffering, and godliness go hand in hand for Kass.

Such is not the case for the scientist and posthumanist Ray Kurzweil: "Whereas some of my contemporaries may be satisfied to embrace aging gracefully as part of the cycle of life, that is not my view. It may be 'natural,' but I don't see anything positive in losing my mental agility, sensory acuity, physical limberness, sexual desire, or any other human ability. I view disease and death at any age as a calamity, as problems to be overcome."[71]

The differences of opinion between Kass and Kurzweil display the oppositional forces at work in the biotechnology debate. Kass celebrates our natural limitations and suffering. Kurzweil cheers our extraordinary powers and their ability to lessen, if not end, suffering. Kass warns against our posthuman future. Kurzweil welcomes its possibilities and its postmodern attitude toward the openness of human existence. Kass emphasizes how this openness and the freedom it makes possible promote a postmodern culture in which the disease of being rotten with perfection can grow all too quickly. Kurzweil, however, perceives this openness and freedom as granting us opportunities to overcome whatever contentment we may feel when we too easily accept our natural limitations and risk the chance of becoming rotten with imperfection. Kass writes as if God is on his side. Kurzweil challenges God-in-the-gaps thinking and the conservative tendency to turn "posthuman" into a devil term. For Kurzweil, the posthuman is associated with how "being human means being part of a civilization that seeks to extend its boundaries. We are already reaching beyond our biology by rapidly gaining the tools to reprogram and augment it." Elaborating on the point, Kurzweil writes,

> If we regard a human modified with technology as no longer human, where would we draw the defining line? Is a human with a bionic heart still human? How about someone with a neurological implant? What about two neurological implants? How about someone with ten nanobots in his brain? How about 500 million nanobots? Should we establish a boundary at 650 million nanobots: under that, you're still human and over that, you're posthuman?
>
> Our merger with our technology has aspects of a slippery slope, but one that slides up toward greater promise, not down into Nietzsche's abyss.[72]

Kurzweil is a very optimistic postmodernist. The posthuman is an extension of the human, not simply its demise. Kurzweil labels the result of this extension the "Singularity": "The Singularity will represent the culmination of the merger of our biological thinking and existence with our technology, resulting in a world that is still human but that transcends our biological roots. . . . If you wonder what will remain unequivocally human in such a world, it's simply this quality: ours is the species that inherently seeks to extend its physical and mental reach beyond current limitations." Kurzweil emphasizes that this human quality has evolved to the point at which it values a moral principle that lies at the heart of "traditional religion" and that must be maintained in the Singularity: the "respect for the consciousness of others."[73] I spoke of this respect earlier when discussing the relationship between human being and otherness. Kurzweil is talking about how we metaphysical creatures are fated to hear and respond to the call of conscience and its attending call of technology.

Kurzweil acknowledges that, as has historically been the case, the challenge here entails dealing wisely with the social, political, and economic problems that necessarily arise with technological progress and its potential to infect us with the disease of being rotten with perfection. The biotechnology debate is a case in point. Like Kass, Kurzweil looks at our natural limitations to inspire his vision. Unlike Kass, however, Kurzweil sees these limitations as indications of what needs to be improved in order to advance the true character of human being. The lived body is open to otherness and its infinity. The ontological dynamics at work here offer a moral directive to Kuzweil the scientist, post-humanist, and postmodernist: we should be as open-minded as possible to how various technological achievements can help us guard against the disease of becoming rotten with imperfection.

The PCB never puts matters this way in its attempt to stimulate public moral argument about the benefits and burdens of biotechnology. Rather, the PCB's rhetoric tends to drift toward the position of erring on the side of caution. Kass' rhetoric affirms the reasonableness of this drift to the point that he recommends a closed-mindedness toward those who would head in the opposite direction. I have too much of a phenomenological, ontological, and postmodern outlook to accept this mind-set without question. Human existence sounds a call of conscience that speaks to us of the moral necessity of being open to otherness. We hear this call as finite beings, but the call itself is enduring, infinite— as infinite as pi, phi, and "the eye of God" found at the center of one of nature's geometric forms, the logarithmic spiral. Is there a purpose to infinity? The phenomenon serves as a catalyst for inciting our metaphysical desire for some sense of completeness. Human existence is structured perfectly to stimulate this desire. The desire, at one and the same time, makes us feel homesick and encourages us to do something about this ill feeling. Orthodox Judaism speaks to us of *Ein Sof*, the Creator of the infinite, as the truly unknowable source of this desire. Christianity, too, acknowledges the wonder of the desire. As the rabbi Jesus Christ is reported to have said shortly before he died, "Verily, verily, I say unto you, he that believeth in me, the works that I do shall he do also; and greater works than these shall he do; because I go unto my Father" (John 14:12).

Greater works: we are called to act in such a way that we overcome the ill effects of being rotten with imperfection. I suspect that as we continue to meet this challenge, there will continue to be many moments of shuddering and repugnance in our lives. With any degree of success, joy, perhaps, might brighten our world. Such joy, however, must not be allowed to instigate a false sense of security whereby we make ourselves susceptible to the disease of being rotten with perfection. Postmodern wisdom offers itself as a reminder of the danger here; it promotes itself as always being up for the challenge. From our finite perspective, the challenge appears infinite. Being the metaphysical creatures that we are, however, the challenge should inspire action on our part. Despite whatever burdens it may bring about, the continuing development of biotechnology is certainly one way to meet the challenge.[74]

Both the PCB and Kass deserve credit for instigating public moral argument that makes us attentive to the potential downside of the biotechnological revolution. As the distinguished bioethicist and legal scholar Nancy King puts it, "If Kass didn't exist, someone would have to invent him."[75] Indeed, is it the case, for example, that these developments will transform the contentment and gratitude associated with being parents? Will the production of "better" children lead us to treat "defective" children unfairly? Will our success in pushing back death result in our becoming less appreciative of the human beauty of character, virtue, and moral excellence? Will the wisdom of repugnance be lost to future generations? Will anything less than perfection be pathology?

I know of no postmodernists or posthumanists who would dismiss the relevancy of such questions. Those included in the PCB's edited volume certainly don't commit the sin.[76] The perfection of human being, its complete way of being incomplete, is forever calling us into question, forever forcing us to deal with our natural limitations and extraordinary powers, forever calling for moral responsibility and open-mindedness. Richard Feynman is right: cosmologically speaking, we "are only in the beginning." "We must maintain an open channel" in order to avoid being "dumb" and "ignorant." We must overcome our tendency to be closed-minded. I cannot see how the Creator of the Infinite (*Ein Sof*) would disagree. Open-mindedness is a necessary condition for appreciating the otherness of infinity and the question of perfection that it raises. Postmodern religious thinkers emphasize this point throughout their writings.[77]

Kass, it seems to me, is too forgetful of the point. His rather shallow reading of postmodern wisdom lacks hermeneutic charity. Who can say for sure that a postmodern future, with its biotechnological developments, is not a part of God's plan? Who can say for sure that human godliness—our ability to exercise speech and reason, freedom in doing and making, and contemplation, judgment, and care—will not be operative as human beings interface ever more closely with our biotechnological inventions? Have we reached the point in human evolution at which our natural limitations cannot be improved without ruining the "true" nature of what we are supposed to be—in the long run?[78] Nature calls. Human existence calls. Otherness calls. With the biotechnology debate we metaphysical creatures find ourselves in a rhetorical situation where the question of perfection is necessarily before us and where public moral argument continues to be essential. "Where art thou?"

CONCLUSION

Owing to the openness, the objective uncertainty, of our spatial and temporal being—to how it is that human being is perfect in its incompleteness—we are fated to hear and respond to such a call of conscience. Kass associates this fate with human "aspiration," which he takes to be "the mother of all aspects of the dignity of being human. Though born of our frailty and bodily neediness, it is sired also by a divine spark to which—miraculously—Being has prepared the human animal to recognize and pursue."[79] Indeed, the lived body is in pursuit of completeness, perfection, a metaphysical all-togetherness that has yet to come to fruition in our earthly existence but that is promised in the Holy Scriptures. The call of conscience that lies at the heart of human being encourages us to remain open to the possibility that the promise will be kept. Is such openness a sign of God's presence? Certainly, without this openness there would be nobody to speak of this presence. For Kass, such a speech act is a supreme demonstration of human dignity. David Gelernter heartedly agrees: "'dignity' in the end is a religious idea . . . we can't be rational and moral animals unless we acknowledge the God of Israel." The field of bioethics "can't possibly be allowed to develop in the secular ghetto where modern intellectuals lives [*sic*]."[80]

Gelernter suggests that the inhabitants of this ghetto encouraged the "murder" of Terri Schiavo: "legal authorities ordered that she be starved to death. . . . Ordinarily, refusing to feed someone who can't feed herself is murder. And virtually all ethical systems require us to help the weak and the sick, not starve them." Expanding on this point, Gelernter writes, "Was Mrs. Schiavo wholly comatose and unresponsive, *beyond a reasonable doubt*? Was it more consistent with human dignity to kill her than to continue helping her to live, *beyond a reasonable doubt*? Was the public's duty to safeguard life overridden by other factors in this case, *beyond a reasonable doubt*? These are simple questions—but if anyone discussed them, I missed it."[81] Indeed, you did! As detailed in the last chapter, these questions attracted much attention in the Schiavo controversy. Medical scientists provided strong evidence that Terri Schiavo did not suffer from starvation because that part of the brain that allows a person to suffer was not functioning in her case. Mercy, not murder, was demonstrated.

The lack of openness in Gelernter's essay is as disturbing as it is in Pinker's review of the Council's report on human dignity. Chairman Pellegrino writes, "Two images of human dignity compete for moral authority. One is the scientific, the other the religious. Neither is likely to capitulate to the other. . . . Extremists on both sides, militant atheists and intransigent dogmatists, insist there can be no common ground. More responsible proponents of both views hope for a productive dialogue and appeal to the necessity of a common ground in the public arena, even while metaphysical foundations remain disputed."[82] Productive dialogue is encouraged by the rhetorical workings of public moral argument. Despite the biases and disagreements that exist among its members and the contributors to *Human Dignity and Bioethics*, I read Pellegrino's words as an indication of the PCB's general goodwill. If I am mistaken in this belief, then I must say, the PCB ought to be ashamed of itself. The genuine pursuit of perfection demands as much. Human existence displays the ontological basis of such noble and dignified action: we are beings who are perfectly incomplete. Lacking definitive evidence and being compelled to act are the prerequisites of the rhetorical situation. At the heart of the biotechnology debate lies such contested terms as the "giftedness of life" and "human dignity." More public moral argument is called for.

Indeed, two days after President Barack Obama's inauguration, the government gave its approval for the first-ever human trials using therapies derived from the controversial area of science known as embryonic stem cell research. According to Dr. Thomas Okarma, president and CEO of Genron, the biotechnology firm that was given permission by the U.S. Food and Drug Administration to begin the research, this approval "marks the beginning of what is potentially a new chapter in medical therapeutics, one that reaches beyond pills to a new level of healing: the restoration of organ and tissue function achieved by the injection of healthy replacement cells."[83] Ongoing stem cell research being conducted by scientists in such countries as Israel, Italy, South Korea, and the United Kingdom supports the potential positive outcomes of Genron's project. Science, however, is not unaware of the caution that is absolutely necessary here. According to Dr. Chuck Murry, codirector of the University of Washington Institute for Stem Cell and Regenerative Medicine, it is "a bold step, and the hard part of this is going to be managing expectations. . . . People have very high hopes for stem cells to do something remarkable. We have to keep in mind—the wonder with working with embryonic stem cells is that they can turn into anything, and the hardest thing with working with stem cells is that they can turn into anything."[84] Public moral argument must have a role in educating us about the risks and rewards of such research.

Those who earn their living studying, teaching, and writing about such argument cannot help but be pleased. Taking pleasure over potentially never-ending arguments has its limits, however, especially when these arguments would have us make certain decisions about the "fate" of human being and how, for example, developments in biotechnology may save us and future generations from a host of life's present-day crises. The biotechnology revolution involves us in the pursuit of perfection. Certainly we want to be careful and take our time here. Expressing perfection as perfectly as possible is a major moral obligation for those who wish to enter the debate and influence its outcome. But time is of the essence when many millions of lives hang in the balance.

Wouldn't it be wonderful if medical science and technology had evolved to the point at which people like Terri Schiavo could now be cured of their ailments and public moral argument concerning their pain, suffering, and salvation was no longer necessary?

This question helped introduce the present chapter. It remains on the table in the biotechnology debate because of how it invites consideration of the consequences that are seen to follow when our "normal" life span is extended. I noted above Kass' shuddering response to this issue. In offering his "standing complaint" against the "enthusiastic" transhumanists who think that such life extension would be a wonderful accomplishment, the bioethicist Daniel Callahan adds this:

> [T]hey defend themselves by hypothesizing a variety of changes in our present way of life that would make our extended lives a kind of heaven on earth. We would be so healthy and energetic we would want to keep working indefinitely. We could start new careers, new families, new ways of life. That we might get tired of it all, or bored, is not allowed into their calculations. Nor is any imaginative effort to image the deleterious social effects allowed. Healthy, affluent people even now usually want to retire from work, not continue indefinitely, and poor people whose work is drudgery want it even more. But they would be forced to continue working unless society and their children were prepared to support them for hundreds of years. Social mobility in every human society has depended on the old making way for the young. . . . I really wish we would be told, when the great day arrives and we have dozens, maybe hundreds of years ahead of us, exactly how it would all work. And to do so without invoking fairy tales. Nature knew what it was doing when it arranged, through natural selection, to have all of us get old and die. That is the price of species survival and vitality, and it has worked well. I don't think we humans can invent a better scenario, but we can surely do much harm in trying.[85]

Like Kass, Callahan is a defender of natural human limitations that enable us to be the dignified creatures that we are. With this position before us, we must continue to struggle with the problem of how to gauge the benefits and burdens of being rotten with perfection versus being rotten with imperfection. The problem is rooted in a fundamental (ontological) truth of human being: the openness of existence that shows itself in our being perfectly incomplete. I conclude my story about perfection by giving further thought to this specific problem of perfection.

CHAPTER TEN

ON BEING AN OXYMORON

The first essay in *Human Dignity and Bioethics* is titled "How to Protect Human Dignity from Science." Its author is the philosopher of science Daniel Dennett, well-known foe of those who abide by the theocon discourse informing the biotechnology debate. Dennett's scholarly reputation and the title of his essay do not seem to go together. The clash here is somewhat oxymoronic, somewhat like a "perfect storm." Dennett is not one to recommend that the nature of anything should be protected from the knowing eyes of science, especially when an understanding of the matter in question (e.g, human dignity) remains shrouded in religious myth. Dennett nevertheless insists in the introduction of his essay that "we can have dignity and science too, but only if we face the conflict [between religion and science] with open minds and a sense of common cause."[1]

Yes, open minds! Our capacity for experiencing and maintaining this state of being has been emphasized throughout this book. Open-mindedness puts us in tune with the truth of our spatial and temporal existence. We are creatures who are perfectly incomplete. We live an oxymoronic existence. Consequently, the being of our lived bodies is forever sounding a call of conscience that challenges us to come to terms with things that are essential to our being and that I have associated with a rhetoric of perfection. Along with the call of conscience there comes the related matters of freedom, ethical responsibility, being open to and acknowledging others, truth, heroism, salvation, beauty, justice, and rhetorical competence. Acknowledging as much is a dignified thing for a soul to do.

Dennett would never put the matter this way. He does not believe in the soul. He is quite clear on this point: "Science has banished the soul as firmly as it has banished mermaids, unicorns, and perpetual motion machines. There are no such things. There is no more scientific justification for believing in an immaterial immortal soul than there is for believing that each of your kidneys has a tap-dancing poltergeist living in it. The latter idea is clearly preposterous."[2] With science on his side, Dennett feels comfortable being closed-minded to religious arguments for the existence of the soul. An ethic of open-mindedness lies at the heart of scientific inquiry, but it eases its moral force as science gets things right and validates its findings about the specific matter at hand. Recall again the Hippocratic teaching: there is science and there is opinion. The first begets knowledge, the second ignorance. Dennett asks, "How can we kindle and preserve a sincere *allegiance* to the ideals of human dignity? And he answers, "The same way we foster the love of a democratic and free society: by ensuring that the lives one can live in such a regime are so manifestly better than the available alternatives."[3] In such a pursuit of perfection, are we better off knowing that the long-comforting religious notion of the soul is "in truth" a ruse? The ontological workings of human existence call for open-mindedness; they say nothing, however, about the worthiness of being closed-minded, other than how this state of being might protect us from the dreadful experience of anxiety. The cost of such protection is the risk of wanting to feel so secure that we become rotten with perfection. This disease promotes a static worldview—one that is out of tune with our dynamic nature of being completely incomplete.

People like Dennett see people like Leon Kass as being carriers of the disease. Kass sees the same in Dennett and those like him who would only give the last word to science. The two groups laugh and shudder at the "false" accusations being lodged against them. Religion is not rotten with perfection as long as it remains open to God's law and acknowledges that it lacks definitive evidence for knowing for sure what exactly this law means from the beginning to the end of time. New and better understandings are always possible. The same goes for the scientific enterprise. It is not rotten with perfection as long as its practitioners remain open to and acknowledge the possibility that their empirical findings lack the requisite definitive evidence to prove their point and therefore may be incorrect. Indeed, new and better understandings are always possible. Science believes that it has acquired enough definitive evidence to dismiss immaterial notions like the soul. Case closed. Religion believes this stance is as arrogant as it is far from the truth. Case closed. There is no getting around the fact that in the biotechnology debate a lot of closed-minded people are willing to speak their minds. In the case of Dennett and Kass, the former is closed-minded in order to make sure that humankind does not become rotten with imperfection. Kass, on the other hand, is closed-minded in order to make sure that humankind does not become deceived into thinking that being rotten with imperfection is necessarily a bad thing to be. Natural limitations ought to be respected. And so, too, things like the soul.

I have no intention of making an argument for or against the existence of the soul. I mention it here because the controversy surrounding it has a place in concluding my story. I must admit that I am not unaffected by certain teachings associated with the Judeo-Christian tradition. "Raising holy sparks," *L'chaim*, and doing "greater works" are, for me, comforting and inspiring ideas. But I am an equally strong supporter of science and its ongoing biotechnological achievements, which, as far as I am concerned, may be considered practical illustrations of these ideas.[4] Such achievements should never be dismissed, curtailed, or halted simply because they call into question traditional religious beliefs. I have yet to meet any enlightened soul who can say with absolute certainty that the perfectibility of human being, our complete incompleteness, is or is not a sign of the Almighty's presence and what exactly this One would have us do with it as we struggle to define lines between being rotten with perfection and being rotten with imperfection. What is a living oxymoron to do?

RELIGION AND SCIENCE AND A RHETORIC TO GO WITH THEM

Consider this: if you were a god and wanted to create a fundamental dynamic of human existence that would ensure that, sooner or later, especially in crisis situations, people would have occasion to give some thought to the possibility of your demanding but still-loving presence, I think it is fair to say that the dynamic of complete incompleteness would be a rather ingenious invention. Human existence is so structured that it continually calls us into question. Your inventive act of creation is rhetorical: the first-ever use of an oxymoron to encourage open-mindedness and responsible thought and action. The Holy Scriptures put this ontological and rhetorical happening into words and narratives: "Where art thou?" "Here I am!" Your act of rhetorical competence encouraged the writing of the most widely read book in the history of humankind. Indeed, the Bible nurtures metaphysical creatures longing for completeness, perfection, in you (whoever or whatever you are). You give and receive the life-giving gift of acknowledgment. You have what you wanted all along. Openness toward others is your most favored way of being. Emmanuel Levinas has this matter in mind when he writes, "One could call this situation religion, the situation where outside of all dogmas, all speculation about the divine or—God forbid—about the sacred and its violences, one speaks to the other."[5] Indeed, the institutions of religion and their various descriptive and prescriptive discourses presuppose the eventful situation in question here: the fundamental relationship of self and other that is, as Levinas puts it, "my pre-originary susceptiveness [to the other] which chooses me before I welcome it" and that is thus the basis for the sociopolitical transformations of the relationships that occur in everyday life.[6]

The dynamic of our complete incompleteness gives rise to religious institutions. But pure religion, true religion, unencumbered by ideological dogma, is always already at work. Personal crises expose us to the dynamic, which is awesome: a source of fear and joy and mystery. Being the metaphysical creatures that we are, we want to know more about all that is going on here. A question may come to mind that was noted early in my story: "Has creation a final purpose at all, and if so why is it not attained immediately, why does perfection not exist from the very beginning?"[7] The twelfth-century rabbinic authority, philosopher, and physician Moses Maimonides, considered the greatest post-Talmudic spiritual leader of the Jewish people, favored a way of answering this question that stressed the importance of scientific inquiry: "He who wishes to attain to human perfection" must study "astronomy and physics" as well as "logic," "mathematics," and "geometry" if you desire to comprehend "the relation between the world and Providence as it is in reality, and not according to imagination."[8]

Science is an invaluable source of wisdom. For the sake of securing its ethical and moral standing in its rational pursuit of knowledge and truth, the enterprise of science must take seriously and appropriate the (God-given?) dynamic of our complete incompleteness. Scientific inquiry is committed to calling itself into question constantly in the face of the objective uncertainty of evolving reality. With the empirical data that it secures in its investigations, science oftentimes feels quite justified in eventually saying, "Okay, enough is enough. The earth is not flat, the Milky Way galaxy is not the center of the cosmos, the lump in your breast is cancer, you had a myocardial infarction (a heart attack), genetics plays a role in human development." The list can go on and on. Such instances of closed-mindedness are not evil doings. Rather, they allow us to move on in the pursuit of bettering our lives. The pursuit is geared to fighting off the disease of being rotten with imperfection. Greater works are needed and called for. The dynamic of complete incompleteness suggests as much with its call of conscience.

Human being is a living oxymoron that at one and the same time is capable of acknowledging "the power and glory of God" and avoiding God-of-the-gaps thinking in order to stay open to the challenge of finding the true empirical nature of things and how we might use the knowledge gained here—for example, to cure horrible diseases. Terri Schiavo would have died earlier than she did if not for the wonders of medical technology.

But Schiavo's percutaneous endoscopic gastrostomy (PEG) tube was only what physicians term a "halfway" technology. As Lewis Thomas notes, such technology consists of the employment of "makeshift" inventions (e.g., dialysis machines, cancer chemotherapy) "to compensate for the incapacitating effects of certain diseases whose cause one is unable to do very much about" because medicine lacks the comprehensive understanding of the mechanisms controlling the diseases in question. Thomas emphasizes that medical care at this level of technology not only requires a great deal of time, effort, and skill on the part of physicians, but also contributes greatly to escalating medical expenditures, since it "involves long periods of hospitalization, lots of nursing, [and] lots of involvement of nonmedical professionals in and out of the hospital." What Terri Schiavo really needed instead is what Thomas terms "the real high technology of medicine." This kind of technology has reached the stage of "curing"; it is the result of basic research in biological science leading to a genuine understanding of disease mechanisms. And when such technology becomes available, notes Thomas, "it is relatively inexpensive, relatively simple, and relatively easy to deliver."[9] Examples would include modern methods of immunization against childhood viral diseases and the use of antibiotics for bacterial infections. Terri Schiavo, unfortunately, needed what the real high technology of medicine has yet to produce. But progress is in the works with the biotechnology revolution.

Did God's call for "greater works" put us on this path of medical and technological progress? Was there, in fact, ever such a call? Where's the definitive evidence? Does the call of conscience that lies at the heart of human existence provide a clue? The openness of our complete incompleteness is certainly something to think about. From openness comes contingency, uncertainty, and mystery—often revealed during personal crises that lead to our being "too far down to fall" any further in life. We are forever being called into question: What am I? What am I failing to do? What should I do? The more our minds crave metaphysical reassurance, the more likely we are to wonder, is there a God? Following Maimonides, we should remain open to the findings of science in answering the question.

I have done as much throughout my story. Recall, for example, that with the big bang things blew outward, not inward, and the resulting openness and material of the cosmos began to take form and expand. It has yet to stop. During its evolution, the Milky Way galaxy in which we live on Earth came into being. The earth is approximately 4.6 billion years old. The galaxy's oldest star (of approximately 200 billion others) is calculated to be approximately 13.2 billion years old. The galaxy is measured to span 100,000 light-years. Light travels 186,000 miles per second. One light-year is approximately 6 trillion miles. The nearest galaxy to the Milky Way is about 2.5 million light-years. Hundreds of billions of other galaxies are scattered throughout space. The farthest galaxies imaged by the Hubble Space Telescope are over 10 billion light-years away. God, it seems, thinks and acts in very big ways.

Indeed, with science we can figure out a crucial point in "the relation between the world and Providence": from "the beginning" to the sixth day, when God created and acknowledged "man," marks a period of billions of years. Humanity's biological history began 3–5 billion years ago, with the rise of the first microscopic life forms. The *human* part of the story begins when the first hominids appear in Africa, approximately 5 million years ago. Those who argue that the Bible supports the "fact" that humankind appeared on Earth only 10,000 years ago are way off base. I am closed-minded on the matter. Evolution is not a debatable point for me, although I am certainly aware of the fact that the fossil record remains incomplete. Nevertheless, science makes clear that evolution does not favor being rotten with imperfection. Things must improve their lives if they are to survive and thrive. The *doing* of science abides by this fact of life. The "true" scientist pledges to be a perfectionist. "All science," writes Paul Davies, "is a search for unification"—for the completeness of perfection.[10] Maimonides' praise of science is warranted. The way of science is arguably the way of God: it is driven by the dynamic of complete incompleteness. Be as open to the world as possible if you want to know its truths!

Having followed this ethical and moral directive, however, science has learned to part company with Maimonides and, in fact, respond to him in a way that would be upsetting to this man of God. The Nobel Prize–winning physicist Steven Weinberg, first discussed in chapter 6, is well known for being eloquent in offering the response. Recall that Weinberg does not believe that science will find an interested God in the final laws of nature, for all "our experience throughout the history of science has tended in the opposite direction, toward a chilling impersonality in the laws of nature." The universe hides no ultimate purpose to its being. As a way of countering the charges of cynicism that he realizes are bound to be evoked by this claim, Weinberg says this:

> But if there is no solace in the fruits of our research, there is at least some consolation in the research itself. Men and women are not content to comfort themselves with tales of gods and giants, or to confine their thoughts to the daily affairs of life; they also build telescopes and satellites and accelerators, and sit at their desks for endless hours working out the meaning of the data they gather. The effort to understand the universe is one of the very few things that lifts human life a little above the level of farce, and gives it some of the grace of tragedy.[11]

In the Judeo-Christian tradition, the "lift" that comes with the "grace of tragedy" marks a moment of epiphany whereby one's suffering becomes instructive for a better life (be it one's own or another's) and thereby enables a person to remain open to, acknowledge, and share an understanding of the loving-kindness of God. The moment is "most appropriate" because it is one in which "the true beauty" of human being is displayed—a beauty whose distinguished purpose is to cultivate "the good" here on earth.[12] The "grace of tragedy" is but an amusing oxymoron when dissociated from this purpose. Recall, an oxymoron is a rhetorical figure employed for effect, for stimulating the attunement of consciousness when making a point. Weinberg's point is that, with the universe in mind, it is pointedly foolish to grant it more than it is worth. There is a beauty, an appropriateness, to the universe that can be acknowledged by scientists and other interested folk who, in turn, can think well of themselves because they can engage in this act. Beyond this, things like rhetorical competence and God don't really matter, unless one chooses to use his or her rhetorical competence to call into question those who think otherwise.

We are at that stage of evolution at which we can think well of ourselves as we produce scientific findings that detail how human beings are, cosmologically speaking, rather insignificant, and how the expanding universe has no point, no purpose. Indeed, as Hume noted long ago, "the life of man is of no greater importance to the universe than that of an oyster." Feeling good about knowing this "fact" is made possible by biological and cognitive capacities that differentiate us from all the other living creatures on earth. We are those beings whose significance lies in our ability to acknowledge the insignificance of "the meaning of it all." There is a *significant insignificance* to our existence. We are more of an oxymoron than what our complete incompleteness makes us out to be.

I must admit that I don't find this discovery especially thrilling. The metaphysical aspect of my being wants something more uplifting. Science tells us that our brains are wired to make possible and encourage this desire. The story of perfection should have a happy ending. Right?

I accept science's finding that we are a significant insignificance, but I do this from a phenomenological standpoint. Our significance presupposes that we are open to the world in such a way that we can ever ponder and announce proudly our insignificance. Such open-mindedness, however, need not be so pessimistic. Our significant insignificance entails a dynamic—a complete incompleteness—that speaks of the importance of being open to other possibilities. We embody this dynamic; it is who *we are* at an ontological level of existence. Our brains have evolved to the point that we can marvel at our openness and read it as a sign of hope rather than as a sign of pointlessness. And we are only in the beginning of that evolutionary stage at which such a thing can happen—that is, where the universe, in and through the opening made possible by human being, becomes ever more conscious of itself. There is so much more to discover. "Normal" life spans may need to be extended.

Openness allows for more than one scientific or religious reading of its nature and worth. Indeed, its very being favors such hermeneutic charity. One can be a strong advocate of science and still be hopeful. Weinberg is hopeful that science will continue to support his assessment of the universe and our role in it. This type of hope abides by very rigorous and rationalistic standards, so much so that it applauds its own dead-end fate. Darwin was a bit more hopeful. Listen, for example, to what he admits regarding his *The Origin of Species* in a correspondence with his friend and colleague, the Harvard botanist Asa Grey:

> With respect to the theological view of the question; this is always painful to me. I am bewildered. I had no intention to write atheistically. But I own that I cannot see, as plainly as others do, and as I should wish to do, evidence of design and beneficence on all sides of us. There seems to me too much misery in the world. I cannot persuade myself that a beneficent and omnipotent God would have designedly created the Ichneumonidae with the express intention of their feeding within the living bodies of caterpillars, or that a cat should play with mice. . . . On the other hand, I cannot anyhow be contented to view this wonderful universe, and especially the nature of man, and to conclude that everything is the result of brute force. I am inclined to look at everything as resulting from designed laws, with the details, whether good or bad, left to the working out of what we may call chance. Not that this notion *at all* satisfies me. I feel most deeply that the whole subject is too profound for the human intellect. A dog might as well speculate on the mind of Newton.[13]

Darwin leaves more of an opening for metaphysical thought than does Weinberg. God is doubted, but not dismissed totally out of hand. Perhaps God is the creator of the laws in question. All that science hopes to discover, however, is what these laws are, without ever making any leaps of faith. If Darwin would have had as much scientific knowledge in his possession as does Weinberg, he might have been much less generous in providing an opening for the God of metaphysical thought (although, empirically speaking, such thought certainly is grounded in the physiology of human brain function, even though its intended object "is too profound for the human intellect").

A bit more open-minded than Darwin in coming to terms with our complete incompleteness are scientists like Stephen Jay Gould, who, much influenced by Darwin, has this to say about the two most fundamental approaches to the issue—religion and science: "I believe, with all my heart, in a respectful, even loving, concordat between the magisterial of science and religion. . . . If religion can no longer dictate the nature of factual conclusions residing properly within the magisterium of science, then scientists cannot claim higher insight into moral truth from any superior knowledge of the world's empirical constitution. This mutual humility leads to important practical consequences in a world of such diverse passions. We would do well to embrace the principle and enjoy the consequences."[14] Humility is an antidote for the disease of being rotten with perfection, for it functions emotionally and reasonably to inform individual selves that they are not as great as they thought themselves to be. The lesson speaks to the importance of being open to others: altruism over egoism.

In his *A Different Universe: Reinventing Physics from the Bottom Down*, the Nobel Prize–winning physicist Robert Laughlin enacts the virtue of humility. He writes, "The great power of science is its ability, through brutal objectivity, to reveal to us truth we *did not anticipate*. In this it continues to be invaluable, and one of the great human creations."[15] Laughlin's research is aligned with the "theory of emergence," which, as noted in chapter 7, involves scientists in "the search for the laws of self-organization and complexity." Laughlin insists that "nature is regulated not only by microscopic rule base but by powerful and general principles of organization. Some of these principles are known, but the vast majority are not." Principles of organization and their consequences can be physical laws that, in turn, can organize themselves into new laws and then into even newer laws. "The laws of electron motion beget the laws of thermodynamics and chemistry, which beget the laws of crystallization, which beget the laws of rigidity and plasticity, which beget the laws of engineering. The natural world is thus an interdependent hierarchy of descent." What this "law of hierarchy" suggests, for example, is "that the fabric of space-time [is] not simply the stage on which life [is] played out but an organizational phenomenon, and that there might be something beyond."[16]

Science must always be in search of this something, the next unarticulated principle of organization. Moreover, as Laughlin puts it, science must learn to "trust Providence" when the search seems to be going nowhere but hope is still alive.[17] Humility must complement the brutal objectivity of science and the closed-mindedness that such objectivity, displayed in "mathematical reductionism," can generate. Laughlin makes the point with humor when he admits that after "years of scholarly labor" he came to understand that the story of Adam and Eve in the Bible is wrong: "What actually happened is that Adam and Eve ate snake in a Chinese restaurant called *Knowledge* and finished up with lychees and fortune cookies. Adam opened his cookie and read, 'Here are the equations of the universe. Good luck with your calculations.' Eve then opened her cookie and read, 'Believe nothing this man says.' Thus began the world as we know it."[18]

The good health and humor of science requires open-mindedness. The same goes for religion. Scientists like Gerald Schroeder encourage such mutual humility in arguing for "the convergence of scientific and biblical wisdom." Schroeder is a physicist who is awed by the "finely tuned mechanics" of the universe that make life possible. For example, science tells us that carbon is the only element that can form the complex chains necessary for the processes of life. In order for this element to form, however, radioactive beryllium must absorb a nucleus of helium and build to carbon. The mean life of a radioactive beryllium atom is quite short: 10^{-16} seconds (0.0000000000000001). Within this life span, a helium nucleus must find, collide with, and be absorbed by the beryllium nucleus, thereby metamorphosing into the atomic staff of life. Human being is impossible without the success of this process. Schroeder writes, "We stand in awe at the beauty of diamond white stars stretching across a velvet black desert night sky. That's our emotional response. These discoveries of science provide a quantifiable basis for that awe. The universe in which we live is very special."[19]

The physicist Schroeder is also a biblical scholar; his interpretations of the Old Testament persuade him that human beings have a purpose on earth and that the finely tuned workings of the universe that make life possible and purposeful are not accidents. Schroeder compares the chances of life being merely a completely random event with the chances of a person winning a national lottery three weeks in a row. It could happen, but the odds are *really* stacked against the possibility. No, the fine-tunings of the universe that lead to human life at this point in time must have a source in something that is itself organizational and harmonic. And, so, Schroeder writes, "Interpretation is as essential for understanding Genesis as it is for understanding nature. It is time for both sides to stop the war. Render unto science that which is science's: a proven method for investigating our universe. But render unto the Bible the search for purpose and the poetry that describes the purpose."[20] For Schroeder the physicist and religious soul, the genius and goodness of science lie in its being second to none in revealing with awesome mathematical precision something of the nature of God. We must not be closed-minded to the very real possibility that intelligent design has always been in the microscopic and macroscopic workings of a universe that, as is the case with human beings, displays a purposeful nature.[21]

Schroeder and like-minded colleagues are very open-minded souls. Too much so, in fact, for less-open-minded scientists. Avoiding God-of-the-gaps thinking is a major rule of right-minded science. When broken, the ire of scientists like Weinberg is raised to a noticeable level. The guilty parties are told, "You may tell me that [rather than some deity like those of traditional monotheistic religions] you are thinking of something much more abstract, some cosmic spirit of order and harmony, as Einstein did. You are certainly free to think that way, but then I don't know why you use words like 'designer' or 'God,' except perhaps as a form of protective coloration." Weinberg is closed-minded to the rhetoric of religion. So much so, in fact, that he claims, "With or without religion, good people can behave well and bad people can do evil; but for good people to do evil—that takes religion."[22] Such closed-mindedness begets more closed-mindedness. With such insults being aired publicly, religion, in turn, is also known to become closed-minded in its consideration of the scientific enterprise, with its notions of "progress" and reductionistic tendencies.[23] It is a tragic mistake on the part of both parties—a mistake that can become quite mean-spirited. For example, in his foreword to physicist Victor Stenger's best-selling book *God, the Failed Hypothesis: How Science Shows That God Does Not Exist*, the cultural critic Christopher Hitchens has this to say about religion and God: "The challenge of our age is the same that confronted all previous ages. How shall we live the good life and how shall we know virtue? In the past millennia of primeval ignorance, pattern-seeking primates proposed a totalitarian solution to this question and threw all responsibility onto a supreme dictator who demanded to be loved and feared at the same time. The story of human emancipation is the narrative of our liberation from this evil myth, and from the greedy, ambitious primates who sought (as they still seek) to rule in its name."[24]

My story about perfection has been more of a story about open-mindedness than closed-mindedness. More about a fundamental way of being that admits an ethical, moral, and rhetorical function and that lies at the heart of genuine religious and scientific inquiry. Human being provides an opening event during which the happening of a much-larger opening event can be witnessed. We are a happening of complete incompleteness engulfed and awed by an infinitely larger happening of complete incompleteness. The openness of the event makes possible our hearing a call of conscience coming from our spatial and temporal existence. The call *calls for* an acknowledging of otherness, which is an ethical, heroic, beautiful, emotional, reasonable, and just thing for humans beings to do. Acknowledgment is a life-giving gift, an act of salvation, something that enables us to construct the dwelling places of interpersonal relationships where we feel comfortable and at home with others and, in being true to our ontological and metaphysical nature, are hopeful of still-better things to come. My story has been about how such a rhetoric of perfection is at work in our existence. This rhetoric admits an epideictic character: a "showing-forth" of humanity at its best.

I am, of course, more than willing to admit that my conception of this rhetoric remains incomplete and is thus not perfect. Indeed, I am awed by and *want to remain true to* the nature of a living oxymoron, an embodied event of complete incompleteness that may be nothing more than a significant insignificance but also may be more than that. I favor the second option, which, to be sure, is a natural thing to do. A perfectionist impulse energizes the lived body, an impulse that, at the very least, began with a big bang billions of years ago when openness first came on the scene. No openness, no life. Openness is good.[25]

The impulse is motivated by our complete incompleteness. Being rotten with imperfection is not a good way to be. Overcompensating to the point that we become rotten with perfection can make matters worse, although the closed-mindedness that is fostered by this disease can be defended for its capacity to have us move beyond arguing over the obvious in our quest for better things to come.

If I have succeeded in telling a story that has been worthwhile enough to get you all the way to this point in the narrative, then perhaps it is correct to assume that you are not suspecting some surprise ending that clarifies beyond a shadow of a doubt why we are metaphysical creatures fated to pursue perfection. I never promised to offer such an ending. A phenomenological assessment of perfection is required to maintain the empirical orientation of science ("to the things themselves") when trying to come to terms with and thereby understand the matter at hand. The complete incompleteness of human being calls for open-mindedness on our part. With this fact in mind, however, I offer one final case study that enables me at least to end my story on a hopeful note. The case, as its title suggests, is particularly fitting for my project: the 1997 Academy Award–winning film and comedy *As Good as It Gets*.[26] Although a work of fiction, the film provides a wonderful illustration of how the lived body is called to come to terms with perfection as it deals with the chaos and order of everyday existence. The film also makes much of how people can suffer from the disease of being rotten with perfection, as well as from the disease of being rotten with imperfection. The Schiavo case also illustrates this sad fact of life. As the final scene fades in *As Good as It Gets*, however, we are supposed to feel good, even though we are not sure what is yet to come of the lived bodies in question. Medical science has a more noticeable role to play in the film than does religion. In fact, the topic of religion *per se* is never mentioned. But its presence is there, nevertheless, and warrants acknowledgment.

As Good as It Gets: A Conclusion

On the cover of its DVD jacket, *As Good as It Gets* is described as "a comedy from the heart that goes for the throat." The film tells the story of Melvin Udall, a very intelligent and successful writer of romance fiction novels. Melvin suffers from the ailment of obsessive-compulsive disorder (OCD) and is thus "fated" to be as perfect as possible with his habitual imperfections, especially as they concern his fear of germs, his passion for neatness and strict behavioral regimen, and his related desire to control his environment and his associations with others.

For example, when washing his hands in scalding hot water in his bathroom, he begins by opening a new cake of Neutrogena soap, passes the bar of soap across each hand three times, throws it away, and then repeats the procedure twice more, selecting a new bar of soap each time. When eating at the one and only restaurant he frequents, which he visits every day, he brings his own plastic-sealed set of plastic eating utensils. He sits at the same table in the restaurant so that he can be waited on by the same waitress. Whenever he returns to his apartment, he twists the dead bolt lock on the front door back and forth five times to make sure that he is safe and sound. His interactions with others are typically marked by his using his extensive vocabulary and quick wit to ridicule their presence and particular ways of being who they are. He always needs to be in command of any situation in order to ensure that his routines are never interrupted. Maintaining strict control is his primary objective every second of the day. When control is lost due to some unforeseen event, the personal and social insecurities hidden by his obsessive-compulsive behaviors surface, exposing a soul that is interpersonally inept, shy, and in desperate need of acknowledgment. He is hard-pressed to receive this life-giving gift, given his mean-spirited ways of dealing with others.

During one of many scenes that present the consequences of events that impede his progress as a prolific and reclusive author, Melvin runs to his psychiatrist's office (making sure that he avoids stepping on cracks in the pavement along the way), barges into a private room where the doctor is studying some notes, and demands an immediate session. The doctor refuses to acquiesce to his ravings and tells him to go home and make a proper appointment. On his way out of the office, he walks through the doctor's waiting room, where a number of patients are sitting quietly, minding their own business. Scanning the room, he asks in an irritated, vindictive, and worried tone, "What if this is as good as it gets?" The scene ends as he leaves the waiting room and as we witness the startled and dejected expressions of those who, in addition to all their other problems, are now also suffering from the effects of his sadistic inquiry. One woman gasps audibly. Contextualized by earlier scenes and dialogue that make clear that he, although an S.O.B., is a "comical" character, his brief address to the other patients comes off as being humorous, albeit in a sick way. Indeed, this is a comedy from the heart that goes for the throat. Melvin's question certainly raises the issue of truth.

Melvin seems to enjoy being a sadist. He feels powerful when he makes others miserable, especially those who "piss him off" because their lives, no matter how dysfunctional they might be, are perhaps still "better" than his. And because his sadism only serves to increase the dislike that others have for him, such behavior becomes at the same time masochistic. Melvin is his own worst enemy; he lives an existence that is severely rotten with perfection. The disease hides the fact that deep down inside Melvin is a person who is dying for the life-giving gift of heart-felt acknowledgment. This nearly extinguished desire, however, becomes his saving grace as certain relationships with others— the waitress, Carol; his gay neighbor, Simon, who lives in an apartment across the hall; and Simon's dog, Verdell—serve to rehabilitate the desire to the point at which Melvin is willing to try to live out an optimistic answer to his earlier-asked and haunting question: "What if this is as good as it gets?"

The film opens with Melvin yelling at and chasing Verdell in the hallway outside of his apartment. Verdell is known to urinate in the hallway (perhaps because he dislikes and fears Melvin, who scares him to death). As Verdell is relieving himself on the wall, Melvin (wearing plastic gloves) catches him, picks him up, and then tosses the helpless creature down the trash chute. No regret is displayed. The call of conscience is not heard, although we hear Simon faintly beckoning to Verdell in the background. Melvin says goodbye to Verdell by reminding him that, hey, "this is New York; if you can make it here you can make it anywhere."

Melvin despises the dog as much as he does its owner, the homosexual Simon, who is a very kind soul and an aspiring and talented artist. Their presence in Melvin's world is bothersome at best and exceptionally disruptive and anxiety provoking at worst. When Simon sees Melvin rushing back to his apartment and inquires about Verdell, Melvin's response makes clear his attitude toward his neighbor's presence, companions, and lifestyle.

SIMON: Verdell!? Where's my good doggie? (*Simon notices Melvin at the far end of the hall and calls to him*)

SIMON: Mr. Udall . . . excuse me. Have you seen Verdell?

MELVIN: What's he look like?

SIMON (*a little taken back*): My dog . . . you know . . . I mean my little dog with the adorable face . . . Don't you know what my dog looks like?

MELVIN (*feigns sudden comprehension*): Oh, I got it. You're talking about your dog. I thought that was the name of the colored man I've been seeing in the hall.

SIMON: Which color was that?

MELVIN: Like thick molasses, with a broad nose perfect for smelling trouble and prison food . . . (*Simon calls to an African American friend who comes over. Simon makes introductions.*)

SIMON: Frank Sachs—Melvin Udall.

MELVIN (*without missing a beat*): How're you doing?

SIMON: Frank shows my work, Mr. Udall, I think you know that. (*Frank is not concerned with Melvin. All of his attention is directed toward Simon.*)

FRANK: Simon, you've got to get dressed.

MELVIN (*to Simon*): What I know is that as long as you keep your work zipped up around me, I don't give a rat's crap what or where you shove your show. Are we done being neighbors for now? (*Suddenly Frank is interested in the conversation. He makes a rush toward Melvin as if to strike him. Simon holds him back.*)

SIMON (*to Frank softly*): It's not worth it. Verdell must be in the apartment. (*As they move toward the apartment, Melvin calls after them.*)

MELVIN: Hope you find him. I love that dog.

(*Simon, terminally nonconfrontational, still finds himself compelled to turn back toward Melvin.*)

SIMON: You don't love anything, Mr. Udall.

The way Melvin speaks when showing contempt for Simon and Frank forms an interesting contrast when we are given a glimpse into Melvin's apartment, which is decorated with large pictures of notable African American figures, including famous jazz musicians and Malcolm X. Indeed, in the privacy of his apartment, Melvin's vulnerability is exposed. He is not the "tough guy" he pretends to be in his interactions with others. Sitting in his apartment writing his romance novels, Melvin is at times overjoyed as he struggles with the art of rhetorical competence and reads aloud as he composes, "Somewhere in the dark, she had confessed and he had forgiven. 'This is what you live for,' he said. 'Two heads on a pillow where there is only the safety of being with each other.' How, she wondered, could she find such hope in the most shameful part of her?" Melvin becomes so engrossed in his writing that he barely reacts to the loud knocking on his door. Simon calls to him, but Melvin continues without hearing him. His fingers fly across the keyboard as he writes, "At last she was able to define love." Melvin pauses to consider the definition of love as the knocking continues. He wrinkles his brow pensively and persists, "Love was . . . ." Melvin's eyes flicker briefly. He is on the verge of a breakthrough, but the knocking finally is too much of an interruption to ignore.

Melvin is in a rage as he stands to answer the door. It's Simon, wanting to inform Melvin that the janitor found Verdell and that he is okay. In one more burst of courage, Simon asks, "Did you . . . do something to him?" As the scene unfolds, we are given another stunning display of lived bodies expressing their stories.

MELVIN: Do you realize that I work at home?

SIMON (*eyes downcast*): No, I don't.

MELVIN: Do you like to be interrupted when you are nancing round in your little garden?

SIMON: No . . . actually, I even shut the phone off and put a little piece of cardboard in the ringer so no one can just buzz me from . . .

MELVIN: Well, I work all the time. So never, never again interrupt me. Okay? I mean, never. Not if there's fire. Not even it you hear a thud from inside my home and a week later there's a smell from in there that can only be a decaying body and you have to hold a hanky against your face because the stench is so thick you think you're going to faint. Even then don't come knocking . . . don't knock . . . not on this door. Not for any reason. Do you get me, sweetheart?

An ethic of being for others is not a quality of Melvin's character. A crisis, however, provides an opening for change. Simon is robbed by hoodlums who break into his apartment and beat him severely, breaking his wrist, bruising his legs, and pummeling his face. Someone has to take care of Verdell while Simon recuperates in the hospital for a few days. Frank confronts Melvin about the situation and, by way of some hilarious intimidation, "persuades" him to become Verdell's temporary caretaker. As he hands over Verdell to Melvin, the latter makes clear how dire the situation is for him, admitting in desperation that "nobody has ever been in [his apartment] before." Melvin is terrified. Verdell is terrified. Melvin has no dog food. Verdell is hesitant to eat the bacon and other people food that Melvin places in a bowl on the floor. Staring at Verdell, Melvin asks, "Where's the trust?" Depressed, Melvin sits down at his piano and begins to play and sing a song that is meant to prepare him for the crisis and challenge before him: "Always Look on the Bright Side of Life." As Melvin plays and sings, Verdell starts to eat the food.

Melvin and Verdell begin to get used to each other and form a bond of friendship. And it is tight: during one scene, Melvin is walking Verdell on the neighborhood streets, wearing plastic gloves as he holds the leash and talking to him in a happy manner: "It is a beautiful day for our walk today. Very nice." Melvin then notices that Verdell is stepping over cracks in the sidewalk as if, like Melvin, he, too, had OCD. Melvin is delighted. "Hey, hey, look at that, look at him." Melvin continues to speak to Verdell, but now in more of a baby-talk manner: "I got to give you something. I got to give you something real good. I got to show it to you." Melvin reaches in his pocket for a bag filled with bacon. His plastic gloves impede the act a bit as he pulls out the treat, picks up Verdell with both hands, holds their faces close together, and lovingly tells him, "Don't be like me. Don't you be like me. Stay just the way you are. You are a *perfect* man and I am going to take you home and get you something to eat." Melvin is being truthful; the dog is better than the man. The scene shifts to two young women who have just witnessed the interaction. One of them is quite moved and adoringly says, "Ah, I'd like to be treated like that." We then see Melvin and Verdell walking back to his apartment, stepping over cracks together. "Let's go home and do some writing," says Melvin in an enthusiastic and joyful voice.

Melvin is back in his apartment writing at his computer as he tries to give a happy ending to his unfinished novel. Verdell is lying down next to him on the desk. Melvin speaks aloud as he writes, "He had made the girl happy, and what a girl. 'You saved my life,' she said. 'You better make it up to me.'" Melvin's faced is filled with glee. He raises his arms in victory: "Done! Done!" He stands up from his chair, points to Verdell, and jokingly says, "Yes, I hate the doggy. I hate the doggy. Sixty-two books, done!" The scene ends as Verdell follows an ecstatic Melvin out of the room.

But Melvin's crisis is far from over. Simon has returned home and joyfully awaits Verdell's presence and affection. Melvin is heartbroken about giving up his caretaking duties. In one scene, right behind his locked front door, he breaks down and cries, has an anxiety attack, and turns the lock back and forth five times. He then sits down at the piano and once again plays his (and Verdell's) song. He stops, stares at Verdell's empty food bowl and his toy bone, and, as he both laughs and cries, speaks: "Over a dog. Over an ugly dog."

Verdell was therapeutic for Melvin. In the company of this dog, Melvin heard and responded to a call of conscience. He assumed the personal responsibility of opening up to another creature and offering him the life-giving gift of acknowledgment. He acted ethically, heroically, reasonably, emotionally, justly. It was a beautiful sight to see. He was a savior. With his words and deeds, he created a dwelling place in which a frightened animal could feel welcome, comfortable, and at home. Melvin demonstrated noble character, and he felt good about himself. He found the right words. He finished his novel. He embodied and displayed a rhetoric of perfection—a showing-forth of humanity at its best. But now things were radically changing again. Change and OCD do not go well together.

Simon is in a wheelchair when he knocks on Melvin's door to pick up Verdell. Melvin makes some sarcastic remarks about Simon's physical appearance as a way of disguising his sadness about giving back Verdell. Simon, nearly in tears, pleads, "Can you take it just a little easy, Mr. Udall?" Simon then calls for Verdell, who is hesitant to leave his new home and who acts strangely once Simon takes him back to his own apartment. The situation is especially dreadful for Simon because he has just learned that he has run out of money and must give up his apartment and art studio. He phones a number of friends, but they can't help. His parents, who he hasn't talked to in a year, are his last option—one that he refuses to take because of too much personal and hurtful family baggage. In the midst of this situation, Melvin steps into Simon's apartment, having just taken Verdell for a walk. Simon wheels himself toward them and thanks Melvin for doing him the favor. But then he has to turn away as he begins to break down, offering the excuse that "he doesn't feel well." A state of being rotten with imperfection is evident. No wonder, notes Melvin: "This place smells like shit." Simon is unable to take any more abuse and screams back, "Go away! Please just leave!" Melvin asks about Simon's "queer party friends." Simon screams again: "Get out of here! There is nothing worse than having to feel this way in front of you." The truth hurts. Melvin responds with experienced authority and rhetorical expertise: "Nellie, you're a disgrace to depression." Simon tells him to "rot in hell." Melvin retorts, "No need to stop being a lady. Quit worrying. You will be back on your knees in no time." Although suffering from the disease of being rotten with imperfection, Simon musters an act of courage. He lifts himself up from his wheelchair and punches Melvin in the head and shoulders, knocking him to the floor.

Melvin is stunned and appears frightened as he stands up and backs away in fear, listening to an angry Simon: "You lucky devil. It just keeps getting better and better. . . . You are here for rock bottom—you absolute horror of a human being." Melvin's facial expressions display a combination of contradictory emotions: disgust for so-called "Nellie," sadness for his plight, domination over his miserable existence, and a little compassion. After much hesitation, kindness wins out for the moment. Melvin explains that "it is not affection" that draws Verdell to him, rather "it is a trick. I keep bacon in my pocket." Simon is greatly relieved. Taking a piece of bacon from Melvin, Simon shows it to Verdell and lovingly calls to him. Verdell nevertheless jumps up on Melvin for affection. Simon is crushed. He looks at Melvin: "Could you leave now, please?" Simon falls back into a severe state of being rotten with imperfection.

It is 3:22 a.m. Melvin wakes up, slides out of bed, puts on his slippers and robe, and knocks on Simon's door carrying a small food container. Simon opens the door, steadying himself with a walking cane. Melvin smiles and says, "I took a chance you were up. I brought you some Chinese soup." Simon thanks him, and they sit down on opposite sides of a wooden bench inside the apartment, near the door. Staring into space, they both look weary and depressed. A brief exchange of truths takes place:

MELVIN: Boy. I've never been this tired in my life. I haven't been sleeping. I haven't been clear in my head . . . or felt like myself. I'm in trouble. It's just not the tiredness. Boy

SIMON (*interrupting and continuing the "conversation"*): Sick. Nauseous . . .

MELVIN: Sleepy . . .

SIMON: Where everything looks distorted and everything inside you kind of aches and you can barely find the will to complain . . .

MELVIN: Yeah! . . . Well, I'm glad we did this.

Melvin stands up and remarks, "Good talking to you," as he walks out of the apartment. Simon looks perplexed and lonely once again. The scene exemplifies how Melvin's selfishness can so easily control and overcome whatever guilt, sympathy, and empathy he may be feeling at the time. Melvin is a survivalist; being rotten with imperfection is not an option for him.

Melvin's all-too-brief "being-for" Simon was also encouraged by feelings that were developing for Carol, the waitress who serves him breakfast every day at his one and only restaurant.

Carol is an attractive, energetic, fast-witted, thirty-something single mother whose young son (Spencer) is oftentimes ill because of asthma that typically receives inadequate medical care whenever he needs to be rushed to the hospital. The two of them live in a small apartment with Carol's mother.

Carol easily holds her own in verbal jousting matches with Melvin, and she does this with humorous sarcasm and a friendly and sly smile. Melvin admires the talent. She is quick and intelligent, more like him than anyone else who works at the restaurant. In a scene early on in the film, however, Melvin offers a demeaning quip about Spencer. Carol's comportment changes immediately, right before our eyes. She sits down at Melvin's table, addresses him as "you fuck," and in a loud voice makes clear that if he ever again talks about here son that way, he will never be allowed back in the restaurant. Melvin cowers as he receives the verbal thrashing. He is unable to maintain eye contact, turns and bends his head in shame and embarrassment, and is unable to speak up until he eventually apologizes and promises never again to be that disrespectful. Still, Melvin's sadomasochistic ways reappear when he and Carol are bantering about such mundane and humorous matters as Melvin's unhealthy dietary lifestyle or how tired Carol looks because of emergency trips to the hospital.

In Carol's company, Melvin feels good, like he does when writing his romance novels. He is smitten by her looks and pleasant manner, and he feels bad about her circumstances. So, without telling her, he makes private arrangements to have his editor's husband, who is a respected physician, visit Carol and her son at their apartment so that he can begin properly helping Spencer deal with his asthma. Carol is ecstatic, although when informed by the doctor that Melvin's connections made possible this longed-for remedy, she eventually becomes extremely nervous, thinking that perhaps Melvin is doing this with the expectation of making a move on her. In the middle of the night she travels in the rain to his apartment, located in a better part of the city, remains outside his apartment door once he opens it, and makes clear that her immense gratitude will never lead to her having sex with him. Melvin is totally unprepared for this interaction. His expressions display dismay, defensiveness, and what perhaps may be the beginnings of a broken heart.

In another scene, we see and hear Carol writing a very long thank you note to Melvin as she worries about the situation. Her mother calls to her; they are supposed to have a night out together. "I am on the last page," answers Carol. "How do you spell 'conscience'?" Her mother replies, "C-O-N-S-C-I-E-N-C-E." Carol continues writing and talking out loud: "I gotta finish this letter or I'll go nuts. . . . This can't be right—'con-science'?" Breaking the word in two this way makes the scene especially fitting for my purposes. Recall that the word "conscience" is derived from the Latin *con-scientia*, meaning "to know with" or "to know together." This is what religious souls try to do with God, and what scientists try to do with their colleagues as they work out their theories, equations, and experiments. Carol is struggling to come to terms with her situation, trying desperately to find the right words to convey to Melvin her overwhelming appreciation of his life-giving gift. It is a struggle for telling the truth in a rhetorically competent way. Melvin has done for Carol what he did for Verdell: he has been open, responsible, ethical, heroic, caring, just, and, to be sure, a savior that is creating a better and more comfortable dwelling place for her and Spencer. A rhetoric of perfection is once again at work. Carol has been struck by the beauty of it all.

The next day, Carol takes the letter to work so she can hand it to Melvin and add some additional words of thanks. Melvin is seated with Frank, who is explaining to him that Verdell has been upset about his change of circumstances and has to go to the veterinarian. Carol walks to the table, interrupts the conversation, and hands the letter to Melvin, explaining briefly what it is: a "thank you note." Melvin is not comfortable with the situation and refuses to take the note. "No thank you note. No, no, no." Carol turns and walks away, disappointed and disturbed. Melvin turns to Frank and says, "Shouldn't that be a good thing, telling somebody 'No thanks required'?" Frank kids Melvin about his "unkindly" behavior and then informs him that Simon has to travel to Baltimore tomorrow to ask his parents for money. "Can you drive him?" asks Frank. Melvin is displeased with the request and responds, "Think white and get serious!" Frank tells Melvin that he can use Frank's car. "It's a convertible." Carol returns to the table to try once again. Melvin informs her about

Frank's request. And Carol lets loose in anger, making her words a bit confusing: "I want your life for one minute, where my big problem is . . . somebody offers me a free convertible so I can get out of this city."

As Melvin tries to make sense of her meaning, Carol walks away again. Melvin than says to Frank, "Okay. I'll do it. I'll take him, I'll take him." Frank leaves the table, and Carol returns. Melvin tells her he is "going to give his queer neighbor a lift to Baltimore" for two days. He then asks, "Hey, what I did for you . . . it's working out?" Carol's mood is transformed from disgust to heartfelt appreciation. You "changed my life," she gladly admits, and she starts to tell him about all that the note contains. She even reads some lines: your action "makes you the most supportive, surprising, generous person I ever met in my life, and . . . you are going to be in our prayers . . . forever." The truth needs to be heard. Displaying great discomfort, Melvin tries to end the scene by telling Carol in an insincere way that her words are "lovely." But she is on an emotional roll, telling him with tears in her eyes that she "is sorry" for all the times that she wasn't a better person for him. Melvin's demeanor changes; he appears to be genuinely moved and sincerely tells her "thank you." Then he announces that he wants her to do something for him. "I want you to go on this trip. . . . I can't do this without you. I'm afraid that [Simon] might pull the stiff 'one eye' on me." Carol is mortified and insists that there is no way she will take the trip. Melvin ensures her that she will just be a "chaperone" and that everything on his part will be, without a doubt, appropriate. Staring at his face and trying to decipher its expressions, Carol asks, "Are you saying that accepting your help obligates me?" Melvin is quick to reply with a wily smile: "Is there any other way to see it?" The ethic of "Where art thou?" "Here I am!" does not come off that well here.

The next scene finds Melvin, Simon, and Carol meeting at Frank's car to begin their trip. Carol and Simon say "Hi" to each other before Melvin can make a formal introduction, which he does by looking quickly at them and saying, "Oh, Carol the waitress, Simon the fag." As they travel to Baltimore, personal stories are shared, and Simon and Carol begin forming a caring friendship. Melvin is jealous. Arriving at the hotel where they are staying, and beginning to unpack their suitcases, Melvin walks into Simon's room.

MELVIN: Can I ask you a personal question?

SIMON: Sure.

MELVIN: You ever get an erection over a woman?

SIMON (*in gentle exasperation*): Melvin . . .

MELVIN: I mean, wouldn't your life be easier if you weren't—

SIMON (*with gentle sarcasm*): You consider your life easy?

MELVIN: All right, I give you that one.

Noticing and admiring the orderly way that Simon has placed his clothes in his suitcase, the obsessive-compulsive Melvin comments, "Nice packin'."

Carol finds outs during a phone call with her mother that Spencer not only is feeling much better, but he was outside playing soccer and scored a goal. Carol is overjoyed, turns to Simon and Melvin, reports the news, and demands, "Take me out for a good time. Take me out dancing." Simon reports that he is exhausted and quite anxious about his upcoming meeting with his parents. There is no way he can go out. Carol gives him a gentle kiss and turns to Melvin: "I'm happy, and you are my date." In a moment of high anxiety, Melvin is speechless and unable to say no. He takes an exceptionally long time showering and getting dressed for his date. Both he and Carol are dressed in good-looking casual attire. They go to a fine neighborhood restaurant filled with many happy customers and staff, are gladly greeted by the head waiter, and are informed that gentlemen are required to wear a tie and jacket. The waiter is willing to provide the clothing to Melvin, who makes it clear that he in no way is willing to get "the plague" by wearing clothes worn by somebody else. The scene is embarrassing and funny as Melvin leaves Carol at the bar, runs out of the restaurant, drives to a men's clothing store, hurryingly purchases and dons a jacket and tie, drives back to the restaurant, and finds her at the bar. They admire each other's appearance from afar. Once they are standing together, Carol says to Melvin: "You look so se . . ." She catches herself before speaking the last word and rephrases, "You look great . . . great! You want to dance?"

Melvin is not confident enough to do so. They thus are seated at their table. The situation is a bit awkward, but it is obvious that they are both happy with the progress so far. Then Melvin notes, "I don't get this place. They make me buy a new outfit and let you in [here] in a housedress." Carol is, of course, insulted and stands up to leave. Melvin frantically explains that he "didn't mean it that way" and pleads for her to sit down. Still angry, Carol sits down and demands, "Pay me a compliment, Melvin. I need one. Quick. You have no idea how much what you just said hurt my feelings."

MELVIN: Okay

CAROL: And *mean* it!

MELVIN (*exceptionally nervous*): Can we order first? (*Carol agrees and Melvin yells out their order to a waiter who is working at another table across the room. As always, Melvin's interpersonal skills are atrocious. Carol's embarrassment is obvious.*)

MELVIN: Okay, now, I got a real great compliment for you. And it's true.

CAROL: I am so afraid you are about to say something awful.

MELVIN: Don't be pessimistic. It's not your style . . . Okay, here I go.

Melvin begins by explaining to Carol for the first time that he "has got this 'ailment'" (OCD). His psychiatrist told him that "in fifty to sixty percent of the cases, a pill [antidepressant] really helps. . . . I hate pills. Very dangerous things, pills. I'm using the word 'hate' here about pills. Hate! My compliment is, that night when you came over and said you would never have . . . Well, you were there, you know what happened . . . Well, my compliment to you is, the next morning I started taking the pills . . ."[27]

CAROL (*looking puzzled*): I don't quite get how that's a compliment for me.

MELVIN (*with an honest smile on his face*): You make me want to be a better man.

The camera closes in on Carol's face, then on Melvin's face, and then back to Carol, who says, "That's maybe the best compliment of my life." Melvin is delighted and notes in a kidding way that "well, maybe I overshot it a little because I was aiming it just enough to keep you from walking out." They laugh together and feel more at ease. Assuming a more confident but curious posture, Carol asks, "How's it going with those pills? Good, I hope, I hope." Melvin struggles with an answer: "It's little by little. . . . It's exhausting talking like this. Exhausting." Melvin puts his head in his hands. Feeling compassionate, Carol moves closer to Melvin and in a loving way asks, "Did you ever let a romantic moment make you do something you know is stupid?" Looking surprised but pleased, Melvin answers, "Never." Carol does not hesistate. "Here's the trouble with 'never,'" she says, as she gently pulls his head toward her and gives him a long and tender kiss on the lips. Remaining silent, a bit unsure, but with a pleasant smile on his face, Melvin remarks, "You don't owe me that." "That wasn't a payment," replies Carol.

She goes on to explain that when Melvin first came to the restaurant for breakfast, she thought he was "handsome." "Then, of course, you spoke. . . . So now that your soft underbelly is all exposed . . . tell me, why did you bring me here?" Melvin stutters. Carol repeats her question. Melvin is silent, not sure what to say. "Okay," says Carol. "If you ask me, I'll say 'yes.'" Stuttering again, Melvin says, "I don't know. There's a lot of reasons." He then goes on to say that "one thought was that if you had sex with Simon . . . maybe . . . Well, it's just one idea."

Melvin's confusion is not helpful. "That's why you brought me?" asks Carol. "Like I'm a what? . . . and I owe you what?" Simon's confusion intensifies as he tries again to explain that it was just "one thought" that came out wrong. Now even more upset, Carol stands up and starts to leave the restaurant. "Forget about what I said about Simon," begs Melvin. "I'll never forget you said it," replies Carol.

Back at the hotel, Simon is leaving a voice mail for his parents. Carol storms into the room. Simon inquires about her evening. "Don't ask," she replies in an angered tone. She informs Simon that she is going to take a "big bath" and order a "big meal." Realizing she is treating Simon unfairly, she apologizes and asks if he is okay. "Don't ask," he replies in a depressed tone. He informs Carol that he needs to find "better thoughts" because, at the moment, he is mostly thinking about "how to die."

Carol heads into the bathroom and begins disrobing and fixing her hair in preparation for entering the tub. The bathroom door is not fully closed, and Simon is able to witness Carol's routine. He is struck by her beauty: her skin, her neck, the line of her back. There is nothing crass going on here. Simon is a gay artist, and in the presence of his new friend Carol he is feeling comfortable and once again inspired to sketch the goodness that he sees. He tells Carol, "I have to draw you." Although flattered, Carol objects. She explains that she is much more shy than people think. Simon is glowing with happiness as he states simply and eloquently, "You are why cavemen chiseled on walls." Simon produces sketch after sketch throughout the evening. We hear Carol say, "We are being naughty here, pal." "No, no," insists Simon. "This is so great." As he breaks off his arm cast so that he can be more careful with his drawing, Simon screams in joy. With Carol's help, he is defeating the disease of being rotten with imperfection.

The next morning, Melvin storms into Simon's room, where Simon is happily eating breakfast while still in his bathrobe. Melvin is upset and direct: "Did you have sex with her?" Carol then enters the room, also wearing a bathrobe. Melvin says he is sorry for interrupting, but then asks again in a demanding manner: "Did you have sex with her?" Carol intervenes: "To hell with sex. It was better than sex. We held each other. What I need he gave me great." Carol walks out of the room. Simon chuckles as he admits, "I just love her," and, after a few seconds, he asks Melvin, "How you doin'?" Melvin remains angry and silent as he leaves the room. For Simon and Carol, however, their being-for each other has brought salvation. Each has become a hero for the other—a beautiful thing to experience. A rhetoric of perfection is evident in their togetherness.

After breakfast Simon again phones his parents, and his mother answers. During the awkward conversation, Simon explains that it was good that his parents didn't answer his call last night. "The important thing" that he wants them to know "is that your son is happy." In the next scene, Simon informs Carol and Melvin that he does not want to go see his parents and ask them for money: "I'll take care of myself." Melvin disagrees, emphasizing in a mean-spirited way that Simon has "real problems" that need immediate attention. Simon is smiling as he turns to his new friend and says, "Carol, a load has been lifted."

Heading back home, they stop at a gas station. Carol buys a baseball cap as a gift for Simon. We see and hear Melvin, upset, talking on an outdoor phone to Frank. He says something about taking Verdell to "the vet." As he returns to the car, Melvin announces, "They sublet your place. You're homeless." Simon looks worried. Melvin adds that Frank has found another place where Simon can live for the time being. "Another place where?" inquires Simon. "Does it matter?" replies Melvin. Simon is smiling as he answers: "No. It doesn't." As they leave the gas station, Melvin, unhappy with the situation, especially the way Carol is ignoring him, puts on a CD. We hear Nat King Cole singing "I love you, for sentimental reasons." Carol reacts immediately: "I don't want to hear that music right now." The scene ends in silence as the car drives down the road.

Arriving back home, Melvin gives Simon the keys to his apartment. Surprisingly, this is where he will be staying temporarily. Melvin tells Simon to go inside; he wants to drive Carol home. Carol tells Melvin she is going to take the bus. He is confused and hurt as Carol continues, "I don't think I want to know you anymore. All you do is make me feel bad about myself." She turns to Simon, who has yet to leave, hugs him, and says, "I love you. You have my number." "I love you, too," Simon replies sadly. Melvin's face continues to display disappointment.

Melvin and Simon enter Melvin's apartment. Verdell greets them both with jumps of joy and kisses. Simon gleefully ensures Verdell that "yes, Mommy and Daddy are home." Melvin directs a stern stare at Simon, who laughs and says, "Sorry. You are just fun to mess with." They walk toward the spare bedroom, which has been decorated and filled by Frank and other friends with many of Simon's belongings. Both Simon and Melvin are quite taken by the overall tasteful and comfortable design of the room. Simon looks at Melvin and, in a very caring voice, says, "Thank you, Melvin. You overwhelm me." Melvin appreciates the comment, and even the one that follows: "I love you." Melvin assumes a totally unprotected physical and psychological posture as he admits, "I tell you, buddy. I'd be the luckiest guy alive if that did it for me." They both smile at each other with sincerity. As Melvin walks out of the room, he pats Simon on the shoulder and tells him, "Make yourself at home." A rhetoric of perfection is forming between "Simon the fag" and Melvin the "absolute horror of a human being."

The scene shifts to Carol's apartment, where she is sharing gifts from the trip with her son and mother. She begins to stare into space, tilts her head, and slowly turns it to the left, giving the impression that she is fondly recollecting a recent experience. Back at Melvin's apartment, the phone rings, and Simon answers it: "Hi! . . . yes, he took me in! . . . Yes. It's Carol for you [Melvin]." Melvin is ecstatic and anxious as he takes the phone, takes a few deep breaths, clears his throat, nervously says, "Hello," and asks, "How are you doing?" Carol explains that she really feels bad about their date and that what she said to Melvin before she took the bus home was "a bad thing." It made her "sick to [her] stomach. And I'd be lying if I didn't say I enjoy your company . . . But the truth is you do bother me enormously," yet, "there were extraordinary kindnesses that did take place." Melvin is staring in shock and disbelief. His last words before they hang up are, "I should have danced with you."

Melvin is distraught. He walks into the kitchen, pulls some bottled water out of the refrigerator, and yells to Simon, "Are you gonna talk to me or not?" "I'm coming," says Simon.

Melvin is venting and admits that "I have to see her . . . I'm dying here":

SIMON: Because you love her?

MELVIN: No! And you people are supposed to be sensitive and sharp?

SIMON: Then you tell me why you're the one who is "dying here."

MELVIN: I don't know. Let me sleep on it.

SIMON: Oh, come on.

MELVIN: I'll figure it out.

SIMON: Oh, please.

MELVIN (*stuttering*): I'm stuck. I can't get back to my old life . . . She's evicted me from my life.

SIMON: Did you really like it that much?

MELVIN: Well, it's better than this. Look, you, I'm very intelligent. If you are gonna give me hope, you gotta do better than you're doing. I mean, if you can't be at least mildly interesting, then shut the hell up. I mean, I'm drowning here, and you are describing the water! (*Melvin is in desperate need of more-inspiring rhetorical competence from Simon.*)

SIMON: Well, picking on me won't help.

MELVIN: If that's true, I'm really in trouble.

SIMON: Melvin, do you know how lucky you are? (*Melvin looks dumbfounded as he shakes his head "no" and listens to another effort in rhetorical competence.*)

SIMON: You know who you want. I would take your seat any day. So do something about it. Go over there now, tonight. Don't sleep on it. It's not always good to let things calm down. You can do this, Melvin. You can do this. Pull out the stops. Tell her how you feel. You can do this!

MELVIN (*growing more confident by the second*): Hey, I'm charged here.

SIMON: Yes you are.

MELVIN: She might kill me if I go over.

SIMON: Then get in your jammies and I'll read you a story . . . Listen, I really think you have a chance here. The best thing you have going for you is your willingness to humiliate yourself. So go over there, do this! Catch her off guard. (*Simon's rhetorical competence is taking effect.*)

MELVIN (*hesitating*): Okay.

SIMON: Okay.

MELVIN (*smiling*): Thanks a lot.

SIMON: Okay.

MELVIN: Here I go. (*Melvin walks to the front door, hesitates, and stares at the doorknob.*)

SIMON: What's wrong?

MELVIN (*looks back at Simon and says with a look of amazement*): I forgot to lock the door. (*He then opens it and walks out.*)

For anyone who suffers from OCD, this last moment in the scene is jubilant. I had tears in my eyes and shouted to myself, "Yes, yes, yes!" Along with the acknowledgment provided by Simon, the pills seemed to be working—for real. Melvin's disease of being rotten with perfection was, at least for the moment, in remission. It is a fantastic feeling. One becomes more hopeful when pondering the question: "What if this is as good as it gets?" Thank goodness for medical science.

In the middle of the night, Melvin goes to Carol's apartment and wakes her up. What they have to say to each other helps them both feel that there is a worthwhile chance that their relationship can develop in a more loving way. They go outside and walk to a bakery that opens early in the morning. When Carol becomes hesitant about the possibility of their future, Melvin makes clear his feelings by telling the truth:

> Hey, I've got a great compliment for you. I might be the only person on the face of the Earth that knows you're the greatest woman on Earth. I might be the only one who appreciates how amazing you are in every single thing that you do, and how you are with Spencer. Spence. And in every single thought you have and how you say what you mean and how you almost always mean something that's all about being straight and good. I think most people miss that about you. And I watch them and wonder how they can watch you bring their food and clean their tables and never get that they just met the greatest woman alive. And the fact that I get it . . . makes me feel good . . . about me.

A large smile forms on Melvin's face. Carol is much moved. As they continue walking to the bakery, we eventually see Melvin stepping on cracks on the sidewalk. The film ends as they enter the shop, in good spirits, to buy "warm rolls."

It is a perfect ending. People feel good as the credits roll. The feeling takes form throughout the movie as three individuals (with the help of a dog) experience a crisis; hear and respond to the call of conscience; open themselves to others; demonstrate responsibility; struggle to be truthful and just; act heroically, beautifully; share the life-giving gift of acknowledgment; become saviors; and dwell together in friendship and love. Importantly, adding to the reality of this perfection is the film's incompleteness. Will Melvin and Carol and Simon all live happily ever after? No one can say for sure. Depending on the ways that we choose or are conditioned by society (and depending, of course, on our genetic makeup) to structure the complete incompleteness of our lives, the diseases of being rotten with perfection and imperfection can infect us at any time. Medical science offers help in dealing with the situation. The biotechnology revolution has made great advances in treating people who suffer from physical and psychological disabilities. Although only a halfway technology, Melvin's antidepressant pills are a case in point: they helped to bring out the best in him; they aided him in answering his own question, "What if this is as good as it gets?"

Life got better for Melvin. The pills, however, were only a part of the remedy. Based on the way he bonded with Verdell, we know that he possessed the potential of embodying a rhetoric of perfection before he began taking the pills. The potential already existed in a more actualized state with Carol and Simon. Without these two individuals, Melvin's answer to his question would have fallen short of where it stands when the film ends. Carol's and Simon's interpersonal and rhetorical relationships with Melvin, their openness toward him, and eventually his openness toward them present a display of what was described earlier, following Levinas, as religion in its purest (preinstitutionalized) form: "the situation where outside of all dogmas, all speculation about the divine . . . one speaks to the other," where "my pre-originary susceptiveness" to the other "chooses me before I welcome it." In short, both science and religion have significant roles to play in the Academy Award–winning and rhetorically competent film we have been considering here.

Such competence serves us in coming to terms with our metaphysical desire for perfection. The desire is motivated by the ontological structure of our existence: its complete (perfect) incompleteness. We live an oxymoronic existence. Life and death go hand in hand. The relationship provokes us to hope for something more than that. Gazing at the heavens, and with the help of science, we learn crucial things about where and how we really stand in the cosmos. It's truly amazing and humbling: evolution has brought us far. In terms of cosmological time, the journey has been quite quick, and we have a long way to go. Still, we have had enough time to become "wise" about certain matters. For example, the earth and its inhabitants are not the center of the universe. Egoism, although it would have us think otherwise, is thus a sham and a shame in the great scheme of things. The self would never materialize without the habitat of otherness. Openness to otherness is who we truly are before we are anything else. This ontological condition can be deciphered as an ethic. Science puts it one way: stay open to the empirical evidence at hand. Religion puts it another way: "Where art thou?" "Here I am!" Science speaks in the name of "progress." Religion calls it "raising holy sparks" and "doing greater good." The ethic of otherness, however, remains the same. The otherness of human being calls on us to be open to its awesome and complex presence. It offers stark evidence that tells us we have much to do in developing our capacities for being as perfect as we can be. At the present time, we cannot say for sure what such a state of being is, in truth. It certainly must be more than what our halfway technologies make possible. It thus is fair to wonder, for example, if human evolution will ever get to the point at which "depression" is a thing of the past, a stage or manner of being that our species had to go through in order to become the humans that we are supposed to be (say, a million years from now). Unless they are "really lost" and "finally gone," the last thing people suffering from depression want in their lives is to remain depressed.

The benefits and burdens of depression and its medical and religious remedies are a much-debated topic.[28] I like to dream of a world in which depression is permanently defeated and, to add but one other example, the life-giving gift of acknowledgment is always practiced by one and all. I hope we are evolving in that direction. I hope that the biotechnological revolution, with its continuing achievements, will take us there. It is too depressing to think that where and how we are now at the present moment of human evolution is as good as it gets. The openness of the future allows us to think that there is a chance that we are headed toward "a better place." Call it "heaven" or whatever you will. The story of Melvin, Carol, and Simon offers suggestions about what it will take to make the journey. The suggestions can be read as a rhetoric of perfection, a rhetoric of what, at least to some extent, it means to be human. The significance of our insignificance—as perhaps only one of many other more highly developed species in the cosmos—lies in the fact that we understand that something *must* be done if the journey is to continue and, one hopes, become better along the way. We are only in the beginning. We must remain open. Surrounded by otherness and dependent on others, we are bound to ask, "Where art thou?" In the name of perfection, we must always be ready to answer, "Here I am!" The well-being of humankind depends on our readiness and the progress it can produce. Looking at the world today, the need for such progress should be perfectly clear.

NOTES

PREFACE

1   Michael J. Hyde, *The Call of Conscience: Heidegger and Levinas, Rhetoric and the Euthanasia Debate* (Columbia: University of South Carolina Press, 2001); idem, *The Life-Giving Gift of Acknowledgment: A Philosophical and Rhetorical Inquiry* (West Lafayette, Ind.: Purdue University Press, 2006).

2   World Health Organization, "Preamble to the Constitution of the World Health Organization," *Official Records of the World Health Organization*, no. 2 (1948): 100; emphasis added. Definition cited at http://www.medical-colleges.net/worldhealth.htm (retrieved May 5, 2009).

3   This belief also motivates such noteworthy intellectual histories and philosophical assessments as Martin Foss, *The Idea of Perfection in the Western World* (Princeton, N.J.: Princeton University Press, 1946); Charles Hartshorne, *The Logic of Perfection* (La Salle, Ill.: Open Court Publishing, 1962); Umberto Eco, *The Search for the Perfect Language*, trans. James Fentress (Oxford: Blackwell, 1995); Jean Baudrillard, *The Perfect Crime*, trans. Chris Turner (New York: Verso, 1996); John Passmore, *The Perfectibility of Man*, 3rd ed. (Indianapolis: Liberty Fund, 2000); Gary A. Anderson, *The Genesis of Perfection: Adam and Eve in Jewish and Christian Imagination* (Louisville, Ky.: Westminster John Knox, 2001); and Russell Jacoby, *Picture Imperfect: Utopian Thought for an Anti-Utopian Age* (New York: Columbia University Press, 2005).

4   Samuel B. Southwell, *Kenneth Burke and Martin Heidegger: With a Note*

against Deconstructionism (Gainesville: University of Florida Press, 1987). I reviewed the book in the *Quarterly Journal of Speech* 75 (1989): 496–97.

5   Kenneth Burke, *Language as Symbolic Action: Essays on Life, Literature, and Method* (Berkeley: University of California Press, 1966), 21. I will have occasion to elaborate on Burke's notion of being "rotten with perfection" throughout this book. Unfortunately, Burke is not referenced in any of the texts cited in note 3 above.

CHAPTER 1

1   David Hume, *Essays: Moral, Political, and Literary*, ed. Eugene F. Miller (Indianapolis: Liberty Classics, 1985), 82–83.

2   Hume, *Essays: Moral, Political, and Literary*, 583.

3   Kenneth Burke, *Language as Symbolic Action: Essays on Life, Literature, and Method* (Berkeley: University of California Press, 1966), 16.

4   Hume, *Essays: Moral, Political, and Literary*, 105–6.

5   Burke, *Language as Symbolic Action*, 16.

6   David Hume, *A Treatise of Human Nature: Being an Attempt to Introduce the Experimental Method of Reasoning into Moral Subjects*, 2nd ed., book 2 (Oxford: Oxford University Press, 1990), 409.

7   Anjula Razdan, "Shiny Happy People: In Our Quest for Self-Improvement, Have We Gone Too Far?" *Utne* (May/June 2005): 59.

8   *Seinfeld*, "The Opposite," episode no. 86, first broadcast 19 May 1994 by NBC. Directed by Tom Cherones and written by Andy Cowan, Larry David, and Jerry Seinfeld.

9   Saul D. Alinsky, *Rules for Radicals: A Practical Primer for Realistic Radicals* (New York: Vintage Books, 1971), 3.

10 Carrie Anne Platt, "Starving for Acknowledgment: A Rhetorical Analysis of Pro Eating Disorder Websites" (M.A. thesis, Wake Forest University, 2004).

11 The King James Version has been used for Scripture quotations throughout.

12 See Eric G. Wilson, *Against Happiness: In Praise of Melancholy* (New York: Farrar, Straus, & Giroux, 2008), for a counterview.

13 Burke, *Language as Symbolic Action*, 3–24.

14 John Rawls, *Lectures on the History of Moral Philosophy*, ed. Barbara Herman (Cambridge, Mass.: Harvard University Press, 2000), 111.

15 John Passmore, *The Perfectibility of Man*, 3rd ed. (Indianapolis: Liberty Fund, 2000), 510.

16 John Locke, *An Essay Concerning Human Understanding*, vol. 2, III.34 (New York: Dover, 1959), 146.

17 Hans Blumenberg, trans. Robert M. Wallace, "An Anthropological Approach to the Contemporary Significance of Rhetoric," in *After Philosophy: End or Transformation?* ed. Kenneth Baynes, James Bohman, and Thomas McCarthy (Cambridge, Mass.: MIT Press, 1987), 441.

18 Isocrates, *Antidosis*, trans. George Norlin, Loeb Classical Library (Cambridge, Mass.: Harvard University Press, 1982), 253–56.

19 George Steiner, *Real Presences* (Chicago: University of Chicago Press, 1989), 160. For a more focused discussion of the "rhetoric of science," see Joseph E. Harmon and Alan G. Gross, *The Scientific Literature: A Guided Tour* (Chicago: University of Chicago Press, 2007).

20 Wilbur S. Howell, ed., *Fenelon's Dialogues on Eloquence* (Princeton, N.J.: Princeton University Press, 1951), 23.

21 Lloyd F. Bitzer, "The Rhetorical Situation," *Philosophy and Rhetoric* 1 (1968): 6–7; emphasis added.

22 Steven Pinker, *The Language Instinct: How the Mind Creates Language* (New York: HarperCollins, 1994), 6, 10, 118, 304. Also see Andrew Newberg, Eugene D'Aquili, and Vince Rause, *Why God Won't Go Away: Brain Science and the Biology of Belief* (New York: Ballantine Books, 2001); and Dean Hamer, *The God Gene: How Faith Is Hardwired into Our Genes* (New York: Doubleday, 2004).

23 Martin Heidegger, *Being and Time*, trans. Edward Robinson and John Macquarrie (New York: Harper & Row, 1962), 58.

24 Heidegger, *Being and Time*, 256–73.

25 Immanuel Kant, "The Metaphysics of Morals," preface to part 1, in *Ethical Philosophy*, trans. James W. Ellington (Indianapolis: Hackett, 1983), 4.

CHAPTER 2

1 Robert Nisbet, *History of the Idea of Progress* (New York: Basic Books, 1980), ix.

2 I offer a case study of this dilemma in chapter 8, in which I discuss the life and death of Terri Schiavo.

3 Karl Jaspers, *Way to Wisdom: An Introduction to Philosophy*, trans. Ralph Manheim (New Haven, Conn.: Yale University Press, 1954), 121.

4 Charles Hartshorne, *The Logic of Perfection* (Chicago: Open Court, 1962), 11.

5 Voltaire, "Épître à l'Auteur du Livre des Trois Imposteurs (Letter to the Author of the Three Imposters)," in *Oeuvres completes de Voltaire*, book 10, ed. Louis Moland (Paris: Garnier, 1877–1885), 402–5.

6 Quoted in Kathleen Freeman, *Ancilla to the Pre-Socratic Philosophers: A Complete Translation of the Fragments in Diels*, Fragmente der Vor-sokratiker (Cambridge, Mass.: Harvard University Press, 1966), 22.

7 Quoted in Freeman, *Pre-Socratic Philosophers*, 23.

8 Quoted in Freeman, *Pre-Socratic Philosophers*, 24.

9 Charles H. Kahn, *The Art and Thought of Heraclitus: An Edition of the Fragments with Translation and Commentary* (New York: Cambridge University Press, 1979), 11.

10 Cited in Kahn, *Art and Thought of Heraclitus*, fragment LIV, 170; fragment CXVIII, 267.

11 Frederick W. J. Schelling, *Of Human Freedom*, trans. James Gutmann (Chicago: Open Court, 1936), 84.

12 Schelling, *Of Human Freedom*, 84; emphasis in original.

13 John Milton, *Paradise Lost*, ed. Alistair Fowler (New York: Longman, 1998), XII, 473–78. For a wonderful discussion of Milton and the Adam

and Eve "myth," see Gary A. Anderson, *The Genesis of Perfection: Adam and Eve in Jewish and Christian Imagination* (Louisville, Ky.: Westminster John Knox, 2001).

14 Abraham Joshua Heschel, *God in Search of Man: A Philosophy of Judaism* (New York: Noonday Press, 1955), 76–78.

15 Heschel, *God in Search of Man*, 160. Also see Abraham J. Heschel, *The Prophets*, vol. 2 (New York: Harper & Row, 1962), 214–26.

16 Robert Jewett, *Christian Tolerance: Paul's Message to the Modern Church* (Philadelphia: Westminster, 1982), 43–67.

17 Thomas Aquinas, "Quodlibetum 3," 27, quoted in F. C. Copleston, *Aquinas* (New York: Penguin, 1955), 228.

18 See Jewett, *Christian Tolerance*, 68–91. See also C. A. Pierce, *Conscience in the New Testament* (London: SCM, 1955).

19 Jack Miles, *God: A Biography* (New York: Vintage Books, 1995).

20 David J. Wolpe, *In Speech and in Silence* (New York: Henry Holt, 1992), 98.

21 James Montgomery Boice, *The Parables of Jesus* (Chicago: Moody Publishers, 1983), 15–20.

22 Heschel, *Prophets*, 218; emphasis in original.

23 Augustine, *On Christian Doctrine*, trans. D. W. Robertson Jr. (Upper Saddle River, N.J.: Prentice Hall, 1997), 4.2.3.

24 Augustine, *On Christian Doctrine*, 4.10.24.

25 Augustine, *On Christian Doctrine*, 4.11.26.

26 Augustine, *On Christian Doctrine*, 4.11.26.

27 Cicero, *De oratore* 3.14.55, trans. H. Rackham, Loeb Classical Library (Cambridge, Mass.: Harvard University Press, 1942).

28 Cicero, *Orator*, trans. H. M. Hubbell, Loeb Classical Library (Cambridge, Mass.: Harvard University Press, 1913), 3.118.

29 Augustine, *Confessions*, trans. Henry Chadwick (New York: Oxford University Press, 1991), 3.4 (7).

30 Cicero, *De officiis*, trans. Walter Miller, Loeb Classical Library (Cambridge, Mass.: Harvard University Press, 1913), 1.7.22.

31 Cicero, *Orator*, 3.12.

32 Cicero, *De officiis*, 1.6.19.

33 Cicero, *De oratore*, 1.8.32.

34 Augustine, *Confessions*, 3.4.7–8.

35 Augustine, *On Christian Doctrine*, 4.3.5.

36 Dietrich Bonhoeffer, *Life Together*, trans. John W. Doberstein (New York: Harper & Row, 1954), 22–23.

37 David A. Cooper, *God Is a Verb: Kabbalah and the Practice of Mystical Judaism* (New York: Riverhead Books, 1997), 29.

38 Midrash Rabbah, Song of Songs 5:3. Irving Greenberg, *The Jewish Way: Living the Holidays* (New York: Simon & Schuster, 1993), 187.

39 Augustine, *Confessions*, 1.1.1.

40 Augustine, *Confessions*, 1.6.10.

41 Augustine, *Confessions*, 2.7.15, 6.4.6.

42 Augustine, *Confessions*, 10.3.4.

43 Augustine, *Confessions*, 10.43.69.

CHAPTER 3

1   Plato, *Apology*, trans. Hugh Tredennick, in *The Collected Dialogues of Plato*, ed. Edith Hamilton and Huntington Cairns (Princeton, N.J.: Princeton University Press, 1961), 40a.

2   Plato, *Phaedrus*, trans. R. Hackforth, in *The Collected Dialogues of Plato*, 270b–272b.

3   Ludwig Edelstein, *Ancient Medicine*, trans C. Lilian Temkin, ed. Owsei Temkin and C. Lilian Temkin (Baltimore: John Hopkins University Press, 1987), 87–110.

4   Plato, *Laws*, IV, 720c–720e, trans. A. E. Taylor, in *The Collected Dialogues of Plato*.

5   W. H. S. Jones, *Hippocrates (The Art)*, vol. 2 (London: William Heinemann, 1923), xiv. Edelstein, *Ancient Medicine*, describes this text as "the [Hippocratic] treatise which documents the physician's rhetorical stance and his rhetorical battle detached from all specifically medical objectives" (101).

6   See Pedro Lain Entralgo, *The Therapy of the Word in Classical Antiquity*, trans. L. J. Rather and John M. Sharp (New Haven, Conn.: Yale University Press, 1970), 139–70. See also Michael Frede, *Essays in Ancient Philosophy* (Minneapolis: University of Minnesota Press, 1987), 232–39.

7   W. H. S. Jones, *Hippocrates (Decorum)*, vol. 2 (London: William Heinemann, 1923), v.

8   W. H. S. Jones, *Hippocrates (Law)*, vol. 2 (London: William Heinemann, 1923), IV.

9   In the Hippocratic oath, one reads, "I will use treatment to help the sick according to my ability and judgment, but never with a view to injury and wrong-doing. Neither will I administer a poison to anybody when asked to do so, nor will I suggest such a course." The prohibition against harming patients is the basis for medicine's ethical stand against euthanasia and physician-assisted suicide. For further background on the Hippocratic oath, see Edelstein, *Ancient Medicine*, 87–110. Also see my work, Michael J. Hyde, *The Call of Conscience: Heidegger and Levinas, Rhetoric and the Euthanasia Debate* (Columbia: University of South Carolina Press, 2001), 124–50.

10 Plato, *Phaedrus*, 260d–260e.

11 Augustine, *Confessions*, trans. Henry Chadwick (New York: Oxford University Press, 1991), 12.31.42.

12 Augustine, *Confessions*, 11.3.5.

13 Augustine, *Confessions*, 12.30.41.

14 For an expanded discussion of the relationship between knowing together, conscience, and acknowledgment, see my work, Michael J. Hyde, *The Life-Giving Gift of Acknowledgment: A Philosophical and Rhetorical Inquiry* (West Lafayette, Ind.: Purdue University Press, 2006).

15 Ludwig Wittgenstein, *On Certainty*, trans. Denis Paul and G. E. M. Anscombe, ed. G. E. M. Anscombe and G. H. von Wright (New York: Harper & Row, 1969), 255.

16 Stanley Cavell, *The Claim of Reason: Wittgenstein, Skepticism, Moral-ity, and Tragedy* (New York: Oxford University Press, 1979), 430, 434.

17 Emmanuel Levinas, *Difficult Freedom: Essays on Judaism*, trans. Sean Hand (Baltimore: John Hopkins University Press, 1990), 9.

18 Clifford Geertz, *The Interpretation of Cultures* (New York: Basic Books, 1973), 19.

19 *Zohar: Annotated and Explained*, trans. Daniel C. Matt (Woodstock, Vt.: Skylight Paths, 2002), 11–12. Also see *The Zohar* (Pritzker Edition), trans. and comm. Daniel C. Matt, 3 vols. (Stanford, Calif.: Stanford University Press, 2004–2006); for the oxymoronic phrase noted here, see "Parashat Be-Reshit," vol. 1, 15a, 107–8. Matt's translation of and commentary on the Zohar is, to say the least, magnificent.

20 Abraham Joshua Heschel, *God in Search of Man: A Philosophy of Judaism* (New York: Noonday Press, 1955), 160.

21 David A. Cooper, *God Is a Verb: Kabbalah and the Practice of Mystical Judaism* (New York: Riverhead Books, 1997), 67.

22 Richard E. Palmer, *Hermeneutics: Interpretation Theory in Schleier-macher, Dilthey, Heidegger and Gadamer* (Evanston, Ill.: Northwestern University Press, 1969), 14.

23 Heschel, *God in Search of Man*, 78.

24 Cooper, *God Is a Verb*, 43, 58.

25 For a clearly illustrated and insightful discussion of gematria, see Marc-Alain Ouaknin, *Mysteries of the Kabbalah*, trans. Josephine Bacon (New York: Abbeville Press, 2000), 335–53.

26 Cooper, *God Is a Verb*, 58.

27 For an excellent discussion and analysis of Luria's life and teachings, see Lawrence Fine, *Physician of the Soul, Healer of the Cosmos: Isaac Luria and His Kabbalistic Fellowship* (Stanford, Calif.: Stanford University Press, 2003). Also see Arthur Green, introduction to *The Zohar* (Pritzker Edition), xxxi–lxxxi.

28 Ouaknin, *Mysteries of the Kabbalah*, 194–96.

29 Fine, *Physician of the Soul*, 128.

30 Rav P. S. Berg, *The Essential Zohar: The Source of Kabbalistic Wisdom* (New York: Bell Tower, 2002), 28.

31 Berg, *Essential Zohar*, 58.

32 Fine, *Physician of the Soul*, 136, 141, 149.

33 Alon Goshen-Gottstein, "Creation," in *Contemporary Jewish Religious Thought: Original Essays on Critical Concepts, Movements, and Beliefs*, ed. Arthur A. Cohen and Paul R. Mendes-Flohr (New York: Free Press, 1987), 116–17. In his historical and groundbreaking account of kabbalistic thought, Gershom Scholem notes, "The decision to emerge from concealment into manifestation and creation is not in any sense a process which is a necessary consequence of the essence of *Ein Sof*; it is a free decision which remains a constant and impenetrable mystery. Therefore, in the view of most kabbalists, the question of the ultimate motivation of creation is not a legitimate one, and the assertion found in many books that God wished to reveal the measure of His goodness is there simply as an expedient that is never systematically developed." Gershom

Scholem, *Kabbalah* (New York: Meridian, 1978), 91. Not accounting for God's "will," however, raises the question addressed above regarding why God's vessels were imperfect before the beginning began. Scholem notes that the question remained "surrounded by controversy, or was consciously obscured" (93). I do not believe that such obscuration should go unchallenged.

34 Lawrence Kushner, *The Book of Words: Talking Spiritual Life, Living Spiritual Talk* (Woodstock, Vt.: Jewish Lights, 1993), 28; emphasis in original.

35 Ouaknin, *Mysteries of the Kabbalah*, 200.

36 Fine, in *Physician of the Soul*, writes, "The role (Luria) played in his community as a diagnostician and physician of the soul" is unique. "While we may be able to find occasional examples of something similar to this type of phenomenon, we know of no figure prior to Luria who served as a spiritual guide in quite this way" (185).

37 Berg, *Essential Zohar*, 59.

38 Heschel, *God in Search of Man*, 136.

39 Emmanuel Levinas makes this point when he notes that to be a Jew is to know the tragedy and horror of "anti-Semitism, which is in its essence hatred for a man who is other than oneself—that is to say, hatred for the other man." In his *Collected Philosophical Papers*, trans. Alphonso Lingis (The Hague: Martinus Nijhoff, 1987), 21, 41.

40 Berg, *Essential Zohar*, 61.

41 Berg, *Essential Zohar*, 27.

42 Scholem, *Kabbalah*, 89.

43 Michael Levin, *The Complete Idiot's Guide to Jewish Spirituality and Mysticism* (Indianapolis: Alpha Books, 2002), 153–54; emphasis in original.

CHAPTER 4

1 Albert R. Jonsen and Stephen Toulmin, *The Abuse of Casuistry: A History of Moral Reasoning* (Berkeley: University of California Press, 1988), 136.

2 Friedrich Schleiermacher, *Hermeneutics: The Handwritten Manuscripts*, trans. James Duke and Jack Forstman, ed. Heinz Kimmerle (Missoula, Mont.: Scholars Press, 1977), 148–49.

3 Jack Miles, *God: A Biography* (New York: Vintage Books, 1995), 87–88.

4 Hans Robert Jauss, *Toward an Aesthetic of Reception* (Minneapolis: University of Minnesota Press, 1982), 19.

5 Barbara Herrnstein Smith, *On the Margins of Discourse: The Relation of Literature to Language* (Chicago: University of Chicago Press, 1978), 151.

6 Gary Wills, *Lincoln at Gettysburg: The Words That Remade America* (New York: Simon & Schuster, 1992).

7 Edwin Black, "Gettysburg and Silence," *Quarterly Journal of Speech* 80 (1994): 21–36.

8   E. D. Hirsch Jr., *Validity in Interpretation* (New Haven, Conn.: Yale University Press, 1967), 8; emphasis in original.

9   Hirsch, *Validity in Interpretation*, 126.

10   E. D. Hirsch Jr., *The Aims of Interpretation* (Chicago: University of Chicago Press, 1978), 80.

11   Hirsch, *Validity in Interpretation*, 244; emphasis added.

12   I expand on this point throughout the remainder of the chapter.

13   Martin Heidegger, *Being and Time*, trans. Edward Robinson and John Macquarrie (New York: Harper & Row, 1962), 256–73.

14   For a detailed discussion of Heidegger's analysis of the scope and function of "the call," see my work, Michael J. Hyde, *The Call of Conscience: Heidegger and Levinas, Rhetoric and the Euthanasia Debate* (Columbia: University of South Carolina Press, 2001), 21–78.

15   Martin Heidegger, "Letter on Humanism," in *Basic Writings*, ed. David Farrell Krell (New York: Harper & Row, 1977), 230.

16   For a critique of "God-of-the-gaps" thinking by a Nobel Prize–winning physicist, see Steven Weinberg, *Dreams of a Final Theory: The Scientist's Search for the Ultimate Laws of Nature* (New York: Vintage Books, 1994), 241–61.

17   Martin Heidegger, *On the Way to Language*, trans. Peter D. Hertz (New York: Harper & Row, 1971), 155. Also see Heidegger, *Being and Time*, 56.

18   Paul Ricoeur, *Interpretation Theory: Discourse and the Surplus of Meaning* (Fort Worth: Texas Christian University Press, 1976), 22.

19   Ricoeur, *Interpretation Theory*, 87–88.

20   Martin Heidegger, *An Introduction to Metaphysics*, trans. Ralph Mannheim (New Haven, Conn.: Yale University Press, 1959), 205.

21   For a comprehensive discussion of this communication problem, see Gerald M. Phillips, *Communication Incompetencies: A Theory of Training Oral Performance Behavior* (Carbondale: Southern Illinois University Press, 1991).

22   Martin Heidegger, *The Principle of Reason*, trans. Reginald Lilly (Bloomington: Indiana University Press, 1991), 113.

23   I deal with this problem in more detail in Hyde, *Call of Conscience*, 74–115. Also see Jean-François Lyotard, *Heidegger and "the Jews,"* trans. Andreas Michel and Mark Roberts (Minneapolis: University of Minnesota Press, 1990); Gunther Neske and Emil Kettering, eds., *Martin Heidegger and National Socialism: Questions and Answers* (New York: Paragon House, 1990); Hans Sluga, *Heidegger's Crisis: Philosophy and Politics in Nazi Germany* (Cambridge, Mass.: Harvard University Press, 1993); Rüdiger Safranski, *Martin Heidegger: Between Good and Evil*, trans. Ewald Osers (Cambridge, Mass.: Harvard University Press, 1998); and Allen Scult, *Being Jewish/Reading Heidegger: An Ontological Encounter* (New York: Fordham University Press, 2004).

24   See Martin Heidegger, "What Is Metaphysics," in *Existence and Being*, trans. Douglas Scott, R. F. C. Hull, and Alan Crick (South Bend, Ind.: Henry Regnery, 1949), 325–61.

25 Kenneth Burke, *Permanence and Change: An Anatomy of Purpose* (New York: Bobbs-Merrill, 1965), 272.

26 Heidegger, *Being and Time*, 318.

27 Commenting on this point, Francoise Dastur writes, "Here there is no metaphor for Heidegger, but, on the contrary, a genuine experience of what voice is. This is because it is not essential that discourse be phonetically articulated to be language (*Sprache*), and because voice (*Stimme*) does not in German have the purely vocal sense of the Greek *phone*, but rather a juridical sense, that of giving one's judgment by a vote. This is why Heidegger emphasizes that 'the voice' is taken rather as a 'giving-to-understand' [Heidegger, *Being and Time*, 316]. Thus there can be a silent voice, which does not speak, as a pure phenomenon of comprehension, a pure phenomenon of meaning, just in the same way there can be an understanding, which is not reduced to a simple acoustic perception." Francoise Dastur, "The Call of Conscience: The Most Intimate Alterity," in *Heidegger and Practical Philosophy*, ed. François Raffoul and David Pettigrew (Albany: State University of New York Press, 2002), 94.

28 Martin Heidegger, *Zollikon Seminars: Protocols-Conversations-Letters*, trans. Franz Mayr and Richard Askay, ed. Medard Boss (Evanston, Ill.: Northwestern University Press, 2001), 215.

29 Heidegger, *Being and Time*, 163–68, 178. Also see Hans-Georg Gadamer, "On the Scope and Function of Hermeneutical Reflection," trans. G. B. Hess and Richard E. Palmer, in *Philosophical Hermeneutics*, trans. and ed. David E. Linge (Berkeley: University of California Press, 1976), 18–43.

30 Martin Heidegger, *Sein und Zeit* (Tubingen: Max Niemeyer Verlag, 1979), 138–39. Macquarrie and Robinson translate "*in der rechten Weise*" as "aright" (Heidegger, *Being and Time*, 178). As indicated above, however, a less-condensed translation is possible: "in a right and just manner." The German *recht* can bespeak the moral sense being emphasized here, as when, e.g., one says, "*Es is nicht recht von dir*" ("It is wrong or unfair of you").

31 Aristotle, *The Politics of Aristotle*, trans. and ed. Ernest Barker (New York: Oxford University Press, 1979), 1281b1–1281b6.

32 For a more detailed discussion of the phenomenon of homemaking, see my work, Michael J. Hyde, *The Life-Giving Gift of Acknowledgment: A Philosophical and Rhetorical Inquiry* (West Lafayette, Ind.: Purdue University Press, 2006), 98–158.

CHAPTER 5

1 Michael J. Hyde, *The Call of Conscience: Heidegger and Levinas, Rhetoric and the Euthanasia Debate* (Columbia: University of South Carolina Press, 2001), 126.

2 Rene Descartes, *Discourse on the Method for Rightly Conducting One's Reason and for Seeking Truth in the Sciences*, part 6, trans. Donald A. Cress (Indianapolis: Hackett, 1993), 62.

3 Peter Gay, *The Enlightenment: An Interpretation*, vol. 2, *The Science of Freedom* (New York: W. W. Norton, 1969), 3–18.

4   A. N. de Condorcet, *Sketch for a Historical Picture of the Progress of the Human Mind*, trans. June Barraclough (London: Library of Ideas, 1955), cited in Isaac Kramnick, ed., *The Portable Enlightenment Reader* (New York: Penguin, 1995), 32.

5   Condorcet, in Kramnick, *Portable Enlightenment Reader*, 30.

6   The watchmaker analogy, which constitutes what many consider the most famous creationist argument, originates with the eighteenth-century theologian William Paley: just as a watch is too complicated and too functional to have sprung into existence by accident, so too must all living things, with their far greater complexity, be purposefully designed. For a critical assessment of Paley's creationist theory, see Richard Dawkins, *The Blind Watchmaker: Why the Evidence of Evolution Reveals a Universe without Design* (1986; repr., New York: W. W. Norton, 1996).

7   Gottfried Wilhelm Leibniz, *The Philosophical Works of Leibniz*, 2nd ed., trans. George Martin Duncan (New Haven, Conn.: Tuttle, Morehouse and Taylor, 1908), 113.

8   Gottfried Wilhelm Leibniz, *The Monadology and Other Philosophical Writings*, trans. Robert Latta (Oxford: Clarendon, 1898), 417.

9   Gottfried Wilhelm Leibniz, *Philosophical Essays*, trans. and ed. Roger Ariew and Daniel Garber (Indianapolis: Hackett, 1989), 115.

10   John Rawls, *Lectures on the History of Moral Philosophy*, ed. Barbara Herman (Cambridge, Mass.: Harvard University Press, 2000), 271.

11   Immanuel Kant, *Religion within the Limits of Reason Alone*, trans. Theordore M. Green and Hoyt H. Hudson (New York: Harper & Row, 1960), 3.

12   Immanuel Kant, *Grounding for the Metaphysics of Morals, with On a Supposed Right to Lie Because of Philanthropic Concerns*, 3rd ed., trans James W. Ellington (Indianapolis: Hackett, 1993), 30.

13   Kant, *Metaphysics of Morals*, 103–4.

14   Kant, *Religion within the Limits of Reason Alone*, 174; emphasis in original.

15   Immanuel Kant, *Ethical Philosophy*, trans. James W. Ellington (Indianapolis: Hackett, 1983), 59–60.

16   Immanuel Kant, "What Is Enlightenment?" in Kramnick, *Portable Enlightenment Reader*, 1.

17   Kant, "What is Enlightenment?" in Kramnick, *Portable Enlightenment Reader*, 1.

18   Immanuel Kant, *Lectures on Ethics*, trans. Louis Infield (Indianapolis: Hackett, 1930), 252–53.

19   Immanuel Kant, "The Metaphysics of Morals," preface to part 1, in *Ethical Philosophy*, trans. James W. Ellington (Indianapolis: Hackett, 1983), 4.

20   Immanuel Kant, *Critique of Judgment*, sec. 47, trans. Werner S. Pluhar (Indianapolis: Hackett, 1987), 177; emphasis added.

21   David Hume, *A Treatise of Human Nature*, 2nd ed., ed. L. A. Selby-Bigge (Oxford: Clarendon, 1978), 458, 470.

22   Adam Smith, *The Theory of Moral Sentiments*, ed. D. D. Raphael and A. L. Macfie (Indianapolis: Liberty Fund, 1982), 113.

23 Smith, *Theory of Moral Sentiments*, 126.
24 Smith, *Theory of Moral Sentiments*, 130–32, 134–37. Also see Vivienne Brown, *Adam Smith's Discourse: Canonicity, Commerce and Conscience* (New York: Routledge, 1994).
25 Kant, *Metaphysics of Morals*, 34, 46.
26 Charles Darwin, *The Descent of Man, and Selection in Relations to Sex* (Princeton, N.J.: Princeton University Press, 1981), 70–106.
27 Darwin, *Descent of Man*, 72.
28 Darwin, *Descent of Man*, 392–94.
29 Darwin, *Descent of Man*, 101.
30 John Poulakos, *Sophistical Rhetoric in Classical Greece* (Columbia: University of South Carolina Press, 1995).
31 Kant, *Critique of Judgment*, sec. 53, n. 63, 198.
32 Aristotle, *Rhetoric*, trans. W. Rhys Roberts (New York: Random House, 1954), 1354a1.
33 Kant, *Critique of Judgment*, sec. 53, 196–97.
34 Kant, *Critique of Judgment*, sec. 53, n. 63, 198; emphasis in original.
35 See Michael J. Hyde and Craig R. Smith, "Aristotle and Heidegger on Emotion and Rhetoric: Questions of Time and Space," in *The Critical Turn: Rhetoric and Philosophy in Postmodern Discourse*, ed. Ian Angus and Lenore Langsdorf (Carbondale: Southern Illinois University Press, 1993), 68–99.
36 W. H. S. Jones, *Hippocrates (Law)*, vol. 2 (London: William Heinemann, 1923), iv.
37 Immanuel Kant, *Immanuel Kant's Critique of Pure Reason*, trans. Norman Kemp Smith (London: Macmillan, 1956 [1787 edition]), 173–74.
38 Raphael Demos, "On Persuasion," *Journal of Philosophy* 29 (1932): 229.
39 Immanuel Kant, *Critique of Practical Reason*, trans. Lewis White Beck (Indianapolis: Bobbs-Merrill, 1956), 155–57.
40 Kant, "Metaphysics of Morals," 84.
41 John Locke, *An Essay Concerning Human Understanding*, ed. Alexander Campbell Fraser (New York: Barnes & Noble, 2004), 424.
42 Locke, *Essay Concerning Human Understanding*, 424.
43 Locke, *Essay Concerning Human Understanding*, 329, 398.
44 Cited in Thomas M. Conley, *Rhetoric in the European Tradition* (Chicago: University of Chicago Press, 1990), 163–64.
45 I expand on this point in my work, Hyde, *Call of Conscience*, 124–25, 274n6.
46 John Durham Peters, *Speaking into the Air: A History of the Idea of Communication* (Chicago: University of Chicago Press, 1999), 88.
47 David Hume, *Essays: Moral, Political, and Literary*, ed. Eugene F. Miller (Indianapolis: Liberty Classics, 1985), 91.
48 Hugh Blair, *Lectures on Rhetoric and Belles Lettres*, lecture 34 (Philadelphia: T. Ellwood Zell, 1862), 377.
49 Blair, *Lectures on Rhetoric*, lecture 2, 16–37.
50 George Campbell, *The Philosophy of Rhetoric* (Boston: Charles Ewer, 1823), 101.

51 Richard Whately, *Elements of Rhetoric: Comprising an Analysis of the Laws of Moral Evidence and of Persuasion, with Rules for Argumentative Composition and Elocution*, ed. Douglas Ehninger (London: John W. Parker, 1846; Carbondale: Southern Illinois University Press, 1963), 115; emphasis in original.

52 Whately, *Elements of Rhetoric*, 39–40, 83–84.

53 Cicero, *De oratore*, trans. H. Rackham, Loeb Classical Library (Cambridge, Mass.: Harvard University Press, 1942), 3.16.61.

54 Cicero, *De officiis*, trans. Walter Miller, Loeb Classical Library (Cambridge, Mass.: Harvard University Press, 1913), 1.6.19.

55 Max Horkheimer, *Eclipse of Reason* (New York: Continuum, 2004).

56 Maurice Hindle, introduction to *Frankenstein: Or, The Modern Prometheus*, by Mary Shelley (New York: Penguin, 1985), 25. Humphry Davy's book is cited as *A Discourse, Introductory to a Course of Lectures on Chemistry* (1802).

57 Hindle, introduction to *Frankenstein*, 41.

58 Mary Shelley, *Frankenstein: Or, the Modern Prometheus* (New York: Penguin, 1985), 85.

59 Shelley, *Frankenstein*, 97–98.

60 Shelley, *Frankenstein*, 101, 102.

61 Shelley, *Frankenstein*, 259.

62 Shelley, *Frankenstein*, 170–72, 187; emphasis in original.

63 Kenneth Burke, *Language as Symbolic Action: Essays on Life, Literature, and Method* (Berkeley: University of California Press, 1966), 18.

64 Marilyn Butler, "Frankenstein and Radical Science," in Mary Shelley, *Frankenstein*, ed. J. Paul Hunter (New York: W. W. Norton, 1996), 307.

65 Butler, "Frankenstein and Radical Science," 311.

66 See, e.g., Jürgen Habermas, *Moral Consciousness and Communicative Action*, trans. Christian Lenhardt and Shierry Weber Nicholsen (Cambridge, Mass.: MIT Press, 1990); and his *The Theory of Communicative Action, vol. 1, Reason and the Rationalization of Society*, trans. Thomas McCarthy (Boston: Beacon Press, 1984).

67 Although Habermas, in my humble opinion, is far from being an eloquent writer.

CHAPTER 6

1 Henry Petroski, *Small Things Considered: Why There Is No Perfect Design* (New York: Vintage Books, 2003), 5–7.

2 Petroski, *Small Things Considered*, 8–9.

3 Petroski, *Small Things Considered*, 14–15.

4 Petroski, *Small Things Considered*, 9.

5 Immanuel Kant, *Critique of Judgment*, sec. 48, trans. Werner S. Pluhar (Indianapolis: Hackett, 1987), 179.

6 Hugh Blair, *Lectures on Rhetoric and Belles Lettres*, lecture 2 (Philadelphia: T. Ellwood Zell, 1862), 16–37.

7 Kant, *Critique of Judgment*, sec. 48, 179; emphasis in original.

8 Kant, *Critique of Judgment*, sec. 48, 179–80.

9   Kant, *Critique of Judgment*, IV, 20.

10 Kant, *Critique of Judgment*, sec. 15, 73.

11 John Passmore, *The Perfectibility of Man*, 3rd ed. (Indianapolis: Liberty Fund, 2000), 15.

12 W. H. S. Jones, *Hippocrates (Decorum)*, vol. 2 (London: William Heinemann; New York: G. P. Putnam's Sons, 1923), v.

13 Plato, *Timaeus*, in *The Collected Dialogues of Plato*, ed. Edith Hamilton and Huntington Cairns (Princeton, N.J.: Princeton University Press, 1963), 68d–69b, 92c.

14 Plato, *Republic*, in *Collected Dialogues of Plato*, x, 596–97.

15 Leon R. Kass, *The Beginning of Wisdom: Reading Genesis* (New York: Free Press, 2003), 11; emphasis in original.

16 Kass, *Beginning of Wisdom*, 37–38; emphasis in original.

17 Kass, *Beginning of Wisdom*, 5–6.

18 Kass, *Beginning of Wisdom*, 18–19.

19 Kass, *Beginning of Wisdom*, 39; emphasis in original.

20 Kass, *Beginning of Wisdom*, 39; emphasis in original.

21 I discuss this point in some detail throughout my work, Michael J. Hyde, *The Life-Giving Gift of Acknowledgment: A Philosophical and Rhetorical Inquiry* (West Lafayette, Ind.: Purdue University Press, 2006).

22 Abraham J. Heschel, *The Prophets*, vol. 2 (New York: Harper & Row, 1962), 216–17.

23 Heschel, *Prophets*, 217; emphasis in original.

24 See, e.g., Russell Jacoby, *Picture Imperfect: Utopian Thought for an Anti-Utopian Age* (New York: Columbia University Press, 2005), 83–111.

25 Bertrand Russell, *Religion and Science* (New York: Oxford University Press, 1961), 216; emphasis in original.

26 Russell, *Religion and Science*, 221–22.

27 For an excellent history and critique of the anthropic principle, see John D. Barrow and Frank J. Tipler, *The Anthropic Cosmological Principle* (New York: Oxford University Press, 1986).

28 Russell, *Religion and Science*, 243.

29 Michael S. Gazzaniga, *The Ethical Brain* (New York: Dana Press, 2005), xviii.

30 Andrew Newberg, Eugene D'Aquili, and Vince Rause, *Why God Won't Go Away: Brain Science and the Biology of Belief* (New York: Ballantine Books, 2001), 37.

31 Leonard Susskind, *The Cosmic Landscape: String Theory and the Illusion of Intelligent Design* (New York: Little, Brown, 2006), 66, 255.

32 Paul Davies, *God and the New Physics* (New York: Simon & Schuster, 1983), 70, 209. Also see Paul Davies, *The Fifth Miracle: The Search for the Origin and Meaning of Life* (New York: Simon & Schuster, 2000).

33 Steven Weinberg, *Facing Up: Science and Its Cultural Adversaries* (Cambridge, Mass.: Harvard University Press, 2001), 242.

34 Charles Darwin, *The Origin of Species by Means of Natural Selection* (New York: Barnes & Noble, 2004), 368, 371–72.

35 Darwin, *Origin of Species*, 369, 383–84.

36 Darwin, *Origin of Species*, 384.

37 Darwin, *Origin of Species*, 383.

38 Richard Dawkins, *A Devil's Chaplain: Reflections on Hope, Lies, Science, and Love* (New York: Houghton Mifflin, 2003), 13.

39 Weinberg, *Facing Up*, 232.

40 Darwin, *Origin of Species*, 384.

41 George Levine emphasizes this point in his introduction to Darwin's *The Origin of Species* (New York: Barnes & Noble Books, 2004), xiii–xxxiii. The rhetorical theorist and critic John Angus Campbell also makes much of Darwin's rhetorical competence. See, e.g., his work, John Angus Campbell, "Charles Darwin: Rhetorician of Science," in *Landmark Essays on Rhetoric of Science: Case Studies*, ed. Randy Allen Harris (Mahwah, N.J.: Lawrence Erlbaum, 1997), 3–18.

42 Steven Weinberg, *Dreams of a Final Theory: The Scientist's Search for the Ultimate Laws of Nature* (New York: Vintage Books, 1992), 245, 250–51.

43 Weinberg, *Dreams of a Final Theory*, 250. For a more conciliatory view of the matter, see Kenneth R. Miller, *Finding Darwin's God: A Scientist's Search for Common Ground between God and Evolution* (New York: Harper Perennial, 1999).

44 Weinberg, *Dreams of a Final Theory*, 261.

45 Weinberg, *Facing Up*, 39.

46 Weinberg, *Dreams of a Final Theory*, 165.

47 Weinberg, *Dreams of a Final Theory*, 243–46, 255.

48 Weinberg, *Facing Up*, 120.

49 Richard Dawkins, *The Selfish Gene*, 2nd ed. (New York: Oxford University Press, 1989), 6, 200, 264.

50 Dawkins, *Selfish Gene*, 196.

51 Dawkins, *Devil's Chaplain*, 12.

52 Dawkins, *Devil's Chaplain*, 13.

53 Dawkins, *Selfish Gene*, 189–201.

54 Dawkins, *Selfish Gene*, 201.

55 President's Council on Bioethics, *Beyond Therapy: Biotechnology and the Pursuit of Happiness* (New York: Regan Books, 2003).

56 Lee Smolin, *The Life of the Cosmos* (New York: Oxford University Press, 1997), 163.

57 Mario Livio, *The Golden Ratio: The Story of Phi, the World's Most Astonishing Number* (New York: Broadway Books, 2002), 117.

58 Quoted in David Blatner, *The Joy of π* (New York: Walker, 1997), 63.

59 Blatner, *The Joy of π*, 2–3.

60 Believing that the mathematical order of the cosmos was based purely on rational numbers, the Pythagoreans considered these other strange numbers to represent some sort of cosmic error that should be suppressed and kept secret. See Livio, *Golden Ratio*, 24–41.

61 Livio, *Golden Ratio*, 75–86; Bülent Atalay, *Math and the Mona Lisa: The Art and Science of Leonardo da Vinci* (Washington, D.C.: Smithsonian Books, 2004), 112–50.

62 Plato, *Timaeus*, 35b–37, 43c–e, 68d–69b, 92c.
63 Brian Greene, *The Elegant Universe: Superstrings, Hidden Dimensions, and the Quest for the Ultimate Theory* (New York: Vintage Books, 1999), 17; emphasis in original.
64 Greene, *Elegant Universe*, 146. "String theory also requires extra space dimensions that must be curled up in a very small size to be consistent with our never having seen them. But a tiny string can probe a tiny space. As a string moves about, oscillating as it travels, the geometrical form of the extra dimensions plays a critical role in determining resonant patterns of vibration. Because the patterns of string vibrations appear to us as the masses and charges of the elementary particles, we conclude that these fundamental properties of the universe are determined, in large measure, by the geometrical size and shape of the extra dimensions. That's one of the most far-reaching insights of string theory" (206).
65 Greene, *Elegant Universe*, 169. Also see Leon M. Lederman and Christopher T. Hill, *Symmetry and the Beautiful Universe* (New York: Prometheus Books, 2004).
66 Greene, *Elegant Universe*, 19.
67 Quoted in John Mansley Robinson, *An Introduction to Early Greek Philosophy: The Chief Fragments and Ancient Testimony, with Connecting Commentary* (New York: Houghton Mifflin, 1968), 96.
68 Greene, *Elegant Universe*, 183.
69 Lederman and Hill, *Symmetry and the Beautiful Universe*, 286.
70 Lederman and Hill, *Symmetry and the Beautiful Universe*, 18.
71 A more detailed phenomenology of "lived experience" is offered in the next chapter.
72 Smolin, *Life of the Cosmos*, 176.
73 Leonardo da Vinci, *Leonardo on Painting*, trans. Martin Kemp and Margaret Walker, ed. Martin Kemp (New Haven, Conn.: Yale University Press, 1989), 9.
74 Leonardo, *Leonardo on Painting*, 10.
75 Leonardo, *Leonardo on Painting*, 32.
76 Leonardo, *Leonardo on Painting*, 35.
77 Leonardo, *Leonardo on Painting*, 16.
78 Leonardo, *Leonardo on Painting*, 120.
79 Leonardo, *Leonardo on Painting*, 153; emphasis added.
80 Leonardo, *Leonardo on Painting*, 144. Also see Sherwin B. Nuland, *Leonardo da Vinci* (New York: Viking Penguin, 2000).
81 Sylvia Nasar, *A Beautiful Mind* (New York: Simon & Schuster, 1998), 388.
82 *A Beautiful Mind*, directed by Ron Howard, produced by Karen Kehela-Sherwood, Todd Hallowell, and Brian Grazer, screenplay written by Akiva Goldsman, based on the book by Sylvia Nasar, Universal Pictures, Universal City, Calif., 2001.
83 Leonardo, *Leonardo on Painting*, 150.
84 Leonardo, *Leonardo on Painting*, 144.
85 Leonardo, *Leonardo on Painting*, 220, 222.

86 Leonardo, *Leonardo on Painting*, 227.

87 Brown's *The Da Vinci Code* (New York: Doubleday, 2003) describes attempts to solve the murder of the renowned curator of the Louvre Museum in Paris. A baffling cipher is found near his body. Investigators attempt to sort out the bizarre riddles and are stunned to discover a trail of clues hidden in the works of Leonardo da Vinci. The book provoked a popular interest in speculation concerning the Holy Grail legend and Magdalene's role in the history of Christianity. The fictional work also was extensively denounced by Roman Catholics and other Christians as a dishonest attack on the Catholic Church.

88 Leonardo, *Leonardo on Painting*, 196.

89 Thomas B. Farrell, *Norms of Rhetorical Culture* (New Haven, Conn.: Yale University Press, 1993), 298; emphasis in original.

90 R. Buckminster Fuller, *Intuition* (New York: Anchor Books, 1973), 10; emphasis in original.

91 Stephen Hawking, *A Brief History of Time* (New York: Bantam, 1998), 190.

CHAPTER 7

1 Crispin Sartwell, *Six Names of Beauty* (New York: Routledge, 2004), 99, 105. Sartwell's meditations are organized around a discussion of the words for beauty in six languages: *beauty* (English, "the object of longing"), *yapha* (Hebrew, "glow," "bloom"), *sundara* (Sanskrit, "whole," "holy"), *to kalon* (Greek, "idea," "ideal"), *wabi-sabi* (Japanese, "humility," "imperfection"), and *hozho* (Navajo, "health," "harmony"). According to Sartwell, "the English world 'beauty' has become somewhat cliche-ridden, and if we are to keep experiencing the beauty of the world we need a kind of refreshment from its linguistic exhaustion" (xiii).

2 Stuart Kauffman, *At Home in the Universe: The Search for the Laws of Self-Organization and Complexity* (New York: Oxford University Press, 1995).

3 Kauffman, *At Home in the Universe*, 26.

4 Kauffman, *At Home in the Universe*, 23, 25–26; also 111–12.

5 Kauffman, *At Home in the Universe*, 23–25, 29.

6 Kauffman, *At Home in the Universe*, 69.

7 Elie Wiesel, *Messengers of God: Biblical Portraits and Legends* (New York: Simon & Schuster, 1976), 11–12.

8 Søren Kierkegaard, *Either/Or: A Fragment of Life*, vol. 1, trans. David Swenson and Lillian Swenson (Princeton, N.J.: Princeton University Press, 1949), 235.

9 Søren Kierkegaard, *Christian Discourses*, trans. W. Lowrie (New York: Oxford University Press, 1939), 80.

10 Emmanuel Levinas, *Time and the Other*, trans. Richard Cohen (Pittsburgh, Penn.: Duquesne University Press, 1987), 69.

11 Levinas, *Time and the Other*, 58.

12 Ronald J. Glasser, *The Body Is the Hero* (New York: Random House, 1976).

13 Ricky Skaggs and Kentucky Thunder, "Too Far Down to Fall," on *History of the Future*, compact disc (Hendersonville, Tenn.: Skaggs Place Productions, 2001).

14 Zygmunt Bauman, *Postmodern Ethics* (Cambridge, Mass.: Blackwell, 1993). I will have more to say about the postmodern in chapter 9 when discussing the biotechnology debate.

15 Ludwig Wittgenstein, *On Certainty*, sec. 471, trans. Denis Paul and G. E. M. Anscombe, ed. G. E. M. Anscombe and G. H. von Wright (New York: Harper & Row, 1969).

16 Martin Heidegger, *Parmenides*, trans. Andre Schuwer and Richard Rojcewicz (Bloomington: Indiana University Press, 1992), 135–36.

17 Martin Rees, *Before the Beginning: Our Universe and Others* (Reading, Mass: Perseus Books, 1997), 177.

18 Paul Davies, *God and the New Physics* (New York: Simon & Schuster, 1983), 55–56.

19 Martin Heidegger, *Being and Time*, trans. Edward Robinson and John Macquarrie (New York: Harper & Row, 1962), 256–73; emphasis in original.

20 Heidegger, *Being and Time*, 318; emphasis in original.

21 Martin Heidegger, *On the Way to Language*, trans. Peter D. Hertz (New York: Harper & Row, 1971), 123.

22 Umberto Eco, *The Search for the Perfect Language*, trans. James Fentress (Oxford: Blackwell, 1995), 7.

23 Heidegger, *Being and Time*, 49–58, 310–25. Also see Heidegger, *On the Way to Language*, 57–136. In this and other later works, Heidegger speaks of the "call of Being" rather than the "call of conscience."

24 Steven Pinker, *The Blank Slate: The Modern Denial of Human Nature* (New York: Penguin, 2002), 424.

25 Fred Adams and Greg Laughlin, *The Five Ages of the Universe: Inside the Physics of Eternity* (New York: Simon & Schuster, 1999).

26 Richard P. Feynman, *The Meaning of It All: Thoughts of a Citizen-Scientist* (Reading, Mass.: Perseus Books, 1998), 25–28; emphasis in original.

27 Feynman, *Meaning of It All*, 28.

28 Feynman, *Meaning of It All*, 49–50.

29 Feynman, *Meaning of It All*, 56–57.

30 Kenneth Burke, *The Rhetoric of Religion: Studies in Logology* (Berkeley: University of California Press, 1979), 274, 305; emphasis in original. For a discussion of the ontological status of Burke's work, see my work, Michael J. Hyde, "Searching for Perfection: Martin Heidegger (With Some Help from Kenneth Burke) on Language, Truth, and the Practice of Rhetoric," in *Perspectives on Philosophy of Communication*, ed. Pat Arneson (West Lafayette, Ind.: Purdue University Press, 2007), 23–36.

31 Kenneth Burke, *Language as Symbolic Action: Essays on Life, Literature, and Method* (Berkeley: University of California Press, 1966), 20.

32 Burke, *Language as Symbolic Action*, 19; emphasis in original.

33 Kenneth Burke, *Permanence and Change: An Anatomy of Purpose* (New York: Bobbs-Merrill, 1965), 44–49.

34 Burke, *Permanence and Change*, 37.

35 Max Horkheimer, *Eclipse of Reason* (New York: Continuum, 1974), 109.

36 Horkheimer, *Eclipse of Reason*, 126.

37 Ernest Becker, *The Denial of Death* (New York: Free Press, 1973), 1, 7, 3; emphasis in original.

38 Becker, *Denial of Death*, 4–5.

39 Becker, *Denial of Death*, 66.

40 Joan Stambaugh, *The Finitude of Being* (Albany: State University of New York Press, 1992), 56.

41 Calvin O. Schrag, *God as Otherwise Than Being: Toward a Semantics of the Gift* (Evanston, Ill.: Northwestern University Press, 2002), 117–18.

42 Elaine Scarry, *On Beauty and Being Just* (Princeton, N.J.: Princeton University Press, 1999), 52–53, 60–61, 109.

43 Scarry, *On Beauty and Being Just*, 28, 69, 90.

44 Lloyd F. Bitzer, "The Rhetorical Situation," in *Philosophy and Rhetoric* 1 (1968): 1–14.

45 Timothy E. Quill, *Death and Dignity: Making Choices and Taking Charge* (New York: W. W. Norton, 1993), 25.

CHAPTER 8

1 David Hume, *Essays: Moral, Political, and Literary*, ed. Eugene F. Miller (Indianapolis: Liberty Classics, 1985), 583.

2 Hume, *Essays: Moral, Political, and Literary*, 583, 585.

3 Hume, *Essays: Moral, Political, and Literary*, 583.

4 See, e.g., James Rachels, *The End of Life: Euthanasia and Morality* (New York: Oxford University Press, 1986); Wesley J. Smith, *Forced Exit: The Slippery Slope from Assisted Suicide to Legalized Murder* (New York: Random House, 1997); Michael J. Hyde, *The Call of Conscience: Heidegger and Levinas, Rhetoric and the Euthanasia Debate* (Columbia: University of South Carolina Press, 2001); Margaret Pabst Battin, *Ending Life: Ethics and the Way We Die* (New York: Oxford University Press, 2005); Garret Keizer, "Life Everlasting: The Religious Right and the Right to Die," in *Harper's* (February 2005): 53–61; and Daniel P. Sulmasy, "Dignity and Bioethics: History, Theory, and Selected Applications," in *Human Dignity and Bioethics*, ed. President's Council on Bioethics (Washington, D.C.: President's Council on Bioethics, 2008), 469–501.

5 Bruce Jennings, "The Long Dying of Terri Schiavo—Private Tragedy, Public Danger," (presentation, the Garrison Colloquium, The Hastings Center, Garrison, N.Y., May 20, 2005): 1–2. This perfect storm controversy was often referenced in the media as it covered the U.S. Supreme Court's January 17, 2006, decision in *Gonzales, Attorney General, et al. v. Oregon et al.*, 546 U.S. 243 (2006). This decision acknowledged the right of a state, conforming to well-detailed and strict regulations, to support the moral action of physician-assisted suicide.

6 Jennings, "Long Dying of Terri Schiavo," 2; emphasis added.

7   Michael Schiavo, *Terri: The Truth*, with Michael Hirsh (New York: Dutton, 2006), 74–78.

8   Mary Schindler and Robert Schindler, *A Life That Matters: The Legacy of Terri Schiavo—A Lesson for Us All*, with Suzanne Schindler Vitadamo and Bobby Schindler (New York: Warner Books, 2006), 202.

9   Schiavo, *Terri: The Truth*, 28–29, 47–48.

10 Schiavo, *Terri: The Truth*, 102–39.

11 The recorded testimonies of Mr. Schindler and his son are included in Schiavo's *Terri: The Truth*, 161–63. The testimonies are not included in Mr. Schindler's book.

12 Schiavo, *Terri: The Truth*, 163.

13 Schiavo, *Terri: The Truth*, xiii; emphasis in original.

14 Schindler and Schindler, *Life That Matters*, xi–xii.

15 For an in-depth rhetorical analysis of the Cruzan case and the court's decision, see Hyde, *The Call of Conscience*, 187–204.

16 Schindler and Schindler, *Life That Matters*, 38; emphasis in original.

17 Schindler and Schindler, *Life That Matters*, 152.

18 Schindler and Schindler, *Life That Matters*, 150.

19 Mr. Schiavo documents incidents of lack of care for Terri throughout his book, Schiavo, *Terri: The Truth*.

20 Schiavo, *Terri: The Truth*, 319.

21 Schindler and Schindler, *Life That Matters*, 218.

22 David Gibbs, *Fighting for Dear Life: The Untold Story of Terri Schiavo and What It Means for All of Us*, with Bob DeMoss (Minneapolis, Minn.: Bethany House, 2006), 15.

23 Søren Kierkegaard, *The Concept of Anxiety: A Simple Psychologically Orienting Deliberation on the Dogmatic Issue of Hereditary Sin*, trans. and ed. Reidar Thomte, in collaboration with Albert B. Anderson (Princeton, N.J.: Princeton University Press, 1980), 188.

24 Schindler and Schindler, *Life That Matters*, 26–27. It should be noted that bulimics tend not to go public about their condition. See Carrie-Anne Platt, "Starving for Acknowledgment: A Rhetorical Analysis of Pro Eating Disorder Websites" (M.A. thesis, Wake Forest University, 2004).

25 Schiavo, *Terri: The Truth*, xiv–xv, 12; emphasis in original.

26 Lawrence O. Gostin, "Ethics, the Constitution, and the Dying Process: The Case of Theresa Marie Schiavo," *Journal of the American Medical Association* 293 (May 18, 2005): 2403–7; Bill Nichols and Andrea Stone, "Schiavo Autopsy Confirms Diagnosis," *USA Today*, June 15, 2005; Abby Goodnough, "Schiavo Autopsy Says Brain, Withered, Was Untreatable," *New York Times*, June 16, 2005.

27 With their argument that God created the world but then leaves matters alone and never intervenes, Deists need not trouble themselves with the phenomenon of acknowledgment.

28 Schindler and Schindler, *Life That Matters*, xii.

29 Schiavo, *Terri: The Truth*, xvi.

30 Schindler and Schindler, *Life That Matters*, 223.

31 Cited in Jay Tolson, "Wrestling with the Final Call," *U.S. News and World Report*, April 4, 2005, 22–23; emphasis in original.

32 Schindler and Schindler, *Life That Matters*, 182–84.

33 Life Legal Defense Foundation, "The Truth about Terri Schiavo," newspaper advertisement, *USA Today*, March 25, 2005, 5A; emphasis in original.

34 Editorial, *Commonweal* 131, April 23, 2004.

35 Anna Quindlen, "The Culture of Each Life," *Newsweek*, April 4, 2005.

36 See my work, Hyde, *Call of Conscience*, 119–50. In the Schiavo case, no living will was ever legally filed.

37 Schiavo, *Terri: The Truth*, 29, 323.

38 Life Legal Defense Foundation, "Truth about Terri Schiavo"; emphasis in original.

39 Kenneth Burke, *Language as Symbolic Action: Essays on Life, Literature, and Method* (Berkeley: University of California Press, 1966), 26.

40 Eugene Kennedy, "Mystery: Terri's Eyes Inflame Our Questioning," *Winston-Salem Journal*, March 26, 2005.

41 Much is made of the phenomenon in Joni Eareckson Tada, *When Is It Right to Die? Suicide, Euthanasia, Suffering, Mercy* (Grand Rapids, Mich.: Zondervan, 1992).

42 Susan Brink, "Inside Terri's Brain," *U.S. News and World Report*, April 4, 2005, 24–25; Benedict Carey, "For Parents, the Unthinkability of Letting Go," *New York Times*, March 20, 2005.

43 John Schwartz and Denise Grady, "A Diagnosis with a Dose of Religion," *New York Times,* March 24, 2005.

44 See my work, Michael J. Hyde, *The Life-Giving Gift of Acknowledgment: A Philosophical and Rhetorical Inquiry* (West Lafayette, Ind.: Purdue University Press, 2006), 117–41.

45 For a detailed discussion of the ontological, metaphysical, and rhetorical nature of heroism, see my works, Hyde, *Call of Conscience*, 187–263; and Hyde, *Life-Giving Gift*, 256–83.

46 Paul McHugh, "Annihilating Terri Schiavo," *Commentary*, June 2005, 29.

47 McHugh, "Annihilating Terri Schiavo," 29–30.

48 Aristotle, *Rhetoric* (1367b37), trans. W. Rhys Roberts (New York: Random House, 1954).

49 McHugh, "Annihilating Terri Schiavo," 31.

50 Hyde, *Life-Giving Gift*, 1–14.

51 McHugh, "Annihilating Terri Schiavo," 32.

52 Hyde, *Call of Conscience*, 204–19.

53 Stephen Drake, "Disabled Are Fearful: Who Will Be Next?" op. ed., *Los Angeles Times*, October 29, 2003. Also see Christopher Kliewer and Stephen Drake, "Disability, Eugenics and the Current Ideology of Segregation: A Modern Moral Tale," *Disability & Society* 13 (1998): 95–111.

54 Drake, "Disabled Are Fearful"; Kliewer and Drake, "Modern Moral Tale."

55 See my work, Hyde, *Life-Giving Gift*, 60–116.

56 James VanTrees, letter to the editor, *USA Today*, April 1, 2005.

57 Martin Foss, *Death, Sacrifice, and Tragedy* (Lincoln: University of Nebraska Press, 1966), 43.

58 *Schiavo v. Schiavo*, 2005 WL 665257 (Fla. 11th Cir. 2005).

59 See, e.g., Phillip Gailey, "Cynical Political Display by Congress," *Winston-Salem Journal*, March 23, 2005; Molly Ivins, "Man Behaving Badly Shouldn't Lecture," *Winston-Salem Journal*, April 21, 2005; Andrea Stone, "Schiavo Autopsy Results Reach a Divided Congress," *USA Today*, June 15, 2005; Dan Gilgoff, "The Schiavo Case Is Just the Latest Front in a Much Nastier War," *U.S. News and World Report*, April 4, 2005, 14–21.

60 James Rachels, *The End of Life: Euthanasia and Morality* (New York: Oxford University Press, 1986), 71.

61 Quindlen, "Culture of Each Life," 62.

62 For an artifact proud to announce such accusations, see the Life Legal Defense Foundation's newspaper advertisement, "Truth about Terri Schiavo." The media feeding frenzy was clearly exhibited in four segments on CNN's *Larry King Live*: "Interview with Michael Schiavo" (March 21, 2005), "Guest Panel Discusses Terri Schiavo Case" (March 23, 2005), "Battle over Terri Schiavo" (March 24, 2005), and "Panel Discusses Battle over Terri Schiavo" (March 25, 2005). The frenzy was also stirred by the media as it gave consideration to how the Schindlers and their supporters took exception to the "message" that was promoted in Clint Eastwood's Academy Award–winning film *Million Dollar Baby*, which was playing during the final weeks of Terri's life. The message spoke of the morality of assisted suicide. For both critical and positive commentary on this film and its relationship to the Schiavo case, see the special issue of the journal *Disability Studies Quarterly* 25, no. 3 (2005). Also see Mary Johnson, *Make Them Go Away: Clint Eastwood, Christopher Reeve, and the Case against Disability Rights* (Louisville, Ky.: Advocado Press, 2003).

63 Quoted in "Bill Might Return Tube: Federal Courts Could Decide Fate of Schiavo," editorial, *Winston-Salem Journal*, March 20, 2005.

64 John Schwartz, "Neither 'Starvation' nor the Suffering It Connotes Applies to Schiavo, Doctors Say," *New York Times*, March 25, 2005.

65 Georges Gusdorf, *Speaking (La Parole)*, trans. Paul T. Brockelman (Evanston, Ill.: Northwestern University Press, 1965), 122.

66 An example of how the point was made is found in Craig M. Klugman's letter to the editor: "The one positive aspect of this case is that Ms. Schiavo has given this country a gift. She has shown to everyone how important it is to have end-of-life conversations with our loved ones and that we must all complete advance-care planning documents." *New York Times*, March 24, 2005.

67 Hans Blumenberg, trans. Robert M. Wallace, "An Anthropological Approach to the Contemporary Significance of Rhetoric," in *After Philosophy: End or Transformation?* ed. Kenneth Baynes, James Bohman, and Thomas McCarthy, 429–58 (Cambridge, Mass.: MIT Press, 1987).

68 John Harris, *Enhancing Evolution: The Ethical Case for Making Better People* (Princeton, N.J.: Princeton University Press, 2007), 3–4; emphasis in original.

69 Editors, "Do We Need Death? The Consequences of Radical Life Exten-
    sion," *Cato Unbound* (December 2007), http://www.cato-unbound.org/.
    Essayists include Daniel Callahan, Ronald Bailey, Diana Schaub, and
    Aubrey De Grey.

70 Francis Fukuyama, *Our Posthuman Future: Consequences of the Bio-
    technology Revolution* (New York: Farrar, Straus, & Giroux, 2002), 7.

CHAPTER 9

1   Gregory Stock, *Redesigning Humans: Choosing Our Genes, Changing
    Our Future* (New York: Mariner Books, 2003), 1–2, 5.

2   Sherry Turkle, *Life On the Screen: Identity in the Age of the Internet*
    (New York: Simon & Schuster, 1995), 263–64.

3   See my work, Michael J. Hyde, *The Life-Giving Gift of Acknowledg-
    ment: A Philosophical and Rhetorical Inquiry* (West Lafayette, Ind.: Pur-
    due University Press, 2006), 239–45.

4   Hans Moravec, *Robot: Mere Machine to Transcendent Mind* (Oxford:
    Oxford University Press, 1999); Ray Kurzweil, *The Singularity Is Near:
    When Humans Transcend Biology* (New York: Penguin, 2006).

5   Max More, "The Extropian Principles (Version 3.0): A Transhumanist
    Declaration," http://www.maxmore.com/extprn3.htm (1998).

6   Laura Bartlett and Thomas B. Byers, "Back to the Future: The Humanist
    Matrix," *Cultural Critique* 53 (2003): 28–46.

7   President's Council on Bioethics, *Beyond Therapy: Biotechnology and
    the Pursuit of Happiness* (Washington, D.C.: Regan Books, 2003), 1.

8   President's Council on Bioethics, *Beyond Therapy*, xvii.

9   President's Council on Bioethics, *Human Cloning and Human Dignity*
    (New York: Public Affairs, 2002), xlii.

10 President's Council on Bioethics, *Beyond Therapy*, ixx–xxi.

11 President's Council on Bioethics, *Beyond Therapy*, 288.

12 Leon R. Kass, *The Beginning of Wisdom: Reading Genesis* (New York:
    Free Press, 2003), 11, 18–19; emphasis in original.

13 Jacques Derrida, "Deconstruction and the Other," in *Dialogues with
    Contemporary Continental Thinkers: The Phenomenological Heritage*,
    ed. Richard Kearney, 107–26 (Manchester: Manchester University Press,
    1984).

14 Leon R. Kass, *The Hungry Soul: Eating and the Perfecting of Our Nature*
    (New York: Free Press, 1994), 6–7; Leon R. Kass and James Q. Wilson,
    The Ethics of Human Cloning (Washington, D.C.: American Enterprise
    Institute Press, 1998), 8–9.

15 Lawrence Vogel, "Natural Law Judaism?: The Genesis of Bioethics in
    Hans Jonas, Leo Strauss, and Leon Kass," *Hastings Center Report* 36
    (2006): 32.

16 Kass, *The Beginning of Wisdom*, 37–38; Leon R. Kass, *Life, Liberty,
    and the Defense of Dignity: The Challenge for Bioethics* (San Francisco:
    Encounter Books, 2002), 240. Also see Leon R. Kass, "Science, Religion,
    and the Human Future," *Commentary* 123 (2007): 36–48; Leon R. Kass,
    "Keeping Life Human: Science, Religion, and the Soul" (Wriston Lecture,

Manhattan Institute for Policy Research, New York City, October 18, 2007); Leon R. Kass, "Defending Human Dignity," *Commentary* 124 (2007): 53–61; and Leon R. Kass, "Looking for an Honest Man: Reflections of an Unlicensed Humanist," 2009 Jefferson Lecture in the Humanities, May 22, 2009, http://www.neh.gov/whoweare/Kass/Lecture.html (retrieved July 20, 2009).

17 Leon R. Kass, "Death with Dignity and the Sanctity of Life," in *A Time to Be Born and a Time to Die*, ed. Barry S. Kogan (New York: Aldine de Gruyter, 1991), 127–29; emphasis in original.

18 Francis Fukuyama, *Our Posthuman Future: Consequences of the Biotechnology Revolution* (New York: Farrar, Straus, & Giroux, 2002); Michael J. Sandel, *The Case Against Perfection: Ethics in the Age of Genetic Engineering* (Cambridge, Mass.: Harvard University Press, 2007).

19 Jürgen Habermas, *The Future of Human Nature* (Oxford: Polity Press, 2003).

20 Leon R. Kass, *Toward a More Natural Science: Biology and Human Affairs* (New York: Free Press, 1985), 348. Also see his "Human Future," "Keeping Life Human," and "Defending Human Dignity."

21 Elizabeth Blackburn, "Bioethics and the Political Distortion of Biomedical Science," *New England Journal of Medicine* 350 (2004): 1379–80; Arthur Caplan, "Rhetoric and Reality in Stem Cell Debates," *Society* 44 (2007): 26–27; Steven Pinker, "The Stupidity of Dignity: Conservative Bioethics' Latest, Most Dangerous Ploy," *New Republic* 238, May 28, 2008, 28–31.

22 President's Council on Bioethics, *Beyond Therapy*, xv–xxi. Also see F. Daniel Davis, "Human Dignity and Respect for Persons: A Historical Perspective on Public Bioethics," in *Human Dignity and Bioethics*, ed. President's Council on Bioethics (Washington, D.C.: President's Council on Bioethics, 2008), 30.

23 Kass, *Defense of Dignity*, 4; Kass, "Keeping Life Human," 1–2.

24 Kass, *Defense of Dignity*, 8.

25 Kass, "Human Future," 46.

26 Kass, *Defense of Dignity*, 5–6.

27 President's Council on Bioethics, *Beyond Therapy*, 37; emphasis in original.

28 Eric Cohen, "Conservative Bioethics and the Search for Wisdom," *Hastings Center Report* 36 (2006): 44–56; Eric Cohen and Leon R. Kass, "Cast Me Not Off in Old Age," *Commentary* 121 (2006): 32–39; Wesley J. Smith, *Culture of Death: The Assault on Medical Ethics in America* (San Francisco: Encounter Books, 2000).

29 Ruth Macklin, "The New Conservatives in Bioethics: Who Are They and What Do They Seek?" *Hastings Center Report* 36 (2006): 38.

30 Kass, *Defense of Dignity*, 32, 37; Kass, "Human Future"; Kass, "Keeping Life Human"; Kass, "Defending Human Dignity." Heidegger's most famous critique of science and technology is his work, Martin Heidegger, *The Question Concerning Technology and Other Essays*, trans. W. Lovitt (New York: Harper & Row, 1977).

31 Kass, *Defense of Dignity*, 274.

32 President's Council on Bioethics, *Beyond Therapy*, 51.

33 President's Council on Bioethics, *Beyond Therapy*, 70; emphasis in original.

34 For a case study centering on this legal issue, see my work, Michael J. Hyde, "A Rhetoric of Risk: Medical Science and the Question of 'Wrongful Life,'" in *Argument and Critical Practices: Proceedings of the Fifth SCA/AFA Conference on Argumentation*, ed. Joseph W. Wenzel (Annandale, Va.: Speech Communication Association, 1987), 129–36.

35 C. Mangel and A. B. Weisse, *Medicine: The State of the Art* (New York: Dial Press, 1984), 196.

36 President's Council on Bioethics, *Beyond Therapy*, 258.

37 See my work, Michael J. Hyde, *The Call of Conscience: Heidegger and Levinas, Rhetoric and the Euthanasia Debate* (Columbia: University of South Carolina Press, 2001); Hyde, *Life-Giving Gift*; and Michael J. Hyde and Sarah McSpiritt, "Coming to Terms with Perfection: The Case of Terri Schiavo," *Quarterly Journal of Speech* 93 (2007): 150–79.

38 President's Council on Bioethics, *Beyond Therapy*, 17.

39 Kass, *Defense of Dignity*, 138–39. Also see Kass, "Defending Human Dignity."

40 Hyde, *Call of Conscience*, 160–76; Leon R. Kass, "The Right to Life and Human Dignity," *New Atlantis* 16 (2007): 23–40.

41 Kass, "Death with Dignity," 140. Also see Cohen and Kass, "Cast Me Not Off in Old Age."

42 Kass, *Defense of Dignity*, 259.

43 President's Council on Bioethics, *Human Cloning and Human Dignity*, 187.

44 Kass, *Defense of Dignity*, 150; Leon R. Kass, "The Wisdom of Repugnance," *New Republic*, June 2002, 17–26.

45 Kass, *Defense of Dignity*, 150.

46 Kass, *Defense of Dignity*, 132, 137, 143.

47 Kass, "Human Future"; Kass, "Keeping Life Human."

48 Adam Briggle, "The President's Council on Bioethics: Science, Democracy, and the Good Life" (Ph.D. diss., University of Colorado, 2006), 172–98.

49 Kass, *Defense of Dignity*, 153.

50 President's Council on Bioethics, *Beyond Therapy*, 55; emphasis in original.

51 President's Council on Bioethics, *Beyond Therapy*, 56.

52 Kass, *Defense of Dignity*, 130–31, 152–53.

53 Yuval Levin, "The Paradox of Conservative Bioethics," *New Atlantis* 1 (2003): 65.

54 President's Council on Bioethics, *Beyond Therapy*, 22–23; Leon R. Kass, "Forbidding Science: Some Beginning Reflections," *Science and Engineering Ethics* (published online April 2, 2009), doi 10.1007/s11948-009-9122-9.

55 President's Council on Bioethics, *Beyond Therapy*, 300.

56 Michael S. Gazzaniga, "Statement of Dr. Gazzaniga," in President's

Notes to pp. 229–237 • 305

Council on Bioethics, *Human Cloning and Human Dignity*, 290. Also see Michael S. Gazzaniga, *The Ethical Brain* (New York: Dana Press, 2005).

57　Ruth Macklin, "Dignity Is a Useless Concept," *British Medical Journal* 327 (2003): 1419–20. Also see Dieter Birnbacher, "Human Cloning and Human Dignity," *Reproductive BioMedicine Online* 10, suppl. no. 1 (2005): 50–55; Richard E. Ashcroft, "Making Sense of Dignity," *Journal of Medical Ethics* 31 (2005): 679–82; and Timothy Caulfield and Roger Brownsword, "Human Dignity: A Guide to Policy Making in the Biotechnology Era?" *Nature Reviews Genetics* 7 (2006): 72–76.

58　F. Daniel Davis, "Human Dignity and Respect for Persons: A Historical Perspective on Public Bioethics," in *Human Dignity and Bioethics*, ed. President's Council on Bioethics, 34; emphasis in original.

59　Pinker, "Stupidity of Dignity," 28–29.

60　Edmund D. Pellegrino, "Letter of Transmittal to The President of The United States," in *Human Dignity and Bioethics*, ed. President's Council on Bioethics, xi–xii.

61　Pinker, "The Stupidity of Dignity," 28.

62　Rebecca Dresser, "Human Dignity and the Seriously Ill Patient," in *Human Dignity and Bioethcs*, ed. President's Council on Bioethics, 507.

63　Pinker, "Stupidity of Dignity," 31.

64　Dresser, "Human Dignity and the Seriously Ill Patient," 508.

65　Pinker, "Stupidity of Dignity," 29.

66　Kass, "Defending Human Dignity," 329.

67　Kass, "Keeping Life Human"; Kass, "Defending Human Dignity," 53–61.

68　Sandel, *Case Against Perfection*, 99–100.

69　Kass, *Defense of Dignity*, 138–39; Kass, "Forbidding Science."

70　Kass, *Defense of Dignity*, 264, 267–68, 272; emphasis in original.

71　Kurzweil, *Singularity Is Near*, 210.

72　Kurzweil, *Singularity Is Near*, 374.

73　Kurzweil, *Singularity Is Near*, 9, 374.

74　Sheila M. Rothman and David J. Rothman, *The Pursuit of Perfection: The Promise and Perils of Medical Enhancement* (New York: Pantheon Books, 2003); John Harris, *Enhancing Evolution: The Ethical Case for Making Better People* (Princeton, N.J.: Princeton University Press, 2007); Rebecca Tuhus-Dubrow, "Designer Babies and the Pro-Choice Movement," *Dissent* (Summer 2007), 37–43. Also see the special issue of the peer-reviewed electronic journal—"Becoming More Than Human: Technology and the Post-Human Condition," special issue, *Journal of Evolution and Technology* 19 (2008)—published by the Institute for Ethics and Emerging Technologies, http://jetpress.org/.

75　Nancy M. P. King (professor, Department of Social Sciences and Health Policy; director, Program in Bioethics, Health, and Society, Wake Forest University School of Medicine, Winston-Salem, N.C.), personal interview with the author, January 6, 2009.

76　See, in particular, the essays by Daniel C. Dennett ("How to Protect Human Dignity from Science"), Patricia S. Churchland ("Human Dignity from a Neurophilosophical Perspective"), and Nick Bostrom ("Dignity and Enhancement"), in *Human Dignity and Bioethics*, ed. President's Council on Bioethics.

77 See, e.g., James Breech, *Jesus and Postmodernism* (Minneapolis, Minn.: Fortress Press, 1989); Emmanuel Levinas, *Of God Who Comes to Mind*, trans. Bettina Bergo (Stanford, Calif.: Stanford University Press, 1998); and John D. Caputo, *On Religion* (New York: Routledge, 2001).

78 Paul Davies, *The Cosmic Jackpot: Why Our Universe Is Just Right for Life* (New York: Houghton Mifflin, 2007).

79 Kass, "Defending Human Dignity," 328.

80 David Gelernter, "The Religious Character of Human Dignity," in *Human Dignity and Bioethics*, ed. President's Council on Bioethics, 404–5; emphasis in original.

81 Gelernter, "Religious Character of Human Dignity," 401–2; emphasis in original.

82 Edmund D. Pellegrino, "The Lived Experience of Human Dignity," in *Human Dignity and Bioethics*, ed. President's Council on Bioethics, 535.

83 Cited in Renay San Miguel, "Feds Approve Stem Cell Tests on Patients with Spinal Cord Injuries," *TechNewsWorld*, January 23, 2009, http://www.technewsworld.com/story/Feds-Approve-Stem-Cell-Tests-on-Patients-With-Spinal-Cord-Injuries-65947.html.

84 San Miguel, "Stem Cell Tests."

85 Daniel Callahan, "Nature Knew What It Was Doing," *Cato Unbound*, December 10, 2007, http://www.cato-unbound.org/2007/12/10/daniel-callahan/nature-kn.

CHAPTER 10

1 Daniel C. Dennett, "How to Protect Human Dignity from Science," in *Human Dignity and Bioethics*, ed. President's Council on Bioethics (Washington, D.C.: President's Council on Bioethics, 2008), 39.

2 Dennett, "How to Protect Human Dignity," 45.

3 Dennett, "How to Protect Human Dignity," 57; emphasis in original. Also see Lee M. Silver, *Challenging Nature: The Clash Between Biotechnology and Spirituality* (New York: Harper Perennial, 2006).

4 I am thus taken, e.g., with essays by Patrick D. Hopkins, "A Moral Vision for Transhumanism," *Journal of Evolution and Technology* 19 (2008), http://jetpress.org/v19/hopkins.htm; Gregory E. Jordan, "The Invention of Man: A Response to C. S. Lewis's *The Abolition of Man*," *Journal of Evolution and Technology* 19 (September 2008), http://jetpress.org/v19/jordan.htm; and Nick Bostrom, "Letter from Utopia," *Journal of Evolution and Technology* 19 (2008), http://jetpress.org/v19/bostrom.htm.

5 Emmanuel Levinas, *Collected Philosophical Papers*, trans. Alphonso Lingis (The Hague: Martinus Nijhoff, 1987), 23.

6 Emmanuel Levinas, *Ethics and Infinity*, trans. Richard A. Cohen (Pittsburgh, Pa.: Duquesne University Press, 1985), 85–122; emphasis in original.

7 Frederick W. J. Schelling, *Of Human Freedom*, trans. James Gutmann (Chicago: Open Court, 1936), 84.

8   Moses Maimonides, *The Guide for the Perplexed*, trans. M. Friedlander (New York: Barnes & Noble, 2004), 1.34.85–86.

9   Lewis Thomas, *The Lives of a Cell: Notes of a Biology Watcher* (New York: Penguin, 1974), 32–33, 35.

10 Paul Davies, *The Cosmic Jackpot: Why Our Universe Is Just Right for Life* (New York: Houghton Mifflin, 2007), 103.

11 Steven Weinberg, *The First Three Minutes: A Modern View of the Origin of the Universe*, 2nd ed. (New York: Basic Books, 1993), 154–55.

12 Warren Zev Harvey, "Grace or Loving-Kindness," in *Contemporary Jewish Religious Thought: Original Essays on Critical Concepts, Movements, and Beliefs*, ed. Arthur A. Cohen and Paul Mendes-Flohr (New York: Free Press, 1987), 229–303; Rudolf Bultmann, *Theology of the New Testament*, vol. 1, trans. Kendrick Grobel (New York: Charles Scribner's Sons, 1951), 156–59, 262–69, 281–94, 329–36.

13 Charles Darwin, *The Correspondence of Charles Darwin*, vol. 8, *1860*, ed. Frederick Burkhardt, Janet Browne, Duncan M. Porter, and Marsha Richmond (New York: Cambridge University Press, 1993), 224.

14 Stephen Jay Gould, *Rocks of Ages: Science and Religion in the Fullness of Life* (New York: Ballantine Publishing Group, 1999), 9–10. For other scientists who display the attitude being emphasized here, see, e.g., Davies, *Cosmic Jackpot*; Joel R. Primack and Nancy Ellen Abrams, *The View from the Center of the Universe* (New York: Riverhead Books, 2006); Kenneth R. Miller, *Finding Darwin's God: A Scientist's Search for Common Ground Between God and Evolution* (New York: Harper Perennial, 1999); and Michael Mallary, *Our Improbable Universe: A Physicist Considers How We Got Here* (New York: Thunder's Mouth Press, 2004).

15 Robert B. Laughlin, *A Different Universe: Reinventing Physics from the Bottom Down* (New York: Basic Books, 2005), xvi; emphasis added.

16 Laughlin, *Different Universe*, xiv, 126.

17 Laughlin, *Different Universe*, 142.

18 Laughlin, *Different Universe*, 203.

19 Gerald L. Schroeder, *The Science of God: The Convergence of Scientific and Biblical Wisdom* (New York: Broadway Books, 1997), 27–28.

20 Schroeder, *Science of God*, 40.

21 For an excellent resource on the debate over intelligent design, see John Angus Campbell and Stephen C. Meyer, eds., *Darwinism, Design, and Public Education* (East Lansing: Michigan State University Press, 2003).

22 Steven Weinberg, *Facing Up: Science and Its Cultural Adversaries* (Cambridge, Mass.: Harvard University Press, 2001), 232, 242.

23 See, e.g., Richard John Neuhaus, "The Politics of Bioethics," *First Things* 177 (2007): 23–28.

24 Christopher Hitchens, foreword to *God, the Failed Hypothesis: How Science Shows That God Does Not Exist*, by Victor J. Stenger (New York: Prometheus Books, 2007), vii.

25 With this point in mind, I feel compelled to share a directive that was sent to me by a friend, who found it on the welcoming sign of a church: "Don't Be So Open-Minded. Your Brains Fall Out." Hermeneutic charity encourages me to see a sense of humor at work in this directive.

26 *As Good as It Gets*, directed by James L. Brooks, produced by John D. Schofield and Richard Marks, TriStar Pictures, Culver City, Calif., DVD format, 1997. Jack Nicholson won an Oscar for "Best Actor in a Leading Role." Helen Hunt won an Oscar for "Best Actress in a Leading Role."

27 The specific type of pill—e.g, Prozac (fluoxetine) or Zoloft (sertraline)—is not identified.

28 See, e.g., Peter D. Kramer, *Listening to Prozac* (New York: Viking Press, 1993); Peter D. Kramer, *Against Depression* (New York: Viking Press, 2005); Carl Elliott, *Better Than Well: American Medicine Meets the American Dream* (New York: W. W. Norton, 2003); Carl Elliott, "Against Happiness," *Medicine, Health Care, and Philosophy* 10 (2007): 167–71; Eric G. Wilson, *Against Happiness: In Praise of Melancholy* (New York: Farrar, Straus, & Giroux, 2008).

INDEX